Economics and Tourism

BUILDING THE FUTURE OF TOURISM

Series Editor: Anukrati Sharma

The world is entering the Third Millennium in which great changes are expected in all areas of human interest, life, and activity. These changes have been brought on by past and present man-made events, which have had both positive and negative consequences. The coming millennium will be marked by significant social, political, demographic, and technological changes and will definitely differ from the last century. The future will bring more leisure time, a higher standard of living and a better quality of life for us all. This series examines recent and the most probable changes and gives a wide range of visionary insights as well as operational takeaways.

Economics and Tourism: New Perspectives in Social Sciences

EDITED BY

FARHANG MORADY
University of Westminster, UK

SİDAR ATALAY ŞİMŞEK
Batman University, Türkiye

İSMAIL ŞIRINER
Batman University, Türkiye

AND

ARMIDA CONCEPCIÓN GARCÍA
Autonomous University of Zacatecas, Mexico

emerald PUBLISHING

United Kingdom – North America – Japan – India – Malaysia – China

Emerald Publishing Limited
Emerald Publishing, Floor 5, Northspring, 21-23 Wellington Street, Leeds LS1 4DL

First edition 2026

British Library Cataloguing in Publication Data
A catalogue record for this book is available from the British Library

ISBN: 978-1-83662-917-7 (Print)
ISBN: 978-1-83662-916-0 (Online)
ISBN: 978-1-83662-918-4 (Epub)

Printed and bound by CPI Group (UK) Ltd, Croydon, CR0 4YY

Contents

Section 2: Gender and Inclusion in Tourism

Section 3: Tourism and Economic Development

About the Editors

Farhang Morady is an Associate Professor in International Development at the University of Westminster, London. His research interests focus on the intersection between global political economy, development, and energy. His academic journey includes BSc Honors from London University and an MA and a PhD in International Political Economy from Leeds University. Having taught and researched for over three decades, he has made a significant impact on higher education through his innovative and student-oriented pedagogical practice. Dr Morady has been acknowledged for his passion for teaching and learning, having been nominated and elected the "Outstanding Teacher" by the Students' Union in 2013, 2016, and 2019. Considering his national and international work in education, he was awarded the National Teaching Fellowship by Advance HE in August 2022 for pioneering and developing the Democratic Education Network (DEN), which aims to integrate students and communities, both in London and worldwide.

Sidar Atalay Şimşek, is a Doctor of the Faculty of Economics at the Batman University, Türkiye (since 2016). With an interest in macroeconomics, environmental economics, econometrics, sustainable tourism, and tourism economy, she has a list of papers presented at international scientific meetings and published in proceedings. In addition, she accredits herself with several national and international publications that include two books, 10 book chapters nine articles in peer-reviewed journals and published seven books as editor position. Dr Atalay Şimşek has also contributed to the organization of international congresses as the Congress Chairperson. She continues to inspire and mentor students and colleagues at Batman University, contributing to the advancement of economic science and the development of sustainable economic policies. Her dedication to academic excellence and community service underscores her role as a prominent figure in the field of economics and tourism.

İsmail Şiriner has extensive experience and a distinguished career in economics, spanning over two decades across various academic and administrative roles. Currently serving as Chair of the Department of Economics at Batman University, Turkey, he has demonstrated exceptional leadership since assuming the position in April 2016. His previous roles include Vice-Dean at both Batman University and Kocaeli University, where he also chaired the Economic Policy Science Field. Professor Şiriner's academic journey is marked by significant contributions to the field of political economy, globalization, and economic policy. He has organized numerous international conferences and workshops, fostering intellectual exchange and advancing research in social sciences. As an accomplished researcher, he has authored and edited several books and contributed extensively to international journals.

Armida Concepción García has a Master's degree in Administration in Autonomous University of Zacatecas, Mexico. PhD in Social Cultural Studies in Autonomous University of Aguascalientes. She is currently a researcher and a Professor for the Development Studies Doctoral Program, an international academic program in the National Council of Science and Technology (CONACYT), México. She has made research stays at the Universidade Federal de Paraíba and the Universidade Federal de Campina Grande, Brazil, collaborating on topics about Informality, precarious work and Textile Production in Mexico and Brazil. She is a member of the National Researchers System (SNI-1) and a member of academic board of Mexican Association of Labor Studies (AMET). Her research lines fall under labor studies (informal labor, labor precariousness) and public policies and labor.

About the Contributors

Muhammad Farooq Akhtar completed his PhD in Consumer and Market Analysis from the Universiti Utara Malaysia and is currently serving as an Assistant Professor at The University of Faisalabad. He has 20 years of experience in academics, research, and industry. He has published numerous papers in internationally reputed journals such as *Social Responsibility Journal* and *The Journal of the Knowledge Economy*. Moreover, he has published book chapters in books related to tourism, climate change, and remedies to overcome environmental issues.

Munise Aksöz, completed her undergraduate studies in German Studies at Çukurova University in 1992. She obtained her Master's degree in 1996 with a thesis on *Emancipatory Tendencies in German and Turkish Children's Books*, and completed her PhD in 2001 at the same university with a dissertation titled *Comparative Analysis of Certain Literary Genres in Turkish and German Literature in the Context of Dictionary Entries*. From 1993 to 1996, she worked as a research assistant at the Department of German Studies at Çukurova University. Subsequently, she held positions as an Instructor (1996–2002), an Assistant Professor (2002–2014), and an Associate Professor (2014–2019). Since 2019, she has been working as a full professor at the Department of German Studies at Çukurova University and has been the head of the Department of Foreign Languages since 2020.

Rabia Arshad is a Lecturer at the National Business School, The University of Faisalabad, Pakistan. She earned gold medal during her graduation. Her research interest are behavioral finance, corporate social responsibility, and sustainable finance. She has also published impact factor publications and book chapters.

Muhammad Ashfaq is currently working as Professor/Dean, Faculty of Management Studies, the University of Faisalabad-Pakistan. He completed his graduation in 1985 and earned MS degree in 1988. He did his training in Marketing from Colorado State University, USA, and later on completed his PhD degree from Australia in 1995. In 2006, he went to University of Laval, Canada, for his post doctorate studies. Dr Ashfaq has also rendered services as consultant to various national and international organizations. He had also won the TWAS

Associateship Award and Australian Alumni Excellence Award for Innovation and Research. He has supervised 14 PhD students and more than 150 MS/MPhil/MSc students. He is the author/co-author of five books; 14 chapters and more than 100 peer reviewed research papers. He is also working as editor/section editor of different journals. He has completed 32 research projects as PI/Co-PI which were funded by national and international organizations.

Mustafa Aslan completed his BSc degree in Astronomy and Space Sciences and his MSc degree in Accounting and Auditing. He currently holds a PhD degree in Business. He has worked in senior executive positions for over 20 years and is currently working as a senior management consultant and teaching various courses in the fields of Aviation Management and Business at Istanbul Bilgi University. His main research areas are Industrial Psychology, Organization Behavior, Aviation Management, Strategic Management, and Decision-Making.

Umut Balcı, completed his Bachelor's degree at Ankara University, Department of German Language and Literature in 2003, his Master's degree at Çanakkale Onsekiz Mart University, Institute of Social Sciences in 2006 and his doctorate at Çukurova University, Institute of Social Sciences in 2010. In 2005, he started his academic life as an assistant in Çanakkale Onsekiz Mart University, Faculty of Education, Department of German Language Teaching. In 2014, he moved to Batman University, Faculty of Tourism. He was appointed as Professor in 2019. He served as the Head of the Department of Tourism Guidance and Dean of the Faculty of Tourism. He is currently working as a professor at Batman University, Faculty of Tourism, Department of Tourism Guidance and has recently been researching mainly on language and tourism, literary tourism and cultural tourism. He is also the editor of *Mesopotamia Journal of Interdisciplinary Studies* and *Cudes* academic refereed journals.

Nuran Öztürk Başpınar is an Associate Professor at Anadolu University. She is currently Head of Department in the Office Management and Secretarial Education program at Eskisehir Vocational School. She completed her Master's degree in 1990 and her doctorate in 1999 at Anadolu University Institute of Social Sciences. She has published several articles in international journals and authored chapters in some international books. Her major areas of study are Management and Strategy, Leadership, Organizational Behavior, Ethics, Office Management.

Demet Cakıroğlu is an Associate Professor at Hacettepe University. She received her Master's degree in 2007 and her PhD in 2017 from Gazi University Institute of Social Sciences, Department of Health Care Management. She has published several articles in international journals and authored chapters in some international books. Her main fields of study are healthcare management and strategy, leadership, organizational behavior, ethics, office management.

Mai Thùy Dương, MA, is a Lecturer in Sociology and Development Studies at the Faculty of International Studies, Hanoi University. She holds a Master's degree in international Affairs from the Geneva Graduate Institute

(Switzerland). Her research centers on environmental sustainability, global governance, multi-culture, and international development, with a particular focus on Vietnam and the broader Asian region.

Hewawasam H. P. K. N. is a Senior Lecturer in Criminology and Criminal Justice at the University Sri Jayewardenepura, Sri Lanka. She obtained a PhD from the same university for her research on financial crimes in the corporate sector. She has presented multiple research papers at local and international conferences. Her research articles have been published in peer-reviewed journals. She has authored five books on various topics, including Crime Victim, Crimes, and Social Problems, Suspects and Their Rights, Evolution of Money and Financial Crime and Criminological Sub Disciplinary.

Sweta Leena Hota, a distinguished academician with a PhD in Commerce, brings over a decade of teaching experience complemented by eight years of professional expertise in the banking sector. Her unique blend of academic and practical knowledge positions her as a versatile educator and researcher. Dr Hota has an impressive portfolio of over 30 research papers published in prestigious international and national journals, including Scopus, Web of Science, and ABDC-listed publications. She has actively contributed to academic discourse by attending and presenting papers at various national and international conferences. Her commitment to education and research excellence highlights her dedication to bridging the gap between academia and industry, making her a respected figure in the fields of Marketing and Banking.

Wondemsew Mesafint Kebadie is a dedicated Lecturer and a researcher at Samara University, Ethiopia, within the School of Tourism and Hospitality Management. His research focuses on tourism and hospitality investment, Halal tourism, and the intersection of technology and tourism. He holds a Master's degree in Tourism Business Administration and a Bachelor's degree in Tourism Management from Bahir Dar University. He actively collaborates with colleagues both within his institution and internationally to advance research in the field. Currently, he is conducting research on hotel investment trends, Halal tourism development, and the role of technology in shaping the tourism and hospitality industry. His work aims to bridge academic insights with practical applications to foster sustainable and innovative tourism strategies.

Sevdiye Kemik, works as a research assistant at the Department of Aviation Management at Topkapi University, Istanbul. In her Master's thesis, she examined commercial aircraft accidents in the prejet era in terms of accident causes and flight phases. She is currently pursuing her doctorate in Aviation Studies and Management. Sevdiye Kemik's academic studies cover various topics such as aviation safety, human factors, sectoral effects of digitalization and circular economy. She has articles, conference proceedings, and book chapters published in national and international journals.

Nohman Khan is an accomplished academic and researcher, with a PhD in Management from the University of Kuala Lumpur (UniKL), Malaysia. With a passion for advancing knowledge in his field, Dr Khan has established himself as an expert in Systematic Literature Reviews and is recognized for his comprehensive research in Digital Tourism and Eco-Tourism. Throughout his academic career, Dr Khan has contributed significantly to the body of knowledge with over 70 published articles in renowned Scopus-indexed journals. His work has helped shape the discourse surrounding modern management practices, with a particular focus on the intersection of digital technology and sustainable tourism practices. Dr Khan's expertise in Systematic Literature Reviews is well-regarded, providing critical insights into various areas of management and tourism. His pioneering research on Digital Tourism and Eco-Tourism is influencing new approaches to sustainable travel and technology's role in enhancing tourist experiences while preserving the environment.

Sze-ee Lee, embarked on her academic career in 2018 as a Senior Lecturer at the School of Architecture, Building, and Design (SABD), Taylor's University in Malaysia. She completed her Postgraduate Certificate in Teaching and Learning in 2020 and PhD in 2024, focusing on interdisciplinary research into the evolving career paths of 21st-century architects. Her research interests encompass social, heritage, and sustainable architecture. In addition to her academic role, Sze-ee is also a practicing architect with over 15 years of diverse experience in residential, commercial, and institutional projects, both locally and overseas. She has worked with international architectural firms in Sydney and London before returning to Malaysia in 2011. Sze-ee believes that thoughtful design and careful planning in architecture bring a better quality of life to people.

Yu-Feng Lin Lee, the Department Head, is the Professor of Economics at the Department of Economics, Applied Statistics, and International Business (EASIB), the Director of Doctor of Economic Development (DED) Program, and the Senior Fellow of Daniels Fund Ethics Initiative (DFEI; by the Bill Daniels Foundation), College of Business, New Mexico State University (NMSU), USA. She also holds as the Distinguished Professor of Bank of America (BoA) at NMSU. Earning her PhD in Economics from Southern Illinois University at Carbondale (SIUC), Lee has joined NMSU since August 2004, and as an award-winning instructor in both the undergraduate and graduate classes, she regularly teaches courses in general and field Economics and International Business, while maintaining her research interests and journal publications in the area including International Business, East-Asian Business Management and Ethics, International Economics, Regional Growth and Development, and Asia-Pacific Economic Integration.

Gobinathan Manickam is currently the subject matter expert with School of Marketing and Management at Asia Pacific University of Technology and Innovation, Malaysia. Gobi also serves as Master Facilitator for Academic Mentoring and a panel member for ISO 9001:2015 internal audit for the university. He has previously managed faculty teams at Brickfields Asia College, Petaling Jaya and Inti International College, Kuala Lumpur. He cofounded a training company and spent a few years as a freelance trainer.

B. Anne Kanchana M. Mendis is a PhD candidate in Labor Studies at the University of Waikato, focusing on female labor force participation in South Asia. With over 15 years of experience as a Human Resources consultant and researcher, she has worked with PwC, Ernst & Young, and the UN FAO Sri Lanka. She holds a Master's in Labor Studies from the University of Colombo.

Nirupama Mohanty, holding a PhD in Social Entrepreneurship, has more than five years of teaching experience is dedicated to creating positive impact through innovative solutions. She has authored eight publications in esteemed journals, showcasing her expertise in sustainable development, social innovation, and entrepreneurial ecosystems.

Pabasara R. P. is a third-year undergraduate studying for his Bachelor's in criminology and criminal justice, at the University of Sri Jayewardenepura, Sri Lanka. Demonstrating his academic capability, he has published numerous research abstracts, and blog articles on crime prevention, sustainability, and social reconciliation. As proof to his academic excellence, he achieved the title "Best Presenter" at two consecutive international research conferences in 2024, including his debut as well.

Alaka Panda is a distinguished academic with over 13 years of teaching experience, known for her dedication to education and research excellence. As the Head of the Department of Commerce for the past five years, she has exhibited outstanding leadership and academic acumen, fostering growth and innovation within her department. Dr Panda's research contributions are noteworthy, with more than 15 publications in esteemed national and international journals. Her active engagement in the academic community is further demonstrated by her participation in over 40 seminars and conferences at both national and international levels, reflecting her commitment to professional development and staying abreast of advancements in her field. Her remarkable blend of teaching, research, and leadership has solidified her reputation as a respected figure in the academic landscape.

Ravindra Kumar Perumal has more than 26 years of professional experience in teaching, learning, research, and curriculum development in three different well-established private institutions for higher education in Malaysia. Currently, he serves as the Senior Lecturer in the School of Global Hospitality and Tourism in Asia Pacific University of Technology & Innovation, Bukit Jalil, Malaysia. He holds a PhD in Management from The LimKokWing University of Creative Technology, Cyberjaya, Malaysia. In addition to being a Senior Lecturer, he is actively involved in conducting Tourism-related research and publication as well as postgraduate research project supervision. Prior to becoming an academic, he has served in the Hospitality and Tourism Industry in Malaysia in various capacity for 10 years.

Yasir Rasool is a researcher and serves as visiting faculty at different universities. His area of interest includes entrepreneurship, marketing, and management subjects. He serves as a mentor and a panel judge at different entrepreneurial platforms. He has published in many impact journals and attended international research conferences. Currently, he is serving as visiting faculty at The Millennium Universal College, Faisalabad Campus.

Smruti Rekha Sahoo is an accomplished Assistant Professor with over 12 years of extensive experience in teaching undergraduate and postgraduate students in the field of Commerce. Known for her academic rigor and dedication to education, she has made significant contributions to research, authoring numerous articles published in Scopus-indexed, ABDC, and UGC-CARE-listed journals. Dr Sahoo has actively participated in the academic community by presenting papers and attending various national and international conferences, showcasing her commitment to knowledge exchange and academic growth. She holds a PhD and serves as a PhD supervisor, mentoring budding researchers in their scholarly pursuits. Currently, Dr Sahoo is engaged in a minor research project sponsored by the Odisha Higher Education Council, further demonstrating her dedication to advancing knowledge in her field. Her scholarly endeavors and teaching excellence make her a respected figure in the academic domain of Commerce.

Maryam Saleem is an Assistant Professor at the National Business School, The University of Faisalabad, Pakistan. Her research interests include workplace status, bottom-line mentality, unethical behaviors, the dark side of leadership, green human resource management practices, and positive organizational Behavior. She has published papers in reputable journals and presented her research at national and international conferences.

Keith Kay Hin Tan, is a UK-registered architect and the author of two previous books about the heritage of Malaysia's colonial-era Catholic mission schools. He obtained a doctorate in Tourism studies from Taylor's University Malaysia in 2017, where he is also an Associate Professor at the School of Architecture, Building and Design. In addition to his teaching role, he is also a member of the university's Liveable Urban Communities (LUC) Impact Lab and is a cluster leader in its Centre for Asian Modernisation (CAM). This has also allowed him to lead and/or participate in research and scholarly activities together with Think City Sdn Bhd and ICOMOS Malaysia. He has a strong interest in the architectural heritage of Southeast Asia and was the editor of several books dealing with these topics. In addition, Keith has a strong publication record in SCOPUS—indexed journals dealing with architectural heritage and tourism and is a regular architectural contributor on Malaysian radio and other media outlets.

Sana Muhammad Tariq is an academician specializing in business management and social sciences. She is the Program Manager for the Business Management & Social Sciences Department at The Millennium Universal College, Faisalabad. Holding an MS in Management Sciences (Silver Medalist), she has extensive experience in higher education. Her research focuses on academic integrity, transnational education, and consumer behavior, with publications in recognized journals. Her latest work, *Impact of Social Media on Tourism Demand*, examines digital influences on the tourism industry.

Nguyen Thi Minh Tien is the Dean of the Faculty of International Studies, Hanoi University, Vietnam. She obtained her Doctor Degree in European Union Law and National Legal System from the University of Ferrara, Italy. She has more than 20 years of teaching and research experience in international and development studies. Her research interest includes sustainable development, labor relations, social inclusion, and public policies.

Nguyen Thi Thanh Thuy is the Vice-Dean of the Multimedia Communication Faculty and Head of the Culture and Communication Department at Vietnam Women's Academy. She holds a PhD in Literature from Hanoi National University of Education and dual Master's degrees in literature and media management. As a respected scholar in cultural studies and communication, her research interests are Vietnamese cultural foundations, gender and cultural development, public relations, and social media communications. Her research contributions include significant work on cultural identity in the integration era and gender sensitivity in modern media.

Ihtisham Ullah has recently joined Asia Pacific University as a Postdoctoral Research Fellow at the Strategic Research Institute. In this role, he aims to further contribute to the field of tourism management, with a particular focus on sustainable development and community-based tourism. During his PhD journey, Dr Ullah published 10 articles in reputable academic journals, reflecting his expertise in areas such as Sustainable Tourism, Community-Based Tourism, Religious Tourism, and Digital Tourism. His extensive research background positions him to make valuable contributions to the advancement of tourism management practices and policies.

Kübra Nur Uzuntaş works as a research assistant in the Aviation Management Department at Istanbul Bilgi University. In her Master's thesis, she focused on the impact of unmanned aerial vehicle usage and applications on aviation safety. She is pursuing a PhD in the Aviation Studies and Management program at Kocaeli University. Her research interests include unmanned aerial vehicles, aviation safety and security, and aviation psychology.

Wijesekara P. D. is a Research Assistant at the International Center for Multidisciplinary Studies of the University of Sri Jayewardenepura since 2017. She obtained her Master of Science degree from the University of Moratuwa, Sri Lanka. Her research interests encompass Social Geography, Human Geography, Cultural Geography, and Land Change Sciences. She has published research papers in indexed and peer-reviewed journals and presented at several local and international conferences.

Introduction

Farhang Morady[a], *Sidar Atalay Şimşek*[b], *İsmail Şiriner*[b] *and Armida Concepción García*[c]

[a]University of Westminster, UK
[b]Batman University, Türkiye
[c]Autonomous University of Zacatecas, Mexico

The tourism industry's fast expansion has created substantial global economic, social, and environmental changes. The World Travel & Tourism Council (WTTC, 2024) reported that tourism contributed 10% to global GDP and supported 300 million employment opportunities before COVID-19. Although this has declined during COVID-19, the figures have returned to a similar level since the end of then.

This anthology deals with various issues and academic research on tourism in the context of globalization, the impact of the introduction of information technologies, and new forms of global tourism. From a critical perspective of the dominant models of tourism development, the authors propose different ways of understanding its problems and development, as well as strategies for dealing with new alternatives in tourism, seeking to promote dialogue and intercultural understanding of tourism in some countries, taking into account the value of the cultural identity of host communities.

Tourism industry is one of the strongest pillars of globalization and a determining factor in the international economy. It plays a key role in economic recovery in times of crisis and sometimes determines and guides political relations between different nations. However, it also reflects economic inequalities and low levels of development and sometimes generates negative impacts, imbalances, problems, and contradictions, as well as a degree of independence in many destinations that have not managed to integrate their traditions alongside tourism growth. Analyzing the impact of this activity on the economy, society, culture, and the environment of localities and countries is an essential task. This is the subject of the contributions brought together by various experts and researchers in the field of tourism.

Economics and Tourism, 1–4

Published under exclusive licence by Emerald Publishing Limited
doi:10.1108/978-1-83662-916-020251001

In the face of accelerating global challenges—such as climate change, gender disparities, digital disruption, and displacement due to conflict or environmental degradation—there is a growing need to reimagine tourism through a more holistic, critical, and sustainable lens.

Scholarly research focuses on four concepts: circular economy, ecolinguistics, inclusive governance, and adaptive climate strategies as tools to rethink sustainable tourism models (Ellen MacArthur Foundation, 2013; Hall, 2008; Stibbe, 2015). Sustainable tourism has evolved to combine ecological responsibility with social fairness and economic strength (UNWTO, 2020). Tourism exists beyond economic activities because it is a transformative mechanism supporting multiple United Nations Sustainable Development Goals (SDGs), including work quality, gender equality, and climate action.

As the world navigates new crises—from climate change to forced displacement—and reconsiders its models of growth and inclusion, tourism has emerged not only as a field of interest for economists and planners but also as a subject of profound social scientific inquiry.

The book contains multiple chapters that critically analyze tourism's changing position in modern society through applied research conducted in Asia, Europe, and other regions. The book is divided into four sections, which explore sustainable tourism and environmental innovation, gender and inclusion in tourism, and tourism economic development, and cultural, social, and global dimensions of tourism. The book examines modern theoretical discussions and policy issues through detailed empirical research. The volume demonstrates how tourism is a transformative power to reshape local economies and reduce environmental degradation while promoting equity and inclusion.

In the first section, the authors explore the imperative of sustainability through innovations in green technology, supply chain reform, and linguistic framing. Contributions such as those by the authors of Chapters 1 and 2 argue for embedding circular economy principles within tourism to shift away from the traditional extractive growth models. These chapters emphasize that sustainability is no longer an aspirational add-on but a necessary policy, investment, and practice framework. Chapter 3 builds on this by critically analyzing the paradox of aviation as both an enabler of global mobility and a significant source of carbon emissions. This tension is addressed through emerging innovations in sustainable aviation fuel and low-emission flight technologies. Chapter 4 offers a linguistic dimension through ecolinguistics, emphasizing that the discourse used in tourism—by marketers, educators, and governments—profoundly shapes tourist behavior and institutional priorities. This underscores the growing importance of communication strategies and semiotic framing in reinforcing ecological values and encouraging responsible consumption patterns. Chapter 5 synthesizes these ideas by offering a macro-level assessment of sustainable tourism trends, arguing for a governance-oriented approach that can operationalize sustainability within global tourism governance regimes. It highlights that aligning tourism development with climate action, social equity, and long-term economic planning requires multi-scalar coordination among local communities, states, and international institutions.

The second section delves into gender equity and social inclusion, interrogating how tourism can function simultaneously as a platform for empowerment and as a site of entrenched structural inequalities. The chapter on Sri Lanka presents a nuanced study of how women-led enterprises foster resilience and collective agency in communities often marginalized by mainstream tourism narratives. It draws on participatory research highlighting how female entrepreneurship can contribute to local well-being and environmental stewardship. Chapters 7 and 8 employ mixed methods and literature reviews to explore the persistent barriers to women's participation in the tourism workforce. These include limited access to capital, inadequate policy support, cultural constraints, and occupational segregation, which disproportionately confine women to low-paid, informal sectors of the tourism economy. Chapter 9 explores these dynamics in the Turkish context, where entrepreneurial support networks, legal frameworks, and training programs are critical in mediating women's entry and advancement in the sector. Thematically, this section builds upon feminist development theory to show how tourism can be reimagined as a tool for equity, inclusion, and transformative justice, provided it is anchored in inclusive policymaking and intersectional analysis.

The third section pivots to the economic and technological evolution of the tourism industry. Chapter 10 critically analyzes golf as a form of elite-driven tourism in China, revealing how leisure practices intersect with national identity, class formation, and political regulation. It sheds light on the broader political economy of sports tourism and the contradictions inherent in state-led leisure projects. Chapter 11 returns to the Sri Lankan case to argue for the economic dividends of empowering women within local tourism economies, linking micro-level enterprise development with macroeconomic stability. It also emphasizes the importance of community-based tourism initiatives that balance entrepreneurial goals with socio-environmental values. Chapter 12 offers a rigorous econometric study from Türkiye, demonstrating that tourism revenues significantly contribute to GDP growth. By employing multiple estimation techniques—FMOLS, DOLS, and CCR—the chapter builds a robust statistical case for strategic investment in tourism infrastructure, workforce development, and digital transformation. Meanwhile, Chapter 13 explores the digitalization of tourism, mapping the transformative impact of social media on destination branding, consumer behavior, and policy responsiveness. Importantly, this chapter also addresses the risks of digital saturation, including misinformation, overtourism, and erosion of cultural authenticity. This section highlights that technology, while a driver of innovation, must be ethically governed to ensure sustainability, equity, and cultural sensitivity.

The final section addresses tourism's cultural, social, and geopolitical dimensions. Chapter 14 investigates how narrative construction influences tourist perception, especially in underrepresented destinations, proposing community-led storytelling as a mechanism for cultural preservation and economic vitality. Drawing from discourse analysis, it advocates for narrative reframing that centers local voices and identities. Chapter 15 deals explicitly with tourism's contribution to the climate crisis, advocating for behavioral and policy-based interventions to reduce the sector's ecological footprint. It explores the tensions between economic growth and environmental preservation, suggesting multilevel governance strategies integrating eco-friendly transport, waste management, and carbon budgeting. Chapter 16 presents an in-depth case study of indigenous tourism in Vietnam, analyzing the tension between cultural preservation and commercial exploitation in the age of globalization. It shows how cultural tourism can commodify and revitalize Indigenous identities, depending on the institutional and market structures mediating these exchanges. Finally, Chapter 17 explores the potential of tourism and hospitality to support refugee integration and economic participation in host countries, using examples from across Europe. This chapter extends the debate beyond financial metrics to include social cohesion, intercultural dialogue, and rights-based approaches to tourism governance. It suggests that ethical frameworks and inclusive planning are essential for ensuring tourism contributes to peacebuilding, not marginalization.

Overall, this collection offers a nuanced, interdisciplinary exploration of the challenges and opportunities shaping global tourism today. The book contributes meaningfully to the growing literature on sustainable and inclusive tourism by bridging academic theory with empirical research and grounded case studies. It is intended as a resource for scholars, students, policymakers, and practitioners who are invested in rethinking tourism as an economic engine and a multidimensional force for social and ecological transformation.

References

Ellen MacArthur Foundation. (2013). *Towards the circular economy: Economic and business rationale for an accelerated transition*. Ellen MacArthur Foundation. https://emf.thirdlight.com/link/x8ay372a3w11-k6778n/@/preview/1?o

Hall, C. M. (2008). *Tourism planning: Policies, processes and relationships*. Pearson Education.

Stibbe, A. (2015). *Ecolinguistics: Language, ecology and stories we live by*. Routledge.

UNWTO. (2020). *International tourism highlights: 2020 edition*. World Tourism Organization. https://www.eunwto.org/doi/book/10.18111/9789284422456

World Travel & Tourism Council. (2024). *Economic impact research 2024: Global trends and sector performance*. WTTC. https://www.wttc.org/research/economic-impact

Section 1

Sustainable Tourism and Green Practices

Chapter 1

Economic Benefits of Sustainable Tourism Practices and Role of Green Technologies

Maryam Saleem, Muhammad Ashfaq and Rabia Arshad

The University of Faisalabad, Pakistan

Abstract

Tourism is a rapidly growing industry that fosters economic growth through GDP expansion and employment creation. However, the sector's growth has also resulted in the depletion of resources and degradation of the environment; thus, the industry is shifting toward sustainable tourism practices. This chapter explores the economic benefits of sustainable tourism practices and the substantial role of green technologies. Green technologies, including energy-efficient appliances, waste management systems, and renewable energy sources, would be important in reducing the carbon emissions generated by tourism activities. By leveraging cutting-edge technology, the tourism industry has the potential to balance economic growth alongside the conservation of the environment and the integration of society.

Keywords: Sustainable tourism; green technologies; economic benefits; sustainability; energy efficiency

Introduction

The tourism industry is widely acknowledged as one of the most dynamic and promising industries on a global scale. It is of the utmost importance to plan and grow tourism in a purposeful and sustainable manner, as it plays a vital role in shaping economic, environmental, and social landscapes in today's world. This chapter mainly focuses on the vital role of sustainable tourism within the South Asian context, which is a biodiverse and culturally rich region, and attempts to formulate ways to tackle the challenges of carbon emissions and depletion of

Economics and Tourism, 7–25

doi:10.1108/978-1-83662-916-020251002

resources. It also highlights the need for community engagement, vocational education, and policy support in attaining sustainable tourism. The chapter emphasizes that sustainable tourism practices and green technology are imperative, both from a moral and economic standpoint, for vibrant, profitable, natural, and cultural resources and sustainable development for future generations. To illustrate sustainable tourism in action, this chapter introduced a case study titled "Tourists' Attitude Towards Cultural Heritage and their Willingness to Pay to Visit: A Case Study of Lahore, Pakistan," which was originally published in the journal "Conservation Science in Cultural Heritage, 20, 125–138." This case study underscores the economic benefits of heritage tourism and demonstrates how well-preserved cultural sites contribute to local economies while promoting sustainable tourism practices. Permission to include this content has been obtained from the copyright owners. This chapter also addresses the questions: "how has sustainable tourism helped a small rural village?" and "what lessons can be learned from the adoption of green technologies in major tourist destinations?" to provide more depth.

Sustainable Tourism and Its Types

Sustainable tourism practices focus on the conservation and protection of the environment to ensure the future viability of the tourism industry (Li et al., 2024). Tourism, although directly linked to three Sustainable Development Goals (SDGs) of the 2030 Agenda, Goal-8 (Decent Work and Economic Growth), Goal-12 (Responsible Consumption and Production), and Goal-14 (Life below Water), holds the potential to impact all SDGs globally, both in direct and indirect ways. Sustainable tourism includes a range of ideas, such as ecotourism, corporate social responsibility, supply chain management, and green tourism (Abd Hamid & Isa, 2020). The various types of tourism have been discussed below.

- *Ecotourism:* The primary goal of ecotourism is to protect the environment or get up close and personal with endangered wildlife. In addition to supporting efforts to increase awareness of the value of preserving natural and cultural capital, ecotourism activities include a significant educational and interpretive component.
- *Green tourism:* includes all forms of tourism activities that evolve in full alignment with the environmental and sociocultural environment of the host region. It is defined as the aggregation of tourist modes designed to augment the social, cultural, and environmental impacts of tourism.
- *Rural tourism* is an effective approach for reconciling tourism demands with environmental preservation and SDGs. Rural tourism broadly denotes vacations undertaken in rural regions. Tourism activities in rural areas are an integral part of sustainable development, as they promote the preservation of natural and cultural resources while ensuring their sustainable consumption. This approach fosters a balance between economic growth and ecological

integrity. Sustainable tourism has significantly contributed to economic growth in rural villages by promoting community-led eco-tourism initiatives. For instance, a rural village, Zlakusa, located in the city of Užice, Serbia, has successfully implemented sustainable tourism through the revival of pottery making, traditional crafts, and local food products. These initiatives have generated employment opportunities, maintained local traditions, and reduced environmental degradation. Sustainable tourism has enhanced the local economy, safeguarded cultural traditions, and advanced environmental practices in Zlakusa. The integration of tourism with community development in the village has established a model for rural sustainability, illustrating that sustainable tourism can significantly contribute to rural growth.

- *Community tourism* emphasizes the engagement of local inhabitants in tourism development tailored to their advantage: they construct and oversee the accommodation facilities and the local services provided to tourists. Local communities retain full control over tourism-generated cash, a significant portion of which is allocated to enhancing communal living circumstances, with particular emphasis on respecting nature and local traditions.
- *Responsible tourism* seeks to improve the surroundings for people to live and visit. Responsible tourism calls for operators, hoteliers, governments, residents, and visitors to embrace accountability and act to make travel more environmentally friendly.

Tourists' Attitude Toward Cultural Heritage and Their Willingness to Pay to Visit: A Case Study of Lahore, Pakistan

This case study pertains to cultural/heritage tourism, which encompasses activities and concepts wherein individuals explore and appreciate the historical significance and distinct identity of a location while also bearing the responsibility to preserve and repair its historic or cultural structures as integral components of tourism resources. Encouraging heritage tourism within a nation contributes to the preservation of heritage sites and positively influences the local environment, society, and economy. The OECD report (2024) for culture and tourism indicates that the primary driving forces behind the development of cultural tourism include the conservation and preservation of heritage, job creation and economic advancement, physical and economic growth, the strengthening and diversification of tourism, population retention, and the enhancement of cultural understanding. This case study examines the perspectives of tourists regarding cultural heritage sites in Lahore, Pakistan, with particular emphasis on the Badshahi Mosque and the Royal Fort. This study analyzes the elements that affect individuals' willingness to pay and assesses the socioeconomic and environmental factors that shape tourism behavior. The analysis of data gathered from 200 respondents indicated that the majority of visitors were young, well-educated, and primarily local individuals. Common reasons for visiting encompass unforgettable experiences, the allure of well-known sites, and the pursuit of cultural discovery. A significant number of visitors reported a positive experience during their stay, emphasizing the appeal and historical importance of the locations they explored. The analysis revealed a positive correlation between willingness to pay and income levels, while high costs and environmental concerns had a detrimental effect. The analysis suggests enhancing site amenities, including pedestrian pathways, landscaping, and traffic control, while utilizing social media for the promotion of tourism. The focus is on channeling tourism revenue back into the preservation of heritage and the advancement of local economic growth. The findings emphasize the promise of cultural tourism as a viable source of sustainable income and its significance in enhancing appreciation for Pakistan's rich cultural heritage. Sustainable tourism seeks to reduce the adverse environmental effects of tourism while enhancing the socioeconomic advantages for local populations. The role of green technologies is essential in facilitating this objective. These energy-efficient and environmentally sustainable technologies can diminish the tourism industry's carbon footprint, mitigate resource depletion, and promote sustainable economic growth. This chapter explores the multifaceted economic advantages of integrating sustainability into tourism operations and the pivotal role of green technologies in driving profitability and resilience.

Economic Impact of Tourism

The tourism industry has demonstrated impressive resilience in the postpandemic era, with global travel experiencing an upward trend. As of 2023, international tourist arrivals hit 89% of prepandemic levels, with a rapid increase to 98% by September 2024. This revival underscores a notable rebound in travel demand worldwide. The travel and tourism sector contributes 7.6% to global GDP and supports nearly 300 million jobs, highlighting its vital importance in tackling societal and economic issues. The importance of the sector is increasing as it supports small- and medium-sized enterprises, with more than 80% of travel and tourism businesses categorized in this way. It plays a crucial role in providing employment for women, youth, migrants, and informal workers, thus making a significant contribution to economic opportunities. The travel and tourism industry serves as a significant catalyst for global connectivity, especially in an era marked by increasing geopolitical tensions and conflicts, alongside a noticeable deceleration in globalization. In the next 10 years, travel and tourism's contribution to alleviating socioeconomic risks is expected to increase significantly, as the World Travel and Tourism Council predicts that the travel and tourism sector GDP will expand at nearly twice the pace of the overall global economy by 2033, resulting in the creation of over 100 million new jobs. According to the World Travel and Tourism Council (WTTC), in 2024 travel and tourism represented $1 of every $10 spent worldwide, as shown in Fig. 1.1 (WTTC Annual research, 2023).

A crucial element of tourism is sustainability, since it aims to meet the requirements of stakeholders while considering economic impacts alongside present, future, and social environmental situations (Liu et al., 2018; World

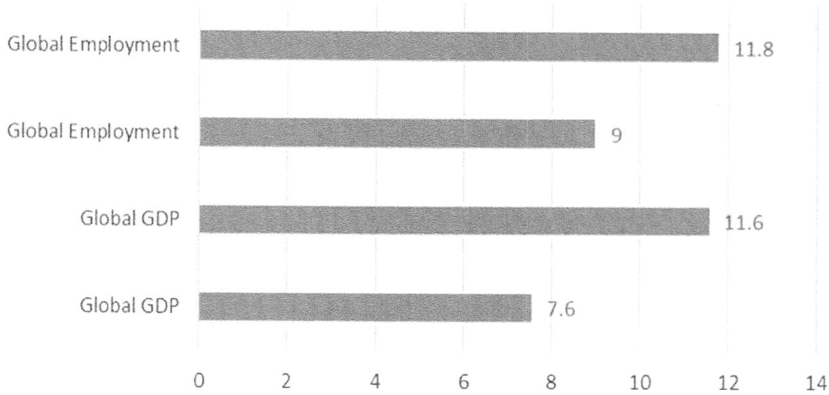

Fig. 1.1. Travel and Tourism Sector's Total Economic Contribution. *Source:* Adapted from World Travel & Tourism Council 2023 Annual Research https://www.weforum.org/stories/2024/01/travel-tourism-role-future-global-prosperity/

Tourism Organization, 2020). Thus, sustainability and the constraints of its expansion remain a persistent issue in the tourism industry. With 334 million jobs and 10.4% of global GDP (US$ 10.3 trillion) attributable to travel and tourism in 2019, before the COVID pandemic, the industry was highly influential. At the same time, in 2019, spending by overseas visitors reached US$ 1.91 trillion. The United Nations World Tourism Organization (UNWTO) verified that foreign visitor arrivals attained 80–95% of prepandemic levels by the end of 2024.

According to the World Travel & Tourism Council (2024) annual report, the travel and tourism industry contributed 9.1% to global GDP in 2023. This was 23.2% higher than 2022 and 4.1% lower than 2019.

- In 2023, 27 million new jobs were created, a 9.1% increase from 2022 and a 1.4% decrease from 2019.
- Domestic visitors spent 18.1% more in 2023 than in 2019.
- International visitor spending rose 33.1% in 2023 but was 14.4% lower than in 2019.

Moreover, compared to the previous year, the industry generated $11.1 trillion in 2024, which accounted for 10% of the global GDP and represented a 12.1% increase, as illustrated in Fig. 1.2 (Statista Research Department, 2024). This upward trend suggests a robust return to prepandemic economic levels, and it may even surpass them. Global travel and tourism employment from 2019 to 2023 and the 2034 projection are also shown in Fig. 1.3 (Statista Research Department, 2024).

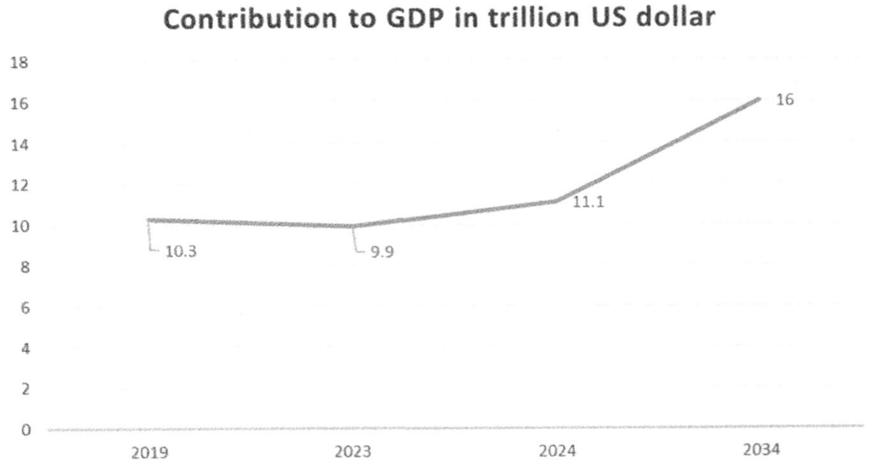

Fig. 1.2. Global GDP Contribution of Travel and Tourism in 2019, 2023 and 2024 With a 2034 Estimate. *Source:* Adapted from Statista Research Department (2024). https://www.statista.com/statistics/233223/travel-and-tourism-total-economic-contribution-worldwide/

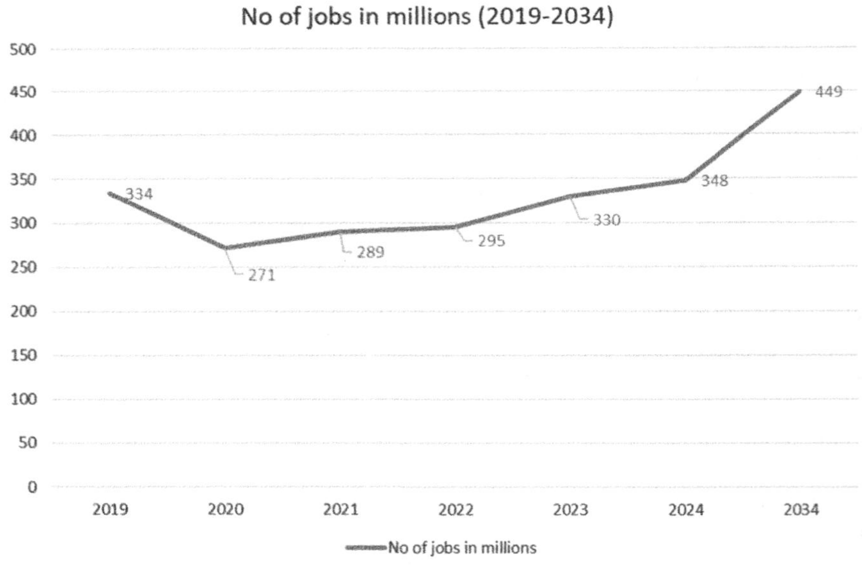

Fig. 1.3. Global Tavel and Tourism Employment 2019–2023, and 2034 Projection. *Source:* Adapted from Statista Research Department (2024). https://www.statista.com/statistics/1268465/number-of-travel-and-tourism-jobs-worldwide/

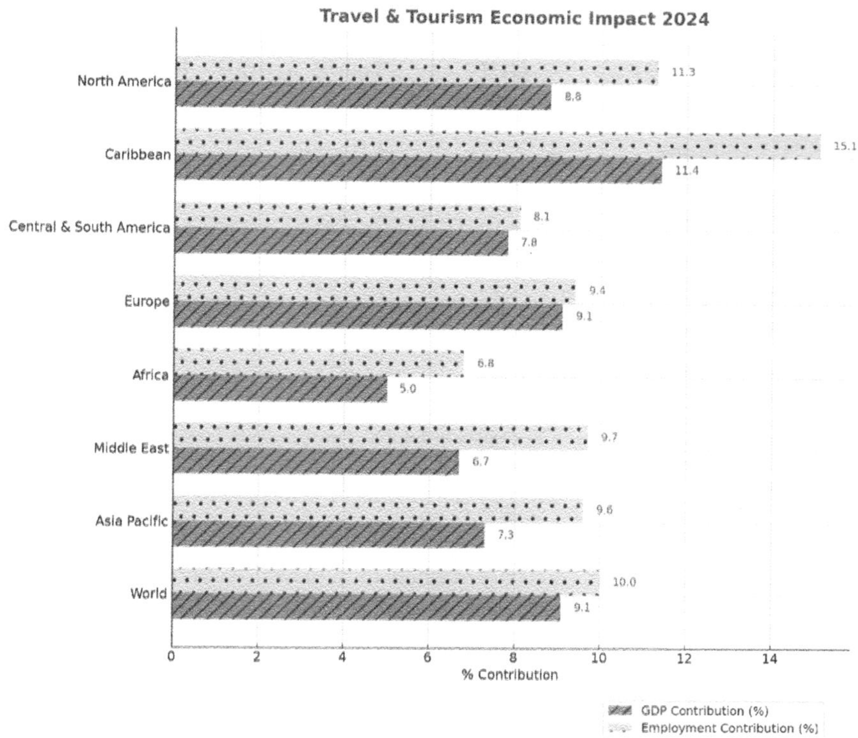

Fig. 1.4. Economic Impact of Travel and Tourism (2024). *Source:* Adapted from World Travel and Tourism Council (2024). https://wttc.org/research/economic-impact

Fig. 1.4 (WTTC, 2024) provides an overview of the global and regional economic impact of travel and tourism, focusing on both GDP contribution and job creation for the year 2023, projected into 2024.

The travel and tourism sector is regaining momentum following the obstacles encountered in recent years. The growth outlook for 2024 appears to be positive. There has been a 17.23% increase in tourist arrivals compared to 2023. International tourist projections are estimated to reach 1.53 billion in 2024, indicating a notable increase compared to the figures from the previous year. In 2023, the industry's contribution to global GDP was 10.6%. For 2024, year-over-year growth forecasts suggest a robust 17.24%, reflecting substantial growth. The travel sector has the potential to generate approximately USD 9.4 billion in revenue (see Table 1.1).

The global travel and tourism market is expected to see a significant rise in revenue soon. It is anticipated that by 2025, the industry will achieve a revenue of

Table 1.1. International Tourist Arrivals 2019–2024.

Years	International Tourist Arrivals	GDP Contributions (%)	Tourist Arrivals Growth (%)	Revenue Growth (USD Billion)
2019	1.5 (billion)	10.4	4 (from previous year)	9.3
2020	381 (million)	1.7	−74.6	2.3
2021	415 (million)	2.15	8.92	2.5
2022	965 (million)	7.6	132.53	5.9
2023	975 (million)	9.1	35.23	8.8
2024	1.53 (billion) expected	10.6	17.24	9.4

Source: Adapted from Trends and Forecasts in Global Tourism, WP Travel (2024). https://wptravel.io/global-tourism-industry-statistics/

US$955.90 billion. The market is projected to achieve a value of US$1,114.00 billion by 2029, reflecting a consistent annual growth rate of 3.90%, indicating a strong recovery and expansion trend.

Tourism in South Asia

Sustainable tourism can foster economic growth by drawing individuals ready to invest in environmentally conscious activities. This is especially true in tourist-heavy regions like Southeast Asia. South Asia is a unique region characterized by a significant contiguous landmass and a variety of physical features, including grasslands, forests, swamps, and deserts. This region is quite appealing overall because of its abundance of natural resources: coastal areas, mountains, beautiful scenery, rivers, and different weather conditions. The tourism sector functions as a catalyst for economic advancement in South Asia, similarly to its function in other emerging countries. Approximately 12% of GDP and 4% of employment in the region are attributed to the tourism sector, which is widely acknowledged as one of the fastest-growing businesses globally (Aini, 2024). There is a great deal of economic potential with an expected 125.78 million tourists per year. Carbon emissions from transportation and energy usage are two areas where this expansion has negative environmental impacts. Projects such as ASEAN Socio-Cultural Community (ASCC) Blueprint 2025, which seeks to promote ecologically responsible city planning, have been inspired by the SDGs of the UN, which promote tourism as an industry with green growth potential (Aini, 2024).

In addition to GDP growth, sustainable tourism has significant economic implications, such as job creation and enhanced connections with local communities. In 2017, the tourist sector accounted for 8.9% ($281.6 billion) of the

GDP in the South Asian region, with a projected growth of 7.2% in 2018. By 2028, it is projected to account for 9.0% of GDP ($301.8 billion), with an additional income growth of 6.2%, ultimately reaching 9.4% of GDP ($579.6 billion), as illustrated in Fig. 1.5 (WTTC Annual Report, 2018).

In 2017, tourism accounted for 7.5% of employment, equating to 49,931,500 jobs, with a projected increase to 7.6% of the job market in 2018, totaling 51,436,500 jobs. By 2028, tourism is projected to constitute 7.8% of the job market, equating to 63,006,000 jobs, as shown in Fig. 1.6 (WTTC Annual Report, 2018).

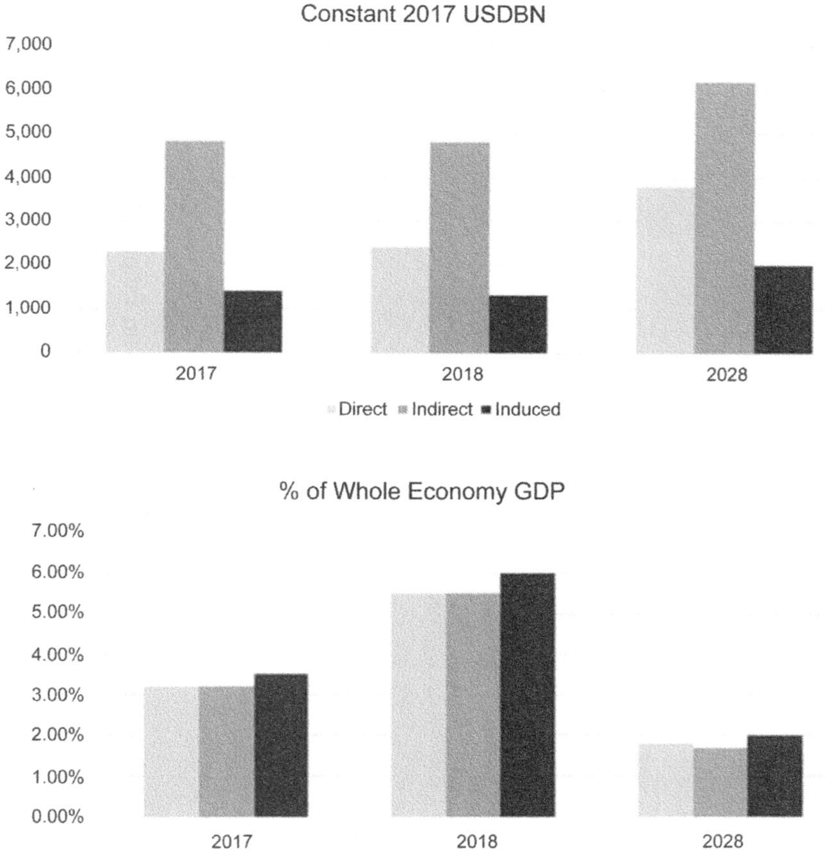

Fig. 1.5. South Asia Contribution to Travel and Tourism GDP 2017–2028. *Source:* Adapted from World Travel & Tourism Council Report (2018). https://www.slovenia.info/uploads/dokumenti/raziskave/world2018.pdf

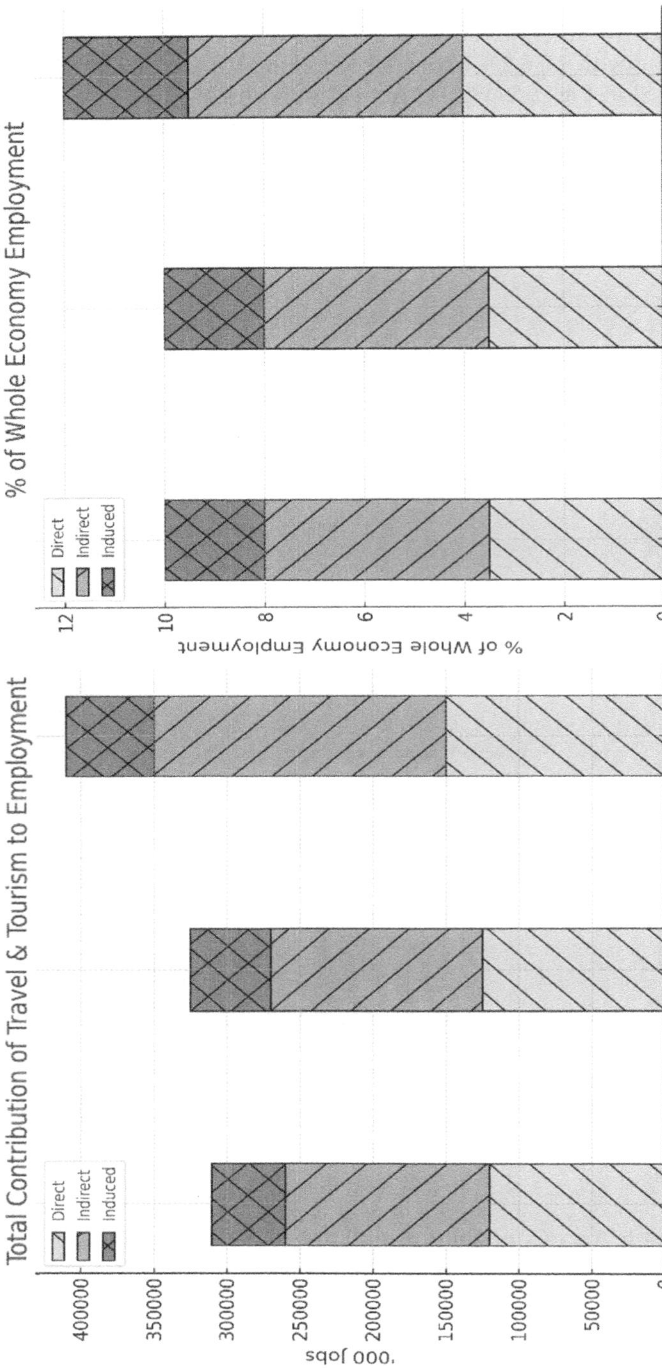

Fig. 1.6. South Asia Contribution to Travel and Tourism Employment, 2017–2028. *Source*: Adapted from World Travel & Tourism Council Report (2018). https://www.slovenia.info/uploads/dokumenti/raziskave/world2018.pdf

An analysis of 11 Southeast Asian nations from 2002 to 2019 using panel data regression revealed that an influx of 22,000 international tourists could result in a 6.14% increase in employment and about $894 million in revenue. However, it was found that this increase would be accompanied by 27 million more tons of carbon emissions per year (Aini, 2024). The rise of CO_2 emission is a critical issue in Southeast Asia, driven by swift industrial growth and urban development. They play a significant role in global warming and negatively impact human health and ecosystems. Consequently, minimizing CO_2 emissions is an essential component of sustainable development in this area. Tourism plays an important role within the economies of Southeast Asia through its contribution of revenue, employment opportunities, and stimulation of local markets (Comerio & Strozzi, 2019). However, unchecked growth in tourism can have environmental consequences and pose a threat to the resources that attract tourists (Baloch et al., 2023; Liu et al., 2022; Teng et al., 2021). This poses the difficulty of achieving maximum economic gains while trying as much as possible to reduce the economic impacts. Therefore, the relevant authorities must promote eco-tourism projects that have the potential to be eco-friendly as well as profitable and encourage the use of renewable energy sources.

Several countries within Southeast Asia have great opportunities for the development of renewable energy sources such as solar and wind. Realizing this potential can help to grow the economy and, at the same time, make sure that the environment is not harmed (Van et al., 2024). Ecotourism and sustainable harvesting can generate revenue while safeguarding the environment, creating additional jobs for rural residents in the bioeconomy. Vocational education and training (VET) shape the skills needed for a thriving economy. PISA-VET, a new OECD (Organization for Economic Co-operation and Development) program evaluates different industries, with a focus on tourism and hospitality (Rausch et al., 2024). The economic benefits of sustainable tourism projects can be enhanced through VET, which focuses on developing domain-specific skills and increasing employability. Sustainable tourism and green technology provide far-reaching economic benefits, including but not limited to the following: increased employment opportunities, stronger communities, and less pollution.

Pakistan is acknowledged for its tourism within the South Asia region. Pakistan is a country of remarkable beauty, and its tourism sector is witnessing considerable expansion. The expansion of international tourism in Pakistan has reached impressive levels. A study reported that 808,000 people visited the area, with a wide variety of sources contributing to this total (Arshad et al., 2018). This figure denotes a 24.4% improvement in relation to the preceding two years. The findings of the survey indicate that Pakistan received 1.75 million tourists in the year 2017. According to the Pakistan Tourism Development Corporation (PTDC), which has confirmed that 30% of visitors come from within the country. According to the World Travel and Tourism Council, Pakistan's tourism industry generated 19.4 billion US dollars in revenue in 2017, which accounted for 6.9% of the country's final gross domestic product. The WTTC forecasts that by the year 2030, this number will have increased to 36.1 billion USD. The development of tourism in Pakistan aims to significantly aid in reducing poverty levels. The tourism sector is integral to the economic development of Pakistan and exhibits a trend of continuous growth.

The Role of Green Technologies in Tourism

The tourism industry has a detrimental impact on climate change and global warming, necessitating the implementation of technological measures to promote sustainable tourism. The tourism sector accounts for 8% of global greenhouse gas emissions within the overall carbon footprint, highlighting the significant environmental impact that persists alongside the economic benefits derived from this industry (Asadi et al., 2020). Fig. 1.7 (Nature Climate Change, 2018) shows the different activities that contribute to tourism's total carbon footprint.

Numerous experts have highlighted the importance of emerging energy technologies, considering increasing concerns regarding climate change (Liu et al., 2024; Nawaz et al., 2021). The implementation of green technology innovation is increasingly acknowledged as a significant approach to lowering CO_2 emissions and attaining carbon neutrality (Puwanendram & Atalay Şimşek, 2024). Green technology encompasses the creation and utilization of products, equipment, and systems aimed at preserving the natural environment and resources, therefore mitigating the detrimental impacts of human activities (Manmohan et al., 2023). Green technology also serves as an alternative to fossil

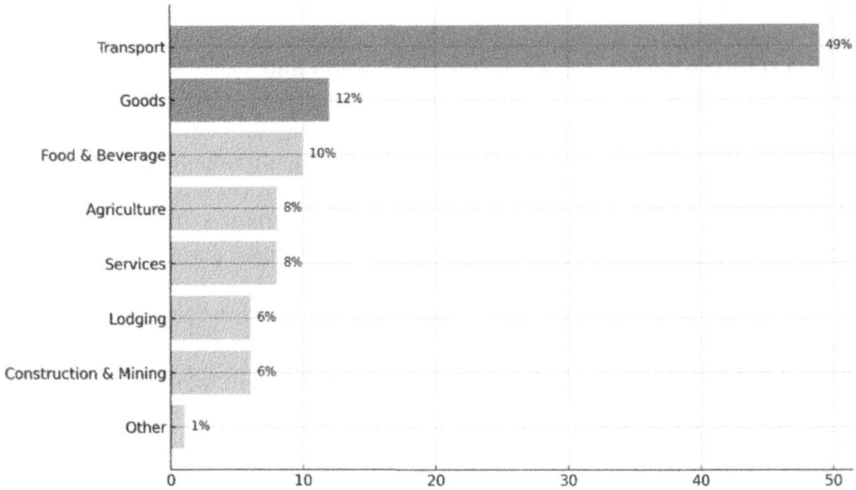

Fig. 1.7. Carbon Footprint of Globnal Tourism. *Source:* Nature Climate Change (2018). Adapted from https://sustainabletravel.org/issues/carbon-footprint-tourism/ This graph shows the different activities that contribute to tourism's total carbon footprint.

fuels, aiming to provide a technological solution that minimizes harm to human health, animal welfare, plant life, and the environment. Furthermore, it is recognized as environmental and clean technology. The adoption of green technology practices has become a significant topic within the tourism sector, driven by the urgent necessity to minimize the carbon footprint produced by industry.

A number of scholars contend that green technologies have the potential to lower expenses related to energy, water, and resources, while also addressing pollution concerns (Miao et al., 2024; Wichaisri & Sopadang, 2018). There is a growing trend among individuals to seek out transportation alternatives that are both environmentally conscious and sustainable, driven by an increased consciousness of their ecological footprint. The tourism sector has the potential to significantly improve its approach to green technology and environmental sustainability through the integration of renewable energy sources such as solar, wind, and hydroelectric power. This methodology has the potential to reduce the carbon intensity associated with tourism endeavors, simultaneously providing more dependable and sustainable electricity sources (Manmohan et al., 2023). Fig. 1.8 (Maksimovic, 2018) shows the main goal of green technology.

The key requirements for sustainable tourism in hotels involve the implementation of energy and water saving measures, the adoption of a zero-waste policy, and participation in solid and organic waste management (Alcieri & Vinci, 2021). For the preservation of this sector, it is vital to put in place

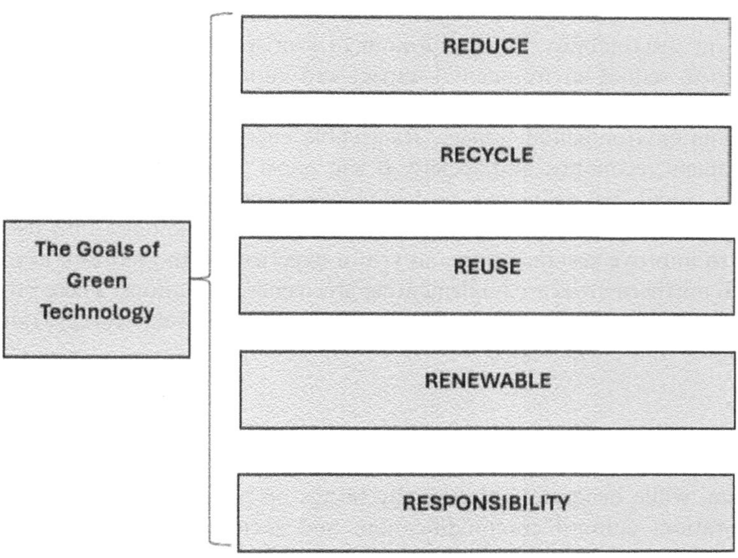

Fig. 1.8. The Key Goals of Green Technology. *Source:* Adapted from Maksimovic (2018). https://link.springer.com/chapter/10.1007/978-3-319-60435-0_12

strategies and technologies that aim to mitigate the negative effects of tourism. For the tourism industry, green technologies are extremely important for several reasons: they increase organizational efficiency and even smooth out the negative aspects of the economy (Forés et al., 2020). Green technology includes pollution controls, ecological restoration, and reconversion industries. Green technological innovation is regarded as a crucial approach for attaining low CO_2 emissions and promoting sustainable development (Chen et al., 2023). The existing literature (Wicki & Hansen, 2019) depicts green technology innovation as all altered approaches to business operations that meet customer needs while producing fewer adverse effects compared to alternative methods.

In the tourism sector, common green technologies include key card systems, room occupancy sensors, centralized air conditioning systems, light-emitting diode (LED) lighting, water restrictors, food decomposers, and other advancements. Green technologies implemented by tourism enterprises are associated with advancements in energy efficiency and environmental sustainability, as well as the creation of smart buildings, all intended to improve efficiency and mitigate environmental pollution (Vachon, 2007). Advanced technologies empower destinations to manage an increased influx of visitors while maintaining ecological balance. This balance fosters enduring sustainability and promotes the welfare of local communities.

The successful implementation of green technologies at popular destinations demonstrates that sustainability and economic growth can coexist. These places exemplify the necessity of renewable energy, water conservation, waste management, and eco-friendly regulations, and community engagement for long-term sustainability. Several prominent tourist destinations use green technologies to reduce environmental impact and improve visitor experiences. For instance, Dubai has invested in renewable energy and water conservation to reduce its environmental impact. Renewable energy in the UAE benefits the environment, economy, and society. It can boost energy security, employment creation, fossil fuel reduction, and innovation and research. Another notable example is Pakistan, which is incorporating green technologies into its tourist sector to improve sustainability and visitor experiences. In Pakistan, key tourist spots in northern areas are implementing green energy solutions. These programs promote sustainable tourism in Pakistan by promoting solar energy, rainwater harvesting, and plastic bans.

Challenges and Opportunities in Tourism

Tourism, while beneficial, additionally brings up issues such as environmental deterioration, cultural commodification, and socioeconomic inequities (Hall, 2008). The overtourism phenomenon in destinations like Venice and Barcelona exemplifies the adverse effects of excessive tourism on local infrastructure and communities (Dodds & Butler, 2019). Environmental concerns are paramount, as mass tourism often leads to habitat degradation, pollution, and resource depletion.

In numerous developing countries, tourism is seen as an essential strategy for diversifying the economy and reducing poverty. Countries like Thailand, Malaysia, and Mexico have effectively leveraged their natural and cultural assets to attract tourists, foster growth, and showcase their distinctive heritage (Jenkins, 2003; Sharpley & Telfer, 2014). This sector is essential for strengthening local economies and supporting the conservation of cultural and historical sites that may otherwise encounter financial difficulties.

The development of tourism in these countries faces significant obstacles, despite its potential. Frequent challenges consist of insufficient infrastructure, ineffective marketing approaches, and political uncertainty. For instance, poorly developed transportation systems and a lack of adequate lodging choices may deter visitors. Political instability presents significant safety hazards, likely dissuading tourists and diminishing investment in the tourism sector. The lack of professional training and skills enhancement in hospitality and tourism management severely hinders industry expansion and service excellence (Rogerson, 2007). Tourism can have significant environmental repercussions, such as pollution and the depletion of natural resources, if it is not effectively managed; unplanned tourism development, especially in areas that are ecologically sensitive, has the potential to lead to biodiversity loss and habitat destruction (Buckley, 2012).

Implementing sustainable tourism practices is essential for optimizing tourism benefits while reducing adverse effects. Emphasizing community participation, environmental protection, and the conservation of cultural heritage is essential. Engaging local communities in the design and implementation of tourism initiatives fosters an equitable distribution of benefits while respecting the needs and values of the community. Studies in sub-Saharan Africa and Southeast Asia emphasize the importance of engaging local populations in tourism initiatives, leading to enhanced sustainability and greater inclusion in development (Tosun, 2000). Policies that advocate for sustainable tourism, bolster local businesses, and safeguard cultural heritage foster the advancement of a fair and sustainable tourism industry in developing countries.

Investigations into the tourism sector in Pakistan reveal a spectrum of potential advantages alongside notable challenges. The nation boasts a profound cultural legacy, a variety of natural terrains, and notable historical landmarks, each presenting considerable prospects for the advancement of tourism. The region boasts remarkable features such as the majestic Himalayas and the formidable Karakoram, alongside the significant archeological sites of Mohenjo-Daro and Taxila. The extraordinary landscapes of Gilgit-Baltistan, marked by majestic mountains and valleys, coupled with cultural festivities such as the Shandur Polo Festival, underscore the unique allure of Pakistan's tourism sector. The tourism industry in Pakistan faces numerous obstacles that hinder its expansion despite its inherent allure. The historical and cultural assets of Pakistan draw tourists; yet, security issues and insufficient infrastructure pose significant obstacles. Poor road conditions and insufficient lodging options dissuade prospective tourists (Ahmed et al., 2022).

Implementing sustainable tourism practices is crucial for aligning development with the interests of local communities and protecting the natural and cultural environment. Engaging local populations in tourism planning and development improves the authenticity of the visitor experience and ensures an equal distribution of benefits (Ali, Shafiq, & Andejany, 2021). Partnerships between the public and commercial sectors may catalyze vital investments in infrastructure, marketing, and training, which are crucial for cultivating a strong and competitive tourism business. By addressing these challenges and leveraging its unique resources, Pakistan can establish itself as a prominent global tourist destination.

Conclusion

Although tourism generates economic advantages, it has also resulted in severe environmental degradation, adverse social and cultural repercussions, and habitat fragmentation. Because of the negative outcomes, people are concerned about the probable future of natural resources, their own health, and their communities' ability to maintain a sustainable economy (Choi & Sirakaya, 2006). Sustainable tourism is both a moral and environmental necessity and an economic strategy for enhancing resilience and assuring the sector's longevity. Effective governance, policies, business engagement, and travelers are essential for planning and managing the development of sustainable tourism practices. Based on the preceding discussion, we propose the following recommendations.

- Promoting sustainable tourism practices is essential for the preservation of both cultural and natural heritage. The global and regional analysis underscores the critical importance of sustainable tourism in employment generation, poverty alleviation, and the promotion of local enterprises. The government must develop policies and implement regulations that promote sustainable tourism and ensure the conservation of natural resources.
- Policies encouraging sustainable travel must be enforced by governments while ensuring the preservation of natural resources. This encompasses imposing strict environmental rules for travel agencies, supporting eco-friendly company models with tax advantages and subsidies, and including sustainability factors into the procedures of tourist licenses and certifications.
- The private sector plays a crucial role in fostering sustainable tourism. Businesses should be encouraged to adopt green certifications, implement energy-efficient technologies, and minimize waste. Financial incentives, such as reduced operational costs for certified eco-friendly businesses and grants for innovation in sustainable tourism, can further motivate businesses to adopt environmentally responsible practices.
- Implement green technologies, such as renewable energy systems and waste management systems, to address carbon emissions, mitigate the adverse environmental effects of tourism, and promote sustainable growth.

- Encourage local community participation in sustainable tourism development.
- Provide vocational training centered on green technologies and sustainable practices for tourism professionals. The integration of vocational education and green technology in tourism improves skill development, operational efficiency, and economic resilience.
- Preserve cultural legacy by improving facilities at sites, including better traffic control, pedestrian walkways, and improved landscapes.
- Encouraging collaborations between the public and private sectors can efficiently leverage resources and expertise in the tourism industry. Public–private partnerships can also play a significant role in developing tourism infrastructure.
- Travelers can promote sustainable tourism by choosing eco-friendly travel. They should be encouraged to assist local businesses, respect cultural legacy, and minimize their environmental impact by means of trash reduction, water and energy conservation, and selection of sustainable transportation choices. Travel guides focusing on sustainable locations, eco-tourism applications, and awareness campaigns can assist tourists in understanding their part in advancing sustainability.

References

Abd Hamid, M., & Isa, S. M. (2020). Exploring the sustainable tourism practices among tour operators in Malaysia. *Journal of Sustainability Science and Management*, *15*, 68–80.

Ahmed, M., Ahmed, S., & Abbas, R. (2022). Tourism in Pakistan, challenges and opportunities. *Journal of Social Sciences Review*, *2*(3), 130–137.

Aini, Y. N. (2024). Sustainable tourism in Southeast Asia: Balancing economic growth, employment, and carbon emissions through evidence-based strategies. *Jurnal Kepariwisataan Indonesia: Jurnal Penelitian dan Pengembangan Kepariwisataan Indonesia*, *18*(1), 157–174.

Aldieri, L., & Vinci, C. P. (2021). Scalability and commercialization in support of sustainable development goals. *Industry, Innovation and Infrastructure*, 979–988.

Ali, M. R., Shafiq, M., & Andejany, M. (2021). Determinants of consumers' intentions towards the purchase of energy efficient appliances in Pakistan: An extended model of the theory of planned behavior. *Sustainability*, *13*(2), 565.

Arshad, M. I., Iqbal, M. A., & Shahbaz, M. (2018). Pakistan tourism industry and challenges: A review. *Asia Pacific Journal of Tourism Research*, *23*(2), 121–132.

Asadi, S., Pourhashemi, S. O., Nilashi, M., Abdullah, N., Samad, S., Yadegaridehkordi, E., Aljojo, N., & Razali, N. S. (2020). Investigating influence of green innovation on sustainability performance: A case on Malaysian hotel industry. *Journal of Cleaner Production*, *258*(17), 253–269.

Baloch, Q. B., Shah, S. N., Iqbal, N., Sheeraz, M., Asadullah, M., Mahar, S., & Khan, A. U. (2023). Impact of tourism development upon environmental sustainability: A suggested framework for sustainable ecotourism. *Environmental Science and Pollution Research*, *30*(3), 5917–5930.

Buckley, R. (2012). Sustainable tourism: Research and reality. *Annals of Tourism Research*, *39*(2), 528–546.

Chen, H., Yi, J., Chen, A., Peng, D., & Yang, J. (2023). Green technology innovation and CO_2. emission in China: Evidence from a spatial-temporal analysis and a nonlinear spatial durbin model. *Energy Policy*, *172*, 113338.

Choi, H. C., & Sirakaya, E. (2006). Sustainability indicators for managing community tourism. *Tourism Management*, *27*(6), 1274–1289.

Comerio, N., & Strozzi, F. (2019). Tourism and its economic impact: A literature review using bibliometric tools. *Tourism Economics*, *25*(1), 109–131.

Dodds, R., & Butler, R. (2019). The phenomena of overtourism: A review. *International Journal of Tourism Cities*, *5*(4), 519–528.

Forés, B., Puig-Denia, A., & Fernández-Yáñez, J. M. (2020). On how to leverage green technologies for sustainability performance in the tourism sector. In *Adapting to environmental challenges: New research in strategy and international business* (pp. 163–188). Emerald Publishing Limited.

Hall, C. M. (2008). *Tourism planning: Policies, processes and relationships*. Pearson Education.

Jenkins, C. L. (2003). The economics of overexploitation: A review of classical literature. *Journal of Economic Surveys*, *17*(1), 5–36.

Li, J., Coca-Stefaniak, J. A., Nguyen, T. H. H., & Morrison, A. M. (2024). Sustainable tourist behavior:A systematic literature review and research agenda. *Sustainable Development*, *32*(4), 3356–3374.

Liu, Z., Mehmood, U., & Nassani, A. A. (2024). How do energy efficiency, technology, natural resources and globalization impact environmental sustainability? Fresh evidence from load capacity curve theory. *Frontiers in Environmental Science*, *12*, 1447808.

Liu, Y., Sadiq, F., Ali, W., & Kumail, T. (2022). Does tourism development, energy consumption, trade openness and economic growth matters for ecological footprint: Testing the Environmental Kuznets Curve and pollution haven hypothesis for Pakistan. *Energy*, *245*, 123208.

Liu, C., Zhang, R., Wang, M., & Xu, J. (2018). Measurement and prediction of regional tourism sustainability: An analysis of the Yangtze river economic zone, China. *Sustainability*, *10*(5), 1321.

Maksimovic, M. (2018). Greening the future: Green Internet of Things (G-IoT) as a key technological enabler of sustainable development. In *Internet of things and big data analytics toward next-generation intelligence* (pp. 283–313).

Manmohan, C., Nikhat, M., Mohammad, N., Gera, R., & Pathani, A. (2023). Green technology and environmental sustainability in the tourism sector: A bibliometric analysis. In *E3S Web of Conferences* (Vol. 391, p. 01179). EDP Sciences.

Miao, C., Chen, Z., & Zhang, A. (2024). Green technology innovation and carbon emission efficiency: The moderating role of environmental uncertainty. *Science of the Total Environment*, 173551.

Nawaz, M. A., Hussain, M. S., Kamran, H. W., Ehsanullah, S., Maheen, R., & Shair, F. (2021). Trilemma association of energy consumption, carbon emission, and economic growth of BRICS and OECD regions: Quantile regression estimation. *Environmental Science and Pollution Research International*, *28*(13), 16014–16028.

Puwanendram, G., & Atalay Şimşek, S. (2024). Sustainable tourism development and emerging technology solutions: With special reference to eco friendly innovations (EFI). *Journal of Current Debates in Social Sciences*, *7*(S1), 68–76. https://doi.org/10.29228/cudes.79961

Rausch, A., Abele, S., Deutscher, V., Greiff, S., Kis, V., Messenger, S., Shackleton, J., Tramonte, L., Ward, M., & Winther, E. (2024). Designing an international large-scale assessment of professional competencies and employability skills: Emerging avenues and challenges of OECD's PISA-VET. *Vocations and Learning*, 1–40.

Teng, Y., Cox, A., & Chatziantoniou, I. (2021). Environmental degradation, economic growth and tourism development in Chinese regions. *Environmental Science and Pollution Research*, *28*, 33781–33793.

Tosun, C. (2000). Limits to community participation in the tourism development process in developing countries. *Tourism Management*, *21*(6), 613–633.

Vachon, S. (2007). Green supply chain practices and the selection of environmental technologies. *International Journal of Production Research*, *45*(18–19), 4357–4379.

Van, T. H., Lichang, L., & Quoc, T. D. T. (2024). Sustainable development in Southeast Asia: The nexus of tourism, finance, and environment. *Heliyon*, *10*(24).

Wichaisri, S., & Sopadang, A. (2018). Trends and future directions in sustainable development. *Sustainable Development*, *26*(1), 1–17.

Wicki, S., & Hansen, E. G. (2019). Green technology innovation: Anatomy of exploration processes from a learning perspective. *Business Strategy and the Environment*, *28*(6), 970–988.

World Tourism Organization. (2020). *International tourism and Covid-19*. https://www.unwto.org/international-tourism-and-covid-19. Accessed on January 5, 2020.

Web Links

https://www.weforum.org/stories/2024/01/travel-tourism-role-future-global-prosperity/

https://www.statista.com/statistics/233223/travel-and-tourism-total-economic-contribution-worldwide/

https://www.statista.com/statistics/1268465/number-of-travel-and-tourism-jobs-worldwide/

https://wttc.org/research/economic-impact

https://www.slovenia.info/uploads/dokumenti/raziskave/world2018.pdf

https://sustainabletravel.org/issues/carbon-footprint-tourism/

https://link.springer.com/chapter/10.1007/978-3-319-60435-0_12

https://wptravel.io/global-tourism-industry-statistics/

Chapter 2

Supply and Value Chains and the Circular Tourism Economy

Mustafa Aslan

Istanbul Bilgi University, Türkiye

Abstract

The integration of supply chain management, value chains, and circular economy (CE) principles in tourism promotes a transition from linear to sustainable circular models. This shift reduces waste and enhances resource efficiency through cross-sectoral synergies. Circular practices optimize energy use, implement shared transport solutions, and improve waste management via recycling and biodegradable materials. Cross-industry collaboration creates closed-loop systems, such as converting hotel food waste into biogas for agriculture. Local loops enhance resource retention, supporting economies and reducing emissions. Success requires collaboration among policymakers, industry, and consumers, supported by policies, innovation, and education to ensure effective implementation of circular strategies.

Keywords: Circular economy; sustainable tourism; resource efficiency; cross-industry collaboration; waste management; local loops

Introduction

Tourism is one of the most important elements of the global economy by influencing a wide range of sectors, including but not limited to hospitality, transportation, entertainment, fashion and textiles, health, cultural heritage, and environmental conservation. The tourism industry contributed about 10.4% to the global Gross Domestic Product (GDP) in 2018 and accounted for generating about 319 million jobs, which means one in every 10 people worldwide is working in the tourism industry (WTTC, 2019). Even these figures are enough to

Economics and Tourism, 27–41

Published under exclusive licence by Emerald Publishing Limited
doi:10.1108/978-1-83662-916-020251003

emphasize the importance of the tourism industry for the global economic system and sustainability.

Although tourism is one of the most important pillars of the global economy, its importance is not limited to economic activities; it plays a very important and critical role in cultural exchange, international understanding, and social cohesion.

This important industry may be characterized as a complex and intricate network of supply chains, which encompass a wide range of goods and services designed to meet the needs of tourists at the right place and time. Unlike traditional industries, where supply chains are often linear and involve straightforward exchanges of goods or services, the tourism industry's supply chains are multidimensional. Within this multidimensional supply chain, numerous stakeholders play critical roles in the creation, distribution, and consumption of products and services. This multidimensionality and complexity are due to the nature of the tourism industry because the value is not just derived from the physical products offered but from the entire experience as well, from initial planning and booking to the actual travel and stay, and even post-visit interactions (Zhang et al., 2009).

While tourism is a vital economic driver, its expansion—often unplanned and uncontrolled—has led to environmental degradation, resource depletion, and social disintegration in many popular destinations. These challenges necessitate a transition to more sustainable management practices. Therefore, while traditional supply chain management practices have often focused primarily on economic efficiency, supply chain management in the tourism industry needs more sustainable approaches that consider the entire lifecycle of products and services. This approach involves integrating environmental, social, and economic sustainability practices and considerations into the supply chain management to minimize the adverse effects and maximize positive outcomes for all stakeholders.

While there are challenges and barriers in implementing such sustainable supply chain management, the outcomes offer significant opportunities for businesses. The businesses may reduce their environmental footprints, enhance social equity, and improve their competitiveness in a growing sustainability-conscious market by implementing a sustainable chain management system. Furthermore, this sustainable supply and value chain management will ensure its sustainability, resilience, and equity, and bring a prosperous future for all stakeholders with the adoption and integration of the circular economy (CE) principles.

Supply and Value Chains in Tourism

The supply and value chains in the tourism industry differ from traditional industries. The complex network of supply chains is designed to meet the customer needs whenever and wherever required; hence, it is not a straightforward exchange of goods or services as in traditional industries. This complexity requires numerous stakeholders to play crucial roles, which causes the supply chains to be multidimensional and mostly interconnected.

Components of Supply Chains in Tourism

Each interconnected component of the tourism industry contributes to the overall tourist experience. This interconnectedness causes challenges in the supply chain management of the tourism industry.

The components of supply chain management in the tourism industry may be divided into four categories: (i) suppliers of the goods, (ii) service providers, (iii) intermediaries, and (iv) end consumers, in this case, tourists. These categories can be explained briefly as follows:

(1) Suppliers of Goods:
These suppliers provide tangible items. Based on the items provided, these suppliers can be divided into two categories:

- *Raw materials and product suppliers* are the suppliers of food, beverages, souvenirs, and other goods that are consumed or purchased by tourists. The sourcing of these products can significantly impact the environment, especially if they are being transported over long distances (Budeanu, 2005), contributing to carbon emissions and resource depletion.
- *Accommodation and facility suppliers* are those who provide the materials and products needed for accommodation facilities, such as furniture, bedding, and bathroom supplies. The supply chain for these items often involves global networks, further increasing the tourism industry's carbon footprint (Gössling, 2002).

(2) Service Providers:
Service providers in the tourism industry can be divided into three categories:

- *Accommodation providers* are hotels, resorts, and other lodging facilities. These facilities are central to the tourism supply chain, and they manage a wide range of services, including but not limited to room maintenance and housekeeping, food service, and guest entertainment.
- Because transportation is a critical component of the tourism supply chain, *transport service providers* are crucial for the tourism industry. Transportation encompasses airlines, cruise lines, car rental agencies, and all public transportation services. The adverse effect of this sector on the environment is substantial. Especially air travel is one of the biggest contributors to greenhouse gas emissions in the globe (Peeters et al., 2019).
- *Tour operators and travel agents* are intermediaries but also service providers, and they play a vital role as well. They are connecting tourists with the products and services they need by curating travel experiences. They often work with a network of local service providers to offer

package deals that include accommodation, transportation, and guided tours (Tapper & Font, 2004).

(3) Intermediaries:

- *Online booking platforms* are businesses that take advantage of digital technology. These online platforms have become crucial intermediaries in the tourism supply chain, and they facilitate the booking process, connecting tourists with accommodation providers, transport services, and other travel-related services (Buhalis & Law, 2008), offering their services to end users from the comfort of their homes.
- *Tourist information centers* provide essential information and services to tourists. These services include maps, guides, and recommendations for local attractions, and they work closely with local businesses to improve the visitor experience (Baggio & Cooper, 2010) and promote tourism.

(4) End Consumers (Tourists):
End users or consumers are the tourists. They are the final component in the tourism supply chain. All the efforts in this supply chain are made to prepare the goods or services to be consumed by them. Their preferences and behaviors significantly influence the supply chain, driving demand for certain types of goods and services and shaping the development of tourism destinations (Prentice, 2004).

The Tourism Supply Chains From the Sustainability Perspective

In the tourism industry, like in all other industries, managing the supply chain effectively and efficiently can lead to significant cost savings and improvements in customer satisfaction (Enz, 2010). This effectiveness and efficiency may have positive effects on the company's financial tables, but it is not always positive. It has substantial adverse environmental, social, and economic effects. These adverse effects may be briefly explained as follows.

Environmental Impacts of Tourism Supply Chains

Tourism supply chains significantly impact the environment, contributing to carbon emissions, resource depletion, and waste generation, particularly in transportation and accommodation services. Food waste in accommodation facilities, often due to overproduction or spoilage (Gössling, 2006), exacerbates greenhouse gas emissions and resource wastage.

The construction and operation of tourism facilities, such as hotels and resorts, require significant amounts of energy, water, and materials, which leads depletion of natural resources. Furthermore, most of the time these facilities require a large amount of land to be cleared, which leads to habitat loss and a decline in biodiversity (Buckley, 2011).

Transportation, especially air travel, is one of the most significant sources of environmental pollution in the tourism supply chain. Aviation by itself is one of the major contributors to global greenhouse gas emissions, accounting for approximately 2.5% of global CO_2 emissions (Gössling & Peeters, 2007). Unfortunately, the tourism industry heavily relies on air travel, since millions of tourists are flying to their tourism destinations around the world each year. The environmental impact of this travel is magnified by the fact that many popular tourism destinations are located in remote areas or near or in fragile ecosystems, such as islands and coastal areas, which are particularly vulnerable to the effects of climate change (Scott et al., 2012).

In addition to carbon emissions, tourism supply chains also contribute to water pollution and waste generation. Like air travel pollutes air, cruise ships and tourism facilities located on land pollute water resources, especially seas and lakes. Cruise ships, like the tourism facilities located on land, are notorious for generating large amounts of waste, including sewage, oily bilge water, and solid waste, and much of it are discharged into the seas, causing harm to marine ecosystems (Butt, 2007). Similarly, the disposal of single-use plastics, such as water bottles and packaging, is a significant problem in many tourist destinations, particularly in developing countries where waste management infrastructure may be inadequate (Juvan & Dolnicar, 2014).

Social and Economic Impacts of Tourism Supply Chains

Tourism contributes to economic growth and job creation but can also lead to social inequality, worker exploitation, and cultural disruption (Bianchi, 2004). Furthermore, one of the most important challenges in managing tourism supply chains is ensuring fair distribution of the economic benefits among all stakeholders. In many cases, the monetary benefits are distributed amongst a few large corporations, and local small businesses receive only a small portion, which leads to social tension, especially in developing countries where tourism is often promoted as a means of economic development (Britton, 1982).

Labor exploitation is another important issue in the tourism industry since many workers, particularly in low-wage jobs such as housekeeping, catering, and retail, are vulnerable to exploitation, especially in developing countries, where labor laws may be weak or poorly enforced, and workers may have little bargaining power (Scheyvens, 2002).

Sustainable Supply Chain Management: Needs and Challenges

There is a need for more sustainable supply chain management due to its significant environmental, social, and economic impacts. This sustainable tourism supply chain management should involve the integration of environmental, social, and economic considerations, aiming to minimize adverse effects and maximize positive outcomes for all stakeholders (Carter & Rogers, 2008).

One of the key principles of sustainable supply chain management is the concept of the triple bottom line. The triple bottom line emphasizes the importance of balancing the economic, environmental, and social goals of businesses in their strategy formulation and implementation process. In the context of the tourism industry, this means that businesses should focus not only on cost efficiency and profitability but also their environmental and social impacts (Elkington, 1997), especially during supply chain activities.

There are also several challenges and barriers in the implementation process of sustainable supply chain management in the tourism industry. The main challenge is caused by the complexity and multidimensionality of the tourism supply chain, because every stakeholder in the supply chain has their priorities, and coordinating these stakeholders and aligning their priorities and goals with sustainability objectives can be difficult, especially where there are power imbalances or conflicts of interest (Tapper & Font, 2004).

The lack of traceability and transparency is another challenge since most of the time it can be very difficult for tourism businesses to trace the origins of the products and services they use, especially when those goods are being sourced from global supply chains (Font et al., 2016).

Because the cost of eco-friendly products or investing in energy-efficient technologies can be higher than the conventional alternatives and may not be financially viable for all tourism businesses, especially for small and medium-sized enterprises (SMEs), the financial and logistical challenges become burdens on the business that wants to implement sustainable supply chain management practices (Revell & Blackburn, 2007).

The Circular Economy

CE promotes the responsible use of resources endorsed by governments (especially in the EU) to minimize environmental impact and boost economic sustainability (Moraga et al., 2019). It offers a framework for reimagining tourism through resource reuse, recycling, and regeneration (Ellen MacArthur Foundation, 2013), ensuring waste minimization and value maximization.

The CE is designed to be regenerative and restorative by intention. It aims to maintain the value of products, materials, and resources in the economy for as long as possible, thereby minimizing waste and environmental impact (Ellen MacArthur Foundation, 2013).

There are three principles of a CE, and they can be summarized as follows:

Designing Out Waste and Pollution is designing the whole process to eliminate waste and pollution as much as possible right from the beginning.

Keeping Products and Materials in use as long as possible by formulating strategies such as recycling, reusing, repurposing resources, and promoting the sharing economy.

Regenerating Natural Systems by restoring, amending, and enhancing ecosystems that have been damaged by the activities of human beings.

Implementing these principles into tourism supply and value chain management can reduce the adverse effects of the tourism industry on the environment, enhance social equity, and contribute to the regeneration of natural systems. Moreover, this implementation also ensures the long-term viability and competitiveness of the tourism sector in an increasingly resource-constrained world.

Integration of Supply and Value Chains With Circular Tourism Economy (CTE)

For effective Circular Tourism Economy (CTE) implementation, supply and value chains must be integrated. Management should oversee the entire process—from raw material sourcing to consumption—ensuring waste minimization and resource reuse (Gössling et al., 2009).

Value chains focus on creating value for customers while maximizing the benefits for all stakeholders. In a CTE, value chains must be designed to enhance the overall customer (tourist) experience while promoting sustainability and social equity. This may be achieved by adopting practices such as sustainable procurement and eco-friendly product and service design (Porter & Kramer, 2011).

The integration of supply and value chains requires a systemic approach. It starts with setting the vision, formulating very well-tailored strategic planning to realize the vision, commitment to sustainability at all levels, and the collaboration of all stakeholders, including governments, businesses, local communities, and tourists themselves (Lew et al., 2020).

For example, governments may formulate and enforce policies and regulations to support circular tourism. These policies and regulations may have standards for sustainable tourism, tax, or other types of incentives to support and promote the implementation of CE principles. Furthermore, governments may invest in infrastructure (like recycling facilities and public transportation systems) to support circular tourism (Gössling & Hall, 2006) as well. Businesses may align their strategies with sustainability. They may integrate the CE principles into their supply and value chains and collaborate with other stakeholders. Collaborating with other stakeholders (e.g., suppliers, NGOs, and local communities) to implement CE principles (Bocken et al., 2016) will also help them to achieve a successful integration.

Challenges in Implementing Circular Economy in Tourism

While integrating CE principles into tourism offers significant benefits, there are also several challenges that may hinder its effective implementation process. These challenges include regulatory hurdles, financial constraints, stakeholder resistance, and unintended consequences. All these challenges should be addressed during the implementation process for a smooth flow and a more balanced approach. These challenges are explained briefly:

Regulatory Hurdles: Complex and, most of the time, outdated or old-fashioned regulatory frameworks often impede the transition to a CE in tourism. Many tourism businesses must comply with local, national, and international regulations, which may not always align with CE principles. Policies governing waste management, emissions, and resource use vary significantly across jurisdictions, making it difficult for businesses to adopt uniform circular practices. Additionally, bureaucratic inefficiencies and the slow pace of regulatory changes can discourage businesses from investing in sustainable solutions.

Financial Constraints: High initial investment cost is one of the most significant challenges in implementing CE practices. Investment in sustainable infrastructure, such as renewable energy sources, water recycling systems, and waste management facilities, often requires substantial capital investments.

Resistance From Stakeholders: The transition to circular tourism requires collaboration among stakeholders, including governments, businesses, local communities, and tourists. However, tourism operators and businesses may not be willing to implement CE practices due to increased costs and operational disruptions. Furthermore, while benefiting from circular practices, local communities may resist if the current tourism models they have been using have provided a steady income.

In addition to the above, while local sourcing and eco-friendly practices are encouraged, switching to CE practices may disrupt existing supply chains, leading to job losses or economic instability in specific sectors. This may also create resistance among businesses, local people, and suppliers.

Addressing these challenges is essential to achieve a smooth transition, and in order to overcome these challenges, policymakers and tourism businesses must develop clear regulatory guidelines, provide financial incentives, and engage in stakeholder collaboration.

Case Studies

Two case studies, namely Bornholm, Denmark, and Ljubljana, Slovenia, were presented here to illustrate how these cities have implemented CE principles and achieved a sustainable tourism industry.

Bornholm, Denmark

Bornholm, often referred to as "the Sunshine Island" due to its favorable climate, is located in the Baltic Sea. It is known for its beautiful landscape, historical sites, and artisanal food products. Bornholm started the transition to become a "circular economy island," implementing sustainable practices across all sectors, including tourism. The main goal was to go zero waste, which means that no waste will be burned or landfilled by 2032 (Christensen et al., 2021). The island also aims to produce all of its energy from zero carbon, which means that all the energy it will use will be obtained from renewable energy sources, primarily wind, solar, and biomass, by 2025 (European Commission, 2021).

Sustainable Waste Management

Bornholm's strategy for achieving sustainable waste management (zero waste) by 2032 initiative involves not only reducing waste at the source but also ensuring that any waste generated is reused, recycled, or composted. Hence, the island has developed an integrated waste management system, which includes comprehensive recycling programs, waste-to-energy initiatives, and community engagement to promote waste reduction practices among residents and tourists alike (Christensen & Munck-Kampmann, 2017).

In the tourism sector, this has translated into efforts to minimize waste generated by hotels, restaurants, and other tourism-related businesses. Many hotels on the island have implemented food waste reduction programs, where leftovers are composted or used to produce biogas, which in turn powers the island's energy grid, while local businesses have started to reuse materials, such as old furniture in renovations (Bohnsack & Pinkse, 2017), to reduce demand for new resources.

Renewable Energy

The island's aim to be entirely powered by renewable energy sources by 2025 will not only reduce carbon emissions but also support the local economy by creating jobs in the green energy sector. The island will primarily rely on wind, solar, and biomass by 2025.

Businesses on the island have actively participated in this transition, and they started to adopt renewable energy technologies such as solar panels and heat pumps, which caused many hotels and resorts to reduce their reliance on fossil fuels. This commitment to renewable energy became a key marketing feature of the island to attract environmentally conscious tourists (Frantál & Urbánková, 2017).

Local Economic Development

The economic development of Bornholm has been closely tied to its CE initiatives. The transition process contributed to the local economy. New economic opportunities in sectors such as renewable energy, waste management, and sustainable agriculture, and hence new jobs were created as a result of its CE initiatives.

Furthermore, this sustainable agriculture triggered agritourism. In agritourism, tourists are invited to visit local farms, learn about organic farming practices, participate in the harvesting of the products, and enjoy farm-to-table dining experiences. This provides a unique attraction for tourists, and, consequently, emphasizes local food production and sustainability (Mundaca et al., 2018). Growing agritourism also motivates and supports local farmers and reinforces the island's CE.

Outcomes

The integration of CE principles into Bornholm's tourism supply and value chains has reduced environmental impact while enhancing the island's economic resilience. The island's reputation as a leader in sustainable tourism has also attracted environmentally conscious tourists, who seek destinations that align with their values. This leadership in sustainable tourism gave Bornholm an advantage in the tourism market and increased its competitiveness on the global stage (Richter & Scholz, 2020).

Ljubljana, Slovenia

Ljubljana is the capital city of Slovenia and the first European Union capital city to adopt a zero-waste goal (Zero Waste Europe, 2015), becoming popular for its commitment to sustainability. The city has been developing and implementing strategies to become a "zero waste city." The city has integrated CE practices into several areas of urban life. Consequently, more than 63% of the waste produced in the city was recycled or composted, one of the top-performing cities in Europe in terms of waste management (EBRD, 2022; Zero Waste Europe, 2015).

The Zero-Waste Program

Ljubljana started its "zero-waste" program back in 2014. The program included very well-designed waste management strategies, including reusing, recycling, and composting the waste produced (EBRD, 2022). Hotels, restaurants, and other tourism businesses have been encouraged to reduce single-use plastics, implement food waste prevention strategies, and provide recycling facilities to guests. The usage of reusable items such as cloth shopping bags and refillable water bottles was promoted to reduce reliance on disposable products (Gamberini et al., 2017).

Resource Efficiency

By definition, resource efficiency is creating more (economic) value with less input of resources (Hirschnitz-Garbers et al., 2013). It is one of the most important components of Ljubljana's implemented CE strategies. The city implemented several methods and measures to optimize the use of resources. For example, many hotels and restaurants have installed energy-efficient lighting systems and appliances, water-saving fixtures, and smart energy management systems to reduce resource consumption. Moreover, a widespread public transportation network, including buses and bike-sharing programs, was established to promote sustainable mobility with the help of the city's pedestrian-friendly infrastructure, which reduced the need for motorized transportation and lowered carbon emissions (Hickman et al., 2017).

Community

The commitment and participation of the local community play a vital role in the success of any project or program, and the success of Ljubljana was no different.

The participation and support of the community were ensured through public awareness campaigns, educational programs, community events, and the participation of guests through providing information and tips on how they can reduce their adverse environmental effects during their stay (Vintar et al., 2019).

Outcomes

Ljubljana's integration of CE principles has improved tourism sustainability, reducing environmental impact and strengthening economic resilience. Implementing CE principles into tourism supply and value chains has positively affected the city's zero-waste goal, and, as a result, the city was able to recycle or compost more than 63% of the waste (EBRD, 2022; Zero Waste Europe, 2015).

The success of the zero-waste program also contributed to Ljubljana's image as a sustainable tourism destination. Consequently, the city was named the European Green Capital in 2016 (European Commission, 2016) and attracted eco-conscious travelers from around the world (Lenzen et al., 2018), which helped to boost Ljubljana's tourism industry.

Conclusion

The transition to a CTE represents a fundamental shift toward sustainability, driven by traditional tourism's environmental, social, and economic challenges. This chapter has tried to provide a comprehensive overview of the potential benefits and challenges associated with adopting a CTE by analyzing the CE principles and exploring how they can be integrated into tourism supply and value chains. Practical examples of how these principles can be successfully implemented to create more sustainable, resilient, and competitive tourism destinations were also given through Bornholm, Denmark, and Ljubljana, Slovenia case studies.

As the introduction highlights, tourism is one of the most significant contributors to the global economy, accounting for a substantial share of GDP and employment worldwide. However, the trade-off, i.e., traditional tourism practices' environmental and social costs, is becoming increasingly apparent. The uncontrolled and, most of the time, destructive growth of tourism has led to severe environmental degradation, including the destruction of natural habitats, overuse of resources, increased carbon emissions, and social inequity. Additionally, the social fabric of many communities has been disrupted by the influx of tourists, leading to cultural erosion, economic inequality, and social tension.

Based on the "take-make-dispose" approach, the traditional linear tourism model is unsustainable due to resource depletion and pollution. CE principles offer a viable framework for sustainable tourism development. The integration of supply and value chains with CE principles is essential for realizing the full potential of a CTE. This sustainable tourism supply chain management should involve integrating environmental, social, and economic considerations to minimize adverse effects and maximize positive outcomes for all stakeholders.

With the triple bottom line in mind, the balance between businesses' economic, environmental, and social goals will be articulated in their strategy formulation and implementation process. In the context of the tourism industry, businesses should focus not only on cost efficiency and profitability but also on their environmental and social impacts (Elkington, 1997), especially during supply chain activities.

Efficient and sustainable supply chain management in tourism can lead to cost reductions, enhanced customer satisfaction, and increased competitiveness. However, traditional supply chain management practices often focus solely on economic efficiency, with little regard for environmental and social impacts. To achieve sustainability, tourism businesses must adopt a more holistic approach to supply chain management that considers the entire lifecycle of products and services, from raw material extraction to disposal or reuse.

Strategic Recommendations for Implementing Circular Economy in Tourism

Although there are several challenges that may hinder the transition to a CTE, following strategic interventions may help its adoption and ensure long-term sustainability.

- Establishing clear and supportive regulatory frameworks addressing CE policies specially tailored for the tourism sector, which may include standardized certifications and incentives (e.g., tax breaks, grants, or subsidies) for businesses implementing CE practices.
- Promoting public-private partnerships to develop waste management systems, sustainable transportation infrastructure, and renewable energy solutions.
- Facilitating financial support and investment in circular tourism, such as establishing green investment funds or low-interest loans for tourism businesses transitioning to circular models.
- Strengthening stakeholder engagement and capacity building by providing education and training programs for tourism operators, local businesses, and employees can enhance awareness of CE benefits and best practices. Additionally, creating collaborative industry forums where businesses can share insights, challenges, and success stories and engage with local communities in decision-making processes to ensure that circular initiatives align with their economic and social needs.
- Encouraging consumer participation and behavioral change to promote eco-friendly travel choices by offering incentives such as discounts for sustainable accommodation or carbon offset programs, developing awareness campaigns highlighting circular tourism's environmental and economic benefits, and integrating smart technologies, such as digital platforms for sustainable travel planning. These interventions can help tourists make informed choices.

The successful integration of CE principles in tourism requires a multi-stakeholder approach, combining regulatory support, financial investment, technological innovation, and behavioral change; by implementing strategic interventions, the industry can transition toward a more resilient, equitable, and sustainable future that balances economic growth with environmental and social responsibility.

References

Baggio, R., & Cooper, C. (2010). Knowledge transfer in a tourism destination: The effects of a network structure. *The Service Industries Journal*, *30*(10), 1757–1771.

Bianchi, R. V. (2004). Tourism restructuring and the politics of sustainability: A critical view from the European periphery (The Canary Islands). *Journal of Sustainable Tourism*, *12*(6), 495–529.

Bocken, N. M., de Pauw, I., Bakker, C., & van der Grinten, B. (2016). Product design and business model strategies for a circular economy. *Journal of Industrial and Production Engineering*, *33*(5), 308–320.

Bohnsack, R., & Pinkse, J. (2017). Value propositions for disruptive technologies: Reconfiguring value for circular economy business models. *California Management Review*, *60*(1), 79–96.

Britton, S. G. (1982). The political economy of tourism in the third world. *Annals of Tourism Research*, *9*(3), 331–358.

Buckley, R. (2011). Tourism and environment. *Annual Review of Environment and Resources*, *36*, 397–416.

Budeanu, A. (2005). Impacts and responsibilities for sustainable tourism: A tour operator's perspective. *Journal of Cleaner Production*, *13*(2), 89–97.

Buhalis, D., & Law, R. (2008). Progress in information technology and tourism management: 20 years on and 10 years after the internet—The state of eTourism research. *Tourism Management*, *29*(4), 609–623.

Butt, N. (2007). The impacts of cruise ship generated waste on home ports and ports of call: A study of Southampton. *Marine Policy*, *31*(5), 591–598.

Carter, C. R., & Rogers, D. S. (2008). A framework of sustainable supply chain management: Moving toward new theory. *International Journal of Physical Distribution and Logistics Management*, *38*(5), 360–387.

Christensen, D., Hjul-Nielsen, J., Moalem, R. M., & Johansen, B. (2021). Circular economy in Denmark: Bornholm's vision to achieve 100 percent reuse and recycling. In S. K. Ghosh & S. K. Ghosh (Eds.), *Circular economy: Recent trends in global perspective*. Springer. https://doi.org/10.1007/978-981-16-0913-8_13

Christensen, T. H., & Munck-Kampmann, B. (2017). Solid waste management and circular economy: A challenge and opportunity for Bornholm. *Waste Management and Research*, *35*(4), 345–348.

EBRD. (2022). Zero-waste strategy: Ljubljana, Slovenia. https://www.ebrd-greencities.com/policy-tool/zero-waste-strategy-ljubljana-slovenia/

Elkington, J. (1997). *Cannibals with forks: The triple bottom line of 21st century business*. Capstone.

Ellen MacArthur Foundation. (2013). *Towards the Circular Economy: Economic and business rationale for an accelerated transition*. https://www.ellenmacarthurfoundation.org/publications/towards-the-circular-economy-vol-1-an-economic-and-business-rationale-for-an-accelerated-transition

Enz, C. A. (2010). *The Cornell School of Hotel Administration handbook of applied hospitality strategy*. Sage Publications.

European Commission. (2016). Ljubljana: European green capital 2016. https://environment.ec.europa.eu/topics/urban-environment/european-green-capital-award/winning-cities/ljubljana-2016_en

European Commission. (2021). *Danish project makes an island community greener*. https://ec.europa.eu/regional_policy/en/projects/europe/danish-project-makes-an-island-community-greener

Font, X., Walmsley, A., Cogotti, S., McCombes, L., & Häusler, N. (2016). Corporate social responsibility: The disclosure-performance gap. *Tourism Management*, *53*, 338–349.

Frantál, B., & Urbánková, R. (2017). Energy tourism: An emerging field of study. *Current Issues in Tourism*, *20*(13), 1395–1412.

Gamberini, R., Gebennini, E., Manzini, R., & Ziveri, G. (2017). Municipal waste management with citizen and stakeholder involvement: A case study in Ferrara, Italy. *Waste Management*, *59*, 64–75.

Gössling, S. (2002). Global environmental consequences of tourism. *Global Environmental Change*, *12*(4), 283–302.

Gössling, S. (2006). Towards sustainable tourism in the Western Indian Ocean. *Western Indian Ocean Journal of Marine Science*, *5*(1), 55–70.

Gössling, S., & Hall, C. M. (2006). *Tourism and global environmental change: Ecological, social, economic, and political interrelationships*. Routledge.

Gössling, S., Hall, C. M., & Weaver, D. B. (2009). *Sustainable tourism futures: Perspectives on systems, restructuring, and innovations*. Routledge.

Gössling, S., & Peeters, P. (2007). It does not harm the environment! An analysis of industry discourses on tourism, air travel and the environment. *Journal of Sustainable Tourism*, *15*(4), 402–417.

Gössling, S., Scott, D., Hall, C. M., Ceron, J. P., & Dubois, G. (2012). Consumer behaviour and demand response of tourists to climate change. *Annals of Tourism Research*, *39*(1), 36–58.

Hickman, R., Hall, P., & Banister, D. (2017). Planning more for sustainable mobility. *Journal of Transport Geography*, *50*, 247–257.

Hirschnitz-Garbers, M., Montevecchi, F., & Martinuzzi, A. (2013). Resource efficiency. In S. O. Idowu, N. Capaldi, L. Zu, & A. D. Gupta (Eds.), *Encyclopedia of corporate social responsibility*. Springer. https://doi.org/10.1007/978-3-642-28036-8_728

Juvan, E., & Dolnicar, S. (2014). The attitude–behaviour gap in sustainable tourism. *Annals of Tourism Research*, *48*, 76–95.

Lenzen, M., Sun, Y. Y., Faturay, F., Ting, Y. P., Geschke, A., & Malik, A. (2018). The carbon footprint of global tourism. *Nature Climate Change*, *8*(6), 522–528.

Lew, A. A., Ng, P. T., Ni, C. C., & Wu, T. C. (2020). The circular economy and sustainable tourism in Asia. *Asia Pacific Journal of Tourism Research*, *25*(3), 271–284.

Moraga, G., Huysveld, S., Mathieux, F., Blengini, G. A., Alaerts, L., Van Acker, K., De Meester, S., & Dewulf, J. (2019). Circular economy indicators: What do they measure? *Resources, Conservation and Recycling*, *146*, 452–461. https://doi.org/10.1016/j.resconrec.2019.03.045

Mundaca, L., Busch, H., & Schwer, S. (2018). Successful' low-carbon energy transitions at the community level? An energy justice perspective. *Applied Energy*, *218*, 292–303.

Peeters, P., Higham, J., Kutzner, D., Cohen, S., & Gössling, S. (2019). Are technology myths stalling aviation climate policy? *Transportation Research Part D: Transport and Environment*, *44*, 30–42.

Porter, M. E., & Kramer, M. R. (2011). Creating shared value. *Harvard Business Review*, *89*(1/2), 62–77.

Prentice, R. (2004). Tourist motivation and typologies. In A. Lew, C. M. Hall, & A. M. Williams (Eds.), *A companion to tourism* (pp. 261–279). Blackwell Publishing.

Revell, A., & Blackburn, R. (2007). The business case for sustainability? An examination of small firms in the UK's construction and restaurant sectors. *Business Strategy and the Environment*, *16*(6), 404–420.

Richter, J. L., & Scholz, R. W. (2020). Environmental consciousness in sustainability-oriented innovation: The case of Bornholm. *Business Strategy and the Environment*, *29*(1), 176–188.

Scheyvens, R. (2002). *Tourism for development: Empowering communities*. Pearson Education.

Scott, D., Gössling, S., & Hall, C. M. (2012). International tourism and climate change. *Wiley Interdisciplinary Reviews: Climate Change*, *3*(3), 213–232.

Tapper, R., & Font, X. (2004). *Tourism supply chains: Report of a desk research project for the Travel Foundation*. Leeds Metropolitan University. https://www.researchgate.net/publication/360783781_Tourism_Supply_Chains_Report_of_a_Desk_Research_Project_for_The_Travel_Foundation

Vintar, M., Žurga, G., & Žižek, N. (2019). The potential of blockchain in the tourism industry: The case of Ljubljana. *Tourism Review*, *74*(3), 585–599.

WTTC. (2019). *Travel and Tourism: Global economic impact and trends 2019*. https://wttc.org/Research/Economic-Impact

Zero Waste Europe. (2015). Ljubljana: First zero waste capital in the EU. https://zerowasteeurope.eu/2015/06/ljubljana-the-first-zero-waste-capital-in-europe

Zhang, H. Q., Song, H., & Huang, G. Q. (2009). Tourism supply chain management: A new research agenda. *Tourism Management*, *30*(3), 345–358.

Chapter 3

Connectivity, Aviation, and Sustainable Tourism Economy

Kübra Nur Uzuntaş[a] *and Sevdiye Kemik*[b]

[a]Istanbul Bilgi University, Türkiye
[b]Istanbul Topkapi University, Türkiye

Abstract

Aviation supports global trade and tourism, driving economic growth, and employment. It has direct, indirect, and induced economic impacts, with airlines boosting tourism and affecting destinations socially, culturally, and economically. Connectivity in aviation fosters new tourist destinations, with low-cost carriers (LCCs) enabling affordable international travel, expanding opportunities for many. This has led to social and economic benefits for major LCC hubs, including business growth, employment, and urbanization. However, tourism poses environmental challenges, such as energy consumption and emissions. Sustainable tourism aims to minimize negative impacts, with aviation addressing its footprint via fuel efficiency, sustainable aviation fuels (SAF), and eco-friendly innovations.

Keywords: Sustainable tourism; aviation; tourism economy; air connectivity; environmental sustainability

Introduction

Aviation is a complex and multi-dimensional transportation system that includes aircraft, operations, maintenance, crews, safety, security, weather, and air traffic management (Rodrigues, 2021). It comprises numerous companies and operations, including airlines, airports, and related services (Papatheodorou, 2021).

Aviation has a role that provides worldwide transportation, contributing to the advancement of global trade and the development of tourism. Air transportation also holds significant social and economic importance. As a global

Economics and Tourism, 43–59

doi:10.1108/978-1-83662-916-020251004

mode of transport, aviation facilitates tourism and trade, contributing to economic growth. Additionally, aviation provides employment, supports GNP (gross national product), and increases revenue from taxes. By enabling the rapid and efficient movement of people and goods around the world, aviation benefits trade and tourism, and it plays a crucial role in the economy of developing countries (Aydın, 2024).

This chapter focuses on the efforts to reduce the environmental footprint of the aviation industry, how sustainable practices can be developed, and the obstacles encountered in this process. It examines the importance of sustainability in the sector, the current state of practices, and the steps that need to be taken in the future. This chapter aims to provide valuable insights for both professionals in the industry and readers interested in sustainability and aviation.

The economic impacts are classified into four categories (İmadoğlu, 2023):

- Direct impact: Includes the first-tier results of the economic activities carried out by the aviation industry (Acar & Karabulak, 2015). These effects result from activities and jobs within the aviation sector. For instance, they include the employment opportunities created by airlines and airports.
- Indirect impact: Includes economic activities outside the aviation sector that contribute to the aviation industry. This covers the activities and employment opportunities of suppliers to the aviation sector. Examples of this impact include airport construction companies, fuel suppliers, suppliers of aircraft sub-components, and services such as call centers or human resources.
- Induced impact: Includes the impact arising from the increase in employment and income resulting from the direct and indirect economic effects of the aviation industry. These effects arise from the spending of individuals who are directly or indirectly employed in the aviation industry.
- Catalytic/Spin-off impact: Relates to how aviation affects and supports the development of other sectors. An example of this would be the impact of aviation on tourism and the revenue generated from tourism.

Among these impacts, catalytic effects are considered the most important. Catalytic effects are examined under two categories: *demand-side* and *supply-side* effects (Bal et al., 2017). Demand-side catalytic effects are the effects of the aviation sector on domestic demand for goods and services. These goods and services are particularly related to trade and tourism. The impact on tourism refers to how airline connections influence tourism and the contribution of expenditures made by tourists using the airport to the GDP. The impact on trade includes facilitating access to distant markets through airline connections and the contribution of products transported by air to the GDP. Supply-side catalytic effects refer to increasing the efficiency of a country's resources through the aviation sector.

Airlines play a catalyst role across multiple sectors, supporting their development and economic growth. One of these areas is the "tourism" sector, which is defined as the movement of individuals for a variety of reasons, such as business, pleasure, or other needs, to locations outside of their typical surroundings. The activities of these visitors, referred to as the "visitor economy," can significantly affect the social, cultural, and economic aspects of the places that are being visited. As was already mentioned, aviation plays an important role in the tourism industry and the global economy by allowing people to travel for leisure or business to places outside of their normal surroundings. Hence, this allows millions of people to have access to job opportunities and also other sources of income. Travelers who visit other nations significantly depend on the services supplied by the aviation industry (Nithya, 2024).

The Aviation Sector

The "Deregulation" initiated in the United States in 1978 paved the way for significant changes in the aviation sector. During this period, the reduction of government intervention in the airline industry contributed to the formation of free market conditions and the rapid growth of the sector. One of the most notable outcomes of deregulation was that airline companies began to operate under competitive conditions. This competitive environment led to a decrease in ticket prices and an increase in demand for air transportation (Uzun, 2019). With the increasing demand, there was a significant rise in passenger capacity, and the aviation sector entered a period of great expansion.

This expansion process has been considered a major step in the development of the aviation sector. The growth in the sector has also enabled airline companies to improve the quality of their services. The development of the aviation sector has positively impacted not only air transportation but also other sectors. For instance, the growth in the aviation sector has increased demand in the tourism sector. Air transportation has become one of the most important elements of tourism and has contributed to the growth of this sector by facilitating access to tourism destinations (Altuntaş & Kılıç, 2021).

Another important factor that triggered the growth of the aviation sector is the increase in average income per capita. Economic development and the rise in income levels have increased people's demand for travel. This economic growth, especially seen in major markets, has significantly increased the demand for air transportation (Macit & Macit, 2017).

In the global economy, the aviation sector is of critical importance not only for passenger transportation but also for the transportation of goods and services. The aviation sector plays a vital role in the development of international trade and the acceleration of economic growth, contributing to the integration of global markets. In countries' economic development strategies, the aviation sector holds great importance and is considered an indispensable tool for economies aiming to integrate with global markets (Saheed & Iluno, 2015).

Airline Service and Its Features

The most important characteristics of the service provided by airline companies are the provision of fast, comfortable, and easy transportation to passengers. The main features of the service offered by aviation can be listed as follows (Güngör, 2023):

- Airline service is personal. Passengers' opinions about the flight vary. These differences in opinion change according to passengers' age, gender, income, expectations, and socioeconomic characteristics (Tsai, 2016).
- Airline service is perishable. An example of perishability is empty seats after the aircraft doors are closed for a flight (Chatwin, 2000).
- The service cannot be stored for later use. Therefore, airline companies must efficiently manage the sale of empty seats (İmadoğlu, 2023).
- Airport-airline strategic partnerships have been shown to provide cost control and competitive advantage (Macit & Basar, 2023).
- Airline service is provided collectively. Meeting customers' demands also increases customer loyalty. While offering services collectively, airline companies must consider the needs and wants of the majority.
- Demand for air travel varies seasonally. The period of highest demand is during the summer months when schools are on vacation. Demand for business-related flights also increases at certain times of the year (Doganis, 2010).
- Aviation activities are influenced by many external factors. These factors can be economic, political, or meteorological events. Examples of events that deeply impacted aviation include the September 11 crisis and the COVID-19 pandemic.
- Establishing and managing an airline business requires high investment and capital. For this reason, until companies reach sufficient capital, airline operations have been managed by the state. Today, the fact that the largest airline fleets are under state control supports this. One of the main costs for airline companies is labor costs. In addition to hiring personnel, airline companies need significant time and financial investment to train this staff (Harvey & Turnbull, 2017).
- Another major cost for airline companies is fuel cost. Fuel cost is the largest expense for airline companies. Therefore, the aviation sector is the most affected by fluctuations in fuel prices. Since fuel costs are the largest expense for airline companies, they tie their economic success to the income they can achieve against this expense (Wolter et al., 2021).
- Airline companies aim to grow, develop, and improve to increase their revenues. Therefore, airline companies should select their human resources in line with this goal. The most important element in aviation is ensuring safety. Airline companies need personnel who possess a safety culture and awareness to ensure the safety of passengers and the flight. The flight crew, technicians, pilots, and other staff must be trained to ensure the flight is conducted safely and securely (Temirkhanova, 2020).

Economic Benefits of Air Transportation

Air transportation makes significant contributions to the global economy, supporting growth and development across a wide range of sectors, from tourism to international trade.

- *Supports Tourism.* Air transportation provides easy access to distant and previously inaccessible destinations. This increased accessibility has led to the growth of global tourism and contributed to local economies benefiting from spending on accommodation, food, and other services (Doganis, 2010).
- *Facilitates International Trade.* Air transportation enables the fast and efficient movement of goods across international borders. This is especially important for high-value and time-sensitive products. For example, air transportation is preferred for the shipment of goods like electronics, pharmaceuticals, and perishable foods. The speed and reliability provided by air transportation support global supply chains and allow businesses to meet customer demands quickly (İmadoğlu, 2023).
- *Creates Employment.* The aviation sector is a significant source of employment, not only within airlines but also in related sectors such as airports, aircraft manufacturing, maintenance, and air traffic control. Additionally, the growth of air transportation creates employment in sectors like hospitality, retail, and transportation services that support air travelers (Tutar et al., 2013).
- *Strengthens Business Connections.* Air transportation facilitates business connections between cities and countries. This enables companies to expand their markets and engage in international trade and investment. Air transportation connects business hubs worldwide, fostering strong business relationships and increasing productivity (ICAO, 2004).
- *Provides Catalytic Impact.* Aviation supports global economic integration by enabling fast and efficient international trade. Air transportation ensures the rapid delivery of time-sensitive products (e.g., electronics, fresh food, pharmaceuticals) to target markets. This increases trade volume between countries and supports the efficiency of global supply chains (Çelik, 2017).
- *Contribution of Airports to Regional Development.* It has been stated that airports not only facilitate trade and tourism but also make significant contributions to regional economic development. These contributions include the creation of employment, increased trade volume, and the development of local businesses in the regions where airports are located (Macit & ve Duran, 2023).
- *Is an Important Source of Revenue for Governments.* This importance stems from the broad economic activities of the sector and the direct and indirect income generated through various tax categories related to these activities (Çelik, 2017).

Connectivity, Aviation, and Tourism

The term "connectivity" describes the degree of connection between two locations. Connectivity, especially in aviation, plays a significant role in tourism, promoting the development of new tourist destinations. Low-cost airline carriers (LCCs) have made affordable international travel by improving connectivity and offering consumers new travel opportunities. A substantial percentage of society that was previously unable to travel overseas for socioeconomic reasons now has the chance to do so thanks to this development. The major LCC destinations have seen an increase in social and economic benefits as a result of the increase in foreign tourist flows (Iñiguez et al., 2014).

The number of enterprises established within a city, the employment rate, and the size of its population are all positively impacted by its air connectivity. In order to increase company productivity, which supports overall area economic growth, there needs to be a strong air connection (Cristea, 2023). Although tourism offers various benefits, it also poses significant challenges, such as high energy consumption and detrimental environmental effects, including contributions to climate change (Streimikiene et al., 2021).

The first definition of sustainable tourism was declared by UNWTO (United Nations World Tourism Organization) in 1996: "tourism which leads to management of all areas, in such a way, that the economic, social and environmental needs are being fulfilled with the cultural integration, ecological processes, biodiversity and supporting the development of societies." Sustainable tourism encompasses principles such as conserving natural resources, protecting cultural heritage, and supporting local economies (Janusz & Bajdor, 2013).

The interaction between connectivity, aviation, and sustainable tourism plays a critical role in shaping the future of the tourism industry. The need for air travel and tourism rises with increased connectivity, placing strain on ecosystems and destinations. To guarantee the long-term sustainability of tourist destinations and reduce adverse effects on the environment and society, it is crucial that the aviation and tourism industries need to embrace sustainable practices. By promoting sustainable tourism practices, stakeholders may enhance the overall travel experience for tourists in addition to supporting local economies and protecting the environment and cultural heritage. The connection between eco-friendly travel and aviation emphasizes how crucial stakeholder cooperation is to reducing negative environmental impacts. Concerns about climate change and the environment are beginning to spread throughout society. As a result, sustainability has become one of the most important concerns. Over the past 10 years, the aviation sector has made significant progress toward achieving sustainability. These steps continue today and will continue in the future. The integration of sustainability into the aviation sector can only be achieved if every part of the industry embraces a common understanding of sustainability (Gemmer, 2019).

The sustainability efforts aim to reduce the direct impacts of air transportation and minimize the industry's environmental carbon footprint. However, sustainability is not limited to the environmental dimension alone. It also encompasses social and economic aspects. Therefore, achieving sustainability in the aviation sector requires collaboration among various stakeholders and a shared vision. Airports serve tourist destinations and facilitate tourist flows. Additionally, airports make significant contributions to economic development. They support tourism activities and promote trade development. Therefore, sustainability efforts in the aviation sector benefit society both environmentally and economically.

Environmental Impacts of Aviation

The temperature of the Earth has increased by about 1°C since 1900. The accumulation of greenhouse gases in the atmosphere is the main cause of this increase, which has led to a global problem known as climate change. With the development of industries and technology, the use of traditional fossil fuels has rapidly increased, resulting in higher emissions of greenhouse gasses (Sher et al., 2021).

In order to mitigate the aviation sector's environmental impact, strategies and procedures have been developed. Implementing sustainable practices, monitoring the process, lowering carbon emissions, and improving aircraft and engine design to improve fuel efficiency are some of these actions. In addition, minimizing environmental impacts can be achieved by improving the infrastructure in aviation and sustainable flight operations. The aviation industry's environmental impact can be reduced through the implementation of these initiatives and measures, opening the door to a more sustainable future (Lynes & Dredge, 2006). Major international agreements that aim to establish sustainability in aviation are summarized in Table 4.1.

Table 4.1. Important Agreements to Establish Sustainability in Aviation.

Date	Agreement/Convention	Description
1997	Kyoto Protocol	In addressing global climate change, the Kyoto Protocol's adoption in 1997 was an important step for sustainability (United Nations FCC, 2013). The clauses of the Protocol, which placed responsibility on the nations, were signed in 1997 and came into effect in 2005. The states involved have committed to reducing their carbon emissions to a certain quantity via this agreement. States agreed to lower their emissions by 5% compared to 1990 for the first period between 2008 and 2012. The EU-15 countries were accountable for cutting it by 8%. In 2001, the United States of America, the nation with the highest global greenhouse gas emissions, declared its rejection of the agreement, although agreeing to a

(Continued)

Table 4.1. *(Continued)*

Date	Agreement/Convention	Description
		7% reduction. The goals of the protocol's second period, which runs from 2013 to 2020, have also been established. The base rate for this period, like with the previous one, was the emission rates for 1990. However, a 20% reduction was the goal for the second term. The primary source of the target rate increase was the rise in emissions between the two periods. In this method, balancing was aimed. While it was included in the second period limitations, civil aviation was not included in the first term limitations (Doğan, 2018)
2016	Paris Agreement	The Paris Agreement, a pact aimed at mitigating and adapting to climate change while also providing funding, was signed in 2015 and came into effect in 2016. It has been agreed by 55 countries (the United States withdrew later on) that are accountable for about 55% of greenhouse gas emissions globally. The purpose was to keep the global temperature rise below 2 degrees compared to the preindustrial period (Doğan, 2018)
2016	The Carbon Offsetting and Reduction Scheme for International Aviation	The international program CORSIA aims to reduce the amount of CO_2 emissions that the aviation industry produces. (Strouhal, 2020). CORSIA seeks to expand forest lands, invest in sustainable technology, and increase the utilization of SAF. The airlines and nations participating have agreed

Table 4.1. *(Continued)*

Date	Agreement/Convention	Description
		reporting their carbon emissions between 2021 and 2026 voluntarily. After 2026, it will be mandatory for all nations to agree to the convention (Doğan, 2018)
2016	ICAO's 39th Assembly adopted Resolution A39	Resolution A39 is a Global Market-Based Measure to address aircraft engine pollution (Abeyratne, 2017). It is an important step in focusing on climate change and aviation emissions. The resolution mandates Monitoring and reporting procedures to ensure transparency and accountability in emissions reporting by airlines. Airlines are required to offset any emissions that exceed 2020 levels by purchasing emission units from accredited carbon offset programs
2021	Net Zero 2050	IATA has pledged to achieve net-zero carbon emissions by 2050, as have many of its member airlines. To achieve net-zero CO_2 emissions by 2050, a strategy combining emission reduction at the source with offsetting and carbon capture technology is necessary. This strategy will rely on 65% of emissions reductions coming from SAF, 13% from new technologies such as electric and hydrogen-powered aircraft, and 3% from improvements in infrastructure and operational efficiencies. The remaining 19% will be addressed through offsets and carbon capture methods (IATA, 2021)

Source: Compiled by the author(s).

Aviation contributes 2–3% of global CO_2 emissions (Stankovic et al., 2021). On the other hand, the demand for air travel rises as the industry emissions also increase. In this regard, environmental issues and measures about climate change are necessary. Significant progress has been achieved in reducing CO_2 emissions in aviation. One of these actions is the usage of composite materials in aircraft, such as the Boeing 787 Dreamliner. These aircraft significantly reduce CO_2 emissions. The material of this aircraft consists of 50% composite materials, and aircraft manufacturers state that the Boeing 787 can reduce CO_2 emissions by between 20% and 25% (Timmis et al., 2015).

Sustainable Aviation Fuel (SAF) is another significant step taken to reduce carbon emissions in aviation. The term "SAF," which is commonly used in the aviation sector recently, refers to a non-traditional aviation fuel. Utilizing SAF in the aviation industry can cut carbon emissions by up to 65% and greenhouse gas emissions by a significant amount (Sharma et al., 2021).

Another environmental issue caused by aviation is noise, referred to as "unwanted sound." Aviation-related noise originates from the sounds generated by aircraft during takeoff, landing, and flight. This noise can lead to various adverse effects on people, especially those living in areas close to airports. Noise pollution can decrease the quality of life for local residents and cause health problems. Noise not only negatively impacts individuals' overall well-being but also disrupts sleep patterns, thereby reducing sleep quality. Over time, sleep disturbances can lead to chronic health issues, such as fatigue, stress, anxiety, and psychological problems like depression (Basner et al., 2017).

Noise pollution also has significant effects on children. Children growing up in noisy environments have been observed to experience attention deficits, learning difficulties, and declines in academic performance. In the long term, this can negatively affect their educational achievements and interfere with their developmental process. Noise is known to threaten not only physical health but also cognitive and emotional well-being. Aviation noise impacts not just humans but also the environment and ecosystems. Parks, open spaces, and natural habitats can be affected by noise pollution. Wildlife, particularly noise-sensitive animals such as birds, can be adversely impacted by this type of noise. Noise can make it difficult for animals to communicate, find mates, feed, and hunt, which are essential life activities. Furthermore, noise pollution may cause animals to leave their natural habitats, disrupting the balance of ecosystems (Mestre, 2008).

Sustainability and Tourism

The connection between tourism and sustainability is growing more and more vital every day. Tourism has the potential to create many positive impacts, such as economic growth, cultural exchange, and social interaction. But tourism can also lead to some negative effects like environmental damage, the destruction of local cultures, and the overuse of natural resources. The objective of sustainable tourism is to minimize these negative impacts while maximizing the benefits that tourism provides (Tahiri & Kovaci, 2017).

Fundamentals of Sustainable Tourism

Sustainable tourism is built on the principles of environmental, economic, and sociocultural sustainability. It seeks to guarantee that tourism-related activities benefit current and future generations. Sustainable tourism is defined by the UNWTO as "a form of tourism that meets the economic, social, and aesthetic needs of present and future generations while preserving environmental integrity, biological diversity, and cultural resources" (UNWTO, 2020).

Environmental Sustainability

It includes managing natural resources in an environmentally responsible manner. Waste generation, water use, and carbon emissions are some of the ways in which tourism affects the environment. For instance, popular tourism destinations are more subject to environmental and cultural degradation over time due to growing tourism (Butler, 1980).

Economic Sustainability

The economic approach aims to ensure that tourism contributes to local economies in a sustainable way. It not only involves ensuring a fair distribution of tourism revenues but also supports the economic independence and development of local communities. Economic sustainability provides long-term economic resilience and stability by reducing local economies' overreliance on tourism (Hall & Lew, 2009).

Socio-Cultural Sustainability

It includes protecting local cultures while also maintaining societal unity. The protection of cultural heritage is a crucial component of the sociocultural sustainability of tourism. Sustainable tourism aims to offer visitors an authentic experience while preserving the cultural identity of local communities. Hence, it is important to prevent the commercialization of local cultures. Sustainable tourism is a long-term approach, and it is based on environmental and social, and economic principles. The objective of this approach is to minimize the negative impacts of tourism while ensuring the preservation of local communities, natural resources, and cultural heritage. The implementation of sustainable tourism policies will guarantee the continued sustainable growth of tourism in the future (Smith, 2009).

Sustainable Tourism Economy

The sustainable tourism economy is based on the concept that the tourism sector should support long-term economic growth and provide lasting benefits for the local communities. Worldwide, tourism is acknowledged as a major economic activity that makes substantial contributions to the GDP of many nations.

However, the economic impacts of tourism must also be balanced with environmental and cultural sustainability (Muhanna, 2006).

The Principles of Sustainable Tourism Economy

Sustainable tourism economy aims to support the economic development of local communities while preserving environmental resources. The key principles of the sustainable tourism economy are as follows:

- Empowerment of the Local Economy: Sustainable tourism ensures that tourism revenues stay within the local economy and benefit local businesses. The goal of sustainable tourism is to lessen reliance on outside sources while improving the financial condition of local communities (Sharpley & Telfer, 2002).
- Long-Term Economic Resilience: While tourism can bring quick gains in the short term, a "sustainable tourism economy" approach offers economic resilience and stability in the long term. Sustainable tourism is more resilient to economic crises and other outside shocks (Dwyer & Forsyth, 2008).
- Equitable Income Distribution: Sustainable tourism supports the fair distribution of tourism revenues and economic opportunities among the local communities. Reducing income inequality is critical to ensuring the sustainability of tourism (Timothy & Tosun, 2003).

The tourism industry's sustainability is determined by its contributions to local economies. Sustainable tourism integrates into the economy by encouraging purchases from local producers, employing local people in tourism businesses, and preserving local cultures. Sustainable tourism practices that support the local economy contribute directly to the welfare of the local population through the revenue acquired from tourism activities (Mowforth & Munt, 2003).

A sustainable tourism economy also includes sustainable investment and financing models. This encompasses elements such as environmentally friendly hotel constructions, energy-saving technologies, and support for local enterprises. Sustainable tourism finance must address not only economic returns but also environmental and social implications (Buckley, 2012).

Financial Sustainability

Financial sustainability refers to the ability of an entity—whether it's a business or a country—to manage its financial resources in a way that ensures long-term stability: generating revenue consistently, controlling or reducing expenses, and having adequate resources to meet future financial needs. This concept involves managing the capacity to meet current financial obligations while also balancing the ability to provide the necessary resources for future growth and development. It is vital for both current and future financial success of organizations (Under30CEO, 2024). It includes the ability to meet existing financial obligations while also securing the resources needed for future growth and development. In the face of challenges such as economic uncertainties and market fluctuations, maintaining financial sustainability helps organizations stay resilient and adaptable, making it key to long-term success (Gleißner et al., 2022).

The key principles of the financial sustainability can be listed as follows:

- Long-Term Planning: Sustaining financial sustainability can be achieved through long-term financial planning and strategic management. Long-term planning includes diversifying revenue sources, maintaining budgeting discipline, and managing financial risks (Sherman, 2010).
- Income-Expense Balance: The sustainability of an organization is achieved when its revenues exceed or at least match its expenses. This balance not only funds daily operations but also creates resources for future investments, and maintaining this balance is crucial for financial sustainability (Hendricks & Singhal, 2005).
- Risk Management: Financial sustainability requires the identification of potential financial risks and the implementation of protective measures against them. Effective management of financial risks secures an organization's financial sustainability (Garrison & Noreen, 2006).

Financial sustainability is closely related to social responsibility. For an organization to be financially sustainable, it must also be capable of fulfilling its responsibilities toward society. Social responsibility and financial sustainability are complementary elements, and financial sustainability is a critical factor for an organization to maintain its positive impact on society. Performance also contributes to fulfilling societal and environmental responsibilities. Therefore, adopting financial sustainability strategies is essential for the long-term well-being of organizations. Financial sustainability is considered a fundamental element for the long-term success and growth of organizations. This concept encompasses financial planning, income-expense balance, risk management, and social responsibility principles. Financial sustainability not only enhances financial and communities (Carroll, 1991).

Conclusion

This book chapter examines the connection between aviation and the sustainable tourism economy, exploring the interactions between these sectors and their environmental and economic impacts. The aviation sector plays a significant role in the global economy and tourism (İmadoğlu, 2023). While aviation activities support economic growth, they also present significant challenges in terms of environmental sustainability (Buckley, 2012). The sustainability of the tourism sector is crucial not only for economic growth and job creation but also for the preservation of natural and cultural resources (Sharpley & Telfer, 2002).

In order to minimize the aviation industry's negative environmental effects and guarantee long-term financial gains, sustainable practices must be employed

(Doğan, 2018). Likewise, the preservation of cultural heritage, the development of local economies, and the conservation of natural resources all depend on the tourism industry's adoption of sustainability principles. An integrated approach to sustainability goals in the aviation and tourism sectors is of great importance for the future success and societal well-being of both sectors (Dwyer et al., 2011).

The widespread use of SAF and the development of environmentally friendly technologies in aircraft design will contribute to reducing carbon emissions in the sector. Additionally, it is necessary to increase sustainability practices in the tourism sector, such as energy conservation, waste management, and efficient use of water resources (Sharpley & Telfer, 2002).

It is important to raise awareness and provide training for employees in both the aviation and tourism sectors to increase sustainability awareness (Sherman, 2010). In this context, relevant stakeholders should be encouraged to acquire knowledge about sustainability and integrate this knowledge into their business processes (Buckley, 2012).

Governments should develop appropriate regulations and policies to promote sustainability in the aviation and tourism sectors (Doğan, 2018). This is a significant step in supporting sustainability initiatives within the sector and reducing environmental impacts (Gleißner et al., 2022). Establishing strong collaborations between stakeholders in the aviation and tourism sectors will play a critical role in achieving sustainability goals. These collaborations will ensure that sectoral developments occur while maintaining the environmental, social, and economic balance (Sharpley & Telfer, 2002).

References

Abeyratne, R. (2017). Outcome of the 39th session of the International Civil Aviation Organization assembly. *Air and Space Law*, *42*(1).

Acar, A. Z., & Karabulak, S. (2015). Competition between full service network carriers and low cost carriers in Turkish airline market. *Procedia-Social and Behavioral Sciences*, *207*, 642–651.

Altuntaş, M., & Kılıç, E. (2021). Havayolu taşımacılığı ile ekonomik büyüme arasındaki ilişkinin incelenmesi: Türkiye örneği. *Afyon Kocatepe Üniversitesi Sosyal Bilimler Dergisi*, *23*(1), 187–202.

Aydın, U. (2024). Havalimanlarında taşınan yolcu sayısı üzerine ağ analizi uygulamaları ve havalimanlarının merkeziliği: Türkiye iç hatları örneği. *Marmara Üniversitesi İktisadi ve İdari Bilimler Dergisi*, *46*(1), 293–312.

Bal, H., Manga, M., & Gümüş Akar, P. (2017). Havacılık sektörü ve ekonomik büyüme: Türkiye örneği. *Akademik Sosyal Araştırmalar Dergisi*, *5*(45), 353–366.

Basner, M., Clark, C., Hansell, A., Hileman, J. I., Janssen, S., Shepherd, K., & Sparrow, V. (2017). Aviation noise impacts: State of the science. *Noise and Health*, *19*(87), 41–50.

Buckley, R. (2012). Sustainable tourism: Research and reality. *Annals of Tourism Research*, *39*(2), 528–546.

Butler, R. W. (1980). The concept of a tourist area cycle of evolution: Implications for management of resources. *Canadian Geographer*, *24*(1), 5–12.

Carroll, A. B. (1991). The pyramid of corporate social responsibility: Toward the moral management of organizational stakeholders. *Business Horizons*, *34*(4), 39–48.

Çelik, D. S. (2017). Havayolu taşımacılığı endüstrisi ve ekonomik etkileri. *Uluslararası Bilimsel Araştırmalar Dergisi*, *2*(8), 82–89.

Chatwin, R. E. (2000). Optimal dynamic pricing of perishable products with stochastic demand and a finite set of prices. *European Journal of Operational Research*, *125*(1), 149–174.

Cristea, A. D. (2023). The role of aviation networks for urban development. *Journal of Regional Science*, *63*(4), 947–980.

Doğan, M. E. (2018). Küresel Kamusal Mal Kapsamındaki Hava Kirliliğine Neden Olan Etkenlerin Havacılık Sektörü Odaklı İncelenmesi. *Gazi Üniversitesi Sosyal Bilimler Dergisi*, *5*(13), 142–156.

Doganis, R. (2010). *Flying off course: Airline economics and marketing* (4th ed.). Routledge.

Dwyer, L., & Forsyth, P. (2008). Economic measures of tourism yield: What markets to target? *International Journal of Tourism Research*, *10*(2), 155–168.

Dwyer, L., Papatheodorou, A., & Forsyth, P. (2011). *Economics of tourism*. Goodfellow.

Garrison, R. H., & Noreen, E. W. (2006). *Managerial accounting*. McGraw-Hill/Irwin.

Gemmer, E. (2019). *Aviation sustainability*. Springer.

Gleißner, W., Günther, T., & Walkshäusl, C. (2022). Financial sustainability: Measurement and empirical evidence. *Journal of Business Economics*, *92*(3), 467–516.

Güngör, H. (2023). Hava taşımacılığı: Havayolu işletmeleri. In H. Güngör (Ed.), *Sivil havacılık yönetiminin temelleri* (pp. 127–154). Akademi Titiz Yayınları.

Hall, C. M., & Lew, A. A. (2009). *Understanding and managing tourism impacts: An integrated approach*. Routledge.

Harvey, G., & Turnbull, P. (2017). Human resource management and industrial relations. In L. Budd & S. Ison (Ed.), *Air transport management* (pp. 307–321). Routledge.

Hendricks, K. B., & Singhal, V. R. (2005). An empirical analysis of the effect of supply chain disruptions on long-run stock price performance and equity risk of the firm. *Production and Operations Management*, *14*(1), 35–52.

ICAO. (2004). *Manual on the regulation of international air transport* (2nd ed., Doc. 9626). International Civil Aviation Organization.

İmadoğlu, T. (2023). Havacılığın dünya ekonomisi için önemi. In H. Güngör (Ed.), *Sivil havacılık yönetiminin temelleri* (pp. 77–99). Akademi Titiz Yayınları.

Iñiguez, T., Plumed, M., & Martínez, M. P. L. (2014). Ryanair and Spain: Air connectivity and tourism from the perspective of complex networks. *Tourism & Management Studies*, *10*(1), 46–52.

International Air Transport Association. (2021). *Fly Net Zero: Commitment to achieve net zero carbon by 2050*. IATA. https://www.iata.org/en/programs/sustainability/flynetzero/

Janusz, G. K., & Bajdor, P. (2013). Towards sustainable tourism – Framework, activities and dimensions. *Procedia Economics and Finance*, *6*, 523–529.

Lynes, J. K., & Dredge, D. (2006). Going green: Motivations for environmental commitment in the airline industry. A case study of Scandinavian Airlines. *Journal of Sustainable Tourism*, *14*(2), 116–138.

Macit, A., & Basar, M. (2023). The effects of the vertical cooperation strategy between airports and airlines on the operating performance of airlines. *OPUS Journal of Society Research*, *20*, 984–1001. https://doi.org/10.26466/opusjsr.1348252

Macit, D., & Macit, A. (2017). Türkiye'de sivil havacılık sektöründe istihdamın mevcut durumu, sorunları ve sorunların çözümüne yönelik öneriler. *Journal of Emerging Economies and Policy*, *2*(2), 74–85.

Macit, A., & ve Duran, Z. (2023). Türkiye'de Yeni İnşa Edilen Havalimanlarinin Sosyoekonomik Etkileri: Tümevarımsal Perspektiften Swot Analizi. *Yönetim Ve Ekonomi Araştırmaları Dergisi*, *21*(3), 196–219. https://doi.org/10.11611/yead.1264153

Mestre, V. (2008). *Effects of aircraft noise: Research update on selected topics* (Vol. 9). Transportation Research Board.

Mowforth, M., & Munt, I. (2003). *Tourism and sustainability: Development and new tourism in the third world*. Routledge.

Muhanna, E. (2006). Sustainable tourism development and environmental management for developing countries. *Problems and Perspectives in Management*, *4*(2), 14–30.

Nithya. (2024). Exploring the role of destination management organizations (DMOs) in leveraging social media as a destination marketing tool: Insights from Himachal Pradesh. *Discovery Researcher Life*. https://discovery.researcher.life/article/exploring-the-role-of-destination-management-organizations-dmos-in-leveraging-social-media-as-a-destination-marketing-tool-insights-from-himachal-pradesh/ebb93458f86b34e9b0962ff773b38611

Papatheodorou, A. (2021). A review of research into air transport and tourism: Launching the annals of tourism research curated collection on air transport and tourism. *Annals of Tourism Research*, *87*, 103151.

Rodrigues, A. (2021). *Aviation investment: Economic appraisal for airports, air traffic management, airlines, and aeronautics*. Taylor & Francis.

Saheed, A. A. A., & Iluno, S. Z. C. (2015). Air transportation development and economic growth in Nigeria. *Journal of Economics and Sustainable Development*, *6*(2), 1–11.

Sharma, A., Jakhar, S. K., & Choi, T. M. (2021). Would CORSIA implementation bring carbon neutral growth in aviation? A case of US full service carriers. *Transportation Research Part D: Transport and Environment*, *97*, 102839.

Sharpley, R., & Telfer, D. J. (2002). *Tourism and development: Concepts and issues*. Channel View Publications.

Sher, F., Raore, D., Klemeš, J. J., Rafi-ul-Shan, P. M., Khzouz, M., Marintseva, K., & Razmkhah, O. (2021). Unprecedented impacts of aviation emissions on global environmental and climate change scenario. *Current Pollution Reports*, 1–16.

Sherman, H. D. (2010). Financial stability: Principles and practice. *The Journal of Economic Perspectives*, *24*(4), 77–90.

Smith, M. K. (2009). *Issues in cultural tourism studies*. Routledge.

Stankovic, M., Ambo-Rappe, R., Carly, F., Dangan-Galon, F., Fortes, M. D., Hossain, M. S., & Prathep, A. (2021). Quantification of blue carbon in seagrass ecosystems of Southeast Asia and their potential for climate change mitigation. *Science of the Total Environment*, *783*, 146858.

Streimikiene, D., Svagzdiene, B., Jasinskas, E., & Simanavicius, A. (2021). Sustainable tourism development and competitiveness: The systematic literature review. *Sustainable Development*, *29*(1), 259–271.

Strouhal, M. (2020). CORSIA-Carbon Offsetting and Reduction Scheme for International Aviation. *MAD-Magazine of Aviation Development*, *8*(1), 23–28.

Tahiri, A., & Kovaci, I. (2017). The theory of sustainable tourism development. *Academic Journal of Business*, *3*(1), 343–349.

Temirkhanova, I. (2020). Employer branding in the airline industry: On the example of Ryanair. *Suleyman Demirel University Bulletin: Social Sciences*, *52*(1).

Timmis, A. J., Hodzic, A., Koh, L., Bonner, M., Soutis, C., Schäfer, A. W., & Dray, L. (2015). Environmental impact assessment of aviation emission reduction through the implementation of composite materials. *International Journal of Life Cycle Assessment*, *20*, 233–243.

Timothy, D. J., & Tosun, C. (2003). *Tourism and community development*. Routledge.

Tsai, T. (2016). Homogeneous service with heterogeneous products: Relationships among airline ticket fares and purchase fences. *Journal of Air Transport Management*, *55*, 164–175.

Tutar, F., Alpaslan, C., Tutar, E., & Erkan, Ç. (2013). Turizm sektörünün istihdam üzerine etkileri. *Global Journal of Economics and Business Studies*, *2*(4), 14–27.

Under30CEO. (2024, March 21). *Financial sustainability*. Under30CEO. Accessed September 9, 2025, from https://www.under30ceo.com/terms/financial-sustainability/

United Nations Framework Convention on Climate Change. (n.d.). *The Kyoto Protocol*. Accessed September 9, 2025, from https://unfccc.int/process-and-meetings/the-kyoto-protocol

Uzun, A. M. (2019). Deregülasyon ve ekonomik etkileri: ABD ve Türkiye havayolu taşımacılığı deneyimi üzerine bir inceleme. *Kafkas Üniversitesi İktisadi ve İdari Bilimler Fakültesi Dergisi*, *10*(19), 474–489.

Wolter, A. H., Ehlers, T., Luetjens, K., & Gollnick, V. (2021). Commodity price pass-through in the US airline industry and the hidden perks of consolidation. *Journal of Air Transport Management*, *95*.

World Tourism Organization. (2020). *UNWTO Regional Conference on Sustainable Development through Tourism – Proceedings, Thimphu, Bhutan, 03 June 2019*. UNWTO, Madrid. https://doi.org/10.18111/9789284421312

Chapter 4

Green Practices: An Eco-linguistic Contribution to the Tourism Economy

Umut Balcı[a] *and Munise Aksöz*[b]

[a]Batman University, Türkiye
[b]Çukurova University, Türkiye

Abstract

Tourism and economics are closely related, as seen in the similarities between university tourism programs. However, the link between tourism, economics, and linguistics is often overlooked. Tourism economics studies the production and consumption of goods by small and medium-sized enterprises, while applied linguistics explores the role of language in various fields. Eco-linguistics, a branch of applied linguistics, examines the relationship between language and environmental issues, emphasizing multilingualism and cultural preservation. Tourist preferences are shaped by factors like recreation, culture, and environmental concerns. The language used in eco-friendly tourism practices influences these preferences, contributing to the tourism economy. This study highlights Eco-linguistics' role in promoting sustainable tourism.

Keywords: Tourism economics; eco-linguistics; destination types; language pragmatics; green practices

Introduction

The Tourism Sector Assessment prepared by Ernst and Young stated that France, Spain, the United States, Italy, and Türkiye were the most visited and

Economics and Tourism, 61–71

Published under exclusive licence by Emerald Publishing Limited
doi:10.1108/978-1-83662-916-020251005

preferred countries in 2022.[1] According to the United Nations World Tourism Organization (UNWTO), Türkiye is projected to be the sixth most visited country in 2023, following France, Spain, the United States, China, and Italy.[2] With this decline, Türkiye regressed to the figures of international tourist arrivals recorded in 2019. Although Türkiye is the fifth or sixth most visited country, there is a contradiction between our country's 14th place in the world ranking with an annual tourism income of $29.8 billion according to 2019 data (Yaşar, 2021, pp. 255–256).

According to the Turkish Statistical Institute report dated January 31, 2024,[3] tourism revenues increased by 6.8% compared to the same quarter of the previous year and reached 12 billion 272 million 673 thousand dollars. Of tourism receipts, 15.2% of tourism receipts were generated by nonresident citizens visiting Turkey. Of the expenditures made by tourists, 9 billion 47 million 94 thousand dollars were personal expenditures and 3 billion 225 million 579 thousand dollars were package tour expenditures. Tourism revenue in 2023 increased by 16.9% compared to the previous year and reached 54 billion 315 million 542 thousand dollars.

Just a few simple facts above are enough to show how important tourism is for the Turkish economy. The crucial aspect for a sustainable tourism economy is to raise awareness of the factors that make Türkiye important and to optimize the tourism goods and services offered in line with demand in order to achieve better results. However, in order to meet these demands, respect for people, culture, the environment, and nature should be the guiding principles, and the pursuit of profit should not override these values. The principal objective of this study is to examine the role of linguistic, ecological, and economic factors in the context of tourism. This will be achieved by evaluating the aforementioned activities in the context of green practices and determining the extent to which contemporary tourism focuses on nature conservation. The study employs document analysis as a qualitative research method. Wach (2013) defines document analysis as a systematic examination of written documents, and this method is used to analyze and evaluate all documents, including printed and electronic materials. As with other methods employed in qualitative research, document analysis necessitates the examination and interpretation of data in order to ascertain meaning to gain insight into the pertinent subject matter, and to generate empirical knowledge (Corbin & Strauss, 2008). In this context,

---

[1]https://www.ey.com/tr_tr/news/2023/11/ey-turizm-sektoru-2023-degerlendirmesi-raporu-yayinlandi. Accessed on June 11, 2024.

[2]https://anlatilaninotesi.com.tr/20240115/2023te-en-cok-ziyaret-edilen-ulkeler-hangileri-1079669928.html. Accessed on June 11, 2024.

[3]https://data.tuik.gov.tr/Bulten/Index?p=Turizm-Istatistikleri-IV.-Ceyrek:-Ekim—Aralik,-2023-53661#:~:text=Turizm%20geliri%202023%20y%C4%B1l%C4%B1nda%20bir,ise%20paket%20tur%20harcamalar%C4%B1%20olu%C5%9Fturdu. Accessed on June 11, 2024.

websites and mobile applications identified as "green" on the Internet were subjected to content analysis, and findings were incorporated into the study.

Demand in Tourism

The production and supply of tourism goods and services are shaped by demand. The demand for tourism originates from the desire to travel and the substantial number of individuals possessing adequate financial means to fulfill this desire. The factors determining the desire to travel, whether positive or negative, are generally divided into three categories. The most important ones are economic factors since the prices of tourism goods and services, the budget available for travel, and the location and quality of the destinations are all determined by economic conditions. Social factors include issues such as education levels, urbanization rates, leisure time, and occupation; however, personal tastes and habits, advertising and promotion by tourism companies, quality and cost of health services, climatic conditions, cultural characteristics, local political situations; for instance, terrorism are among the most influential factors (İçöz, 2005; Kaya & Canlı, 2013, p. 43; Kozak et al., 2001; Lim 1997).

There are weaknesses and strengths determining the demand for a tourist destination. The factors identified by Yaşar (2021 p. 259) based on the data of the State Planning Organization for 2001, which do not reflect the actual situation, should be summarized and corrected as follows:

- Environmental factors such as nature, climate, and historical artifacts,
- The socio-economic importance of tourism is understood by a large part of society,
- Türkiye's rich cultural heritage,
- The hospitality of the people,
- A dynamic and youthful population capable of rapidly adapting to the tourism phenomenon,
- Unique socio-cultural qualities, the coexistence of exotic tourism assets of the East and the West,
- Awareness in the main markets; high market share and presence of travel agencies and airlines with expertise in Türkiye in the international tourism market,
- Newer and better quality facilities compared to competitors in the Mediterranean hinterland,
- Coastal areas favorable for the development of yachting tourism,
- New places for tourists in remote corners that have yet to be discovered,
- Handicraft products such as clothing, carpets, jewelry, and leather,
- Geographical structure and transport facilities offering opportunities for tourism diversification,
- Adaptation to the changing structure of demand in international tourism.

The results of Öztürk and Tuna's (1999) research on the British market are more realistic in terms of showing the strengths and weaknesses of Turkish tourism. According to this research, the advantages include hospitality, affordability, natural beauty, beaches, sun, Turkish food, historical artifacts, and cultural values. The disadvantages determined in this study cover political and social turmoil, human rights violations, competition among tour operators, inadequate and poorly maintained highways, insufficient railway transport, poor quality of service at airports, over-crowdedness in some tourist regions, Türkiye's negative international image, lack of qualified personnel, seasonal challenges, inadequate infrastructure, service problems, coastal pollution, non-compliance with cleaning, and health rules in some establishments, inadequacy of camping sites and apart-hotels, cheap marketing of the country, and relative distance of Türkiye from European tourist markets. It is possible to claim that the negative aspects mentioned in this survey, which is quite old, are still relevant and have even increased. Irregular migrants/refugees coming to Türkiye from many countries of the world, especially from Syria, spoil the image of Türkiye and thus damage the tourism economy.

Tourism and Foreign Languages

One of the driving forces of the tourism economy is the marketing of tourism goods and services, as well as the quality of marketing. The main factor assigning this quality is tactile/olfactory/visual/gustatory communication (Balcı & Balcı, 1997, 2021; Balcı & Yavuz, 2008). In the tourism sector, one of the most important communication channels is foreign languages.

In Türkiye, many studies have been conducted on the problems in tourism education and on the proposed solutions. In one of these studies, Balcı (1998) identified the lack of foreign language skills of the personnel providing tourism services as one of the main problems. The reason for this issue is that foreign language education is not given enough importance in the undergraduate and postgraduate curricula related to tourism (Babayiğit & Balcı, 2023; Gültekin Talayhan & Babayiğit, 2023), and tourism is considered to be only an economic field. Akgöz and Gürsoy's (2014) study on "foreign language learning, willingness, and determination in tourism education" at Selçuk University, and Beyşehir, Yücel and Arıkan's (2019) research on the foreign language needs of tourism personnel in Antalya also directly or indirectly address the similar problems. Altürk et al. (2016) analyzed the curricula of all existing tourism faculties and colleges in Türkiye in terms of foreign languages, and stated that tourism-oriented foreign language education should be given much more importance, and serious changes should be made in terms of course curriculum.

Environment and Ecology

According to the Turkish Language Association, the word "environment" has eight different meanings. The definition related to our subject is "All natural, social, and cultural external factors that are effective in the development of life[4]." The term "ecology" is defined as follows: "The branch of science that studies the relationships of living things, individually or collectively, to each other and to their environment." This definition is more limited in scope compared to the term "environment." Eco-linguistics, called "environmental linguistics" in Turkish language, is never mentioned in the dictionary of the Turkish Language Association.

In the German DWDS dictionary, "Ecologie" is defined as: "The science of the relationships between the systems of organisms and their environment."[5] The term "Ecology" does not appear in this dictionary. There is, however, the term "human ecology," which is defined as "the science of the relationships between social groups and their natural environment." Both of these definitions show how intertwined the human being, social relations, nature, and language are.

Language ecology was introduced in the 1970s by the sociolinguist Einar Haugen (Eliasson, 2015). Haugen argues that languages, like other living things, live, develop, interbreed, and die. Eco-linguistics is a very broad interdisciplinary field. In parallel with the definition of environment mentioned earlier, Eco-linguistics is concerned with the relationship between linguistics and natural, social, and cultural factors that are effective in the preservation and development of every element of the universe. Factors such as the explanation of linguistic processes, linguistic change, the decline or death of languages, and multiculturalism are significant issues that directly affect the environment and ecological balance.

Although it had no theoretical basis at the time, the father of Eco-linguistics is considered to be the German philosopher Humboldt (Makkai, 1996, p. 83). In the 1980s, however, Alwin Fill rescued the term Eco-linguistics from its purely metaphorical use, and he directly linked linguistics to the ecosystems of nature and cultures (Fill, 1996). According to Fill (1996, p. 3), the architect of Eco-linguistics, biological and linguistic diversity, multilingualism, indigenous languages, pidgin languages, rhetorical figures (especially metaphor), language change, language conflict, the death of dialects and minority languages, code switching, interference, feminist linguistics, queer linguistics, and interculturality can be included in the field of Eco-linguistics.

The Concept of "Green": Reflection of Eco-linguistic Elements on Tourism

Particularly, since the 1970s, the concept of "green" has been attributed many different embellishing meanings. For this reason, it is also possible to use the term "green linguistics" instead of Eco-linguistics. This beautiful color evokes nature, life, youth, freshness, newness, sharing, harmony, tolerance, trust, hope,

---

[4]https://sozluk.gov.tr/. Accessed on June 12, 2024.

[5]"Wissenschaft von den Beziehungen der Systeme von Organismen zu ihrer Umwelt." https://www.dwds.de/wb/%C3%96kologie. Accessed on June 12, 2024.

peace, comfort, success, tranquillity, goodness, respect, love, and joy. Therefore, "green" is more than a signifier of a color, but it is a kind of activism that adopts the principle of struggling against the prevailing mediocrity and the tyrannical great power. The term "Green" stands for the small and the weak, the defenseless and the victimized, and the oppressed and the different. For example, the "green agenda" blog of "Yeşil Gazete[6]" includes the following categories: climate crisis, nature, ecology, agri-food, energy, animal rights, women, LGBTI, civil society, and city.

The following issues reported in Yeşil Gazete's blogs may be directly related to tourism and may hold a positive or negative impact on the tourism economy: The Marmara Sea is "sick," the ecological equilibrium threshold has been exceeded/Extreme weather conditions caused $41 billion damage in six months/ The four horsemen of the climate crisis: heat waves, droughts, fires, and floods/If there are no bees, there is no us/Will we be able to communicate with whales?/five ways to get in touch with nature for holidaymakers in Istanbul/TEMA's call: We need forest and water resources/EKAD's call for volunteers for Caretta carettas/ Fethiye's water and Muğla bees are in danger/The revised EIA report is incomplete, irregular, and inconsistent/Implement court decisions, close thermal power plants!/"No" to cyanide mining!/IKEA destroys Romanian Carpathian forests for cheap and easy furniture/Approval for WPP project in Muğla: 12,000 trees to be cut down/Famous water buffalo of Çaycuma and its registered product, water buffalo yoghurt, are disappearing/Clean Cooking Summit organized in Europe: Half a million lives could be saved in Africa/Study: New fossil fuel projects completely unnecessary/Animal rights activists in Urfa stand up for dogs: There are no more dogs on the streets/Release arrested rights activist, Özgünlü, immediately/Massacre law cannot be legitimized on the pretext of rabies: Maximum two cases per year/Denmark includes women in military service under the pretext of "gender equality"/Statement on homophobic attacks during Newroz: No Halay is free without us/We're in Kastamonu and Sinop with the "Environment and Climate Journalism School"/Coastal Movements Solidarity Network calls for all coasts against commercialization/IPEC2024 Conference will discuss "derivation economy"/Civil society rolled up its sleeves for a clean and livable Asi River Basin/Kadıköy Environment Festival 2024 started with the theme "Sustainable City and Urban Resilience" etc...

Whether we are aware of it or not, we are confronted with the interaction between language and environment on a daily basis. These relationships will affect tourism either immediately or in the long term.

The environment does not spontaneously intervene and harm people. Nature does not disturb its own equilibrium; it is man who disturbs the equilibrium. Therefore, humans can damage the environment directly or indirectly. Besides, if nature harms human beings, it is caused by human beings. In other words, the destruction that human beings cause in nature comes back to them in the form of

[6]https://yesilgazete.org. Accessed on June 12, 2024.

fire/flood/drought. Unfortunately, these natural disasters also cause great damage to the tourism industry.

Sometimes, people do things with good intentions to protect and improve the environment. For example, the first open-source artificial intelligence language model, "ClimateGPT" was developed as a contribution to the environment and ecologists. This model, which we place within the framework of computational linguistics, corpus linguistics, and Eco-linguistics, aims to contribute to the fight against the climate crisis by supporting efforts to mitigate human damage to nature and the effects of global warming on the environment. There are many disciplines aiming to live in peace, fraternity, and cooperation with humans, animals, plants, and rivers, essentially with every element of nature. Examples may incorporate ecological agriculture, sociolinguistics, queer linguistics, feminist linguistics, and eco-linguistics.

No one would ever say that they were trying to damage nature. In fact, people misuse language by making positive statements to cover up their bad intentions. To indicate a tourism-related instance: describing an ordinary tomato as an organic tomato, cow's cheese as goat's cheese, and farm eggs as village eggs to tourists is nothing but deception. Balcı (2006) highlights the following examples of environmentalist or counter-environmentalist words or discourses that can be associated with environmental linguistics at the semiotic level: Field tomato, village bread, eco-friendly/new generation engine, global warming, dog esthetics, meat eater, social justice, globalization, microbial weapon, ecosystem, exotic creature, genetic diversity, dung, urban waste, rural area, environmental concern, healthy/unplanned urbanization, green belt, migration, concretization, biodiesel, biomedical, bioclimate, biofascism, biofuel, bioecology, bioproduct, biosafety, biodiversity, bio-oil, biogod, bio-waste, bioweapon, biopile, biomimicry, biobank, biolaw; eco-club, eco-ethics, eco-product, eco-neighborhood, eco-fuel, eco-farming, eco-village, eco-economy, eco-tourism, eco-anarchy, eco-settlement, etc.

Although mass tourism based on sea, sand, and sun is the largest contributor to Türkiye's tourism economy, it is rather crucial to diversify tourism. Yaşar (2021, p. 261) cites cruise tourism, health tourism, nature tourism, winter and mountain tourism, religious and cultural tourism, congress and sports tourism, and gastronomic tourism as examples of diversification. For Turkey to effectively compete with countries such as France, Spain, Italy, and Greece, and to enhance its tourism industry, it is imperative to emphasize its distinctive characteristics rather than striving solely for esthetic superiority. As the concepts of beautiful and good are relative, being different means being unique, and turning to new destinations that emphasize these differences will make our tourism economy stronger. For example, Antakya, which boasts more than 600 types of food, can be promoted as a gastronomic destination. Batman/Hasankeyf and Şanlıurfa can act as significant cultural heritage destinations. Adana, Ankara, and many other cities with strong health services are candidates to make a major contribution to a sustainable tourism economy.

The "Nature Tourism Web Application"[7] launched by the Ministry of Agriculture and Forestry draws attention to how rich Türkiye is in terms of nature tourism, with its national and nature parks, wetlands, caves, and flora and fauna specific to these areas. In Hatay alone, there are 10 destinations for nature tourism: AltınözüWildlife Development Area, Belen Pass Nature Park, Gölbaşı Lake Wetland, Hassa Lava Tube Caves Nature Area, Hatay Mountain Gazelle Wildlife Development Area, Haydaralar Lake Wetland, İskenderun-Arsuz Wildlife Development Area, Mileyha Reed Wetland, Şahin Hill Nature Park, and Tekkoz-Kengerlidüz Nature Reserve.

Health tourism refers to all kinds of tourism activities for a healthy life. Health tourists go to a foreign country to receive treatment and surgery in hospitals, relaxation and rehabilitation services in thermal facilities, geriatric treatment, and long stays in natural environments such as plateaus and to engage in social activities. Although health tourism means traveling from one country to another for the purpose of treatment in order to regain health, health tourists' travels are not limited to receiving health services, yet people like changes as much as they like stability. Therefore, combining the health service to be received with a different environment and geography in terms of cultural and natural beauties, and "killing two birds with one stone" provides psychological relief, especially for substance addicts, chronic patients, the elderly, and the disabled, and this increases the desire to hold on to life and live.

According to the Health Tourism Sector Report of the Association of Turkish Travel Agencies (TÜRSAB),[8] the most preferred countries by health tourists are Türkiye, South Korea, India, Mexico, Thailand, Israel, Malaysia, and Singapore. Of course, among many other reasons, low cost is the biggest factor in this preference.

The Ministry of Trade's report on health tourism[9] states that Türkiye has become a global center, and 1.4 million health tourists came to our country in 2023, increasing the export of health services to $2.3 billion. According to the data of the International Health Services Incorporated Company USHAŞ based on the data of the Turkish Statistical Institute, TÜİK, a total of 1,538,643 people came to Turkey to receive health services in 2023, and an income of 3,006,092, thousand USD was earned from them.[10] These data indicate that health tourism is rather significant for a sustainable tourism economy and should be promoted more. At this point, it is essential to integrate these services with other cultural tourism packages, such as nature tourism, religious tourism, or ecological tourism, during the marketing phase of health tourism services. It is imperative

---

[7]https://ekotaban.tarimorman.gov.tr/. Accessed on June 13, 2024.

[8]https://www.duendedijital.com/wp-content/uploads/2023/12/TURSAB-SAGLIK-TURIZMI-RAPORU.pdf. Accessed on June 13, 2024.

[9]https://ticaret.gov.tr/haberler/saglik-turizminde-kuresel-merkez-turkiye#:~:text=%C3%9Clkemiz%2C%202022%20y%C4%B1l%C4%B1%20sa%C4%9Fl%C4%B1k%20hizmeti,2%2C3%20milyar%20dolara%20y%C3%BCkselmi%C5%9Ftir. Accessed on June 14, 2024.

[10]https://www.ushas.com.tr/saglik-turizmi-verileri/. Accessed on June 14, 2024.

for Türkiye to exert greater efforts in promoting cultural tourism products to enhance its share in the tourism market (Bal & Dilek, 2021). Mosques, inns, baths, tombs, aqueducts, registered building streets, monumental trees, fountains, caravanserais, clock towers, ancient cities, castles, city walls, theaters, necropolises, acropolises, temples, churches, cisterns, museums, local languages, and many tangible and intangible values such as dialects, holidays, folklore, festivals, weaving such as carpets and rugs, earthen and wooden artifacts, copper and stone processing products, and jewelry are essential for a sustainable tourism economy. Although the number of cultural tourists is lower than the other types, it has been observed that their purchasing power is higher.

However, there are a great deal of aspects to consider; it is necessary to curb globalization, which may appear innocent, but in our view, it is destroying the ecological balance with all its power for the pursuit of more profits. In other words, it is of the utmost importance to prevent the adverse consequences of industrialization, rapid urbanization, and second home disease (Meydan Uygur & Baykan, 2007).

Conclusion

Türkiye is one of the world's most important tourist destinations, ranking sixth in the world. Considering Turkey's current economic problems, it is evident that a sustainable tourism economy to be carried forward is entailed. For a stronger and more sustainable tourism economy, Turkish tourism should be diversified with cruise, health, nature, religious, cultural, congress, sports, and gastronomic tourism. The Ministry of Tourism should focus on new destinations with potential for nature, faith, and cultural tourism, especially those that emphasize diversity, multilingualism, multiculturalism, and cultural heritage.

Tourism is not a sector that can exist in isolation; in fact, interdisciplinary work is essential for the sustainability of tourism. Ecology is an example of such disciplines, as it seeks to protect all kinds of organisms, living or nonliving things, abstract or concrete beings, individual or social possessions, and all kinds of values. In the field of linguistics, a branch of applied linguistics called eco-linguistics has emerged to protect and develop ecological values through language, and it is dedicated to nature and human beings; however, it is not restricted to preserving and improving nature through language. Thus, it opposes the exploitation of nature and the manipulation of people through the misuse of language and favors the small, the weak, the defenseless, the victim, and the oppressed.

Improving the quality of tourism education is essential for the sustainability of the tourism industry. Therefore, tourism education curricula should cover the topics such as language learning, multilingualism, and multiculturalism. It is difficult for those working in tourism to contribute to a sustainable tourism economy if they do not hold environmental awareness and consciousness within the broad framework outlined by eco-linguistics. This awareness and consciousness should primarily be possessed by the people who receive tourism services. Especially in alternative tourism destinations, it is essential for sustainability that cultural heritage, nature parks, and wildlife, which are the apple of nature tourism, not be damaged. As a suggestion for further investigations, it is indicated that Türkiye, ranking sixth globally in tourism, confronts economic challenges that underscore the imperative for a sustainable tourism approach; thus, studies exploring diversification into cruise, health, nature, religious, cultural, congress, sports, and gastronomic tourism sectors are entailed, and within this goal, boosting facilities in academic genres should be taken into consideration. In addition, new destinations emphasizing diversity, multilingualism, multiculturalism, and cultural heritage preservation should be developed and presented by the Ministry of Tourism in Türkiye since it may be possible for human beings to come up with various perspectives for the mentioned topics. Also, it is highlighted that Eco-linguistics, as an interdisciplinary field, advocates for ecological conservation through language and opposes exploitative linguistic and environmental practices; therefore, tourism education should be integrated with language acquisition, multilingualism, and multicultural perspectives processes, and awareness within cultural heritage, nature reserves, and wildlife in the scope of Eco-linguistics should be boosted. Thus, academicians and curriculum programmers have to take urgent actions in the academic field.

References

Akgöz, E., & Gürsoy, Y. (2014). Turizm Eğitiminde Yabancı Dil Öğrenme İstek ve Kararlılıkları: Selçuk Üniversitesi Beyşehir Örneği. *Journal of Tourism and Gastronomy Studies*, *1*(2), 21–29.

Altürk, A., Yel, G., Arık Yüksel, T., & Balcı, U. (2016). Turizm Fakülte ve Yüksekokullarında Yabancı Dil Eğitimi. *International Periodical for the Languages, Literature and History of Turkish or Turkic*, *3*(11), 139–150.

Babayiğit, M. V., & Balcı, U. (2023). Yabanci Dil Eğitiminde Dil Kaygisi Üzerine Bibloyografik Bir Çalişma: Turizm Fakülteleri Örneği. In M. Tosun & C. Doğan (Eds.), *Kültürlerarasılık & Dil* (1st ed., pp. 199–218). Paradigma Akademi.

Bal, F., & Dilek, S. E. (2021). Awareness level of residents on cultural heritage: The case of Diyarbakır. *Mesopotamia Journal of Interdisciplinary Studies*, *1*(1), 45–67.

Balcı, T. (2021). Sprechakte unter besonderer Berücksichtigung der Höflichkeit. *Diyalog. Interkulturelle Zeitschrift für Germanistik*, *1*(9), 108–121.

Balcı, T. (1998). *Türkiye'de Germanistik ve Turizm Eğitimi. Sorunlar ve Somut Çözüm Önerileri*. Çukurova Üniversitesi Eğitim Fakültesi Yayınları.

Balcı, T. (2006). Ekodilbilim ya da Çevredilbilim. *Cumhuriyet Bilim ve Teknik*, *988*, 11.

Balcı, T., & Balcı, H. (1997). Tarihsel Süreçte Kadın Erkek Eşitsizliğinin Kadın Dili ile Erkek Diline Yansıması ve Sosyo-Kültürel Nedenleri. *Cukurova University Faculty of Education Journal*, *15*(1), 40–55.

Balcı, T., & Yavuz, N. (2008). İşletme Dilbilimi: Antipazarlama Dilbilimi. *Pazarlama ve İletişim Kültürü Dergisi (pi)*, *2*, 12–18.

Corbin, J., & Strauss, A. (2008). *Basics of qualitative research: Techniques and procedures for developing grounded theory*. Sage.

Eliasson, S. (2015). The birth of language ecology: Interdisciplinary influences in Einar Haugen's "The ecology of language". *Language Sciences*, *50*, 78–92.
Fill, A. (1996). Ökologie der Linguistik – Linguistik der Ökologie. In A. Fill (Ed.), *Sprachökologie und Ökolinguistik* (pp. 3–16). Stauffenburg.
Gültekin Talayhan, Ö., & Babayiğit, M. V. (2023). Foreign language teaching in Türkiye historical development problems and solutions. *Uluslarası Bilim ve Eğitim Dergisi*, *6*(3), 246–260.
İçöz, O. (2005). *Turizm İşletmeleri ve Yönetimi*. Turhan Kitabevi.
Kaya, A. A., & Canlı, B. (2013). Türkiye'ye Yönelik Uluslararası Turizm Talebinin Belirleyenleri: Panel Veri Yaklaşımı. *Anadolu Üniversitesi Sosyal Bilimler Dergisi*, *13*(1), 43–54.
Kozak, M., Bowen, D., & Rimmington, M. (2001). *Tourism marketing: An Asian-Pacific perspective*. Continuum.
Lim, C. (1997). Review of international tourism demand models. *Annals of Tourism Research*, *24*(4), 835–849.
Makkai, A. (1996). Die Welt als Bewusstsein und Paraphrase. In A. Fill (Ed.), *Sprachökologie und Ökolinguistik* (pp. 77–91). Stauffenburg.
Meydan Uygur, S., & Baykan, E. (2007). Kültür Turizmi ve Turizmin Kültürel Varlıklar Üzerindeki Etkileri. *Gazi Üniversitesi Ticaret Ve Turizm Eğitim Fakültesi Dergisi*, *2*, 30–49.
Öztürk, Y., & Tuna, M. (1999). Türkiye Turizminin İngiliz Pazarında Kuvvetli ve Zayıf Yönleri Üzerine Bir Araştırma. *Anatolia: Turizm Araştırmaları Dergisi*, *1* (10), 47–52.
Wach, E. (2013). Learning about qualitative document analysis. https://opendocs.ids.ac.uk/opendocs/bitstream/handle/20.500.12 413/2989/PP%20InBrief%20 13%20QDA%20FINAL2.pdf?sequence=4. Accessed on May 11, 2024.
Yaşar, İ. (2021). Türkiye'ye Gelen Yabancı Turistlerin Tatil Tercihleri ve Satın Alma Davranışları Üzerine Bir Değerlendirme. *Sosyal, Beşerî ve İdari Bilimler Dergisi*, *4*(3), 252–272.
Yücel, E., & Arıkan, A. (2019). Turizm Personelinin Yabancı Dil Gereksinimleri: Antalya Örneği. *Bingöl Üniversitesi Sosyal Bilimler Enstitüsü Dergisi*, *17*(9), 657–668.

Chapter 5

Sustainable Tourism Development: Trends and Prospects

Nguyen Thi Minh Tien and Mai Thùy Dương

Hanoi University, Vietnam

Abstract

Under globalization and interconnectedness, tourism fosters cross-cultural understanding and drives economic growth while promoting inclusive and sustainable development. As a result, sustainable tourism, which prioritizes more than profit-seeking, has gained increasing support from governments and citizens. Despite its potential, challenges such as governance gaps, social stratification, and climate risks persist, particularly in Asia. This chapter explores key trends, principles, and types of sustainable tourism through global examples. It examines its advantages over traditional tourism and discusses the prospects of sustainable tourism. Through comparative analysis, this study highlights sustainable tourism's role in achieving long-term development goals.

Keywords: Sustainable tourism; economic growth; traditional tourism; responsible and regenerative tourism; climate conscious travel

Introduction

Prior to COVID-19, it was reported that 10.4% of global GDP (equivalent to 10.3 trillion USD) belonged to the Travel and Tourism sector (World Travel & Tourism Council, n.d.). Global tourism reached an all-time high in 2019, with 1.76 billion international arrivals (Herre & Samborska, 2023). Despite a sharp decline in 2020 during the pandemic, the global travel and tourism industry has strongly bounced back, generating nearly 880 billion USD in revenue across hotels, holiday packages, vacation rentals, and camping (Statista, 2025). Given the significant contribution of tourism to GDP, as well as its continued

Economics and Tourism, 73–87

doi:10.1108/978-1-83662-916-020251006

attractiveness—considering the consistently high number of tourist arrivals—tourism plays an essential role in global development and economic growth.

All of these challenges require a sustainable tourism development approach, which stresses the importance of an equitable form of tourism that balances interactions between economic, social, and environmental aspects. Under the sustainable tourism framework suggested by the International Council on Monuments and Sites (ICOMOS), tourism activity levels should be maintained over the long term, ensuring "a net benefit for the social, economic, natural, and cultural environments of the area in which it takes place" (as quoted from GDRC, n.d.). This is especially crucial to ensure that future generations have the opportunity to continue enjoying natural beauty and experiencing global wonders in their travels, both within and across countries.

Although sustainable tourism development or sustainable tourism has become a frequent theme in various forums and discussions on tourism and hospitality, there remains a strong focus on the realization of sustainable tourism as the way forward for the industry. This is particularly relevant for developing countries, where natural wonders remain pristine and services are often diverse and affordable. These countries have seen increasing tourist visits and growing travel interest, especially from backpackers and travelers from Western and developed nations.

However, the opportunities associated with the expansion and growth of tourism and hospitality also come with risks. Therefore, this chapter aims to explore the trends, principles, and models of sustainable tourism, as well as analyze the extent to which opportunities and challenges can be balanced. The insights drawn from this chapter will provide fresh perspectives on various examples of sustainable tourism practices worldwide through a comparative analysis of tourism models, coupled with a case-study-driven approach that highlights best practices and emerging strategies.

Principles and Frameworks of Sustainable Tourism

Definition of Sustainable Tourism

The World Tourism Organization (UNWTO, n.d.) defines sustainable tourism as tourism that "takes full account of its current and future economic, social, and environmental impact, addressing the needs of visitors, the industry, the environment, and host communities." Unlike mass tourism, which is profit-driven and strongly focused on industry expansion, sustainable tourism considers the long-term impacts of tourism on society and the environment. When discussing mass tourism and sustainable tourism, some scholars (Butler, 1980, 1991; Goodwin, 2016; Gössling et al., 2018) adopt an "oppositional view," arguing that mass and sustainable tourism are inherently conflicting in nature. Others (Bramwell & Lane, 1993; Sharpley, 2009; Swarbrooke, 1999; Weaver, 2011) take a "moderate view," suggesting that sustainable tourism can complement mass tourism by integrating sustainability principles, making the two approaches compatible.

From a traditional academic perspective, Butler (1993) defined sustainable tourism as "tourism which is developed and maintained in an area in such a manner and at such a scale that it remains viable over an indefinite period and does not degrade or alter the environment." In another conceptualization, Swarbrooke (1999), in Sustainable Tourism Management, described sustainable tourism as "a form of tourism that seeks to minimize negative economic, environmental, and socio-cultural impacts while maximizing positive benefits to local communities and environments."

Swarbrooke's definition takes a more pragmatic approach, emphasizing impact minimization and benefit maximization, whereas Butler adopts a structural and theoretical perspective, focusing on destination life cycles and the consequences of unregulated tourism growth. Despite the different viewpoints scholars take and the evolving conceptualizations of sustainable tourism over time, there is a general consensus that tourism must incorporate sustainability to prevent long-term damage—an essential principle in understanding sustainable tourism.

Besides the commonly used definition of sustainable tourism by the UNWTO and various interpretations by academic scholars, the evolution of sustainable tourism as a concept is closely linked to the idea of sustainable development, which was introduced in the Brundtland Report (1987). In this report, the World Commission on Environment and Development (WCED) defines sustainable development as "development that meets the needs of the present without compromising the ability of future generations to meet their own needs." Although the report does not specifically address tourism, its emphasis on balancing environmental, economic, and social dimensions has influenced changes in development approaches across various industries, including tourism.

Core Principles of Sustainable Tourism

The principles of sustainable tourism are based upon the three main dimensions, including environmental conservation, economic viability, and socio-cultural responsibility. Similar to the holistic framework of sustainable development, sustainable tourism also tackles multiple dimensions that would affect the long-term development of the tourism industry. In other words, sustainable tourism should not solely generate economic benefits, but it has to consider the consistent financial benefits in the long run without compromising environmental and social sustainability.

The Principle of Economic Viability would depend on stakeholder collaboration, diversification, and responsible business strategies. The engagement of multiple stakeholders, such as government–private partnerships for sustainable tourism, is crucial and has been highlighted by Akande and Ijeuru (2024) as a key driver of greater economic impact. In an increasingly competitive tourism market, where customer demand is rising alongside growing socio-environmental concerns, diversification in strategies is essential for the long-term viability of the industry. A prime example of this is Singapore's tourism model, which has successfully positioned itself as an economically resilient destination by integrating diversification, government-private partnerships, and responsible tourism investments into its long-term growth strategy. Rather than relying solely on mass tourism, Singapore has developed multiple high-revenue tourism sectors, including eco-tourism, medical tourism, cultural tourism, and MICE (Meetings, Incentives, Conferences, and Exhibitions), ensuring resilience against economic fluctuations (Chang, 2002; Henderson, 2007; Sugimoto, 2017).

The Principle on Socio-cultural Responsibility: While sustainable tourism fosters opportunities for cultural exchange and learning across communities and nations, it also prioritizes the preservation of local cultures and traditions. Ethical responsibility, respect for indigenous traditions, cultural heritage, and historical values, along with the active participation of local communities in safeguarding their cultural assets, are fundamental aspects of this approach. As highlighted in UNESCO's World Heritage and Sustainable Tourism Programme (UNESCO, n.d.), sustainable tourism requires integrated planning and stakeholder collaboration to balance heritage conservation and tourism development. Without responsible management, there is a significant risk of cultural commodification and erosion, particularly in destinations rich in traditions, historical landmarks, and indigenous cultures. Beyond the proper management of cultural heritage sites, sustainable tourism must actively involve local communities by creating incentives that allow them to economically benefit from tourism while empowering indigenous groups to preserve their cultural identity.

The Principle on Environmental Conservation: Sustainable tourism should strive to address environmental challenges arising from tourist-related activities by promoting eco-friendly practices and conservation-focused policies. As a resource-intensive industry that relies heavily on natural landscapes, biodiversity, and ecological balance, the travel and tourism sector is responsible for 8% of global carbon emissions (World Travel & Tourism Council, n.d.), significantly contributing to climate change. Therefore, sustainable tourism must prioritize natural conservation, the promotion of renewable energy use, the development of smart and green infrastructure, and the implementation of educational programs to raise public awareness about environmental sustainability. These measures are essential to alleviating the pressure and mitigating the negative impacts of tourism on natural landscapes and ecosystems.

Types and Models of Sustainable Tourism

Sustainable tourism can be divided into some major types, including Eco-tourism, Community-Based Tourism, and Cultural and Heritage Tourism. According to the Statista Research Department (2024) recent data has indicated a strong interest among travelers in eco-friendly accommodations. Specifically, as of February 2022, 78% of global travelers would intend to stay at least once in a green or eco-friendly lodging in the upcoming year, despite the differences in willingness to pay a premium for such accommodations.

Although there are numerous models and frameworks in the literature, this chapter will focus on the Tourism Area Life Cycle (TALC) and the Carrying Capacity Models.

Tourism Area Life Cycle (TALC): Developed and revised by Richard Butler (1980, 1991), this model illustrates the six stages of tourism growth—from initial exploration and development to stagnation and eventual decline or rejuvenation. In the final stage, Butler argued that destinations may either decline due to congestion and environmental decay or experience rejuvenation if innovative management strategies are applied. Based on his life cycle analysis, the model examines tourism's predictive patterns and underscores the need to incorporate sustainability strategies into tourism development to avoid overexploitation of resources. Although the model does not explicitly mention "sustainable tourism" in its title, it nonetheless advocates for sustainability strategies in tourism management.

The Carrying Capacity Model: The Carrying Capacity Model has been widely used in tourism management to define the maximum number of visitors a destination can sustain without causing excessive damage to its environment, economy, infrastructure, and social fabric. Originally developed as a concept in ecology, "carrying capacity" was later applied to tourism by J. J. O'Reilly (1986) and has since been further developed in sustainable tourism literature. This model serves as a management tool for policymakers to set visitor limits, protect local communities, and promote sustainable tourism. In fact, to counter over-tourism and regulate visitor numbers, the Carrying Capacity Model has often been employed by UNESCO, national parks, and major tourist destinations. In contemporary times, there have been many accounts of the successful adoption of this model by top destinations—such as Machu Picchu (Peru), the Galapagos Islands (Ecuador), Komodo National Park (Indonesia), and Mount Everest Base Camp (Nepal and Tibet)—to balance tourist growth with long-term sustainability. Specifically, Komodo National Park in Indonesia, which is home to the endangered Komodo dragons, has faced significant pressure from over-tourism, leading to issues such as wildlife stress, ecosystem degradation, and illegal poaching. Applying the principles of carrying capacity, the Indonesian government has implemented various measures to alleviate pressure on both tourism management and the environment, including setting an annual visitor quota (up to 200,000 people) and increasing entrance fees to 250 USD per person to limit mass tourism (Yuniar, 2022).

Trends in Sustainable Tourism

There has been growing interest in sustainable tourism among travelers, hospitality service providers, and governments. This is reflected in several notable trends in sustainable tourism, which have been discussed extensively in academic research, sustainability journals, and UNWTO reports. Those include (i) Regenerative Tourism, (ii) Climate-Conscious Travel, and (iii) Smart Tourism and AI for Sustainability.

Growth of Responsible and Regenerative Tourism

This trend moves beyond the traditional sustainable tourism framework—which emphasizes only the minimization of negative impacts—by also focusing on the active restoration and improvement of destinations across environmental, social, and economic dimensions. This concept has been explored by many scholars, including Anna Pollock (2019) and Harold Goodwin (2016). Drawing a distinction between sustainability and regeneration, Pollock (2019) highlights in her work on regenerative tourism that "sustainable practices address symptoms and enable us to do less harm," whereas regeneration aims to create a net positive impact. Examples of regenerative tourism can be found in many destinations across Asia, including Bali, Indonesia, with its *Regenerative Tourism Model*; Bhutan, which follows the *High-Value, Low-Impact Model*; and Koh Tao Island, Thailand, with its *Sustainable Tourism and Coral Reef Restoration Model.*

Regenerative Tourism Model (Bali, Indonesia): Bali has emerged as a pioneer in regenerative tourism by integrating the Tri Hita Karana philosophy to balance environmental sustainability, community well-being, and economic resilience (Pickel-Chevalier, 2017). Unlike conventional sustainable tourism, Bali's regenerative approach actively restores ecosystems through sustainable agroforestry, biodiversity conservation, and waste reduction programs that address the long-term impacts of mass tourism (Suta et al., 2021). Community-driven tourism plays a crucial role in this transition by ensuring that development aligns with local traditions and environmental preservation while empowering residents as key stakeholders (The Other Side of Bali, n.d.; UNDP Indonesia, 2024). Additionally, collaborative partnerships between businesses, policymakers, and local communities have fostered a circular economy, reinforcing responsible tourism practices that regenerate rather than exploit Bali's resources (Pickel-Chevalier, 2017). These integrated efforts establish Bali as a global model for regenerative tourism, demonstrating how destinations can shift from extractive tourism models to community-driven, restorative tourism that prioritizes cultural integrity and ecological regeneration (The Other Side of Bali, n.d.).

High-Value, Low-Impact Model (Bhutan): A strategic approach to preserving cultural heritage and environmental integrity is exemplified while generating economic benefits through controlled tourism (Dorji, 2001). The model was designed to balance modernization with Bhutan's unique identity, ensuring that tourism development aligns with national priorities under the Gross National Happiness (GNH) framework (International Trade Centre, 2011). A core element of this model is the Sustainable Development Fee (SDF), which helps fund essential public services, conservation programs, and infrastructure projects, thereby ensuring that tourism directly supports Bhutan's broader development goals (Bhutan Tourism Council, 2023). Through this deliberate policy framework, Bhutan has positioned itself as a leading example of regenerative tourism, demonstrating how well-managed tourism policies can sustain long-term economic stability while safeguarding cultural and natural assets (International Trade Centre, 2011).

Sustainable Tourism and Coral Reef Restoration Model (Koh Tao Island, Thailand): Koh Tao Island, a renowned diving destination in Thailand, is a prime example of how sustainable tourism can coexist with marine conservation. Drawing between 300,000 and 500,000 visitors annually, the island's coral reefs face significant environmental pressures from human activity and climate change (Biodiversity Finance Initiative - BIOFIN, 2024). In response to ecological degradation from unregulated tourism, the island introduced a 20-Baht (approximately 0.50 USD) conservation fee in April 2022, generating substantial funds for marine protection efforts (BIOFIN, 2024). Moreover, initiatives such as the Koh Tao Model have been developed to integrate responsible tourism with active reef restoration. Conservation programs—including those run by the *New Heaven Reef Conservation Program*—emphasize habitat rehabilitation, eco-conscious diving practices, and public education to mitigate environmental damage (Hein et al., 2020; New Heaven Reef Conservation Program, 2024). These efforts demonstrate how balancing economic benefits from tourism with ecological responsibility can create a sustainable future for marine ecosystems, offering valuable insights for other coastal destinations worldwide.

Low-Carbon and Climate-Conscious Travel

This trend is reflected in both travelers' preferences and the practices of hospitality service providers in recent years. According to a 2023 report by Booking.com—a well-known travel agency—76% of travelers are likely to choose more sustainable travel options in the next year, while research by the World Travel & Tourism Council (WTTC, 2024) shows that 74% of tourism companies now have a sustainability strategy aimed at reducing their carbon footprint. Best practices promoting low-carbon and climate-conscious travel have been implemented worldwide. For instance, France has banned short-haul flights and promoted rail alternatives; specifically, recent government legislation (2023) banned domestic flights on routes where train alternatives exist (Jennifer, 2023). Furthermore, efforts have been made to increase the number of high-speed rail (TGV) trips as a replacement for air travel. Airlines in France are also being encouraged to invest in Sustainable Aviation Fuel (SAF) and carbon offset programs (Jennifer, 2023).

Another example comes from *the Maldives*—a popular tourist destination in Asia that is also one of the most climate-vulnerable countries. Tourism accounts for about 40% of the nation's total emissions and is described as a "luxury service-based industry that requires significant energy consumption for transport, cooling/freezing, and desalination" (Ministry of Environment, Republic of Maldives, 2019). To address this environmental pressure, some resorts have taken measures to become carbon neutral by adopting solar energy, desalination, and zero-waste practices (Ministry of Climate Change et al., 2024). Additionally, a portion of tourism revenue is used to fund coral reef restoration projects. Specifically, tourists pay a "Green Tax" when staying in Maldivian resorts, hotels, or vessels, with the collected funds directed toward environmental projects, island sanitation, and water research. It is estimated that a total of 21 million USD was collected through this "Green Tax" scheme in 2020 (Hilmi et al., 2023).

Smart Tourism and AI for Sustainable Travel

AI-powered tools have become a key area of discussion, emerging as the driving force behind sustainable tourism for governments, businesses, and travelers, as they enable stakeholders to make data-driven sustainability choices (Gretzel et al., 2015). AI and big data have been recognized as essential drivers of smart tourism ecosystems, allowing destinations to optimize visitor flows, enhance energy efficiency, and improve environmental sustainability. In the explanation by Gretzel et al. (2015), "Smart tourism relies on the ability to not only collect enormous amounts of data but to intelligently store, process, combine, analyze, and use big data to inform business innovation, operations, and services."

In fact, countries have attempted to apply AI in sustainable tourism, with *Singapore* standing out as a leading example in ASEAN. The evolution of Singapore as a Smart Tourism City, through the integration of technology and innovation in tourism, serves as an exemplary case in an ASEAN country. Thanks to advances in technology and the integration of AI, Singapore has been able to promote sustainable tourism by optimizing tourist flow and traffic management, enhancing energy efficiency, and advancing environmental management. Singapore has established itself as a leading *Smart Tourism City* by integrating AI-driven technologies to enhance visitor experiences and operational efficiency. The *Singapore Tourism Board* (STB) has embraced AI to elevate service standards and drive growth within the tourism sector, including the development of personalized travel itineraries and advanced chatbots to assist visitors (Chiew, 2023). In a significant move, Singapore's government announced an investment exceeding $1 billion in AI as part of Budget 2024, aiming to transform various sectors, including tourism. This substantial investment underscores the nation's commitment to leveraging AI for economic and service excellence (Singapore Business Review, 2024).

Beyond large-scale AI-driven initiatives, smart applications are also playing a key role in enhancing visitor experience and sustainability. For instance, *MySentosa*, a real-time consumer data platform, provides visitors with instant updates on crowd levels and waiting times, enabling them to adjust their itineraries dynamically to reduce congestion and improve travel efficiency. This integration of AI-powered consumer insights not only enhances tourist convenience but also contributes to sustainable destination management by reducing overcrowding and optimizing resource allocation (Weltman et al., 2024).

Prospects of Sustainable Tourism Development

Sustainable tourism development focuses on creating a balance between the growth of the tourism industry, the needs of local communities, and the preservation of the environment. As the world becomes increasingly aware of the importance of sustainability, the prospects for sustainable tourism development are becoming more promising and multifaceted; some are discussed below.

Growing Tourists' Demand

There is a rising trend among tourists who seek eco-friendly travel options. Travelers are increasingly choosing sustainable accommodations, eco-tours, and destinations that prioritize environmental responsibility. Moreover, there's an increasing Gen Z influence on tourism, younger generations prioritize sustainability in their travel choices, which drives businesses in the tourism sector to adopt sustainable practices to meet their demand. Localities, at the same time, promote propaganda about responsible tourism through the development of guidance documents and specific codes of conduct. For instance, the installation of a multilingual information sign system at monuments in Luang Prabang (Laos) helps visitors comprehend the history and significance of each project; in Bhutan, every visitor is given a handbook on Buddhist culture and proper conduct at monasteries; in New Zealand's Maori cultural villages, visitors are shown educational videos about local rituals and customs prior to their visits, assisting them in understanding and respecting local cultural values. Each of these approaches encourages visitors to help preserve cultural landmarks and tourist destinations.

Economic Opportunities for Local Communities

Sustainable tourism development can provide job opportunities for local communities while fostering economic diversification away from industries that are less environmentally friendly, and by promoting local cultures and traditions, sustainable tourism can enhance the economic viability of cultural heritage, incentivizing its preservation.

For this aspect, many localities are now developing the models of community tourism cooperatives that help small business households develop together and share resources and experiences, thereby improving the competitiveness and ensuring sustainable development. The government has assisted residents in Maori cultural villages in New Zealand in forming tourist cooperatives, enabling them to take the initiative in creating and overseeing cultural tourism offerings. The Hmong people in Sapa, Vietnam, have benefited from the community tourism cooperative model by creating hiking trips that incorporate cultural experiences, boosting their income, and taking a more active role in protecting their identity. Specifically, these cooperatives' training programs on marketing, product creation, and financial administration have improved the community's ability to conduct business. In addition, diverse communication campaigns through mass media channels, social networks, and community activities to disseminate knowledge about cultural values and the importance of preserving local identity have been organized; sustainable development is integrated into tourism activities, helping both residents and tourists realize the importance of protecting the environment and maintaining cultural values and ensuring long-term economic benefits for the community. In the Toraja cultural village (Indonesia), periodic community meetings on the importance of preserving traditional longhouse architecture have helped people better understand the value of heritage. Through raising awareness, people will voluntarily participate in preserving and promoting cultural values, contributing to building a sustainable and rich tourism industry.

Government Policies and Support

Many governments are beginning to adopt policies and build comprehensive legal frameworks with various legal documents to promote sustainable tourism practices based on each country's situation and characteristics. Typically, in New Zealand, the government has enacted the "Maori Heritage Act" to protect intellectual property rights for indigenous culture and specific regulations on the exploitation of these values in tourism. Besides, there are currently financial incentives applied for businesses that commit to sustainable practices, including grants, subsidies, and favorable tax policies. Some countries apply financial support policies through the establishment of investment funds for conservation and development, such as the Bhutan Heritage Conservation Fund model, which is formed with sustainable tourism fees.

In addition, at the local level, authorities have been given greater autonomy in managing tourism activities while building effective coordination mechanisms among stakeholders. In Kyoto (Japan), the city government has established a Cultural Tourism Management Board with the participation of representatives of relevant parties. This helps to effectively coordinate tourism activities and cultural preservation.

Aside from that, more sophisticated systems have been implemented to equitably share advantages with nearby communities through tax, fee, and profit-sharing regulations. One typical example is Nepal's program, which requires the Sherpa community to receive a percentage of the money earned from climbing Mount Everest. The Ifugao cultural villages in the Philippines, where residents are empowered to choose tourism activities along rice terraces, are an example of how community involvement is promoted in tourism management.

Culture Preservation and Promotion

Sustainable tourism can support the conservation of natural and cultural resources and help create revenue streams that incentivize the protection of ecosystems and endangered species. Various comprehensive and long-term conservation plans for each specific cultural heritage have been developed. Typically, in Luang Prabang (Laos), the government has implemented a project to preserve ancient urban architecture with the support from UNESCO, including creating detailed records of works and strict regulations on construction and reparations. In Maori cultural villages in New Zealand, the "Living

Heritage Preservation" program is implemented to record and teach traditional rituals and arts for the younger generation.

Some countries have encouraged the use of technology in cultural preservation, such as digitizing intangible cultural heritage in craft villages in Kyoto (Japan), which helps preserve sophisticated craft techniques for future generations. In addition, the creation of conservation funds with revenue from tourism activities has also been practiced. In Bhutan, a portion of sustainable tourism fees is set aside to fund the preservation of Buddhist culture and support monasteries in maintaining traditional spiritual practices. In Hoi An (Vietnam), a portion of the entrance fee is used to restore monuments and support artisans, which has helped to maintain traditional crafts.

Technological Innovations and Investment in Green Infrastructure

Through resources like smartphone apps that recommend eco-friendly travel options, technological advancements can improve the sustainable tourism experience. The quality of the tourist experience has increased as a result of the use of technology in tourism development. A virtual field trip introducing history in Ifugao cultural villages (Philippines) is one example. In addition, the infrastructure and utilities that support tourism have been increasingly modernized and digitalized. Examples of this include the development of tourist bus routes, the addition of bilingual signage, and improved roadways. At the same time, the development of contemporary tourist information centers with automated interpretation systems and smartphone apps to assist with sightseeing will make it easier for travelers to obtain information and have a more satisfying trip. Digitalization in tourism contributes to the development of databases of tourist attractions, online platforms for booking tours and services, and the use of technological effects in heritage performances, such as virtual reality (VR) and augmented reality (AR). In order to help tourists better comprehend the history and Inca culture, a mobile application was created in Cusco, Peru, that offers information about the Machu Picchu relic in multiple languages. It also uses AR technology. Many nations are using big data and artificial intelligence (AI) technology to examine the demands and behaviors of tourists in order to make the necessary modifications to the creation of tourism products. In Singapore, trends and tourist satisfaction in Chinatown are monitored using tourism data analytics, which enhances the traveler experience and service quality.

Active Cooperation in Sustainable Tourism Development

Participation in global initiatives such as the United Nations Sustainable Development Goals (SDGs) encourages countries and businesses to commit to sustainable tourism practices, whereas collaboration between public and private sectors, NGOs, and local communities can foster innovative approaches to sustainable tourism that benefit all stakeholders. The cooperation is demonstrated through various responsible investment projects to strengthen public-private cooperation in the establishment of connecting models between the government, businesses, and local people. The government plays a role in guiding and creating a legal corridor while businesses invest in infrastructure and marketing, and local people participate in providing tourism services. Typically, in Bhutan, the cooperation model between the government and travel companies in developing high-end cultural tours has contributed to preserving Buddhist culture and creating sustainable revenue. In Hoi An (Vietnam), the cooperation between the government and businesses in developing typical tourism products such as craft village tours and art shows has contributed to promoting local culture.

The cooperation mechanism, along with a common digital information system, will allow data sharing on visitor numbers, tourist attractions, and services among tourism destinations that would help coordinate visitor numbers, optimize experiences, and allocate resources. Apart from that, inter-regional cultural and tourism events such as festivals and periodic exhibitions can be organized under the cooperation of various tourism organizations to share experience, provide professional support, and build common standards for service quality, cultural preservation, and sustainable development. In Japan, the "Heritage Road" program connecting traditional craft villages in Kyoto with other cultural tourism destinations has created unique tourism products and increased visitors' length of stay.

In addition, more research, online networks, and exchanges of experiences between localities and countries have been conducted through the organization of international seminars, study tours, or forums to share management models, development policies, and solutions for sustainable tourism development. For instance, the community-based tourism concept in New Zealand has been enhanced by initiatives to share Maori cultural tourist management practices with other indigenous groups, or the network of collaboration between cultural villages in Southeast Asia has made it possible to exchange knowledge and generate distinctive travel experiences.

Conclusion

Sustainable tourism development presents a wealth of prospects driven by changing consumer preferences, technological innovation, and growing awareness of global challenges. As stakeholders in the tourism industry continue to embrace sustainability, the potential for a more responsible, inclusive, and environmentally friendly tourism model is promising. This shift not only benefits the planet but also enhances the travel experience for future generations and supports the well-being of local communities worldwide. While it holds significant promise for balancing economic growth, environmental preservation, and social equity, sustainable tourism development also faces various challenges that can hinder its effective implementation. These may include the challenges in balancing the conflict between pursuing sustainable practices and maintaining financial viability or the goals of economic development, while investors want to maximize the value of tourism trade, which can cause the loss of originality of indigenous culture or natural habitats. The balance between tourism development and cultural space preservation is another challenge. Due to commercialization pressure, many traditional cultural values have become neglected or distorted. Low capability and awareness of local people and tourists, which leads to disrespect for local culture or irresponsible consumption behavior and environmental protection, are also a challenge for sustainable tourism development. While those challenges are significant, addressing them is crucial for achieving a balance between tourism growth and environmental and social sustainability. Collaborative efforts among government, businesses, communities, and travelers are essential to navigate these challenges successfully. By fostering awareness, implementing effective policies, and promoting responsible practices, the tourism industry can work toward a more sustainable future.

References

Akande, O. A., & Ijeuru, U. C. (2024). *Stakeholder engagement and sustainable tourism in developing countries: Insights from Old Oyo National Park*. Research Gate.

Bhutan Tourism Council. (2023). *Sustainable development fee & tourism policy updates*. https://www.visitbhutan.com/page.php?id=68

Biodiversity Finance Initiative (BIOFIN). (2024). *Koh Tao: A model for sustainable tourism and coral reef conservation*. https://www.biofin.org/news-and-media/koh-tao-model-sustainable-tourism-and-coral-reef-conservation

Bramwell, B., & Lane, B. (1993). Sustainable tourism: An evolving global approach. *Journal of Sustainable Tourism*, *1*(1), 1–5. https://doi.org/10.1080/09669589309450696

Butler, R. W. (1980). The concept of a tourism area life cycle of evolution: Implications for management of resources. *Canadian Geographer*, *24*(1), 5–12.

Butler, R. W. (1991). Tourism, environment, and sustainable development. *Environmental Conservation*, *18*(3), 201–209. http://www.jstor.org/stable/44521393

Butler, R. W. (1993). Tourism – An evolutionary perspective. In J. G. Nelson, R. W. Butler, & G. Wall (Eds.), *Tourism and sustainable development: Monitoring, planning, managing* (pp. 27–44). University of Waterloo (Department of Geography Publication 37).

Chang, T. C. (2002). Regionalism and tourism: Exploring integral links in Singapore. *Asia Pacific Viewpoint*, *39*(1), 73–94. https://doi.org/10.1111/1467-8373.00054

Chiew, S. (2023). Transforming Singapore's tourism sector with AI. *The Edge Singapore*. https://www.theedgesingapore.com/news/sector-focus/transforming-singapores-tourism-sector-ai

Dorji, T. (2001). Sustainability of tourism in Bhutan. *Journal of Bhutan Studies*, *3*(1), 84–104. https://d1i1jdw69xsqx0.cloudfront.net/digitalhimalaya/collections/journals/jbs/pdf/JBS_03_01_03.pdf

Global Development Research Center. (n.d.). *Defining sustainable tourism*. https://www.gdrc.org/uem/eco-tour/sustour-define.html

Goodwin, H. (2016). *Responsible tourism: Using tourism for sustainable development*. Goodfellow Publishers.

Gössling, S., Scott, D., & Hall, C. M. (2018). Global trends in length of stay: Implications for destination management and climate change. *Journal of Sustainable Tourism*, *26*(12), 2087–2101. https://doi.org/10.1080/09669582.2018.1529771

Gretzel, U., Sigala, M., Xiang, Z., & Koo, C. (2015). Smart tourism: Foundations and developments. *Electronic Markets*, *25*(3), 179–188. https://www.researchgate.net/publication/280719315_Smart_tourism_foundations_and_d evelopments

Hein, M. Y., Beeden, R., Birtles, A., Gardiner, N. M., Le Berre, T., Levy, J., Marshall, N., Scott, C. M., Terry, L., & Willis, B. L. (2020). Coral restoration effectiveness: Multiregional snapshots of the long-term responses of coral assemblages to restoration. *Diversity*, *12*(4), 153. https://doi.org/10.3390/d12040153

Henderson, J. C. (2007). Uniquely Singapore? A case study in destination branding. *Journal of Vacation Marketing*, *13*(3), 261–274.

Herre, B., & Samborska, V. (2023). *Tourism* [Online resource]. https://ourworldindata.org/tourism

Hilmi, N., Basu, R., Crisóstomo, M., Lebleu, L., Claudet, J., & Seveso, D. (2023). The pressures and opportunities for coral reef preservation and restoration in the Maldives. *Frontiers in Environmental Economics*, *2*, 1110214. https://doi.org/10.3389/frevc.2023.1110214

International Trade Centre. (2011). Bhutan: A model for sustainable tourism development. https://www.intracen.org/news-and-events/news/bhutan-a-model-for-sustainable-tourism-development

Jennifer, L. (2023). *France bans short-haul flights to slash aviation CO2 footprint*. https://carboncredits.com/france-bans-short-haul-flights-to-slash-aviation-co2-footprint/

Ministry of Climate Change, Environment and Energy, Republic of Maldives. (2024). *Paving the way for a just energy transition in Maldives. Road map for the energy sector 2024-2033*. https://www.environment.gov.mv/v2/wp-content/files/publications/20241107-pub-energy-roadmap-maldives-2024-2033-.pdf

Ministry of Environment, Republic of Maldives. (2019). *Maldives first biennial update report to the United Nations framework convention on climate change*. https://unfccc.int/sites/default/files/resource/Maldives%20First%20Biennial%20Update%20Report.pdf

New Heaven Reef Conservation Program. (2024). *Koh Tao reef status*. https://newheavenreefconservation.org/learning-resources/explore-topics/koh-tao-reef-status NZ

O'Reilly, A. M. (1986). Tourism carrying capacity: Concepts and issues. *Tourism Management*, *7*(4), 254–258. https://doi.org/10.1016/0261-5177(86)90035-X

Pickel-Chevalier, S. (2017). Can tourism enhance "nature" in Bali? Toward a new paradigm through the interculturation process. In *Tourism in Bali and the challenge of sustainable development* (pp. 132–160). Cambridge Scholars Publishing.

Pollock, A. (2019). *Flourishing beyond sustainability: The future of tourism*. European Travel Commission. https://etccorporate.org/uploads/2019/02/06022019_Anna_Pollock_ETCKrakow_Keynote.pdf

Sharpley, R. (2009). *Tourism development and the environment: Beyond sustainability?* Earthscan.

Singapore Business Review. (2024). Singapore's tourism embraces $1 billion AI boost. https://sbr.com.sg/videos/singapores-tourism-embraces-1-billion-ai-boost

Statista. (2024). Share of travelers worldwide who plan to stay in eco-friendly or green accommodations in the next year. https://www.statista.com/statistics/1055777/sustainable-travel-travelers-staying-in-green-lodging-in-the-next-year/

Statista. (2025). Total number of international tourist arrivals worldwide. https://www.statista.com/statistics/209334/total-number-of-international-tourist-arrivals/

Sugimoto, K. (2017). Development of tourism and MICE in Singapore. *E-journal GEO*, *12*, 246–260. https://doi.org/10.4157/ejgeo.12.246

Suta, W. P., Abdi, N., & Astawa, I. P. M. (2021). *Sustainable tourism development in importance and performance perspective: A case study in Bali.* https://www.researchgate.net/publication/351315254_Sustainable_Tourism_Development_in_Importance_and_Performance_Perspective_A_Case_Study_Research_in_Bali

Swarbrooke, J. (1999). *Sustainable tourism management*. CABI Publishing.

The Other Side of Bali. (n.d.). Preserving the essence of old Bali: A regenerative tourism model. https://theothersideofbali.com/preserving-the-essence-of-old-bali-a-regenerative-tourism-model/

United Nations Development Programme (UNDP) Indonesia. (2024). *Harmonizing forest conservation and culture: The role of regenerative tourism in achieving FOLU net sink targets 2030.* https://www.undp.org/indonesia/press-releases/harmonizing-forest-conservation-and-culture-role-regenerative-tourism-achieving-folu-net-sink-targets-2030

United Nations Educational, Scientific and Cultural Organization (UNESCO). (n.d.). *World heritage and sustainable tourism programme*. UNESCO World Heritage Centre. https://whc.unesco.org/en/tourism/

Weaver, D. B. (2011). Can sustainable tourism survive mass tourism? The case for enlightened mass tourism. *Journal of Sustainable Tourism*, *19*(1), 5–16.

Weltman, T., Hwang, Y.-H., Sciacca, A., & Schipani, S. (2024). *Smart tourism ecosystem development readiness in Southeast Asia* (ADB Briefs No. 296). Asian Development Bank. https://doi.org/10.22617/BRF240230-2

World Commission on Environment and Development (WCED). (1987). *Our common future*. Oxford University Press. https://sustainabledevelopment.un.org/content/documents/5987our-common-future.pdf

World Tourism & Travel Council (WTTC). (2024). A net zero roadmap for travel & tourism. In *Proposing a new target framework for the travel & tourism sector* (2nd ed.). https://cdn.prod.website-files.com/6329bc97af73223b575983ac/673de26f81610cd1b3e248d9_NetZero191124-Final%20(1).pdf

World Tourism Organization (UNWTO). (n.d.). *EU guidebook on sustainable tourism for development*. UNWTO. https://www.unwto.org/eu-guidebook-on-sustainable-tourismfor-development.

World Travel & Tourism Council (WTTC). (n.d.). *Sustainable travel & tourism – Research, insights and actions*. https://wttc.org/sustainability

Yuniar, R. W. (2022, July 17). Indonesia's Komodo dragons are endangered. But are tourists willing to pay US$250, instead of $10, to see them? *South China Morning Post*. https://www.scmp.com/week-asia/article/3185546/indonesias-komodo-dragons-are-endangered-are-tourists-willing-pay-us250

Section 2

Gender and Inclusion in Tourism

Chapter 6

Empowering Women Through Sustainable Tourism: Special Reference to Sri Lanka

B. Anne Kanchana M. Mendis

University of Waikato, New Zealand

Abstract

Sustainable tourism offers a powerful avenue for empowering women and promoting gender equality in Sri Lanka, where the industry drives economic growth and cultural preservation. However, women face challenges such as limited financial resources, cultural norms, inadequate skills, and restricted market access. This study examines strategies to overcome these barriers, emphasizing the role of women-led tourism enterprises in enhancing local economies, community well-being, and sustainable development. The research provides actionable insights to foster inclusive growth and leverage tourism as a catalyst for women's empowerment and societal progress by evaluating policy frameworks, support mechanisms, and digital technologies.

Keywords: Sustainable tourism; women's empowerment; women-led enterprises; inclusive growth; cultural preservation; gender equality

Introduction

Overview of Tourism as a Catalyst for Community Development

Tourism is widely recognized as a powerful driver of community development, particularly in regions rich in natural, cultural, and historical assets (Bujdosó et al., 2015). As illustrated in Fig. 7.1, tourism contributes significantly to communities' social and economic well-being by fostering economic growth, creating employment opportunities, and enhancing infrastructure. It facilitates direct income generation through tourism-related businesses, such as hospitality,

Economics and Tourism, 91–113

doi:10.1108/978-1-83662-916-020251007

transport, and local crafts, and supports indirect employment in supply chain industries (Agarwal et al., 2023).

This diagram illustrates tourism's multidimensional impacts, including economic growth, cultural preservation, social equity, and environmental sustainability, and their interconnected roles in fostering inclusive development.

Beyond economic benefits, tourism serves as a cultural exchange and preservation platform. Communities often leverage their unique traditions, heritage, and local knowledge to attract visitors, reinforcing cultural pride and identity. Investments in tourism can also lead to improved public infrastructure, including better roads, sanitation facilities, and communication networks, which enhance the quality of life for residents (Agarwal et al., 2023).

Moreover, tourism fosters social cohesion and inclusivity by empowering marginalized groups, such as women and Indigenous populations, to participate actively in economic activities (Tiwari & Nguyen, 2024). Community-based tourism emphasizes local ownership and management, ensuring that benefits are equitably distributed while promoting sustainable practices (Tiwari & Nguyen, 2024). For example, homestays and eco-tourism initiatives often involve training residents and enhancing their skills and self-reliance.

However, tourism-driven development must be approached cautiously to avoid adverse effects like environmental degradation, cultural commodification, and social inequities (Alamineh et al., 2023). As shown in Fig. 7.1, adopting sustainable tourism practices prioritizing community involvement, environmental stewardship, and cultural preservation ensures that tourism remains a long-term, inclusive development catalyst. By striking this balance, tourism can transform communities, fostering resilience and shared prosperity.

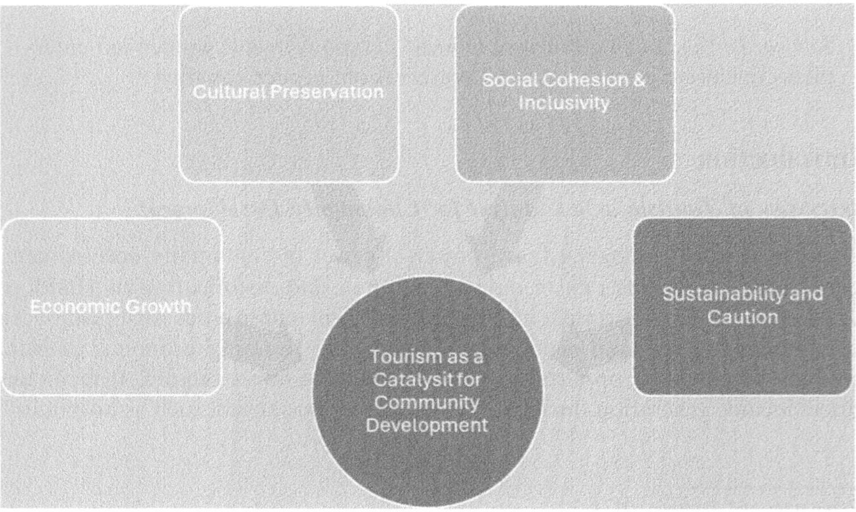

Fig. 7.1. Conceptual Map—Tourism as a Catalyst for Holistic Community Development: Key Drivers and Interconnections. *Source:* Prepared by the author.

Importance of Sustainable Tourism in Sri Lanka

Sustainable tourism is vital for Sri Lanka, which is celebrated for its rich biodiversity, cultural heritage, and scenic landscapes. As a major contributor to the national economy, tourism has the potential to drive economic growth, create employment opportunities, and support rural development. However, the rapid growth of mass tourism poses significant risks to the country's natural and cultural assets, necessitating a shift toward sustainability (Baloch et al., 2023).

Sri Lanka's unique ecosystems, including rainforests, pristine beaches, and wildlife sanctuaries, are critical for attracting tourists (Liyanage & Fernando, 2014). However, these environments are susceptible to over-tourism, pollution, and unregulated development (Baloch et al., 2023). Sustainable tourism minimizes environmental impact by promoting eco-friendly practices such as waste management, renewable energy use, and conservation initiatives (Baloch et al., 2023). It also supports the preservation of cultural heritage by encouraging responsible tourism practices that respect local traditions, crafts, and lifestyles (Liyanage & Fernando, 2014).

For Sri Lankan communities, sustainable tourism offers opportunities for equitable economic development. Community-based tourism models empower local populations by creating direct income opportunities and fostering entrepreneurial ventures (Sriyani, 2022). Initiatives such as homestays and agro-tourism allow rural communities to benefit directly from tourism revenue, reducing income inequalities.

Moreover, sustainable tourism aligns with Sri Lanka's goals of fostering inclusivity, enhancing resilience to climate change, and achieving long-term economic stability. By integrating sustainability principles into tourism planning and management, Sri Lanka can ensure that its natural and cultural treasures are preserved for future generations while maximizing benefits for its people. This approach is essential for the sector's viability and the country's overall development trajectory.

Harnessing the Power of Sustainable Tourism for Women's Empowerment and Inclusive Economic Growth in Sri Lanka

Sustainable tourism is vital for empowering women and fostering inclusive growth in Sri Lanka (Silva et al., 2017). The sector's inherent reliance on cultural, natural, and human resources provides unique opportunities for women to participate in and benefit from economic activities (ILO Country Office for Sri Lanka and the Maldives, 2016). In a country where women often face barriers to equitable employment, sustainable tourism can be a platform to break gender norms and enhance economic participation.

Women's involvement in tourism-related activities, such as hospitality, handicrafts, and eco-tourism, promotes financial independence and skill development. Community-based tourism initiatives, including homestays and village tours, allow women to utilize their local knowledge and cultural expertise to create unique visitor experiences. Such engagement improves household incomes and builds women's confidence and decision-making capabilities.

Moreover, sustainable tourism's emphasis on inclusivity ensures that marginalized groups, including women, are not left behind in the development process (Bhatt et al., 2024). It prioritizes equitable resource distribution, capacity-building programs, and leadership opportunities for women in the sector (Bhatt et al., 2024).

Sustainable tourism in Sri Lanka contributes to broader developmental goals by addressing gender disparities and fostering inclusive growth. It generates economic benefits and strengthens social cohesion and community resilience. As such, embedding gender equality and inclusivity into sustainable tourism strategies is essential for ensuring that the sector drives long-term, equitable growth while empowering women as key stakeholders.

Women's Role in Sustainable Tourism

The Untapped Potential of Women in Tourism

Sustainable tourism in Sri Lanka holds significant potential to empower women, address entrenched gender disparities, and foster inclusive economic growth and community resilience (Hemachandra & De Silva, 2021). Despite their critical contributions to the sector, such as preserving cultural heritage, creating artisanal products, and providing authentic local experiences, many women remain confined to low-paying, informal roles with limited leadership opportunities globally (World Tourism Organization, 2019). Addressing this imbalance is a moral and strategic necessity for maximizing the tourism sector's potential.

This diagram illustrates the interconnected pathways through which women engage in tourism homestay management, culinary tourism, craft production, and cultural storytelling, and how these roles foster economic, social, and cultural empowerment.

Community-based and inclusive tourism approaches offer transformative opportunities for women, particularly in rural areas (Vujko et al., 2024). As shown in Fig. 7.2, initiatives like homestays, eco-tourism, and agritourism enable women to leverage their unique skills and cultural knowledge to generate sustainable incomes while fostering local ownership and entrepreneurial growth (Quang et al., 2023). Examples from Sri Lanka illustrate how women successfully manage tourism ventures such as traditional cooking classes, handicraft workshops, and guided nature tours, creating economic and social value.

Access to training, digital tools, and financial resources is critical to empowering women in the tourism sector (Kumar & Mittal, n.d.). Skill development programs and policies that promote gender equity, such as fair wages, equal access to financing, and representation in leadership, can help women transition from informal roles to formal employment and entrepreneurial success.

By integrating women into the tourism value chain and prioritizing gender-focused policies, Sri Lanka can create a more inclusive and sustainable

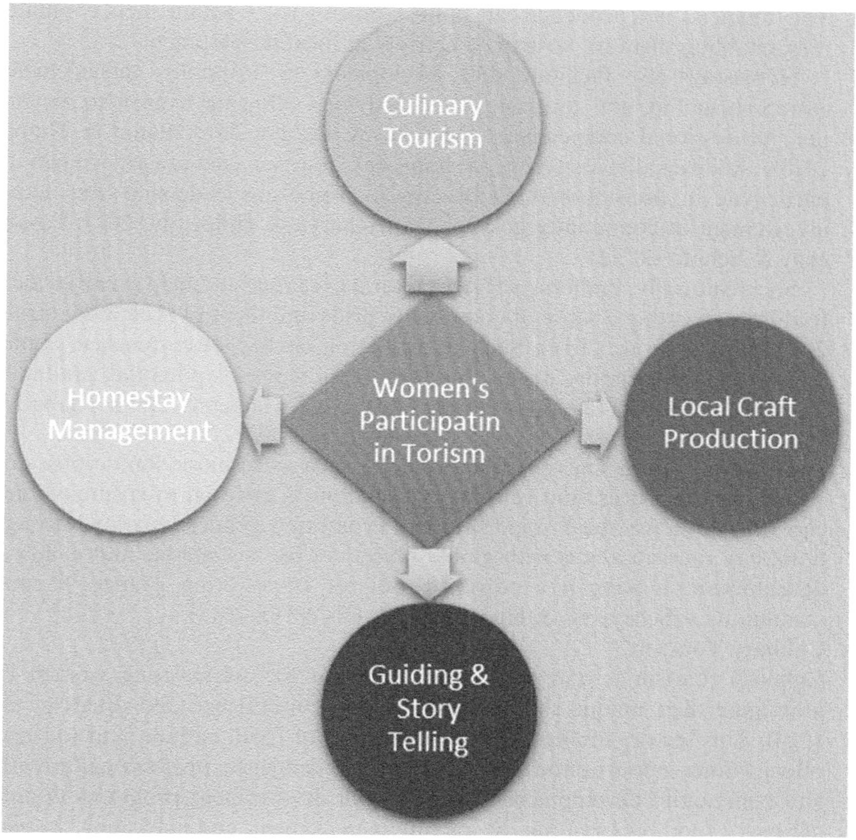

Fig. 7.2. Conceptual Map—Pathways to Women's Empowerment in Tourism: Roles and Opportunities. *Source*: Prepared by the author.

tourism industry. Harnessing women's potential in tourism drives economic growth and contributes to national development by advancing gender equity and fostering social cohesion.

Key Areas for Women's Participation in Sustainable Tourism

- Homestay Management
  Homestays serve as a transformative avenue for empowering women by creating direct economic and social opportunities. Economically, they provide women with income and resources, enhancing their ability to contribute to household welfare and improving long-term prospects such as education and healthcare for their families (Pasanchay & Schott, 2021; Shukor et al., 2014).

This financial independence can uplift women's roles within their communities, enabling them to participate actively in local development.

Homestays also facilitate skill development in hospitality management, entrepreneurship, and tourism-related activities, allowing women to expand their professional competencies (Movono & Dahles, 2017; Panta & Thapa, 2018). Additionally, engaging in homestay tourism encourages women to participate in decision-making processes, promoting leadership and active involvement in community governance (Acharya & Halpenny, 2013; Pasanchay & Schott, 2021).

Socioculturally, homestays foster cultural exchange and help preserve local traditions, creating a sense of community pride and identity (Leh & Hamzah, 2012; Shukor et al., 2014). Such participation challenges entrenched gender roles and discriminatory norms that often limit women's potential, gradually dismantling barriers to empowerment (Acharya & Halpenny, 2013; Thapaliya et al., 2013).

However, addressing systemic obstacles such as resource limitations, discriminatory practices, and cultural expectations is essential to ensure women can fully leverage these opportunities. Promoting gender equality through homestay tourism aligns with global objectives for sustainable and inclusive development, making it a powerful tool for empowering women in rural communities (Scheyvens & Hughes, 2019; UNWTO, 2019).

- Culinary Tourism

  Culinary tourism is a revolutionary platform for empowering women by leveraging their unique skills, creativity, and cultural heritage (Bhatt et al., 2024). This sector, situated at the intersection of food, culture, and tourism, offers women opportunities for economic independence, professional growth, and community development. Through skill development programs in culinary arts, food preservation, hospitality management, and marketing, women can enhance their employability and embark on entrepreneurial ventures, such as catering services, food trucks, or artisanal businesses. Access to microfinancing, grants, and mentorship further supports women entrepreneurs in overcoming structural barriers and reaching broader audiences through platforms like farmers' markets, online marketplaces, and culinary festivals.

  A key aspect of culinary tourism is preserving and promoting culinary heritage. As custodians of traditional recipes and cooking techniques, women are instrumental in leading gastronomic tours and workshops celebrating regional cuisines while fostering cultural understanding. This form of tourism, characterized by dining experiences, wine tastings, and gastronomic routes, highlights a region's culinary uniqueness, sustains rural areas, conserves biodiversity, and empowers local stakeholders. Gastronomy tourism has emerged as a distinct market segment (UNWTO, 2017) and is increasingly recognized for enhancing the value of a region's culinary offerings (INE, 2023). Spain's gastronomic heritage, driven by iconic products with Protected Designations of Origin (PDO) and Protected Geographical Indications (PGI), exemplifies how culinary tourism supports regional identities and economic development (Muñoz Benito et al., 2023; Spanish Ministry of Agriculture, Fisheries and Food, 2024).

Women's historical role in preserving culinary traditions has faced challenges, including balancing work and family responsibilities and limited mentorship in professional kitchens (Haddaji et al., 2017; Monica & et al., 2013). However, strides toward gender equality in gastronomy tourism have narrowed gender gaps in agriculture and rural sectors, reflecting the growing recognition of women's contributions (UNWTO, 2023). For example, initiatives like "Raíz Culinaria" and "Campo y Alma" in Spain aim to promote local products and traditional techniques, supported by high-end restaurants and social media, which attract tourists and enhance visibility (Kim et al., 2023; Vieira et al., 2023).

Culinary tourism can empower women, preserve cultural heritage, and drive sustainable development by addressing challenges and fostering inclusive policies. Through education, entrepreneurship, and collaborative initiatives, women's active participation in culinary tourism enriches the sector while transforming their communities. As gastronomy tourism grows, its potential to empower women and support rural development becomes even more significant.

- Local Craft Production

Craft production in the tourism industry can empower women by facilitating the preservation and promotion of cultural heritage, enhancing economic independence, and improving social standing (Vujko et al., 2024). Women often occupy a central role in the maintenance of traditional craft-making techniques, which are crucial to the cultural identity of their communities (Tzanidaki & Reynolds, 2011). The tourism sector provides a valuable platform through which these crafts can be showcased to a global audience, increasing their cultural and economic value (Tzanidaki & Reynolds, 2011). By producing handmade souvenirs, clothing, and accessories highly sought after by tourists, women can directly access markets, resulting in increased income and economic empowerment (Vujko et al., 2024). This direct access to markets reduces reliance on intermediaries and strengthens the local economy, particularly in rural or underserved areas.

Furthermore, craft production allows women to establish small businesses, fostering entrepreneurial activity and granting them greater control over their work schedules and growth opportunities. This entrepreneurial shift enhances their financial independence and facilitates the development of critical business skills, such as design, marketing, and management (Tzanidaki & Reynolds, 2011). Through targeted training and capacity-building initiatives, women acquire knowledge that extends beyond the tourism sector, empowering them in broader socioeconomic contexts.

Socially, women engaged in craft production are frequently recognized as community leaders, a recognition that challenges traditional gender roles and enhances their visibility as contributors to both economic and cultural development (Mehra, 1993). Their involvement in craft production can also advance gender equality, enabling them to transcend domestic boundaries and elevate their standing within the community. Moreover, craft production is often associated with sustainable practices, including using local materials and eco-friendly production methods (Fernández Bellver et al., 2023). This aligns with the increasing demand for ethical tourism practices and creates inclusive opportunities for marginalized women, enabling them to participate in the workforce and access economic opportunities that may have previously been unavailable. Craft production within the tourism industry empowers women economically and socially and contributes to broader socioeconomic transformation, benefiting both individual women and the industry.

- Guiding and Cultural Storytelling
Cultural storytelling in tourism can empower women by enabling them to reclaim and share their narratives, fostering a sense of identity, autonomy, and agency (Vujko et al., 2024). Through storytelling, women can actively participate in preserving and disseminating their cultural heritage, which is often intertwined with their lived experiences, traditions, and roles within their communities (Rieger et al., 2023). In many societies, women's voices and perspectives have been marginalized or silenced; however, tourism provides a platform for women to assert their stories, allowing them to challenge dominant narratives and reshape public perceptions of their roles and contributions (Seow & Seow, 2020). Women can influence their communities' representation through cultural storytelling, highlighting their leadership, resilience, and cultural significance.

Moreover, cultural storytelling can economically empower women, particularly in communities where tourism is a significant industry (Vujko et al., 2024). By sharing their stories with tourists, women can generate income through guided tours, workshops, or cultural performances, contributing to personal financial independence and local economic development. This economic empowerment process fosters broader social empowerment as women gain visibility and recognition, challenging traditional gender norms and roles. Furthermore, storytelling can be a transformative tool for building women's confidence and public speaking skills, facilitating personal growth and leadership development (Shackelford et al., 2023).

In addition, cultural storytelling within the tourism context can contribute to the breaking down of gender stereotypes, particularly in societies where women are often relegated to passive or subordinate roles (Shackelford et al., 2023). Through their involvement in storytelling, women can present themselves as knowledgeable custodians of their culture, positioning themselves as active agents in the cultural and economic landscape. This empowerment through storytelling strengthens women's agency and fosters a sense of collective empowerment within communities as women collaborate and support each other in creating and sharing cultural narratives. As such, cultural storytelling in tourism has the potential to catalyze both personal and collective empowerment, enhancing women's social, economic, and cultural standing within their communities and beyond.

Breaking Barriers: Empowering Women for Gender Equity in Tourism

Empowering women in tourism requires a comprehensive approach to addressing the barriers that limit their participation and advancement in the sector. Societal norms and cultural expectations often confine women to traditional roles, restricting their engagement in tourism (Silva et al., 2017). These norms frequently discourage women from pursuing careers in leadership, technical, or nontraditional roles within the industry, where they can significantly contribute to innovation and growth (Silva et al., 2017). Overcoming these challenges necessitates a shift in societal attitudes and the promotion of gender equity through awareness campaigns and inclusive community practices (Seow & Seow, 2020).

This diagram illustrates the systemic barriers to women's empowerment (societal norms, limited access to resources, and occupational segregation) and the strategies to address them, including policy reforms, education, and inclusive practices.

Another critical barrier is women's limited access to resources and education. Many women, particularly in rural or underprivileged areas, lack access to the financial resources, training, and networking opportunities required to thrive in the tourism sector (Nordbø, 2022). Education and skill development are essential to empowering women, equipping them with the capabilities to excel in various roles, from entrepreneurs managing homestays to professionals in travel technology and sustainable tourism planning. As shown in Fig. 7.3, governments,

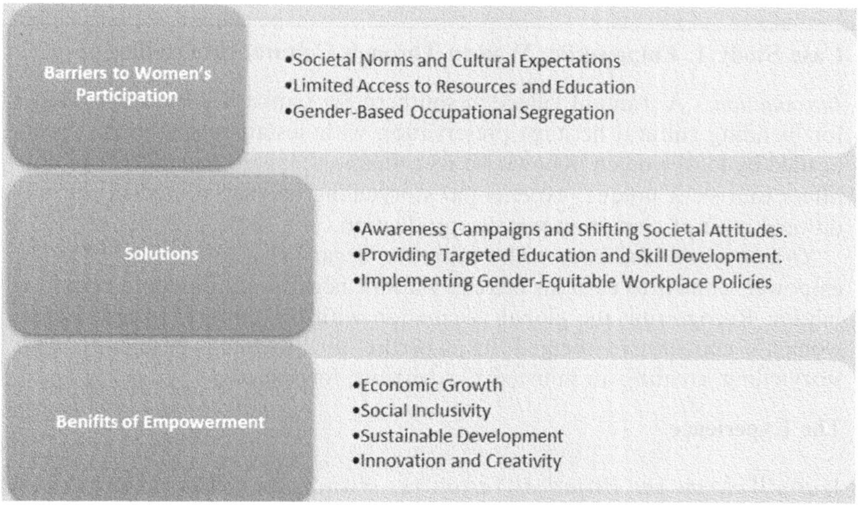

Fig. 7.3. Conceptual Map—Overcoming Barriers and Advancing Gender Equity. *Source:* Prepared by the author.

nongovernmental organizations, and industry stakeholders must collaborate to provide targeted training programs, scholarships, and mentorship opportunities for women aspiring to build careers in tourism.

Gender-based occupational segregation further exacerbates inequalities in the tourism industry (Silva et al., 2017). Women are often relegated to low-paying, labor-intensive roles with limited prospects for career growth, while men dominate managerial and decision-making positions (Silva et al., 2017). This segregation not only restricts women's economic empowerment but also denies the industry the diverse perspectives and talents that women bring. Tackling this issue involves implementing workplace policies that promote gender equality, such as transparent recruitment and promotion processes, flexible work arrangements, and equal pay for equal work.

As Fig. 7.3 visualizes, empowering women in tourism has far-reaching benefits. Leveraging women's potential to drive innovation and creativity enhances economic growth, promotes social inclusivity, and fosters sustainable development. Addressing societal norms, expanding access to education and resources, and breaking down occupational segregation, the tourism sector can become a powerful platform for advancing gender equity and creating lasting positive change in communities worldwide.

Women-Led Initiatives and Community Development

Case Studies of Successful Women-Led Tourism Ventures

Case Study 1: Empowering Women Through Cultural Storytelling

Introduction – A tranquil village in southern Sri Lanka has become a model for blending cultural heritage preservation with sustainable tourism, spearheaded by local women. Known for its cinnamon plantations, the village now offers tourists a unique, experiential storytelling journey rooted in the traditional craft of cinnamon powder production.

Origin of the Initiative—The initiative began as a grassroots effort to empower women to earn an income without neglecting household responsibilities. Recognizing the global fascination with Sri Lankan spices, a local women's cooperative merged its expertise in cinnamon processing with storytelling, creating an immersive experience for visitors.

The Experience

Warm Welcome and Historical Narratives—Visitors are welcomed into homes or community spaces and introduced to the history of cinnamon in Sri Lanka, enriched by personal anecdotes and folklore passed down through generations.

Demonstrations and Storytelling—The women showcase the intricate cinnamon powder production process while narrating stories about its cultural and historical significance. One might demonstrate peeling and grinding cinnamon, while another shares tales of ancient trade routes where cinnamon was valued more than gold.

Family Involvement—The initiative's family-oriented nature is evident as children assist with small tasks, blending family life with entrepreneurship.

Balancing Roles and Responsibilities—The women seamlessly juggle their roles as storytellers, demonstrators, and homemakers. Between sessions, they attend to household chores, such as cooking, helping children with homework, or tending vegetable gardens. This balance is maintained through mutual support within the cooperative, ensuring no one is overwhelmed.

Impact of the Initiative

Economic Empowerment—Additional income from tourism has improved living standards and enabled families to invest in education.

Community Leadership and Cultural Ambassadorship—The women have gained recognition as cultural ambassadors, fostering a more profound appreciation among tourists for their craft and heritage.

Conclusion

This initiative exemplifies how cultural storytelling and skill-based demonstrations can empower rural women, promote sustainable tourism, and preserve intangible cultural heritage. It emphasizes rural women's potential to flourish as economic contributors and cultural custodians while balancing their personal and professional lives.

Case Study 2: Women's Empowerment Through Homestays in Ella, Sri Lanka

Ella, a scenic town in the central highlands of Sri Lanka, has become a notable destination for community-based tourism. It offers visitors a blend of cultural immersion and natural beauty. One of Ella's most prominent forms of tourism development is the homestay model, where families provide bed-and-breakfast accommodations to travelers. Women have been at the forefront of this model, utilizing homestays to achieve economic independence, strengthen community ties, and contribute to sustainable tourism. This case study explores how women operating homestays in Ella have empowered themselves economically and socially, highlighting their ability to balance business responsibilities with traditional household duties.

(*Continued*)

(Continued)

Economic Empowerment and Social Impact

Homestays in Ella give women a unique opportunity to generate income while staying rooted in their communities. Through these ventures, women manage essential aspects of the business, such as guest services, culinary offerings, and marketing. The resulting income supports their families by covering expenses for children's education, healthcare, and household improvements. This dual role as caregivers and business owners positions them as central figures in their families' economic stability.

In addition to economic benefits, the homestay model fosters social empowerment. Through interactions with guests, women gain exposure to diverse cultures and perspectives. This exposure enhances their confidence, decision-making skills, and ability to engage with broader networks within and outside their communities. By successfully managing their businesses, they challenge traditional gender roles and serve as role models for other women in the area.

Balancing Household Duties and Business Responsibilities

One remarkable aspect of women's involvement in homestay operations is their ability to balance business responsibilities with traditional household duties. Women often seamlessly integrate their business activities into their daily routines, using their existing skills and resources. For instance, preparing meals for guests becomes an extension of their household cooking while maintaining the homestay, which aligns with their regular housekeeping practices.

Moreover, some women have innovatively structured their homestays to ensure a balance between work and family life. They share responsibilities and strengthen familial bonds by incorporating family members into their operations. In other instances, the flexible nature of the homestay business allows women to prioritize household tasks during specific times of the day, reserving business-related activities for later. This adaptability is a testament to their resilience and resourcefulness in navigating multiple roles.

Impact on Sustainable Tourism

The contributions of women-led homestays extend beyond individual empowerment to influence Ella's tourism landscape and sustainability goals. Homestays emphasize cultural authenticity by offering guests locally prepared meals, opportunities to engage in traditional cooking, and insights into Sri Lankan customs. These experiences resonate with tourists seeking meaningful connections, further enhancing Ella's appeal as a destination.

Additionally, many women incorporate environmentally conscious practices into their homestays, such as using organic ingredients, minimizing plastic waste, and adopting energy-saving methods. This commitment to sustainability aligns with global tourism trends and reinforces Ella's reputation as a hub for eco-friendly tourism.

Conclusion

The success of women-led homestays in Ella illustrates the transformative potential of community-based tourism in fostering economic and social empowerment. By leveraging their skills and resources, women have created a sustainable business model that benefits their families and communities. Their ability to balance household responsibilities with business management demonstrates their resilience and adaptability.

The homestay model in Ella serves as an exemplary case of how tourism can empower women, strengthen cultural ties, and promote sustainable practices, ultimately contributing to the broader goals of gender equality and community development in rural Sri Lanka.

Case Study 3: Women Empowering Sustainable Tourism Through the Traditional Lace-Making Industry of Galle, Sri Lanka

Introduction

Galle, a historic city in Sri Lanka's southern province, is celebrated for its centuries-old lace-making tradition. Introduced during the Portuguese colonial era, this artisanal craft has become a symbol of cultural heritage and economic empowerment for women. By integrating their craft into sustainable tourism, women artisans have transformed lace-making into a thriving industry that promotes cultural preservation, financial independence, and community development.

Women's Role in the Lace-Making Industry

Women are the backbone of Galle's lace-making industry, contributing to economic growth while preserving the region's cultural legacy. The craft provides women a unique opportunity to generate income by producing handmade items like tablecloths, garments, and decorative pieces. With minimal infrastructure requirements, lace-making is accessible to women of varying economic backgrounds, especially those managing household responsibilities. Sustainable tourism is crucial in expanding the market for handmade lace products. Tourists visiting Galle seek authentic cultural experiences, and women artisans meet this demand through workshops,

(*Continued*)

(*Continued*)

demonstrations, and sales of handcrafted goods. These efforts enhance the economic value of the craft while promoting women's financial independence.

Economic Empowerment Through Sustainable Tourism

Women in Galle have leveraged sustainable tourism to revitalize the lace-making industry and achieve economic empowerment. Their ability to market handmade products to local and international buyers has transformed lace-making into a profitable enterprise. By engaging in this heritage-based industry, women contribute to household incomes, improve their quality of life, and participate actively in Galle's tourism-driven economy. Success stories illustrate how women have harnessed the potential of sustainable tourism to enhance their livelihoods:

Entrepreneurial Leadership: One woman modernized her family's lace-making tradition by introducing contemporary designs and using online platforms to market her products. Starting with a small investment, she trained other women in her community, expanded her operations, and secured international orders. Her efforts strengthened her family's financial stability and inspired other women to pursue similar ventures.

Cooperative Model: Another woman established a cooperative with 10 artisans, pooling resources to fulfill bulk orders from hotels and retailers. This collective approach allowed members to share workloads, negotiate better prices, and achieve economic independence while preserving traditional lace-making techniques.

Balancing Household Responsibilities With Craftsmanship

Lace-making offers women the flexibility to balance their professional and personal responsibilities. Many women manage household tasks in the mornings and dedicate afternoons and evenings to their craft. Family members, including daughters and mothers, sometimes participate in lace-making, fostering collaboration and strengthening familial bonds. Cooperative models also alleviate individual burdens by distributing workloads during peak periods, such as festival seasons or significant tourist events. This adaptability enables women to pursue financial independence without neglecting their household roles, making lace-making a unique blend of tradition and empowerment.

Preserving Culture Through Tourism

Women artisans are not only economic contributors but also cultural custodians. By teaching younger generations and hosting workshops for tourists, they ensure the continuity of this heritage craft. Lace-making demonstrations have become a popular attraction for visitors seeking authentic experiences in Galle, further integrating the craft into the tourism industry. The sale of handmade lace items as souvenirs enhances the craft's economic value, while its visibility in cultural tourism secures its future as a sustainable industry. Women artisans thus play a vital role in preserving Sri Lanka's cultural identity and enhancing its appeal as a tourist destination.

Broader Impacts on Women's Empowerment

The lace-making industry's integration into sustainable tourism has empowered women in multiple ways:

- *Economic Independence:* Women earn an income that enables them to contribute to household finances and invest in education.
- *Social Recognition:* Women gain respect and recognition as cultural ambassadors and entrepreneurs.
- *Sustainability Leadership:* Women promote low-impact production methods that align with sustainable tourism practices.

Conclusion

The traditional lace-making industry in Galle exemplifies how heritage crafts can empower women and promote sustainable tourism. Women artisans have revitalized a centuries-old craft, creating economic opportunities and ensuring cultural preservation. By blending entrepreneurship with cultural stewardship, women in Galle demonstrate the transformative potential of sustainable tourism to foster gender equity, financial resilience, and community development.

Socioeconomic Benefits of Women-Led Initiatives

Women-led initiatives, particularly in traditional crafts and community-based tourism, drive socioeconomic transformation. These ventures uplift individual women and contribute to their communities' broader economic and social fabric. The lace-making industry in Galle and homestay enterprises in Ella, Sri Lanka, are prime examples demonstrating such initiatives' multifaceted benefits.

This conceptual map illustrates the interconnected benefits of women-led ventures, including economic empowerment, cultural preservation, and sustainable development.

(1) Economic Empowerment and Financial Independence
Women-led initiatives provide a direct pathway for women to earn an income, enhancing their financial independence and economic security.

- In Galle, women involved in traditional lace-making generate steady incomes by selling artisanal products to local and international markets. Many women have transitioned from subsistence livelihoods to economically sustainable ventures by leveraging their skills.
- Similarly, in Ella, women operating homestays have diversified their income streams, using earnings to invest in children's education, healthcare, and home improvements.

The economic stability gained through these initiatives reduces dependence on male breadwinners and strengthens women's bargaining power within their households.

(2) Social Empowerment and Community Leadership

By leading business ventures, women challenge traditional gender norms and emerge as community role models.

- The lace-making cooperatives in Galle demonstrate how collective efforts can amplify women's influence. These cooperatives foster collaboration and elevate women into leadership positions, where they manage production, finances, and marketing.
- Women-led homestays in Ella showcase how women can navigate hospitality demands while engaging with diverse cultural groups, enhancing their confidence and decision-making capabilities.

These roles contribute to breaking down societal stereotypes and encouraging other women to take up leadership roles in economic and social spheres.

(3) Preservation of Cultural Heritage

Women-led initiatives often play a critical role in preserving and promoting cultural traditions, turning them into a source of pride and economic opportunity.

- The lace-making industry in Galle, sustained primarily by women, safeguards a centuries-old craft while adapting it to contemporary markets. Women artisans pass down their skills to younger generations, ensuring the continuity of this cultural heritage.
- In Ella, women-led homestays integrate local traditions into the tourist experience, such as offering authentic Sri Lankan meals and sharing cultural practices. These efforts not only preserve intangible heritage but also attract culturally conscious tourists.

Through their involvement, women act as custodians of cultural identity, reinforcing the unique appeal of their communities.

(4) Contribution to Sustainable Development

Women-led initiatives align with sustainable development goals by promoting inclusive economic growth, reducing inequalities, and fostering environmental sustainability.

- In Ella, women incorporate eco-friendly practices into their homestays, such as minimizing waste and using locally sourced materials. These

practices contribute to sustainable tourism, benefit the environment, and support local supply chains.
- In Galle, lace-makers create handcrafted, low-impact products that cater to growing consumer demand for sustainable goods.

Such initiatives demonstrate how women can drive sustainable practices in traditionally male-dominated industries, creating long-term economic and environmental benefits.

(5) Work-Life Balance and Resilience
Women-led initiatives often highlight innovative ways to balance professional and domestic responsibilities, showcasing resilience and adaptability.

- Women lace-makers in Galle work from home, seamlessly integrating their craft into daily routines. Involving family members in production fosters a collaborative household dynamic that strengthens familial bonds.
- In Ella, women running homestays manage flexible schedules to prioritize household duties alongside business activities. Many delegate tasks to family members, ensuring that neither sphere is neglected.

This ability to balance work and home life enables women to sustain their businesses while maintaining familial responsibilities, creating a holistic empowerment model.

The socioeconomic benefits of women-led initiatives are transformative, extending beyond individual empowerment to include community development, cultural preservation, and sustainable growth. Lace-making in Galle and homestays in Ella illustrate how women can harness traditional skills and entrepreneurial spirit to drive progress in diverse sectors.

As illustrated in the Conceptual Map—Socioeconomic Impact of Women-Led Initiatives (Fig. 7.4), these initiatives create a ripple effect: economic empowerment fosters social leadership, cultural preservation enhances sustainable tourism, and flexible work models enable resilience. By supporting and scaling such initiatives, policymakers and stakeholders can unlock women's potential as change agents and foster inclusive and equitable development across Sri Lanka and beyond.

Strategies for Empowering Women in Sustainable Tourism

Empowering women in sustainable tourism requires a multifaceted approach to address persistent barriers such as gender-based occupational segregation and limited resource access. Fig. 7.5 illustrates three core strategies: gender-sensitive policies, targeted interventions, and digital innovation, forming the foundation for systemic change.

These policies should tackle systemic inequalities, including wage disparities, gender-based violence, and restricted access to leadership roles. Ensuring women's participation in decision-making processes, such as establishing quotas

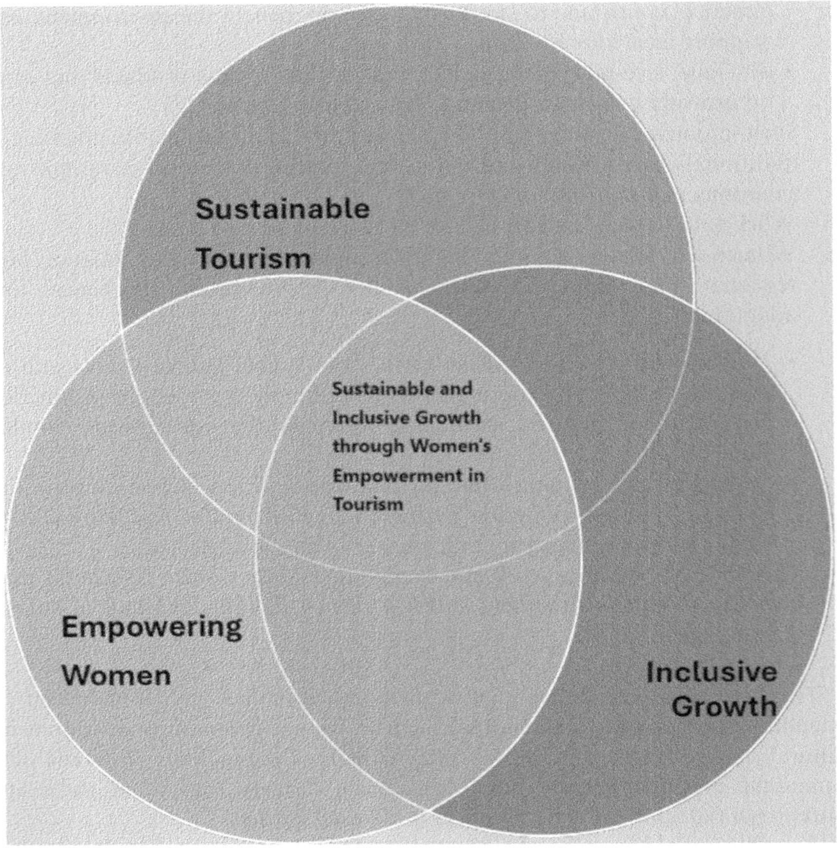

Fig. 7.4. Conceptual Map—Socioeconomic Impact of Women-Led Initiatives. *Source:* Prepared by the author.

for female representation in tourism governance, is essential. Additionally, designing infrastructure that prioritizes women's safety and comfort, such as well-lit public spaces, childcare facilities, and separate restrooms, can significantly enhance their involvement. Engaging local communities in tourism development ensures that benefits are equitably distributed and tailored to meet women's needs.

Targeted interventions are another critical strategy for empowering women. Skill development programs focused on hospitality, cultural preservation, digital marketing, and leadership can equip women with the expertise required for tourism roles. Providing free or subsidized training opportunities ensures inclusivity, enabling women from diverse socioeconomic backgrounds to participate. Microfinance initiatives further support women by offering access to

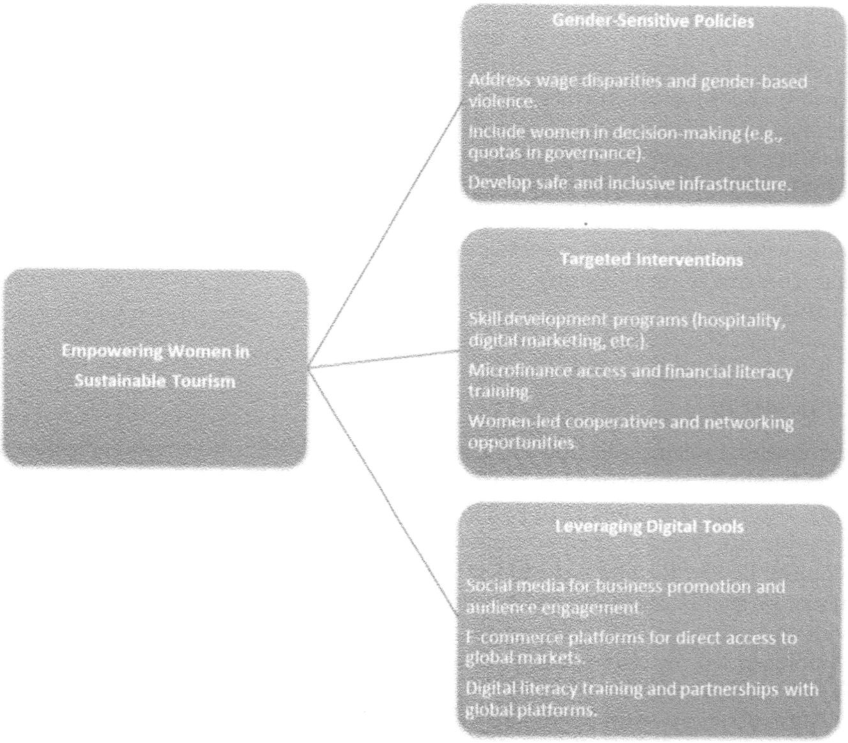

Fig. 7.5. Conceptual Map—Empowering Women in Sustainable Tourism: Gender-Sensitive Policies, Targeted Interventions, and Digital Innovation. *Source:* Prepared by the author. Interconnected strategies for empowering women in sustainable tourism. Gender-sensitive policies create enabling environments, targeted interventions build capacity, and digital tools amplify reach, collectively fostering equitable growth.

credit, allowing them to establish or expand tourism-related enterprises like homestays, artisanal crafts, and culinary experiences. To complement these efforts, financial literacy workshops can foster sustainable business practices. Networking opportunities, such as women-led tourism cooperatives and mentorship programs, can also play a pivotal role in promoting collaboration and market access. At the same time, conferences and forums amplify women's voices in the sector.

Leveraging digital tools presents a transformative opportunity for empowering women in tourism. Social media platforms enable women to promote businesses, share cultural heritage, and engage with global audiences. Training women in content creation and digital marketing can significantly enhance the visibility of their initiatives. Additionally, e-commerce platforms allow women to sell local crafts and tourism services directly to international customers, bypassing traditional intermediaries. Partnerships with global platforms like Airbnb and Etsy can further expand their reach. To maximize impact, digital literacy programs must be accessible to women in underserved communities, ensuring they can fully utilize these tools to overcome geographical and structural barriers.

By integrating gender-sensitive policies, targeted interventions, and digital tools, women can achieve economic empowerment, promote sustainable tourism, and contribute meaningfully to their communities while preserving cultural heritage.

Conclusion

Empowering women through sustainable tourism is critical to achieving inclusive and equitable development in Sri Lanka. As a key driver of the nation's economy, tourism offers immense potential to address gender disparities while contributing to broader socioeconomic goals. However, realizing this potential requires deliberate and targeted efforts to dismantle structural barriers that hinder women's full participation. Initiatives must focus on equipping women with the necessary skills, resources, and opportunities to thrive in the sector, complemented by community awareness programs to challenge traditional gender stereotypes.

Global success stories provide valuable insights into how women's involvement in sustainable tourism can enhance household incomes, foster leadership, and contribute to community development. Lessons from Morocco, Peru, Nepal, and Jordan illustrate the transformative impact of women's participation, showcasing how it can break traditional gender roles and empower women economically and socially. These examples underscore the importance of adapting best practices to the Sri Lankan context, ensuring that initiatives align with the country's unique cultural, economic, and social landscape.

Sustainable tourism aligns with global development priorities, particularly the United Nations' Sustainable Development Goals, by promoting gender equality (SDG 5), decent work and economic growth (SDG 8), and sustainable communities (SDG 11). Women's tourism empowerment strengthens social cohesion and community resilience and creates opportunities for education, healthcare, and broader societal advancements.

For Sri Lanka, integrating women into sustainable tourism practices is not merely an economic strategy but a transformative approach to fostering social inclusion and equity. Policies supporting women entrepreneurs to ensure equal pay and increase representation in decision-making are essential. Moreover, community-based tourism initiatives, where women lead homestays, cultural tours, and eco-tourism projects, offer practical solutions to reduce gender-based economic disparities and reshape societal perceptions of women's roles.

Ultimately, empowering women through sustainable tourism has far-reaching implications for Sri Lanka's future. It enhances the sector's economic contribution, promotes cultural preservation, and drives environmental sustainability. By prioritizing women's participation, Sri Lanka can unlock the full potential of its tourism industry, ensuring that the benefits are equitably distributed across communities. This approach will position tourism as a catalyst for long-term, inclusive development, reinforcing the critical role of gender equality in shaping a sustainable and prosperous future.

References

Acharya, B. P., & Halpenny, E. (2013). Homestays as an alternative tourism product for sustainable community development: A case study of women-managed tourism product in rural Nepal. *Tourism Planning & Development*, *10*(4), 367–387. https://doi.org/10.1080/21568316.2013.779313

Agarwal, S., Isha, T., Lrappa, T. V., & Akaremsetty, S. (2023). The impact of tourism on local communities: A literature review of socio-economic factors. *Journal of Harbin Engineering University*, *44*(8), 1851–1859. https://doi.org/10.5281/zenodo.8314700

Alamineh, G. A., Hussein, J. W., Mulu, Y. E., & Taddesse, B. (2023). The negative cultural impact of tourism and its implication on sustainable development in Amhara Regional State. *Cogent Arts and Humanities*, *10*(1). https://doi.org/10.1080/23311983.2023.2224597

Baloch, Q. B., Shah, S. N., Iqbal, N., Sheeraz, M., Asadullah, M., Mahar, S., & Khan, A. U. (2023). Impact of tourism development upon environmental sustainability: A suggested framework for sustainable ecotourism. *Environmental Science and Pollution Research*, *30*(3), 5917–5930. https://doi.org/10.1007/s11356-022-22496-w

Bhatt, K., Seabra, C., Kumar, J., Ashutosh, K., & Kumar Kabia, S. (2024). Tourism-led inclusive growth in emerging and developing economies: A systematic literature review. *Sage Open*, *14*(2). https://doi.org/10.1177/21582440241252516

Bujdosó, Z., Dávid, L., Tőzsér, A., Kovács, G., Major-Kathi, V., Uakhitova, G., Katona, P., & Vasvári, M. (2015). Basis of heritagization and cultural tourism development. *Procedia – Social and Behavioral Sciences*, *188*, 307–315. https://doi.org/10.1016/j.sbspro.2015.03.399

Fernández Bellver, D., Prados-Peña, M. B., García-López, A. M., & Molina-Moreno, V. (2023, January 1). Crafts as a key factor in local development: Bibliometric analysis. *Heliyon*, *9*. https://doi.org/10.1016/j.heliyon.2023.e13039

Haddaji, M., Albors-Garrigós, J., & García-Segovia, P. (2017). Women chefs' experience: Kitchen barriers and success factors. *International Journal of Gastronomy and Food Science*, *9*, 49–54. https://doi.org/10.1016/j.ijgfs.2017.06.004

Hemachandra, P. V. N. S., & De Silva, D. C. H. (2021). Sustainable tourism assisting national development in Sri Lanka – (STAND SL). In *Proceedings of international conference on business management* (Vol. 17). https://doi.org/10.31357/icbm.v17.5258

ILO Country Office for Sri Lanka and the Maldives. (n.d.). *ILO country Office for Sri Lanka and the Maldives*.

INE (Instituto Nacional de Estadística). (2023, March). Overnight stays in non-hotel tourist accommodation. *EOAT*. https://www.ine.es/en/daco/daco42/ocuptr/eoat0323_en.pdf

Kim, W., Che, C., & Jeong, C. (2023). Restaurant customers' food leftover reduction intention derived from nature connection and biospheric values: A comparison between men and women. *Frontiers in Psychology*, *14*, 976102. https://doi.org/10.3389/fpsyg.2022.976102

Kumar, R., & Mittal, K. (n.d.). Women empowerment and financial literacy empowering women through tourism: A journey of transformation. https://www.researchgate.net/publication/377416839

Leh, F. C., & Hamzah, M. R. (2012). Homestay tourism and pro-poor tourism strategy in Banghuris, Selangor, Malaysia. *Elixir International Journal*, *45*, 7602–7610.

Liyanage, S., & Fernando, J. (2014). *Wetland ecotourism in Sri Lanka: Issues and challenges*. https://www.researchgate.net/publication/258511406

Mehra, R. (1993). *Gender in community development and resource management: An overview*. International Center for Research on Women.

Monica, D. M. F., Tendani, E., & Zengeni, N. (2013). The absence of females in executive chef positions in Zimbabwean hotels: A case study of rainbow tourism group (RTG). *Australian Journal of Business and Management Research*, *3*(10), 1–18.

Movono, A., & Dahles, H. (2017). Female empowerment and tourism: A focus on businesses in a Fijian village. *Asia Pacific Journal of Tourism Research*, *22*(6), 681–692. https://doi.org/10.1080/10941665.2017.1308397

Muñoz-Benito, R., Navajas-Romero, V. M., & Hernández-Rojas, R. D. (2023). Traditional gastronomy in Alto Guadalquivir: Origin of contemporary recipes in Cordovan cuisine. *International Journal of Gastronomy and Food Science*, *32*, 100720. https://doi.org/10.1016/j.ijgfs.2023.100720

Nordbø, I. (2022). Female entrepreneurs and path-dependency in rural tourism. *Journal of Rural Studies*, *96*, 198–206. https://doi.org/10.1016/j.jrurstud.2022.09.032

Panta, S. K., & Thapa, B. (2018). Entrepreneurship and women's empowerment in gateway communities of Bardia National Park, Nepal. *Journal of Ecotourism*, *17*(1), 20–42. https://doi.org/10.1080/14724049.2017.1299743

Pasanchay, K., & Schott, C. (2021). Community-based tourism homestays' capacity to advance the sustainable development goals: A holistic sustainable livelihood perspective. *Tourism Management Perspectives*, *37*, 100784. https://doi.org/10.1016/j.tmp.2020.100784

Quang, T. D., Phan Tran, N. M., Sthapit, E., Thanh Nguyen, N. T., Le, T. M., Doan, T. N., & Thu-Do, T. (2023). Beyond the homestay: Women's participation in rural tourism development in Mekong Delta, Vietnam. *Tourism and Hospitality Research*. https://doi.org/10.1177/14673584231218103

Rieger, K. L., Horton, M., Copenace, S., Bennett, M., Buss, M., Chudyk, A. M., Cook, L., Hornan, B., Horrill, T., Linton, J., McPherson, K., Rattray, J. M., Murray, K., Phillips-Beck, W., Sinclair, R., Slavutskiy, O., Stewart, R., & Schultz, A. S. H. (2023). Elevating the uses of storytelling methods within indigenous health research: A critical, participatory scoping review. *International Journal of Qualitative Methods*, *22*. https://doi.org/10.1177/16094069231174764

Scheyvens, R., & Hughes, E. (2019). Can tourism help to "end poverty in all its forms everywhere"? The challenge of tourism addressing SDG1. *Journal of Sustainable Tourism*, *27*(7), 1061–1079. https://doi.org/10.1080/09669582.2018.1551404

Seow, D. Y., & Seow, D. (2020). *The role of gender, patriarchy and culture in the Asian female travel experience*. Copyright statement.

Shackelford, L., Kothari, A., & van Meenen, K. (2023). Gathering stories: Creating spaces for young women to connect and build community through multimodal storytelling. *Social Sciences*, *12*(9). https://doi.org/10.3390/socsci12090487

Shukor, H., Abdeshahian, P., Salih, N., & Yusoff, W. M. W. (2014). Biobutanol production from palm kernel cake (PKC) using Clostridium saccharoperbutylacetonicum N1-4 in batch culture fermentation. *BioResources*, *9*(3), 5325–5338. https://doi.org/10.15376/biores.9.3.5325-5338

Silva, S., & Mendis, K. (2017). Women in tourism industry-Sri Lanka. *An International Peer-Reviewed Journal*, *25*. www.iiste.org

Spanish Ministry of Agriculture, Fisheries and Food. (2024). *Agri-food and fisheries exports reached a record €70.43 billion in 2023* (Press release, 18 March 2024). Government of Spain.

Sriyani, G. T. W. (2022). Impact of community-based tourism projects' empowerment on the adoption of sustainability practices by community tourism entrepreneurs in Sri Lanka. *Wayamba Journal of Management*, *13*(1), 114. https://doi.org/10.4038/wjm.v13i1.7555

Thapaliya, M., Rai, G. S., Shrestha, A., Parajuli, B., & Pande, O. (2013). Homestay: Assessment in Lwang Ghalel. *Nepal Tourism and Development Review*, *2*(1), 105–140. https://doi.org/10.3126/ntdr.v2i1.7382

Tiwari, S., & Nguyen, T. P. L. (2024). *Towards social equity and sustainable economic prosperity through ecotourism: A case of caste diversified community along Annapurna Sanctuary Trail (AST)* (Vol. 34). World Development Perspectives. https://doi.org/10.1016/j.wdp.2024.100592

Tzanidaki, D., & Reynolds, F. (2011). Exploring the meanings of making traditional arts and crafts among older women in crete, using interpretative phenomenological analysis. *British Journal of Occupational Therapy*, *74*(8), 375–382. https://doi.org/10.4276/030802211X13125646370852

UNWTO. (2017). *Tourism for development – Volume I: Key areas for action*. World Tourism Organization (UNWTO).

UNWTO. (2019). *Global report on women in tourism* (2nd ed.). World Tourism Organization (UNWTO). https://doi.org/10.18111/9789284420384

UNWTO. (2023). *International tourism highlights, 2023 Edition: The impact of COVID-19 on tourism (2020–2022)*. World Tourism Organization (UNWTO). https://doi.org/10.18111/9789284424986

Vieira, B. M., Borges, A. P., & Vieira, E. P. (2023). The role of social networks for decision-making about tourism destinations. *International Journal of Internet Marketing and Advertising*, *18*(1), 1–27. https://doi.org/https://doi.org/https://doi.org/https://doi.org/https://doi.org/https://doi.org/https://doi.org/https://doi.org/https://doi.org/https://doi.org/https://doi.org/https://doi.org/10.1504/IJIMA.2023.128148

Vujko, A., Karabašević, D., Cvijanović, D., Vukotić, S., Mirčetić, V., & Brzaković, P. (2024). Women's empowerment in rural tourism as key to sustainable communities' transformation. *Sustainability*, *16*(23), 10412. https://doi.org/10.3390/su162310412

World Tourism Organization. (2019). In *Global report on women in tourism* (2nd ed.). World Tourism Organization (UNWTO). https://doi.org/10.18111/9789284420384

Chapter 7

Women in Tourism Industry: Opportunities and Barriers

Hewawasam H. P. K. N., Wijesekara P. D. and Pabasara R. P.

University of Sri Jayewardenepura, Sri Lanka

Abstract

Women represent a significant portion of the global economy, and such participation is important for sustainable development. Since the tourism industry contributes to sustainable economies, this chapter aims at the scholarly identification of women's participation in tourism, using secondary data (50 journal articles) from Taylor & Francis, Emerald, and SAGE published since 2000. The study establishes that women in tourism have positive career progress. However, certain barriers to women's participation were identified, particularly socioeconomic, cultural, and political, and especially in developing countries. Hence, to achieve sustainable development, this paper calls for a transformation where women's potential is fully realized within tourism.

Keywords: Tourism; women empowerment; challenges; opportunities; sustainable development; gender equality

Introduction

The socially given concept termed as "Gender" has come to be adopted as a major phenomenon in studies across disciplines. It is defined as the "socially constructed and historically variable relationships, cultural meanings, and identities through which biological sex differences become socially significant" (Laslett & Brenner, 1989, as cited in LaPan et al., 2021). By generating two stereotypical genders of male and female, the sexual division of labor has shaped multiple social contexts based on gendered behavior and gender expectations. Though universal definitions regarding empowerment cannot be found in the

Economics and Tourism, 115–130

doi:10.1108/978-1-83662-916-020251008

academic literature, scholars have defined it from various perspectives. Tegland (2008, as cited in Moswete & Lacey, 2014) identified empowerment "based on increased control over the determinants of the quality of an individual's life in respect to health, knowledge or freedom". This umbrella term of empowerment has several categories within it. Citing Scheyvens' (1999) seminal conceptualization of empowerment, Seyfi and others (2020) demonstrate the economic, social, political, and psychological aspects of empowerment, as associated with tourism development. The empowerment of women is a key topic of contemporary global political discourse (McMillan et al., 2011). This terminology has been defined by various scholars from different perspectives. Women's empowerment is defined as a "continuous, ongoing process entailing enhanced abilities to control choices, decisions and actions" (Al-Dajani & Marlow, 2013, as cited in McMillan et al., 2011). This emphasizes what positive change women's empowerment can play in transforming the role of women and society at large. Since some cultural practices deter women from economic activities, ensuring inclusivity and empowerment for such excluded social groups is essential to achieve sustainability together with inclusive growth. Bhatt and others (2024) point out, citing Uduji et al. (2021) that the concept of women's empowerment has received worldwide attention specifically with their incorporation with UN Sustainable Development Goals (SDGs). As Seyfi and others (2020) write, insights regarding empowerment, and women's empowerment, in particular, are included in the core understandings of sustainability and SDGs. On one hand the tourism industry has been identified as a harbinger of inclusive growth (Bhatt et al., 2024). On the other, shedding the light of sustainability in the tourism industry is essential. Hence, tourism needs to be understood and managed with a wider context of sustainability (Higgins-Desbiolles, 2018 as cited in Janjua et al., 2021). This innovative form of tourism utilizes more appropriate strategies and ensures effective role plays in a way that resource management benefits both the present and future. Meanwhile, sustainable tourism has developed with several innovative practices, including community-based tourism (Simons & de Groot, 2015), regenerative tourism (Nitsch & Vogels, 2022), community-based eco-tourism product (CBET), rural tourism, homestays, and women entrepreneurship (Janjua et al., 2021), and has focused on empowering communities and accomplishing power shifts, as Simons and de Groot (2015) explains. The tourism sector comprises 54% of women, which is in strong contrast with the broader economy, which only accounts for 39% (UNWTO, n.d., as cited in Nitsch & Vogels, 2022). However, despite the higher number of women in the tourism industry, they are employed as unskilled in low-paid jobs, explain Cave and Kilic (2010). Rather than empowering women, tourism has contributed to objectifying women, write Even Nitsch and Vogels (2022). However, sustainable tourism can be considered as a means of empowering women. It helps women negotiate spatial and moral boundaries associated with gender (Tucker, 2007, as cited in LaPan, 2021). Hence, women are employed in a spectrum of activities within the tourism industry, ranging from leaders to entrepreneurs (Moswete & Lacey, 2014). Women's entrepreneurship in tourism is a prominent means of empowerment as it significantly alleviates all forms of human poverty, including that of physical and mental health poverty, cultural literacy poverty, and participation in public affairs poverty, living environment poverty, and self-value, as Xu et al. (2018) explains. Hence, involvement in commercial hospitality has become a "vehicle for the empowerment of women" (McMillan et al., 2011).

Literature Review

Economic Contributions of Women in Tourism

Women's participation in the tourism industry fosters economic growth through job creation, small and medium enterprise development, and the promotion of unique local experiences. Mostly, women are significantly seen as entrepreneurs, employees, and cultural ambassadors in this industry. Women in tourism challenge established gender roles and challenge economic, cultural, social, and symbolic capital while aiming for economic development (Al-Dajani & Marlow, 2013). Empowering women in tourism helps to advance gender equality and community resilience while boosting local economies. Al-Dajani and Marlow (2013) make it clear that gender relations, the patriarchy, and exile are the factors that directly affect both potential and the driving forces behind women's entrepreneurship in developing their own business. Additionally, these women are often confined to the traditional female gender role of housekeeper and guest attendant, restricting their engagement in entrepreneurship to the lowest hierarchy of such activities (International Labour Organization, 2017). As Karatas-Ozkan et al. (2024) has emphasized, women's empowerment through tourism is not advocating only for the individual, but for the society as a whole. Vukovic et al. (2023) point out that in countries with underdeveloped tourist production, income from tourism for women is restricted as a result of the peculiarities of the economic, psychological, and social structures that shape these societies in the developing countries. However, some women voluntarily choose to work in the industry, driven by a desire for independence, skill development, and career advancement (Silva Dos Santos et al., 2024). Women who overcome societal barriers demonstrate that tourism can be a platform for women's empowerment, enabling economic independence and professional growth.

Despite the popular social expectations and work environments, women who work in the sector have significant potential for empowerment (Kodagoda & Jayawardhana, 2022). As is evidenced by the case studies of Moswete and Lacey (2014) on women's involvement in cultural tourism in Botswana, policies that promote community-based cultural tourism in a Botswana safari context raise considerable empowerment potential for women. Not only do women entrepreneurs in tourism pursue activities for purposes of achieving gender equality and environmental sustainability, but they also help in culture preservation. The tourism and hospitality sector of the Maldives has witnessed an almost steady inclusion of women in the workforce, including in management positions. This has been a shift in the course of social and cultural change even in an Islamic nation (Nagar, 2021).

Women in Tourism Entrepreneurship

Tourism entrepreneurship contributes to societal shifts such as changing perceptions about the conventional woman's role as well as entrepreneurial development that is sustainable in nature. A large number of women are able to find employment in tourism and hospitality industries for both direct opportunities and small and medium enterprises (SMEs), empowering income generation and leadership positions. Women also dominate tourism entrepreneurship, taking advantage of their creative ability, cultural endowment, and administrative skills to develop different models for tourism experiences.

Tourism provides opportunities for women in various settings. Much of the intangible cultural heritage, including the crafts, performing arts, and rituals, allows rural women to be economically and socially more developed and empowered. These include women of Haiyuan County practicing Hui embroidery to support the cultural and tourism sectors and uplift their region's standards (Su et al., 2020). Female hosts of homestays involved in mountain tourism in the Hunza Valley are empowered to take charge of finances, decision-making and have enhanced self-esteem (Ali et al., 2024). Likewise, women in rural Nepal are responsible for the homestays, the cultural shows, and sales of handicrafts, thus improving their social and economic status (Acharya & Halpenny, 2013). Female labor is an essential factor for Beeralu lace and Dumbara weaving, which are tourist attractions in Sri Lanka (Handapangoda et al., 2019; Maruyama & Woosnam, 2020). These activities also act as ways of conserving the cultural identity, apart from having the economic benefits that help women to gain more chances as well as visibility in the tourism industry.

Tourism Policies and Gender Equality

To empower women in tourism, the United Nations World Tourism Organization (UNWTO) launched the Global Report on Women in Tourism that celebrates the areas where women are gaining ground, such as wages, leadership, and entrepreneurship (World Tourism Organization, 2022). The countries that have adopted gender equality in the sector of tourism have realized an appreciation in the participation of women in decision-making. For instance, the Botswana community-based cultural tourism policy has socially empowered women in the community (Moswete & Lacey, 2014), while the Bhutanese government seeks gender mainstreaming in tourism policy to safeguard women, youths, and disabled persons. However, Belize's 2019 National Tourism Policy spells out the word 'inclusiveness' with no pointed plans on the gender concerns (Tourism Civil Aviation Ministry, 2019). UN Women also partners with the World Bank for visions of democratic and shared governance, scholarships for women leaders, and funds for women business persons (World Tourism Organization, 2019). Females are among the labor force categories in the tourism industry, especially in the developing world (United Nations Entity for Gender Equality and the Empowerment of UN Women, 2021; United Nations World Tourism Organization, 2022). Trade-related assistance through AfT projects is important for the realization of SDG 5 on Women Empowerment through empowering women through trade resources and opportunities in products such as tourism (WTO, 2022).

Challenges Faced by Women in the Tourism Industry

Women in the tourism industry find a number of challenges that affect their ability to gain recognition, equal opportunities, and promotions within the sector. Although the tourism sector provides huge potential for employment and entrepreneurship, gender-based obstacles continue. Even though women constitute over half of the world's labor force working in tourism, a lack of barriers to leadership roles and decision-making positions exists. Their representation on boards of companies is 15.2% on average (Equality in Tourism, 2013). Cultural barriers are also one of the common issues (Moswete & Lacey, 2014). As an example, women's empowerment at the UNESCO World Heritage site, Osun Grove, has been significantly hindered by various challenges, including insufficient formal education, inadequate entrepreneurship and occupational training, limited access to financial support or micro-finance schemes, and entrenched cultural barriers that have long suppressed their entrepreneurial potential (Aleshinloye, 2023). Even though Nagar (2021) found that women's participation has increased in the tourism and hospitality industry in the Maldives. Women managers face significant barriers, including cultural expectations, challenges in balancing work and family responsibilities, and persistent under-representation in leadership positions. World Tourism Organization (2019) highlights that women in the tourism industry face a significant wage gap, earning on average 14.7% less than their male counterparts. Addressing these challenges requires comprehensive measures, including stringent policies, awareness programs, support systems for reporting incidents, and fostering a culture of respect and equality to ensure a safer and more inclusive industry.

Future Trends in Tourism

The tourism industry is shifting away from traditional roles, embracing diverse and inclusive workforce models. Tourism in rural Nepal has increasingly shifted into the domain of women, marking a sociological paradigm shift in the country's sociocultural outlook. This shift is particularly evident in home-based tourism businesses, which challenge traditional perceptions of rural women's roles in community development and contribute to reshaping their social and economic status (Acharya & Halpenny, 2013). Khoo et al. (2023) suggest the delivery of gender-inclusive digital competency training for female entrepreneurs in tourism to promote greater involvement and achievement of women in tourism. Nagar (2021) points out that the change in social attitude and the increasing acceptance of women in professional work create an environment where it is becoming possible for more women to take part in a tourism career. Although there remain challenges, increasing involvement, public endorsement, and skill development, positive and beneficial media depictions of successful women's careers could also contribute to the promotion of gender equality in the sector.

Identified Research Gaps in Existing Literature

Although numerous studies have explored the role of women in the tourism industry, significant gaps still remain in the research. While some countries have integrated gender considerations into tourism policies, a comparative analysis of these strategies and their effectiveness across regions is lacking. Yet although much literature addresses gender-based violence, there is insufficient research on the effectiveness of mitigation strategies and policy frameworks to overcome harassment and improve workplace ethics in the tourism industry. Quantitative analyses to measure impacts such as wage gaps, entrepreneurial outcomes, and leadership progressions are also sparse. Success stories of women in tourism should also be measured using a quantitative approach compared to the men in the same industry. Studies lack depth in assessing how community-based tourism reshapes gender norms in patriarchal systems over time. Furthermore, it is crucial to understand the opportunities and the barriers prevailing in the tourism industry in the existing condition. Following the research gap, this study has focused on identifying the challenges, barriers and opportunities for women in the tourism industry and making recommendations to overcome the situation.

Further, the present study depends on secondary data from 50 journal papers available in Taylor & Francis, Emerald, and SAGE databases since 2000. The journal papers have been selected through the above data based on the particular websites using the keywords of "Women," "Women Empowerment," and "Tourism industry." The analysis was conducted based on identified main themes as challenges and opportunities, which fit the general conceptual framework of the qualitative approach toward analysis.

Results

Challenges Toward the Women in Tourism Industry

Cultural and Family Expectations

Cultural barriers that confine women to family responsibilities rather than a career further reduce their chances of participating in the tourism sector, especially in Turkey (Cave & Kilic, 2010). Husbands are settlers, while wives are caretakers of children and the home, which greatly hinders Asian women from getting a job or seeking a promotion. This woman-oriented division of work reduces her chances of getting employment under a normal work environment and employee benefits, hence acting as a demerit to sectors such as tourism, which has adverse working conditions, including long working hours and unsociable hours of work. They profoundly restrict women from pathways to realization of paid work, education, and other spheres (Bhatt et al., 2024).

For instance, lack of social capital, such as cheap childcare, discourages women from fully capitalizing on economic opportunities of huge tourism booms (Ferguson, 2011). Therefore, while tourism as a sector offers the possibility for women to flourish in the sector, structural barriers in society and inadequacies in the provision of infrastructure hinder the entry and promote the under-representation of female workers in the sector. This cultural limitation of women's economic participation is a major challenge to the tourism sector in many contexts.

"Double Burden" of Work

Working in tourism did not necessarily relieve women of their domestic responsibilities, leading to an increased workload for many (Tucker, 2007). Even though the women are full-time engaged in tourism careers, they are still expected to maintain domestic duties, leading to increased workloads for women. Beedle and others (2013) explain this as a "double burden" of work, and Lapan et al. (2021) mention the same situation as a "double shift," where they are expected to manage both paid work and their traditional domestic duties. This contributes to the perception that women's work in tourism is supplementary to their primary role as caregivers and homemakers (Cave & Kilic, 2010). Instead of liberating women from the perceived constraints, this double burden (Lapan et al., 2021) ultimately acts as a barrier toward the full integration of women into tourism and limits their career prospects (Beedle et al., 2013).

Male Dominance in the Workforce

This study revealed that female participants in the tourism industry face many barriers to career mobility because of the prevailing culture and tradition, just like their male counterparts who may have similar academic qualifications and professional competence. These stereotypical images are further compromised as a part of the tourism images where men are depicted as overbearing and women as homebound (Cave & Kilic, 2010; Xu et al., 2017). Experiences from areas such as Nicaragua and Cape Verde which reveal the sexism in tourism and women's stakeholders (Moswete & Lacey, 2014). There is unfavorable treatment of women where they are locked out of meaningful work, even in such sectors as handicraft production, in micro enterprises which are perceived to empower them' (Ferguson, 2011). Nepali women, for instance, have done trekking and tour guiding, becoming confident and hence disrupting those traditional patriarchal roles (Hillman & Radel, 2021). Although for women, tourism prospects can provide some economic power, in terms of social and political power, tourism is much restricted. Policies must include unpaid work and relations of power for the parity; for this reason, they have to go beyond mere economic liberalism (Ali et al., 2024; Ferguson, 2011). It is clear that tourism-related activities are strongly stratified by gender; men dominate higher paid and managerial roles, while women are over-represented in lower tier positions.

Cave and Kilic (2010), in their study in Antalya, Turkey, illustrated that even when women reach the management positions, they are often confined to departments like human resources rather than operations or finance, which are traditionally held by men. There is a considerable barrier for women to meaningfully participate and be empowered even in the microenterprises like the handicrafts production industries (Ferguson, 2011). This gender bias and a lack of transparent promotion systems led to a glass ceiling effect where women are confined to lower level positions despite having acquired the qualifications and experience needed for advancement (Cave & Kilic, 2010).

Problems that affect women engaged in tourism businesses include some of these women lacking starting capital, lacking education or having poor education, and having grouped control of tourist centers (Moswete & Lacey, 2014). Among them are resistance toward gender equity, insufficient financing, and lack of institutional support (Wilson, 2020). The financial systems are impregnated with systematic discrimination to bar women from receiving credit or training, or other professional prospects. In Thailand, poverty Input Stream Women engage in sex tourism due to poverty and lack of education and job opportunities, which make them work as the family breadwinners. This commodification continues to promote gender inequalities, stigmatization, and exploitation just like what can be previewed in countries like the Philippines, the Dominican Republic, and Brazil (O'Malley, 1988).

Challenges in the Workplace

Female employees in the industry are often employed in lower status, temporally or casually situated roles such as cleaning and serving food and beverages, thus they are also disadvantaged by gender (Cave & Kilic, 2010; Ferguson, 2011). The gender pay gap remains a burning concern, with women limited to low-skilled and low-paid employment and no gender-sensitive policies to foster career mobility (Beedle et al., 2013; Lapan et al., 2021). All these challenges are more so seen in the Global South societies. High working demands, unpredictable working conditions, and shift work inconvenience in the tourism sector make working conditions for women worse by trying to balance working schedules with family obligations that do not include childcare or parental leave benefits (Cave & Kilic, 2010). Analyzing with regard to sex, females are dominating in research activities—67% in contrast to men—33%, but female scholars speak rarely as key-speakers, and their visibility in leadership positions is scarce (28%) (Basurto-Barcia & Ricaurte-Quijano, 2017). Some of the challenges that women in management encounter include culture, family responsibilities, and someone to guide or sponsor positive change (Nagar, 2021). Traditionally, male-dominated roles still persist to shape gender expectations that pose strict restrictions on women on their operations. Still, for women, sustainable tourism creates fair and effective employment, emphasizing the role of the community, as well as calling for development policies (Karatas-Ozkan et al., 2024).

Opportunities

Tool for Gender Equality and Economic Empowerment

Tourism supports the women in marginalized communities in tourism areas to gain economic power and, by the way, to support their families and contribute to the decision-making within their family structure. As described by Surti et al. (2024), women are traditionally marginalized, but they are capable of conveying indigenous craft, fable, and all other types of cultural communication. As a development tool and contributor to socioeconomic development, including and beyond absolute and relative poverty (Lagos & Wang, 2023), the impact and contributions of tourism to gender equity and women's enhancement are conditioned (Tucker & Boonabaana, 2011). Ferguson (2011) argues that tourism can indeed contribute to empowering women, but this potential is underutilized due to the current development paradigms. Tourism brings implications of changing gender roles and the societal status of women. Despite having many economic benefits, Lapan and others (2021) observed that women are often typecast into performances of traditional business occupations such as weaving or artisanship. Women, in particular, can find that tourism can open up the opportunity to be self-employed and to take charge. Concerning the economic empowerment and occupation opportunities in this case, they may alleviate other social, cultural, and institutional barriers toward gender inequality (Wilson, 2020). Women's empowerment in tourism entails breaking down hindrances that include sociocultural factors and ensuring resource equity to women globally (Kim et al., 2019). Yet it is believed that women's entrepreneurship in tourism can provide economic opportunities for personal and social transformation. By involvement in tourism, rural women have opportunities to learn new skills and improve their literacy and cultural knowledge, which also serves to improve their confidence and professional competence (Xu et al., 2018). Tourism offers important sources of employment for local women as they financially foster their families or communities' needs (Beedle et al., 2013; Doran, 2016; Seyfi et al., 2020). Agricultural accommodation like farmhouses and homestays is preferred; that also helps women in earning money regarding household chores, which leads to economic independence and minimizes poverty (Bhatt et al., 2024; Janjua et al., 2021; Xu et al., 2018). These activities help to enhance children and educational systems as well as quality and women to fully control financial resources at home (McMillan et al., 2011).

Hillman and Radel (2021) have also described income generation and women's independence through tours such as trekking guides and crafts in Nepal. Likewise, in Guatemala, rural tourism is not highly beneficial for women due to the persistent gender discrimination. But those women have some financial freedom and appreciation of their labor (Lapan et al., 2021). The employment tasks without division into male and female characters and paid work offered them autonomy and power.

Stepping Beyond Domestic Boundaries

Apart from economic empowerment, tourism allows women to interact with people from different cultures, learn, and, subsequently raise their awareness. Hillman and Radel (2021) mentioned that this social and cultural exchange is a major element for the new definition of women's roles in Nepal. Tucker (2007) emphasized the long-term trend of expanding the tourism industry in the village of Göreme, a space formerly perceived as a man's domain. Women participating in small-scale entrepreneurial activities, such as selling handicrafts, cleaners, and kitchen helpers, also began taking on more visible roles, such as hotel receptionists and restaurant servers. This was facilitated by broader social changes, such as education for young women, inspirations for migration, and exposure to modern lifestyles through media influence. They have participated in transgressing old boundaries of women and reshaping the gender dynamics in Göreme (Tucker, 2007). The women engaged in agro-tourism and vegetable production are mostly women. Domestic boundaries are challenged when these entrepreneurs are offered with vocational training and resources supporting agro-tourism. Doran (2016) discusses how women negotiate traditional gender roles and the challenges that women face in claiming a space for themselves within this male-dominated industry of adventure tourism. Adventure tourism provides a means for women to experience self-development through the pursuance of hobbies, the development of skills, and the achievement of personal goals. Further, the experience helps to increase their self-understanding, pride, strength, and confidence, which are essential to empowerment (Doran, 2016). Female venture development empowers them and offers economic worth by contributing to family and rural development (Xu et al., 2018). Nepali women are empowered in male-streamed industries, including trekking and tour guiding, confidence build-up, and dealing with patriarchal policies (Hillman & Radel, 2021). Sustainable tourism gives women leadership chances and a better say in tourism initiatives by raising local participation (Bhatt et al., 2024). In the most significant ways, leading tourism businesses assist women in breaking gender barriers and encouraging gender equality within the sector (Del Casino & Hanna, 2000). However, promoting tourism participation enhances confidence, accomplishment, and enables women to transform and attain their vision (Moswete & Lacey, 2014). Female business owners use tourism to introduce change and establish social status for women and children in cultures where they are marginalized (Wilson, 2020).

Apart from women working as tourism service providers, female tourists have not been left out either, as they have played a substantial part in redefining the landmarks of women's participation in the tourism industry. Betty Hagglund, in her book *Tourists and Travelers: Women's Fictional and Non-Fictional Writing*, highlights the significant role women travelers played in transforming gender perceptions (Moutray, 2012). Their opinions alone are also sources of evidence on the exoticization of specific places, depicting the significance of women's opinions in developing the tourism narratives (Moutray, 2012). Moreover, tourism generates more roles than the domestic sphere and reconstructs the familial and communal roles optimistically (Beedle et al., 2013; Hillman & Radel, 2021). Diverse sectors' involvement enhances women's networking and social power and opens up channels for partnership.

Leadership and Social Recognition

Women get local and industry recognition since they acquire leadership and entrepreneurial positions. Hence, tourism becomes instrumental in a change toward better livelihood and therefore improvements in the social status of women and gender equity. Tourism policies in various African countries, including Ghana, Nigeria, and Cameroon, support women's empowerment through the use of collaborative networks. These networks provide access to finance, skill development, and business management resources, which help women entrepreneurs overcome challenges (Kim et al., 2019; Moswete & Lacey, 2014). Women in rural tourism also participate more in public and community affairs, which allows them to take part in new experiences and opportunities (Xu et al., 2018). Further, women entrepreneurs experience a sense of fulfillment and improved mental health (Xu et al., 2018) by managing their businesses and achieving personal goals. The economic stability and the status they gained from tourism may release them from the economic burdens that come from the family. Though it is initially demanding, tourism entrepreneurship has contributed to significant improvements in women's physical and mental well-being over time. Women's entrepreneurship plays a pivotal role in enhancing the competitiveness of tourism destinations by fostering innovation, diversifying offerings, and promoting inclusive growth. According to Kim et al. (2019), women entrepreneurs bring unique perspectives and skills to the tourism industry, creating distinctive experiences that cater to a wide range of consumers while also contributing to sustainable development. In many rural areas, linking tourism with agriculture, such as through agritourism, has empowered women who are involved in farming. This creates new income streams for women by integrating them into tourism value chains (Bhatt et al., 2024). Community-based tourism involves the participation of local communities in tourism activities around protected areas, mainly on natural resources or areas enriched with biodiversity. Gidebo (2023) further points out that community-based tourism allows women and other members of the community to take part in decision-making, ownership, and management of tourism ventures, thus promoting economic benefits and biodiversity conservation. Women can actively participate in this type of tourism because they are closer to protected areas, unlike men, who often move away in search of employment opportunities. Women play a key role in sustaining cultural tourism, such as offering authentic cultural experiences through homestays. Their participation ensures that traditions are preserved while fostering cultural exchanges (Janjua et al., 2021). Heritage tourism, Intangible Cultural Heritage (rituals, ceremonies, and festivals/storytelling and oral histories/live cultural performances such as music, dance, and theater), culinary tourism, crafts and handicrafts, religious and spiritual tourism, and community-based cultural experiences are some of the cultural tourism initiatives.

Conclusion

Women employed in the industry are hugely constrained by cultural and societal factors that essentially lock them out from participating in the economic ventures, especially in Turkey, Asia, and Brazil, because they have to undertake some chores like childbearing and raising, as well as performing most of the domestic tasks. Such pressures aggravate the gender disparities and elevate the status of womanhood in the difficulty of maintaining family life and work life. Juggling work and home responsibilities is commonly referred to as the 'double burden' of women in the workplace and does not enable women to progress up the corporate ladder in a particular male-dominated sector. Barriers that are recurrent include: gender discrimination, funding constraints, and lack of support from organizations limit women's advancement and promotion in the tourism industry. Nevertheless, the problem stated above has its lights: tourism enables women who live in such districts, to raise their economic activity levels by such actions as selling handmade products or offering their households to tourists, fighting poverty, and promoting children's schooling through investments. Tourism also leads to the liberation of women, whereby they can build confidence and also have the chance to gain the necessary skills, hence professional competence. It also helps them to precipitate a departure from the historical type of gender roles since they can now exercise the status of managers and leaders; which improves their integration into the making of decisions on family and other communal matters. Female managers in rural tourism engender employment in the local economy of a country and play a role model to other women who intend to embrace the tourism business. It also acts as an escape from those oppressive cultural practices and norms that harm women socially, psychologically, and physically. Specialized tourist products, including ecotourism and agro-tourism, are pioneering sustainable livelihoods by tapping into women's creativity for the improvement of folks and the environment. Cultural tourism in this case involves women in tour guiding, preparation of the native foods, crafting, and other cultural integrity which assists in standardizing cultural tourism and reducing the intercultural barriers.

Thus, to eradicate barriers, strategies should entail nondiscriminatory policies of recruitment, eradication of gaps between male and female employees' wages, and promotion of leadership training for women. For women to be able to conquer the double burden, the following arrangements must be made available: providing flexible work arrangements, parental leave, and childcare services. It is only possible if women receive monetary support in the form of micro-financing or have governments and NGOs to partner with. Enhancing opportunities for education, skills development, training in trade and vocation, and tourism, especially in the areas of environmental conservation, would provide more opportunities to women. Awareness creation together with working with leaders at the grassroots level may help neutralize culturally ingrained restrictive norms. The enhancement of women's needs can stimulate their mental and health fitness, as well as recognition of their achievements in handling their problems. Furthermore, simplification of gender-sensitive research and data collection would go a long way in the development of sustainable and healthy tourism models. In turn, these strategies would help change the lives of women through the involvement in tourism, promoting their economic, social, and cultural empowerment.

References

Acharya, B. P., & Halpenny, E. A. (2013). Homestays as an alternative tourism product for sustainable community development: A case study of women-managed tourism product in rural Nepal. *Tourism Planning & Development*, *10*(4), 367–387. https://doi.org/10.1080/21568316.2013.779313

Al-Dajani, H., & Marlow, S. (2013). Empowerment and entrepreneurship: A theoretical framework. *International Journal of Entrepreneurial Behavior & Research*, *19*(5), 503–524. https://doi.org/10.1108/IJEBR-10-2011-0138

Aleshinloye, K. D. (2023). Women's role in Africa's tourism industry: Overcoming gender disparities, empowerment, and entrepreneurship challenges at a UNESCO world heritage site. *Tourism Planning & Development*, *21*(4), 485–502. https://doi.org/10.1080/21568316.2023.2230454

Ali, A., Iqbal, Z., & Ali, I. (2024). Women in mountain tourism: Exploring the links between women tourism entrepreneurship and women empowerment in Hunza Valley. *Tourism Recreation Research*, 1–17. https://doi.org/10.1080/02508281.2024.2386869

Amani, D., & Mfumbilwa, E. E. (2024). Destination promotion videos and tourism knowledge: A road toward residents' empowerment in emerging tourism destinations. *Sage Open*, *14*(3). https://doi.org/10.1177/21582440241276182

Basurto-Barcia, J., & Ricaurte-Quijano, C. (2017). Women in tourism: Gender (in) equalities in university teaching and research. *Anatolia*, *28*(4), 567–581. https://doi.org/10.1080/13032917.2017.1370781

Beedle, J., Kline, C., Cardenas, D., Byrd, E. T., & Schneider, P. (2013). An exploration of gendered systems theory on women-owned businesses in emerging tourism destinations: Future directions. *Journal of Tourism and Cultural Change*, *11*(3), 170–186. https://doi.org/10.1080/14766825.2013.808644

Bhatt, K., Seabra, C., Kumar, J., Ashutosh, K., & Kumar Kabia, S. (2024). Tourism-led inclusive growth in emerging and developing economies: A systematic literature review. *Sage Open*, *14*(2). https://doi.org/10.1177/21582440241252516

Cave, P., & Kilic, S. (2010). The role of women in tourism employment with special reference to Antalya, Turkey. *Journal of Hospitality Marketing & Management*, *19*(3), 280–292. https://doi.org/10.1080/19368621003591400

Del Casino, V. J., & Hanna, S. P. (2000). Representations and identities in tourism map spaces. *Progress in Human Geography*, *24*(1), 23–46. https://doi.org/10.1191/030913200673388638

Doran, A. (2016). Empowerment and women in adventure tourism: A negotiated journey. *Journal of Sport & Tourism*, *20*(1), 57–80. https://doi.org/10.1080/14775085.2016.1176594

Equality in Tourism. (2013). *Women in the boardroom in the tourism industry*. Equality in Tourism. https://www.equalityintourism.org/wp-content/uploads/2013/07/Sun_Sand_Ceiling_F.pdf

European Bank for Reconstruction and Development. (2020). Addressing gender-based violence and harassment (GBVH) in the hotels. *Catering and Tourism (HCT) Sector*. https://www.ifc.org/content/dam/ifc/doc/mgrt/sectorbrief-addressinggbvh-hct.pdf

Ferguson, L. (2011). Promoting gender equality and empowering women? Tourism and the third Millennium development goal. *Current Issues in Tourism*, *14*(3), 235–249. https://doi.org/10.1080/13683500.2011.555522

Gidebo, H. B. (2023). Linking livelihood and biodiversity conservation in protected areas: Community based tourism development perspective from developing country. *Tourism and Hospitality Research*, *23*(3), 361–375. https://doi.org/10.1177/14673584221102699

Hagglund, B. (2012). *Tourists and travellers: Women's non-fictional writing about Scotland, 1770–1830*. Channel View Publications. 2010. *Women's Studies*, *41*(4), 498–502. https://doi.org/10.1080/00497878.2012.662879

Handapangoda, W. S., Bandara, H. M., & Kumara, U. A. (2019). Exploring tradition in heritage tourism: The experience of Sri Lanka's traditional mask art. *International Journal of Heritage Studies*, *25*, 415–436. https://doi.org/10.1080/13527258.2018.1481132

Hillman, W., & Radel, K. (2021). The social, cultural, economic and political strategies extending women's territory by encroaching on patriarchal embeddedness in tourism in Nepal. *Journal of Sustainable Tourism*, *30*(7), 1754–1775. https://doi.org/10.1080/09669582.2021.1894159

International Labour Organization. (2017). *Decent work in the tourism sector in South Asia: Challenges and opportunities*. International Labour Organization. https://www.ilo.org/sites/default/files/wcmsp5/groups/public/@asia/@ro-bangkok/@ilo-colombo/documents/publication/wcms_551675.pdf

Janjua, Z. U. A., Krishnapillai, G., & Rahman, M. (2021). A systematic literature review of rural homestays and sustainability in tourism. *Sage Open*, *11*(2). https://doi.org/10.1177/21582440211007117

Karatas-Ozkan, M., Tunalioglu, R., Ibrahim, S., Ozeren, E., Grinevich, V., & Kimaro, J. (2024). Actioning sustainability through tourism entrepreneurship: Women entrepreneurs as change agents navigating through the field of stakeholders. *Central European Management Journal*, *32*(1), 31–56. https://doi.org/10.1108/CEMJ-12-2021-0159

Khoo, C., Yang, E. C. L., Tan, R. Y. Y., Alonso-Vazquez, M., Ricaurte-Quijano, C., Pécot, M., & Barahona-Canales, D. (2023). Opportunities and challenges of digital competencies for women tourism entrepreneurs in Latin America: A gendered perspective. *Journal of Sustainable Tourism*, *32*(3), 519–539. https://doi.org/10.1080/09669582.2023.2189622

Kim, S., Whitford, M., & Arcodia, C. (2019). Development of intangible cultural heritage as a sustainable tourism resource: The intangible cultural heritage practitioners' perspectives. *Journal of Heritage Tourism*, *14*, 422–435. https://doi.org/10.1080/1743873X.2018.1561703

Kodagoda, T., & Jayawardhana, S. (2022). Forced or voluntary reluctance or voluntary preference to work? Women in hotel industry: Evidence from Sri Lanka. *Gender in Management*, *37*(4), 524–534. https://doi.org/10.1108/GM-01-2021-0011

Lagos, K., & Wang, Y. (2023). International tourism and poverty alleviation: Cross-country evidence using panel quantile fixed effects approach. *Journal of Travel Research*, *62*(6), 1347–1371. https://doi.org/10.1177/00472875221119978

LaPan, C., Morais, D. B., Wallace, T., Barbieri, C., & Floyd, M. F. (2021). Gender, work, and tourism in the Guatemalan Highlands. *Journal of Sustainable Tourism*. https://doi.org/10.1080/09669582.2021.1952418

Maruyama, N. U., & Woosnam, K. M. (2020). Representation of "mill girls" at a UNESCO world heritage site in Gunma, Japan. *Journal of Sustainable Tourism*, *29*(2–3), 277–294. https://doi.org/10.1080/09669582.2020.1738443

McMillan, C. L., O'Gorman, K. D., & MacLaren, A. C. (2011). Commercial hospitality: A vehicle for the sustainable empowerment of Nepali women. *International Journal of Contemporary Hospitality Management*, *23*(2), 189–208. https://doi.org/10.1108/09596111111119329

Mkono, M. (2010). Zimbabwean hospitality students' experiences of sexual harassment in the hotel industry. *International Journal of Hospitality Management*, *29*(4), 729–735. https://doi.org/10.1016/j.ijhm.2010.03.002

Moswete, N., & Lacey, G. (2014). "Women cannot lead": Empowering women through cultural tourism in Botswana. *Journal of Sustainable Tourism*, *23*(4), 600–617. https://doi.org/10.1080/09669582.2014.986488

Moutray, T. J. (2012). Betty hagglund. Tourists and travellers: Women's non-fictional writing about Scotland, 1770–1830: Bristol: Channel view Publications, 2010. *Women's Studies*, *41*(4), 498–502. https://doi.org/10.1080/00497878.2012.662879

Nagar, K. (2021). Representation of women managers in hospitality and tourism: A content analysis of related magazine articles. *Gender in Management*, *36*(3), 329–348. https://doi.org/10.1108/GM-10-2019-0180

Nitsch, B., & Vogels, C. (2022). Gender equality boost for regenerative tourism: The case of Karenni village Huay Pu Keng (Mae Hong Son, Thailand). *Journal of Tourism Futures*, *8*(3), 375–379. https://doi.org/10.1108/jtf-01-2022-0032

Nsom Kimbu, A., Zisuh Ngoasong, M., Adeola, O., & Afenyo-Agbe, E. (2018). Collaborative networks for sustainable human capital management in women's tourism entrepreneurship: The role of tourism policy. *Tourism Planning & Development*. https://doi.org/10.1080/21568316.2018.1556329

O'Malley, J. (1988). Sex tourism and women's status in Thailand. *Loisir et Société* [*Society and Leisure*], *11*(1), 99–114. https://doi.org/10.1080/07053436.1988.10715292

Scheyvens, R. (1999). Ecotourism and the empowerment of local communities. *Tourism Management*, *20*(2), 245–249. https://doi.org/10.1016/s0261-5177(98)00069-7

Seyfi, S., Hall, C. M., & Vo-Thanh, T. (2020). The gendered effects of statecraft on women in tourism: Economic sanctions, women's disempowerment and sustainability? In *Gender and tourism sustainability* (pp. 285–302). Routledge. https://doi.org/10.1080/09669582.2020.1850749

Silva Dos Santos, C., Lugosi, P., & Hawkins, R. (2024). Trust, traditions and indigenous women's leadership in sustainable tourism management. *Journal of Sustainable Tourism*, 1–17. https://doi.org/10.1080/09669582.2024.2309200

Simons, I., & de Groot, E. (2015). Power and empowerment in community-based tourism: Opening pandora's box? *Tourism Review*, *70*(1), 72–84. https://doi.org/10.1108/tr-06-2014-0035

Su, M. M., Wall, G., Ma, J., Notarianni, M., & Wang, S. (2020). Empowerment of women through cultural tourism: Perspectives of Hui minority embroiderers in Ningxia, China. *Journal of Sustainable Tourism*, *31*(2), 307–328. https://doi.org/10.1080/09669582.2020.1841217

Surti, T., Pratomo, D. S., Santoso, D. B., & Pangestuty, F. W. (2024). Unlocking the economic potential of cultural heritage: Women's empowerment in the creative economy of developing countries. *Journal of Ecohumanism*, *3*(3), 1794–1816. https://doi.org/10.62754/joe.v3i3.3631

Tourism and Civil Aviation Ministry. (2019). *National sustainable tourism master plan for Belize 2030*. Government of Belize.

Tucker, H. (2007). Undoing shame: Tourism and women's work in Turkey. *Journal of Tourism and Cultural Change*, *5*(2), 87–105. https://doi.org/10.2167/jtcc089.0

Tucker, H., & Boonabaana, B. (2011). A critical analysis of tourism, gender and poverty reduction. *Journal of Sustainable Tourism*, *20*(3), 437–455. https://doi.org/10.1080/09669582.2011.622769

UN Women. (2021). *Tourism sector in Timor-Leste: Women's participation and opportunities*. UN Women. https://asiapacific.unwomen.org/sites/default/files/Field%20Office%20ESEAsia/Docs/Publications/2021/03/tl-TOURISM-SECTOR-s.pdf

Vukovic, D. B., Petrovic, M., Maiti, M., & Vujko, A. (2023). Tourism development, entrepreneurship and women's empowerment – Focus on Serbian countryside. *Journal of Tourism Futures*, *9*(3), 417–437. https://doi.org/10.1108/JTF-10-2020-0167

Wilson, B. (2020). Gender equality and tourism beyond empowerment In S. Cole (Ed.). *Current issues in tourism* (pp. 1011–1013). CABI Publications. https://doi.org/10.1080/13683500.2020.1821492.

World Tourism Organization. (2019). *Global Report on women in tourism – Second edition*. UNWTO. https://doi.org/10.18111/9789284420384

World Tourism Organization. (2022). *Gender-inclusive strategy for tourism businesses*. UNWTO. https://doi.org/10.18111/9789284423262

World Trade Organization. (2022). *Aid for trade global review: Gender equality, women's economic empowerment and sustainable trade*. Rue de Lausanne.

Xu, H., Wang, C., Wu, J., Liang, Y., Jiao, Y., & Nazneen, S. (2018). Human poverty alleviation through rural women's tourism entrepreneurship. *Journal of China Tourism Research*. https://doi.org/10.1080/19388160.2018.1507860

Xu, H., Wang, K., & Ye, T. (2017). Women's awareness of gender issues in Chinese tourism academia. *Anatolia*, *28*(4), 553–566. https://doi.org/10.1080/13032917.2017.1370780

Chapter 8

Female Workforce Participation, Challenges, and Opportunities in the Tourism Industry

Nirupama Mohanty and Sweta Leena Hota

Kalinga Institute of Industrial Technology, India

Abstract

Tourism has become a vital global economic force and a key driver of development. Its rapid growth presents valuable opportunities for women entrepreneurs to impact local and national economies. Beyond its economic role, tourism promotes social awareness, cultural exchange, and international cooperation. In India, tourism significantly contributes to income generation and helps address unemployment. While the industry employs many women, they are often confined to low-wage, low-skill roles. Despite the sector's potential, women's participation in leadership and entrepreneurship remains limited. This paper explores the reasons behind this imbalance and suggests ways to increase women's involvement in tourism. Women face challenges such as job segregation, lower wages, and limited access to resources. Deep-rooted social norms also restrict their advancement. Still, the sector offers promising opportunities for women to launch businesses, assume leadership roles, and gain education and training. To foster lasting change, collaboration among policymakers, industry leaders, and community groups is essential. Together, they can build a more inclusive and equitable tourism industry where women can truly thrive.

Keywords: Women empowerment; tourism; entrepreneurship; equality; employment; SDG

Economics and Tourism, 131–141

Published under exclusive licence by Emerald Publishing Limited
doi:10.1108/978-1-83662-916-020251009

Introduction

Tourism is a multifaceted phenomenon encompassing social, cultural, and economic aspects, where individuals travel to places outside their regular surroundings for purposes such as leisure, business, or professional activities. These individuals, known as visitors, include both tourists and excursionists, whether they are residents or nonresidents. Tourism encompasses their activities, often involving expenditure related to their travels. It can also be defined as "the actions of people who journey to and stay in places outside their usual environment for a period not exceeding one consecutive year, for leisure, business, or other purposes unrelated to the economic activities of the destination."

This study aims to examine women's current participation in the tourism industry by analyzing their employment roles and entrepreneurial engagement. It also seeks to identify barriers to their advancement, including wage disparities, limited leadership opportunities, and sociocultural constraints. Additionally, the research explores opportunities for empowering women through tourism by highlighting initiatives and strategies that promote their economic and social development. Furthermore, it assesses the role of various stakeholders in fostering gender equity by evaluating collaborative efforts to enhance women's participation and address existing inequalities within the sector.

Currently, tourism stands as one of the fastest expanding industries and serves as a major source of employment, largely due to the transformative effects of globalization on the tourism landscape. This field has evolved from focusing solely on air travel and overnight stays to encompass the full range of experiences associated with travel destinations. This noticeable shift is driven not only by rising income levels but also by changing lifestyles and a new generation of travelers. More and more individuals are venturing around the globe in pursuit of enriching experiences related to culture, nature, and education. This trend has created a new type of traveler who seeks to immerse themselves in the destination by interacting with locals and learning about various cultures and communities. Consequently, this emerging trend opens up fresh opportunities for the tourism industry, as the number of both domestic and international travelers continues to rise. However, despite the growing demand, there exists a disparity between supply and demand, as there is a shortage of qualified tourism professionals to meet the needs of this expanding sector.

Travel has emerged as a significant global economic powerhouse, acknowledged for its swift, sustainable expansion and ability to foster development. In India and various other developing countries, it acts as an essential source of foreign currency and enhances both local and national economies. The tourism industry has shown its capacity to generate employment and promote income-generating opportunities that advantage local communities in tourist destinations. The tourism and hospitality sector stands out as one of the most recognized segments within India's services industry.

Methodology

The research utilizes a qualitative methodology, mainly relying on secondary data gathered from scholarly articles, industry publications, and earlier research concerning women's engagement in the tourism field. By conducting a thorough literature review, the study highlights significant themes such as job trends, entrepreneurial opportunities, obstacles, and prospects for women in the tourism sector. The examination centers on comprehending the socioeconomic and cultural elements that influence women's participation and advancement within the industry.

Tourism as an Entrepreneurship

Tourism enterprises are business ventures associated with the tourism industry, operating according to specific business principles. According to Sinclair and Stabler (1997), a tourism enterprise is "a combination of products that include accommodation, natural resources, catering, transport, entertainment, and other facilities and services, such as tour operators, shops, and banks." Individuals or groups involved in creating and managing tourism-related products are known as tourism entrepreneurs. These entrepreneurs must exhibit all the qualities of a typical entrepreneur, along with specialized expertise in the service sector.

Shaw and Williams (2002) suggest that proficiency in the service sector revolves around two fundamental aspects: the first pertains to the industry's economic structure, particularly the dominance of certain activities and ownership groups, while the second focuses on understanding the broader framework of financial power structures.

Entrepreneurship tourism can be explained as the process of developing ideas pertaining to tourism and applying specialized skills and expertise to establish a new business or grow an existing one, with the goal of creating employment, generating wealth, and fostering social goodwill. In simpler terms, it involves the activities of key stakeholders in the service sector, primarily aimed at balancing the demands and supply of tourism while achieving competitive professionalism and a profitable socioeconomic standing.

In simple terms, tourism entrepreneurship involves all activities related to setting up and running legitimate tourism businesses. It excludes any tourism activities that go against the commonly accepted laws of the land. Tourism entrepreneurship plays a key role in promoting economic growth and maximizing the use of local resources, providing a boost to the local economy.

Women's Participation in Tourism

Tourism has proven effective in generating employment and creating income opportunities that benefit local communities in popular travel destinations. However, there has been limited attention to the unequal sharing of these benefits between men and women, particularly in developing nations. The tourism sector provides women with valuable job opportunities and avenues for self-employment through small and medium-sized enterprises, playing a crucial role in reducing poverty among women and within local communities in these areas.

Tourism presents both opportunities and challenges in promoting gender equality and empowering women. Although women's involvement in the business sector has increased in recent years, their presence in leadership and managerial roles remains limited. In the tourism industry, women make up a large portion of the workforce but are often confined to low-paying, unskilled jobs. Despite this, the sector offers many avenues for women to secure employment and engage in self-employment through small and medium-sized income-generating activities.

Unlocking the full potential of tourism requires meeting specific conditions through the collaborative efforts of various stakeholders. These include governments, intergovernmental organizations, local authorities, the tourism industry, trade unions, community groups, NGOs, and community-based tourism initiatives. As a labor-intensive sector, this expansion has led to rapid job creation and development. Globally, tourism is a significant sector, particularly for females, who constitute 46% of the workforce in this industry—more than their representation in the overall labor force, which ranges from 34% to 40% (according to ILO data). The proportion of women employed in tourism varies widely between countries, ranging from as low as 2% to over 80%. While clear regional trends are scarce, but it seems that in countries with a more developed tourism industry, women typically constitute around 50% of the workforce. Future tourism development should prioritize optimizing its benefits while protecting the natural environment, conserving cultural heritage, and promoting social and economic equity.

Opportunities for Women in Tourism Sector

Although women contribute significantly to the tourism sector, several critical issues need to be addressed during tourism development. These include:

- Women's achievements in the tourism industry many times go unnoticed, not due to the lack of expertise or skills, but due to the scarcity of opportunities available to them.
- Family and friends' support and encouragement are essential in boosting women's confidence and enabling their success in the tourism industry.
- Gender stereotypes and male dominance frequently confine women to low-paying, insecure, and low-status jobs, such as roles in food preparation, housekeeping, and customer service.
- Advancing gender equity can improve the overall quality of the tourism experience, driving increased profitability and fostering sustainable growth.
- Females are many times perceived as more suited to clerical roles and less likely to advance to professional positions, resulting in lower average wages compared to men.

- Despite higher representation at ministerial levels compared to other sectors, much progress remains to achieve full gender equity in tourism.
- In family-owned tourism businesses, women often perform significant unpaid labor that goes unnoticed.
- Women's contributions to community development need greater acknowledgment and appreciation.
- Gender pay gaps persist in the tourism industry, and eliminating this discrimination is essential.
- Cases of sexual intimidation and requests for nonconsensual or official favors from female workers are on the rise and require immediate attention.
- Technology offers promising solutions for reducing gender disparities in the sector.
- Numerous startups in the tourism industry are now being successfully run by women.
- Policymakers and NGOs are increasingly focusing on gender empowerment, supported by growing feminist movements.
- The feminization of poverty is gradually declining as more women gain financial independence through tourism-related jobs.

Women's Occupations and Positions in the Tourism Industry

Similar to many other industries, the tourism sector displays pronounced horizontal and vertical gender segregation in its workforce. Horizontally, men and women are directed toward distinct job roles—women frequently work as cleaners, waitresses, flight attendants, or travel agency staff, whereas men are commonly employed as drivers, gardeners, pilots, or construction workers. Vertically, the industry resembles a "gender pyramid," with women concentrated in lower-tier positions offering limited prospects for advancement, while men dominate senior managerial roles. This vertical segregation aligns with global labor market trends. The United Nations World Tourism Organization (UNWTO) defines gender equality as ensuring that women, men, girls, and boys have equal rights, responsibilities, and opportunities.

Although women have attained higher levels of education and make up more than 40% of the global labor force, their presence in management roles remains significantly underrepresented, with only a small percentage managing to break through the "glass ceiling." Various interconnected factors sustain this gender segregation, including societal stereotypes, traditional gender roles, and perceptions of gender identity. Females are frequently perceived—and perceive themselves—as better suited for particular types of jobs. Furthermore, traditional expectations often place the primary responsibility for childcare, eldercare, and household tasks on women, pushing them toward casual, part-time, or seasonal work.

Community-based tourism initiatives frequently rely on preserving natural resources, protected areas, and national parks, which are essential for sustaining the livelihoods of those involved in tourism. Similarly, conserving local cultures and heritage sites is vital, as they form the foundation of many tourism activities.

The seasonal nature of tourism can sometimes be advantageous for women, as it allows them to balance various responsibilities. However, this is not universally applicable. In many cases, women and mothers cannot depend on seasonal work to provide a stable income and must find ways to generate earnings year-round to support their households.

Challenges Faced by Women

Women constitute 59% of the tourism workforce, with their representation rising to 61% in accommodation services and 64% in travel companies. Within the EU's accommodation and food service sectors, women account for 53% of informal workers. The tourism industry, characterized by high turnover rates, seasonal employment, unstable contracts, and part-time work, disproportionately affects women compared to men. For instance, men are more likely to work in well-developed tourist regions where wages are generally higher. Women face both horizontal and vertical segregation in the sector, resulting in a 14.7% wage gap despite having higher education levels than men. They earn less than men for equivalent roles, and this disparity widens with increased education. Although studies indicate that companies with female leaders perform better, men continue to dominate managerial positions.

Literature reviews show that female entrepreneurs encounter numerous challenges. Terms like barriers, difficulties, issues, and limitations are often used to describe the obstacles they face. Ahmad (2013) defines these challenges as difficulties and constraints, including socioeconomic issues. Winn (2004) emphasizes that limited access to capital and family support are significant obstacles for women launching businesses. Female entrepreneurs face critical challenges, including inadequate funding and cash flow difficulties during operations (Gundry et al., 2002; Helms, 1997). Van der Merwe and Saayman (2003) highlights other barriers, such as insufficient financial and family backing, unfavorable sociocultural perceptions, and low self-confidence. Despite these findings, there is a lack of research dedicated to exploring these specific challenges in depth.

For the tourism industry to achieve sustainable growth, it must guarantee equal involvement of women in the development process. However, various obstacles impede women's advancement. These challenges include:

- *Low female literacy:* Many women are unable to complete their education, which is crucial for securing jobs, due to family responsibilities or early marriages.
- *Gender stereotypes:* In many developing countries, women are still perceived as unfit for certain jobs due to traditional beliefs.
- *Pay disparities:* Females are often paid less than men for the similar job or work, which is a significant barrier to progress.

- *Lack of male support:* One of the major obstacles to women's success in the tourism business is the insufficient support from their male counterparts.
- *Traditional mindsets:* Beliefs such as women should not interact with tourists or strangers, especially in household settings, remain widespread. Addressing these misconstructions will be a major issue to solve for policymakers.
- *Religious constraints:* Cultural or religious views, such as the belief that women are impure during menstruation and should not work during that time, also need to be addressed.

Women's Empowerment Through Tourism

The tourism industry is crucial in achieving the United Nations' 2030 Sustainable Development Goals, especially in promoting gender equality and women's empowerment, as emphasized in Goal 5. As a specialized UN agency, the UN Tourism organization is dedicated to maximizing tourism's benefits for women and advancing gender equality, aligning with the vision of SDG 5 to empower all women and girls. The United Nations World Tourism Organization (UNWTO) defines women empowerment as tourism that can empower women by providing jobs and income-generating opportunities, thereby contributing to gender equality and economic independence.

Women represent a significant majority (60–70%) of the tourism workforce globally (UNWTO, 2008). With the industry poised for substantial growth (World Travel & Tourism Council, 2017), tourism presents vast opportunities for women's employment and empowerment in diverse settings, from rural and urban areas to cultural destinations. By prioritizing women's empowerment, the WTO is undertaking a vital initiative that can harness tourism's potential as a powerful tool for promoting gender equality and economic opportunities for women.

Despite global efforts to advance women's rights, women continue to disproportionately face poverty, hunger, and illiteracy, according to the United Nations Population Fund (UNFPA, 2009). Women often encounter significant barriers to essential resources, including healthcare, economic opportunities, education, and protection from violence. Empowering women is therefore essential to bridging the gender equality gap and promoting a more just and equitable society.

The UN defines empowerment as a fundamental aspect of gender equality, where both men and women enjoy equal opportunities, rights, and responsibilities in all areas of life. Gender equality is realized when both genders equally share in power, have the same opportunities for financial independence, and have equal access to education and the ability to pursue their goals. Empowering women is essential for fostering gender equality and sustainable development, and tourism can play a significant role in this process.

Tourism contributes to achieving Sustainable Development Goals (SDGs) by improving livelihoods, reducing poverty, promoting environmental sustainability, and empowering women. However, no region in the developing world has fully achieved gender equality in legal, social, and economic rights. This gender gap impacts access to resources, political influence, economic opportunities, and power dynamics, ultimately disadvantaging society as a whole. So, how can tourism address these challenges?

- *Increasing control over natural resources:* In developing nations, women are generally tasked with obtaining water, food, and fuel, along with overseeing family health and nutrition. Tourism development can encourage environmentally conscious practices, teach women how to preserve resources, and introduce sustainable practices that can generate income. Women can also become suppliers in the tourism industry's value chain by improving agricultural techniques.
- *Economic empowerment:* More women than men live in poverty (UNFPA, 2008), and much of the unpaid work falls on women, who face daily discrimination in economic spheres. Tourism can be a catalyst for economic upliftment by creating new markets for marginalized enterprises and supporting microcredit programs to reduce the gender economic gap.
- *Educational empowerment:* Women make up about two-thirds of illiterate adults globally (UN, 2010). Education for women is linked to lower infant mortality, reduced fertility, and greater economic opportunities for their children. Tourism can provide educational opportunities by training women at various levels to acquire skills for the industry, such as language proficiency, hospitality, guiding, and project management.
- *Political empowerment:* Women still do not enjoy equal rights with men in many social and legal institutions, affecting their access to land, employment, earnings, and decision-making processes. Tourism projects can address this by including women in planning and decision-making, giving them a voice in the process and enabling them to influence their community's development and livelihoods.

Although gender encompasses both male and female equally, much of the focus in tourism expansion has centered on empowering women (L. Ferguson, 2010). Tourism is seen as a powerful tool for addressing issues that predominantly affect women, earning it the title of a "vehicle for gender equality and women's empowerment" (UN Report). According to research by M. B. Swain and V. L. Smith, the tourism industry deals with the roles that primarily require human interaction, and since women are often recognized for their strong interpersonal skills, they are expected to excel in these roles. Tourism activities such as guiding, providing accommodation, and food services are often routine tasks for women, making them well-suited to these roles (W. B. Lama). Additionally, since tourism in many areas, it is a part-time activity, women can engage in it during their spare time after completing household duties.

It is argued that women have a closer connection to nature than their counterparts, due to their frequent interaction with nature when gathering food, caring for livestock, and managing domestic chores (R. Scheyvens). This connection makes women more empathetic toward nature, which is why women are often seen as more suited to managing nature-based tourism, such as eco-tourism, agro-tourism, and rural tourism (K. F. Kahn, A. Gordon). In developing countries, where women face significant challenges and inequalities, tourism has been providing a source of hope by uplifting women economically, socially, and politically (R. Scheyvens).

Tourism also creates valuable supply chains that offer both formal and informal job opportunities for women. It provides a platform for women to express their views and take on leadership roles, often offering more opportunities than other industries (A.M. Hjalager, S. Andersen). Additionally, tourism supports women's entrepreneurship by improving access to credit, land, and property, and offering essential training and resources to help women expand their businesses. While data on women's education in tourism development is scarce, the number of women and girls graduating in tourism-related fields is increasing, and the unpaid labor traditionally carried out by women is gaining recognition through tourism.

In their study, K. M. Gentry highlights the various roles women take on in both mass tourism and foreign-owned alternative tourism ventures. However, the employment landscape in tourism often remains gendered, reinforcing women's lower social status (S. Chant). Gentry's research suggests that the tourism industry benefits from traditional gender norms, especially regarding the segregation of jobs by sex, the relegation of women to domestic roles, low wages, and long working hours. Nevertheless, factors such as family financial decision-making, social collaboration, business ownership, and increased independence are creating opportunities for women to challenge these societal norms. Many studies have shown that women are generally employed in "female" roles, while men dominate the higher positions in mass tourism (A. Bolles; S. Chant).

Conclusion

In conclusion, recognizing that gender segregation in labor markets is a widespread issue should not imply that it should be overlooked in the context of tourism. Achieving necessary changes requires efforts across all sectors. However, the tourism industry stands out as a particularly strong candidate for promoting women's advancement. Women have better representation and participation in tourism than in other sectors, but this does not mean that no improvements are needed for women in the industry. There are several key issues that must be addressed to empower women in tourism, as highlighted in the challenges section of the paper. The tourism industry's large scale, rapid growth, and diverse, dynamic nature provide significant flexibility, allowing it to develop initiatives that can support the advancement of women. These initiatives could serve as models for other industries seeking to make similar strides. Lastly, it is essential to implement measures that ensure both gender equality and the sustainable growth of the sector.

References

Ahmad, R. (2013). Working with Pierre Bourdieu in the tourism field making a case for 'third world' tourism. *Cultural Studies*, *27*(4), 519–539.

Bolles, A. (1997). Women as a category of analysis in scholarship on tourism: Jamaican women and tourism employment. *Tourism and Culture: An Applied Perspective*, 77–92.

Chant, S. (2005). Gender and tourism employment in Mexico and the Philippines. In *Gender, work and tourism* (pp. 119–177). Routledge.

Elshaer, I., Moustafa, M., Sobaih, A. E., Aliedan, M., & Azazz, A. M. (2021). The impact of women's empowerment on sustainable tourism development: Mediating role of tourism involvement. *Tourism Management Perspectives*, *38*, 100815.

Ferguson, L. (2010). Interrogating 'gender' in development policy and practice: The World Bank, tourism and microenterprise in Honduras. *International Feminist Journal of Politics*, *12*(1), 3–24.

Ferguson, L. (2011). Promoting gender equality and empowering women? Tourism and the third millennium development goal. *Current Issues in Tourism*, *14*(3), 235–249.

Figueroa-Domecq, C., Pritchard, A., Segovia-Pérez, M., Morgan, N., & Villacé-Molinero, T. (2015). Tourism gender research: A critical accounting. *Annals of Tourism Research*, *52*, 87–103.

Gentry, K. M. (2007). Belizean women and tourism work: Opportunity or impediment? *Annals of Tourism Research*, *34*(2), 477–496.

Gundry, L. K., Miriam, B. Y., & Posig, M. (2002). Contemporary perspectives on women's entrepreneurship: A review and strategic recommendations. *Journal of Enterprising Culture*, *10*(01), 67–86.

Hall, C. M. (2005). Rural wine and food tourism cluster and network development. In *Rural tourism and sustainable business* (pp. 149–164). https://doi.org/10.21832/9781845410131-012

Helms, M. M. (1997). Women and entrepreneurship: The appealing alternative. *Business Perspectives*, *10*(1), 16–20.

Hjalager, A. M., & Andersen, S. (2001). Tourism employment: Contingent work or professional career?. *Employee Relations*, *23*(2), 115–129.

Hota, S. L., Mohanty, N., Kumar, A., & Panda, K. (2024). Achieving sustainability in newly founded start-up businesses: Navigating challenges and gaining insights. *Recoletos Multidisciplinary Research Journal*, *12*(1), 1–7.

Kahn, K. F., & Gordon, A. (1997). How women campaign for the U.S. Senate: Substance and strategy. In P. Norris (Ed.), *Women, media, and politics* (pp. 59–76). Oxford University Press.

Kulkarni, R. (2022). A study on challenges and opportunities of women entrepreneurs in tourism sector. *Journal of Positive School Psychology*, 6732–6743.

Lama, W. B. (2000). Community-based tourism for conservation and women's development. In P. Godde, M. F. Price, & F. M. Zimmermann (Eds.), *Tourism and development in mountain regions* (pp. 221–238). CABI Publishing.

McArthur, J. W. (2014). The origins of the millennium development goals. *SAIS Review of International Affairs*, *34*(2), 5–24.

MDG Monitor. (n.d.). *Promoting gender equality and empowering women.* http://www.mdgmonitor.org/mdg-3-promote-gender-equality-and-empower-women. December 28, 2024.
Mohanty, N., Parida, J. K., Sahu, R., Kumar, A., & Debyani, D. (2024). Sustainable development and zero hunger: A focus on India's social entrepreneurship initiatives. *Journal of Information and Optimization Sciences*, *45*(6), 1717–1725. https://doi.org/10.47974/JIOS-1707
Mohanty, N., Parida, J. K., Sahu, R., Kumar, A., & Hota, S. L. (2023). Catalysts of change: Social entrepreneurs shaping quality living. *European Economic Letters*, *13*(5), 895–900. https://doi.org/10.52783/eel.v13i5.848
Mohanty, P., Swain, S. K., & Besra, S. (2018). Women at work: Exploring the issues and challenges of women employees in travel and tourism. *Indian Journal of Economics and Development*, *6*(1), 1–5.
Nassani, A. A., Aldakhil, A. M., Abro, M. M. Q., Islam, T., & Zaman, K. (2019). The impact of tourism and finance on women empowerment. *Journal of Policy Modeling*, *41*(2), 234–254.
Ramchurjee, N., & Paktin, W. (2011). *"Tourism" a vehicle for women's empowerment: Prospect and challenges*. University of Mysore.
Roe, D., & Urquhart, P. (2001). *Pro-poor tourism: Harnessing the world's largest industry for the world's poor*. IIED.
Scheyvens, R. (2000). Promoting women's empowerment through involvement in ecotourism: Experiences from the Third World. *Journal of Sustainable Tourism*, *8*(3), 232–249.
Scheyvens, R. (2007). Exploring the tourism-poverty nexus. *Current Issues in Tourism*, *10*(2–3), 231–254.
Shaw, G., & Williams, A. M. (2002). *Critical issues in tourism: A geographical perspective* (p. 371). Blackwell Publishing.
Sinclair, M. T., & Stabler, M. (1997). *The economics of tourism.* Routledge.
Swain, M. B. (1989). *Gender roles in indigenous tourism: Kuna Mola, Kuna Yola, and cultural survival.*
United Nations Population Fund. (2009). *UNFPA annual report 2008*. UNFPA.
United Nations Statistics Division. (2010). Education (Chapter 3). In *The world's women 2010: Trends and statistics*. United Nations.
UNWTO. (2008). *International recommendations for tourism statistics 2008 compilation guide* [Compilation Guide]. United Nations Statistics Division.
Van der Merwe, P., & Saayman, M. (2003). Determining the economic value of game farm tourism. *Koedoe*, *46*(2), 103–112.
Winn, J. (2004). Entrepreneurship: Not an easy path to top management for women. *Women in Management Review*, *19*(3), 143–153.
World Tourism Organization (UNWTO). (2011, March 11). Tourism: A vehicle for gender equality and women's empowerment, UN reports. http://europe.unwto.org/news/2011-03-11/tourism-vehicle-gender-equality-and-women-s-empowerment-un-reports. Accessed on December 25, 2024.
World Tourism Organization (UNWTO). (2019). *Global report on women in tourism* (2nd ed.). World Tourism Organization (UNWTO).
World Travel & Tourism Council. (2017). *Travel & tourism economic impact: World* (pp. 1–20). World Travel & Tourism Council.

Chapter 9

Women's Employment and Entrepreneurship in the Tourism Sector: The Case of Türkiye

Demet Cakıroğlu[a,*] *and Nuran Öztürk Başpınar*[b,†]

[a]Hacettepe University, Türkiye
[b]Anadolu University, Türkiye

Abstract

When we look at the employment of women employees and entrepreneurs in the tourism sector, we see significant differences in gender inequalities and entrepreneurial opportunities. This study aims to analyze the current state of women's entrepreneurship and employment in the tourism sector and provide recommendations that can increase the representation of women in the sector and reduce the challenges they face in Türkiye. Based on a literature review, the study will evaluate the effectiveness of strategies and policies and existing support programs to strengthen the role of women in the tourism sector and reduce gender inequality.

Keywords: Female labor force; female employment; female entrepreneurship; tourism sector; Türkiye

Introduction

Increasing women's labor force and employment and supporting women's entrepreneurship in ensuring economic development in societies are of great importance for the effective participation of women in the process. In societies where female labor force is ignored, and gender is discriminated against, this

*http://orcid.org/0000-0003-3959-7062
†http://orcid.org/0000-0002-0913-4350

Economics and Tourism, 143–160

doi:10.1108/978-1-83662-916-020251010

causes a significant economic loss. Gazi Mustafa Kemal expressed this in the following words: "If a society is contented with only one of the sexes obtaining the necessities of our century, that society will be weakened by half," and "If only men have modern rights in a society, it weakens more than half of the society" (Ünsay, 2017). "Full equality. Women's rights are the same as those of men. They earned their freedom by right. It would not be appropriate for half of the nation to remain alien and distant from social life" (as cited in Tayhani, 2009).

Atatürk's other words on this subject are as follows: "Human society is made up of two kinds of people, men, and women. Is it possible to advance one part of this mass and neglect the other so that the whole mass can advance?," "Is it possible that as long as one half of an object is tied to the earth with chains, the other half can rise to the skies?" (as cited in Yangil & Başpınar, 2022). These words of Mustafa Kemal clearly show that women should take their rightful place in the social and economic spheres.

Industrialization and migration have encouraged women to join the labor force, but women's employment is still lower than men's in Turkiye and around the world. Women, who have lower levels of education than men, tend to work in low-paid, precarious, temporary jobs in the informal sector or remain unemployed. The limited number of jobs available to women in the labor market makes it difficult for women to find work, while men are given priority in hiring, and women are the first to be laid off in times of economic crisis. In addition to these inequalities related to gender roles, regulations such as the export-oriented industrialization model, downsizing of the public sector, and privatization have further deepened the problems of poverty and unemployment among women (Aşkın & Aşkın, 2017). Therefore, the fact that women, who still make up half of the world's population, do not participate or cannot participate in the labor force indicates that there are some problems related to the structure and functioning of society within the framework of gender discrimination. This is defined as discrimination, which is the valuation of an individual's nonproductive characteristics in the marketplace. Statistics and reports published by the International Labor Organization, the World Bank, the World Economic Forum, the European Commission, and Social Watch show that gender inequalities persist in the labor markets of all countries in the world, both globally and regionally, and that more women are working in the informal sector than men. The World Economic Forum's 2023 Global Gender Gap Report, which aims to assess gender inequality by dividing countries into eight regions, shows that gender equality varies across regions. Europe tops the list (76.3%), North America is at parity (75%), and sub-Saharan Africa has the lowest score (68.2%). In Eurasia and Central Asia, gender equality is highest in Moldova and lowest in Tajikistan and Turkiye. Overall, economic participation and opportunities have improved, but the gender gap remains at 68.8% (https://www3.weforum.org). Women's entrepreneurship and employment are also important opportunities to reduce women's unemployment and poverty. Many studies in this area have emphasized the importance of gender-sensitive policies, such as developing women-friendly policies and raising social awareness, taking steps toward women's economic and social empowerment, removing barriers faced by women in this sector, and increasing educational opportunities. Various policies and practices have been put in place to facilitate and encourage the participation of women, who are one of the disadvantaged groups in the labor market, in employment. Although some sectors, such as the tourism sector, have been highlighted as an opportunity to increase women's employment and ensure their economic and social empowerment, it is known that these inequalities are still prevalent in Turkiye. This situation plays an important role in deepening and sharpening gender inequalities by blocking women's path to economic freedom (Çelik Uğuz & Topbaş, 2016). In this study, the position of the still underemployed female labor force in the tourism sector is examined with the help of numerical data, and the position of female entrepreneurship in the tourism sector is evaluated.

General Structure of Female Labor Force and Female Employment in Turkiye

As of December 31, 2023, 49.9% (42 million 638 thousand 306 people) of the population of Turkiye is female, and 50.1% (42 million 734 thousand 71 people) is male. How much of the total population participates in the labor force is of great importance for the quality of labor market coverage. The labor force participation rate is defined as the ratio of the labor force to the active population, which is the sum of those who are employed and those who are unemployed and looking for a job (Ayta & Şen, 2023). Looking at the labor force participation rate of women aged 15 and above in Turkiye since 2000, it is seen that it was 26.6% in 2000, 23.3% in 2005, 27.6% in 2010, 31.5% in 2015, and 30.9% in 2020 (https://biruni.tuik.gov.tr/medas/?kn=72&locale=tr). These rates show that the labor force participation rate of women has increased over time. However, it should be noted that due to the impact of the COVID-19 pandemic, the female labor force participation rate, which was 34.4% in 2019, decreased to 30.9% in 2020. It increased to 32.8% in 2021 and 35.1% in 2022. These rates can be interpreted as an increase in the female labor force participation rate in Turkiye, but it is still insufficient. The labor force participation rates in Organization for Economic Cooperation and Development (OECD) and EU countries in 2022 are 52.9% and 51.9%, respectively. According to the data of the International Labor Organization (ILO) in 2023, the global female labor force participation rate is 48.7% (www.ilo.org). Looking at TURKSTAT data in Turkiye, as seen in Table 9.1 (TURKSTAT, 2022b, 2023b), women's labor force participation rate increases as their education level increases.

According to the TURKSTAT National Education Statistics Database 2022, the proportion of women aged 25+ who have completed at least one level of education is 86.7% of the total population. According to the same database, the proportion of the population aged 25+ who are graduates of colleges and faculties with master's and doctoral degrees, is 23.5% of the total population. Of these, 21.6% are women.

The extent to which the labor force can participate in economic activities, that is, the employment rate, is also very important. The employment rate can be

Table 9.1. The Participation Rate of Women 25+ by Educational Attainment (2022, 2023).

Education Status (2022)	**Labor Force Participation Rate (%)**	**Education Status (2023)**	**Labor Force Participation Rate (%)**
Illiterate	12.8	Illiterate	13.9
Less than high school	25.3	Less than high school	27.1
High school	32.5	High school	36.1
Vocational or technical high school	38.5	Vocational or technical high school	43.0
Higher education	67.6	Higher education	68.8

Source: Household Labor Force Survey (2022a, 2023a) and Turkish Statistical Institute (TURKSTAT).

defined as the ratio of employed persons to the noninstitutionalized working-age population (Ayta & Şen, 2023). Looking at the employment rate of women aged 15 years and above in Turkiye since 2000, it is seen that it was 24.9% in 2000, 20.7% in 2005, 24.0% in 2010, 27.5% in 2015, and 26.3% in 2020 (https://biruni.tuik.gov.tr/medas/?kn=72&locale=tr).

Fig. 9.1 shows that in 2022, the employment rate of women in Turkiye will be less than half that of men. In the same year, the female employment rate in the OECD will be 64.9%, while the highest female employment rate in the EU

Fig. 9.1. Female Labor Force Participation Status.
Source: TURKSTAT, Labor Force Statistics cited by Bektaş, 2024.

countries will be 78.1% in the Netherlands and 54.4% in Romania (https://data-explorer.oecd.org/?pg=0&bp=true&snb=247&tm=women). According to the labor market statistics of the OECD, the country with the highest female employment rate in OECD countries in the third quarter of 2023 is Iceland, with 68.8%, while the average of OECD countries is estimated to be 51.0% (Bektaş, 2024). According to the results of the Household Labor Force Survey (2022a), the total employment rate of women is 30.4%. In the last quarter of 2023, this rate increased to 36%. The above rates show that Turkiye's female employment rate is at the bottom of the OECD and EU rankings. According to TURKSTAT data, the employment status of working women in Turkiye is shown in Fig. 9.2.

According to Fig. 9.2, by type of employment, the rate of employers is only 1.77%, while the rate of self-employed is 9.32%. The total ratio of employers and self-employed, i.e., entrepreneurs, is 11.09%. Data on women's employment by sector are shown in Table 9.2.

In 2022, the share of part-time workers in total employment was 9.9%, of which 16.4% were women. In 2023, the share of part-time workers in total employment was 9.8%, of which 16.1% were women. The percentage ratio of the difference in wages or earnings between men and women to the wages or earnings of men is defined as the gender wage or earnings gap. In this context, according to TurkStat's "Earnings Structure 2022 Statistics," the highest difference for the indicator calculated with the average annual gross wage-salary was realized among the university graduates with 17.1%, and the lowest difference was realized among the primary school graduates and below with 12.4%. For the indicator calculated based on average annual gross earnings, the highest difference was 19.6% for tertiary education graduates, and the lowest difference was 14.5% for primary education graduates and below.

The factors affecting the gender pay gap in the tourism sector in Turkiye are as follows (Çelik Uğuz & Topbaş, 2016):

- Discrimination: In studies conducted in Turkiye, issues such as attitudes toward gender discrimination and identifying the departments where women work most are among the causes of wage discrimination.

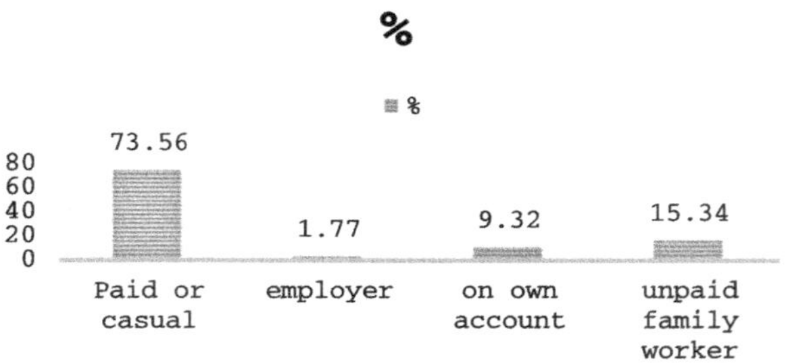

Fig. 9.2. Employment Status of Female Workers (2023). *Source:* Turkish Statistical Institute (TURKSTAT). Labor Force Statistics.

Table 9.2. Female Employment by Sector (%).

Sector	2020	2021	2022	2023	2024
Agriculture	17.7	17.2	15.8	14.8	14.6
Industrial	20.5	21.3	21.7	21.2	20.8
Construction	5.8	6.2	6.0	6.3	6.6
Service industry	55.9	55.3	56.5	57.6	58.0

Source: Turkish Statistical Institute (TURKSTAT). Women in Statistics.

- Experience: It has been found that men have approximately 25% more experience than women in the tourism sector, which may contribute to the wage gap.
- Continuity of employment: Women's shorter tenure in the sector may lead to lower wages.
- Educational level: Although women in Turkiye generally have a higher level of education than men, women in the tourism sector have 4.3% less education than men.

General Structure of Female Entrepreneurship in Turkiye

Entrepreneurship plays a driving role in the economy of all countries and is becoming increasingly important in creating new areas of employment, reducing unemployment, and ensuring economic growth. An entrepreneur is a person who brings together the resources necessary to produce goods or services, aims to make a profit, creates value, and assumes the risks associated with this venture. Entrepreneurship is an effective way to combat unemployment and poverty through self-employment. Woman entrepreneur is a person who owns a business in their name and account, establishes direct relationships with other organizations for the supply of goods/services produced/marketed, provides employment opportunities for others, and has a say in the business (Kumkale, 2015). Women's entrepreneurship increases employment by mobilizing the idle labor force. It is known that the women's entrepreneurship movement can be traced back to the 1840s and the United States, from where it spread to Europe, germinated after World War II, and strengthened with international migration mobility in the 1960s (Gündüz & Karadeniz, 2022). Depending on the development of technology, women had more entrepreneurial opportunities in the following decades. The 1980s were the years when women's entrepreneurship accelerated. Women's entrepreneurship, which is seen as a way to provide economic freedom to women in Turkiye and reduce the high unemployment rate among women, as well as a means of political intervention to prevent the deepening of poverty among poor urban families, began in the 1990s (Seçkin Halaç & Meşe, 2021, p. 59). In 2015, it grew with the support of microcredit for women entrepreneurs (Düzgün, 2021). Today, women take the women who became entrepreneurs before them as a model, and the number of women entrepreneurs is increasing day by day.

There are various external and internal factors that push women to become entrepreneurs (Özkaya, 2009). Extrinsic factors can be listed as economic (insufficient family income, etc.), family structure (death of spouse/divorce, single-person households, single nuclear families, etc.), organizational (lack of flexible work opportunities in the current job, etc.), and gender discrimination (prioritizing male employment, etc.). These are factors over which individuals have no direct control. Intrinsic factors that make entrepreneurship attractive to women are the Entrepreneurial drive, the drive to do something new, the drive to achieve social status, and the drive for self-realization, etc. However, there are several challenges that women entrepreneurs face in the process of starting and sustaining their business activities, both before and after they start entrepreneurship (Nxopo & Iwu, 2015). In the Turkish context, the patriarchal family structure of Turkish society and the lack of gender equality remain a primary challenge, but inexperience and lack of knowledge, lack of capital, and difficulties in accessing capital are also challenges.

While the number of employed women in Turkiye is 10 million 546 thousand, the total number of employed women entrepreneurs is 1 million 170 thousand. In other words, the rate of women entrepreneurs is 10%. In other words, 1 out of 10 employed women is an entrepreneur. Of these women entrepreneurs, 22.4% are in Istanbul. This is the most important indicator that women entrepreneurs are not evenly distributed across the country. Women entrepreneurs are risk-averse and rely more on personal or family financing. This has a negative impact on women's ability to grow their businesses and create more jobs (Filimonau et al., 2024).

Taking into account the needs, problems, and expectations of the labor market, the National Employment Strategy Document (NES), prepared by the Ministry of Family, Labor and Social Affairs, General Directorate for the Status of Women, emphasized that women entrepreneurs have a very important place by addressing women entrepreneurs on the axis of increasing employment of groups requiring special policies. Within the framework of the NES (2014–2023), policies for women entrepreneurs are defined as shown in Table 9.3 (Republic of Türkiye Ministry of Labour and Social Security, 2024).

Table 9.3. Measures to Increase Employment of Groups With Special Policy Needs.

Measure and description	Areas of women's entrepreneurship will be identified on a regional basis, and measures will be taken to promote women's entrepreneurship with the support to be provided. Women's entrepreneurship will not be limited to traditional sectors, and it will be ensured that the existing entrepreneurial potential of women is effectively used in accordance with the requirements of the time.

(Continued)

Table 9.3. *(Continued)*

Measure and description	Ensure that women's entrepreneurship is not limited to traditional sectors and that the existing potential of women entrepreneurs is effectively utilized in accordance with the needs of the time. Training will be provided to support women's entrepreneurship, especially women working in the agricultural sector, and the training pillar will be supported by information and advisory services on access to financial resources.

Source: Republic of Türkiye Ministry of Labor and Social Security, National Employment Strategy (NES).

In addition to the policies for women entrepreneurs identified in the NES (2014–2023), a strategic action plan was prepared under the coordination of the Ministry of Family and Social Policies (now the Ministry of Family and Social Services), as detailed in Table 9.4 (Strategy Document on the Empowerment of Women, 2018–2023). This action plan was prepared in five dimensions: education, health, economy, participation in decision-making mechanisms, and media, and was presented to public institutions and organizations, local governments, universities, civil society organizations, professional organizations, the private sector, and other relevant organizations.

Table 9.4. Strategic Action Plan for Women's Empowerment.

Strategy	Title	Action
3	Strengthen women's economic empowerment and develop economic and social policies to combat informality, especially unpaid family work.	Efforts to strengthen women's cooperatives will be continued and intensified. Support for agricultural development cooperatives and production and business cooperatives established by women entrepreneurs in areas such as training, entrepreneurship, and consultancy will be further expanded.

Table 9.4. *(Continued)*

Strategy	Title	Action
		Efforts will be made to cooperate in the marketing of products, especially with local governments.
5	Developing women's entrepreneurship and strengthening women's economic empowerment, particularly through the expanded use of information and communication technologies.	An effective system will be established to provide counseling and guidance services to women entrepreneurs in their business development processes. The system will include counseling and guidance services that identify the business development needs of women entrepreneurs.
		Awareness-raising activities will be carried out to develop a culture of entrepreneurship among women. Printed and visual materials such as information exchange meetings, spot films, documentaries, brochures, posters, etc. will be prepared, and women will be informed about support mechanisms for entrepreneurship.
		A system will be established to facilitate women entrepreneurs' access to government support. The system will be structured in a holistic and user-friendly manner to ensure more effective use of support for women entrepreneurs.
		Regional development agencies will prioritize programs and projects that support women's entrepreneurship. In cooperation with the public

(Continued)

Table 9.4. *(Continued)*

Strategy	Title	Action
		sector, the private sector, and NGOs, women's entrepreneurship, especially small-scale women's entrepreneurship, will be supported through projects that take into account local dynamics.

Source: Kadının Güçlenmesi Strateji Belgesi ve Eylem Planı (2018–2023). (https://www.aile.gov.tr/media/6315/kad%C4%B1n%C4%B1n-gue%C3%A7lenmesi-strajesi-belgesi-ve-eylem-plan%C4%B1-2018-2023.pdf).

With the various efforts mentioned above, according to TURKSTAT Labor Force Statistics, while the share of women entrepreneurs in total was 6.4% in 2009, it increased to 8% in 2013 and 8.9% in 2014. In 2023, it will increase to 17.4%. The main organizations supporting women entrepreneurs in Turkiye can be listed as follows: Public institutions and organizations such as the Small and Medium Enterprises Development Organization (KOSGEB), nongovernmental organizations such as the Women Entrepreneurs Association of Turkiye (KAGİDER), the Foundation for the Evaluation of Women's Work (KEDV), the Foundation for Solidarity with Women (KADAV), the Association of Entrepreneurial Businesswomen (ANGİKAD), and the World Bank and the United Nations Development Program (UNDP).

Employment of Women in the Tourism Sector

Tourism is defined as a set of events and relationships resulting from people's travel outside the places where they live, work, and meet their usual needs, and their temporary stay in these places, usually by demanding goods and services produced by tourism enterprises (Kozak et al., 2012). Tourism is a large revenue-generating sector that covers a variety of areas, including accommodation, travel, food and beverage, and recreation. In addition to direct service providers, the tourism sector also includes boutique businesses, establishments that offer local products, and boutique shops where gifts are offered and sold. In addition to generating income, tourism has various employment opportunities in finding solutions to unemployment and contributes to economic growth. This is because the tourism sector receives contributions from many sectors and provides inputs to many sectors. For this reason, all countries see tourism as a means of salvation that will pull their economies out of the bottleneck.

According to 2012 data from the International Labor Organization (ILO), 120 million people were directly employed in tourism (travel agencies, accommodation, food and beverage, leisure, etc.), and 328 million people were indirectly employed in tourism. The tourism sector consists of various components such as accommodation, food and beverage, recreation, health, and travel. Facilities offering local products, souvenirs, and handicrafts, as well as their promotion and sale, are also part of the tourism sector. In the global context, it is known that women who set up their businesses in various fields such as accommodation, food and beverage, souvenirs, and the promotion and sale of local products are increasingly participating as entrepreneurs in the tourism sector, and in general, women entrepreneurs provide employment opportunities for women in their businesses (Tekeli & Yılmaz, 2021). Tourism is an important factor in the economy and labor market of many countries. In many countries around the world, tourism plays an important role in the economy. For many states, tourism has been an important driver of the national economy and labor market. Periods of economic slowdowns and crises in the past decades and the COVID-19 pandemic and global crisis in recent years have also hit the tourism sector hard.

An analysis of the sectors in which women entrepreneurs work shows that they are mostly in the service sector. According to 2019 data from the World Travel and Tourism Council (WTTC), the tourism and travel sector accounts for 10% of total employment worldwide. In Turkiye, the number of women employed in the tourism sector accounted for 25.2% of total employment in 2019 (Ardıç Yetiş & Çalışkan, 2020). In 2021, while this rate is 54% in the world (Kutlu et al., 2022), it is 33% in Turkiye. In the accommodation sector, which accounts for the largest share of employment in tourism, this rate has reached 35.6% (https://www.turob.com/tr/), which is far below the world average. These data show that Turkiye lags far behind both the world as a whole and the European Union member states in terms of the proportion of women employed in the tourism sector.

According to UNWTO 2019 data, women in tourism are concentrated in low-level jobs and earn 14.7% less than men. In many countries, including OECD member states, women are 16% less likely to be employed in the sector than men, and their average hourly wage is significantly lower than men's; however, compared to developed economies, the employment level in Turkiye is 14.83% higher (Kutlu et al., 2022).

In OECD countries, women account for 60% of employment in the tourism sector. Temporary, part-time, and other forms of nonstandard employment are major problems in the tourism sector. Nonstandard forms of employment are particularly prevalent among women, young people, and the low-skilled. Insecure employment relationships and informal working arrangements are other major challenges to the promotion of decent work in tourism (https://www.sbb.gov.tr). Through their participation in tourism, women entrepreneurs have the potential to improve gender equality and achieve sustainable economic development. Supportive government policies and mentoring programs are needed to further strengthen women's entrepreneurship in tourism (Ali et al., 2024). To reduce the gender pay gap in the tourism sector, social and cultural barriers need to be addressed by increasing education levels. To reduce the gender pay gap in the tourism sector in Turkiye, it is necessary to increase the level of education.

However, for this process to be successful, social and cultural barriers also need to be eliminated (Çelik Uğuz & Topbaş, 2016).

Women Entrepreneurship in Tourism

Entrepreneurship can be defined as the process of identifying and exploiting opportunities to create value for new or existing organizations. Tourism, regardless of its purpose, emphasizes the movement of people and human communities. The movement of people and human communities, in the historical process and today, reveal the very different needs of people. It is believed that the needs and the necessity to meet these needs, the diversity of needs, and the fulfillment of needs in full and in time, under appropriate conditions and qualities, have also revealed a new understanding of entrepreneurship under the title of Tourism Entrepreneurship (Ünüvar, 2020). Tourism entrepreneurship can be defined as a value-creation process that aims to utilize tourism resources by the demands of tourists to ensure the development of the destination and is realized through factors such as risk investment, innovation, competition, and efficiency. It is also known that women's tourism entrepreneurship, which is a different structure of tourism entrepreneurship, is a very important individual career field where entrepreneurs use their initiative and creativity to reduce income poverty and human poverty (Xu et al., 2018). Table 9.5 illustrates the evolution of tourism policies in development plans, highlighting its strategic role for women entrepreneurs in Türkiye (Presidency of the Republic of Turkey, 2023).

Table 9.5. Tourism in Development Plans.

Development Plan No	Years	Status
Preplanned period	1923–1962	Not enough progress was made.
1	1963–1967	Results in failure.
2	1968–1972	Resulted in failure.
3	1973–1977	It led to failure.
4	1979–1983	However, the Tourism Incentive Law No. 2634 of 1982 played an important role in bringing the sector to its current level.
5	1985–1989	Favorable conditions were created for foreign investment, efforts were made in the areas of promotion and coastal protection, and diversification of tourism gained importance.
6	1990–1994	In order to diversify tourism, incentives have been implemented for this important sector.

Table 9.5. *(Continued)*

Development Plan No	Years	Status
7	1996–2000	Efforts have been made to increase bed capacity, make effective use of superstructures, and solve problems facing the tourism industry through policies to protect natural capital.
8	2001–2005	Efforts have been made to eliminate deficiencies in construction, to reduce the destruction of the natural and historical environment and the phenomenon of urbanization in tourist centers, to certify tourism training and quality, and to focus on the establishment of a national tourism organization.
9	2007–2013	The aim is to increase the bed capacity, to evaluate the potential in the field of cultural tourism, to evaluate the ecological potential, and to observe the balance between protection and use.
10	2014–2018	The possibility of developing health tourism, the promotion of sustainable tourism, the development of health tourism and alternative types of tourism, the decisions of local administrations, NGOs, and the public on tourism, and the improvement of the quality of the workforce have been highlighted.
11	2019–2023	Tourism has been identified as a priority area for development, and it is stated that the contribution of tourism to the economy will increase by increasing the diversity and quality of tourism services. Efforts have been made to empower women in society and ensure gender equality.

Source: Presidency of the Republic of Turkiye, Directorate of Strategy and Budget. Development Plans.

As you can see, tourism and tourism entrepreneurship have an important place in our development plans. Tourism is a growing value for women entrepreneurs, despite the difficulties they face due to the nature of the sector. International organizations such as UN Women, ILO, World Tourism Organization, and OECD define tourism as a sector that should be promoted due to its potential to empower women (Tekeli & Yılmaz, 2021).

The presence of women entrepreneurs in the tourism sector in Turkiye began with their activities in the agricultural sector; women entrepreneurs have found a place for themselves in the tourism sector for reasons such as Turkiye's historical and cultural richness, remarkable destination features such as natural beauties, differentiation of living conditions, meeting of individuals from different business sectors, formation of a holiday understanding, increase in labor law and leisure time, and ease of vacation for the population belonging to economically different income groups. The relationship between tourism, which is a service sector, and entrepreneurship can be explained as follows: As entrepreneurship develops, tourism develops, and as the development of tourism accelerates, interest in tourism entrepreneurship increases. Since tourism is a sector that stimulates economic development and women's entrepreneurship is often effective in local development, women's entrepreneurship and tourism are closely intertwined. The areas where women entrepreneurs are intensively involved in the tourism sector in Turkiye are accommodation, restaurants and cafe, tour guiding, handicraft and souvenir production, health and wellness tourism, ecotourism and nature tourism, training, and consultancy tourism, technology, and digital platforms of tourism (Çıkmaz, 2024). The main reasons why women choose entrepreneurship in this sector are as follows (Soysal, 2010; Yadav & Unni, 2016): The service sector requires relatively less capital than other sectors, many women entrepreneurs have experience and/or knowledge in this sector, and it is not a sector that requires high technical knowledge (Soysal, 2010). However, since tourism is consumed where it is produced, tourism entrepreneurs need to develop different marketing methods than entrepreneurs in other sectors and determine what tourists want to experience.

The main types of tourism entrepreneurs are classified as follows (Koh & Hatten, 2002): Creative Tourism Entrepreneurs (bringing a completely new product to the industry—American Express traveler's checks), Innovative Tourism Entrepreneurs (bringing a new approach to an existing product—Disneyland), Follower Tourism Entrepreneurs (restaurants, cafes, or souvenir shops that operate in the same or slightly different way), Social Tourism Entrepreneurs (public and private not-for-profit museums, those who set up aquariums, art galleries, etc.), Informal Tourism Entrepreneurs (street vendors in the informal economy, unlicensed tour guides, etc.), and Potential Tourism Entrepreneurs (those who are looking to start a business in the informal economy), informal tourism entrepreneurs (street vendors in the informal economy, unlicensed tour guides, etc.), potential tourism entrepreneurs (those who are not yet involved in the process), lifestyle entrepreneurs (those who take initiatives that support their preferred lifestyles, hobbies, and interests. For example, someone who loves to cook opens a restaurant). Examples of successful women's entrepreneurship in the tourism sector in Turkiye include local products, accommodation, especially pensions, food and beverage, and souvenir businesses established by women in provinces and districts such as the Beypazarı district of Ankara, Çanakkale, Kars, Cappadocia, Şanlıurfa, Edirne, Kastamonu, etc.

Conclusion

Improving the position of women in Turkiye and ensuring that they live under equal conditions with men is of great importance both for themselves and for the development of our country. Since the establishment of the Republic, various steps have been taken and legal provisions have been made in this regard. Although the rate and level of education of women have increased as a result of these efforts, it can be seen that these facts are not fully reflected in the employment of women. The gender phenomenon also plays an important role in the fact that women's employment and women's entrepreneurship have not yet reached the desired level in Turkiye.

According to the statistics on the nonparticipation of women in Turkiye, 47.1% of women are engaged in domestic work, and the fact that domestic work, taking care of children, elderly, sick, and disabled people is considered a woman's responsibility is very important for women's participation and employment (Ayta & Şen, 2023). It has been found that the presence of a person in need of care at home increases women's responsibilities and significantly limits their social life (Işık, 2020). These findings indicate the need for family-friendly policies and regulations regarding access to care services. Public service announcements can be made to challenge the notion that housework and care are women's work, and awareness-raising training can be provided from primary school onwards. The importance of the contribution of women's participation in the workforce to society and the country should be explained, and the perceptions and roles against women that have been ingrained in society for years should be broken down. The issue of gender equality should be included in educational curricula at all levels in order to change the traditional mindset that still prevails in the country. Although it can be said that the employment rate of women in Turkiye has increased over time, and many legal regulations have been made, it can be seen that the regulations made are not sufficient, and more efforts should be made in this regard compared to other countries.

Women's entrepreneurship aims to ensure that women have equal opportunities in the business world and to reduce gender discrimination. Incentives, microcredits, and training provided by various national and international institutions and organizations are enabling women to participate in the tourism sector as entrepreneurs in increasing numbers. As a labor-intensive sector, tourism is classified as a service sector. In the 12th Development Plan, under the heading "Turkiye in 2053," it is stated that within the framework of the long-term development strategy of our country, the weight of the service sector in the sectoral distribution is expected to continue to increase with fundamental changes in the structure of employment and to exceed 70% by the end of the period. In another article under the same heading, it is stated that the main goals include a Turkiye where equal opportunities in employment, wages, and career development are fully ensured and work–life balance is established for all individuals in the active labor force... and that the female labor force participation rate will exceed 60% with a comprehensive transformation that will facilitate women's entry into the labor force. In another article, it is stated that policies to promote labor force participation, especially among women and youth, will be put into practice in order to make the population not included in the labor force active in the economy, and that the incentive system will be made simple and effective by increasing the weight of incentives for women, youth and disabled people. All this shows that tourism is considered an attractive sector for women and that this demand is expected to increase in the coming years, with the incentives and loans provided to the tourism sector. However, in order to increase the number of women entrepreneurs, it is also important to organize entrepreneurship training programs for women and encourage them to become entrepreneurs. While there are various projects in this regard, diversifying and increasing the number of such programs can help increase women's employment. While empowering women can increase the number of women entrepreneurs by contributing to reducing gender inequality, increasing the number of women entrepreneurs will also contribute to reducing gender inequality. It can be said that women's entrepreneurship in Turkiye is supported and seen as a way to fight poverty and unemployment, especially by institutions dealing with entrepreneurship such as KOSGEB, and the targets to increase the number of women entrepreneurs in development plans, but it is important that this support is done by prioritizing gender equality.

References

Ali, A., Iqbal, Z., & Ali, I. (2024). Women in mountain tourism: Exploring the links between women tourism entrepreneurship and women empowerment in Hunza Valley. *Tourism Recreation Research*, 1–17.

Ardıç Yetiş, Ş., & Çalışkan, N. (2020). Turizm sektöründe kadın istihdamı: Mevcut duruma ilişkin bir değerlendirme. *Manisa Celal Bayar Üniversitesi Sosyal Bilimler Dergisi*, *18*(3), 105–119. https://doi.org/10.18026/cbayarsos.601634

Aşkın, U., & Aşkın, E. Ö. (2017). Toplum yararına programların kadın işsizliği ile mücadeledeki etkinliği: Tokat ili araştırması. *The Journal of Industrial Relations and Human Resources*, *19*(48), 23–48.

Ayta, F., & Şen, M. (2023). Türkiye'de kadın istihdamının genel görünümü: İstihdamın artırılması kapsamında seçilmiş ülke örnekleri. *Uluslararası Ekonomi ve Yenilik Dergisi*, *9*(2), 421–454. https://doi.org/10.20979/ueyd.1344210

Bektaş, H. (2024). *İstatistiklerle kadın girişimciliği*. İstanbul.

Çelik Uğuz, S., & Topbaş, F. (2016). Turizmde kadın istihdamı ve ücret ayrımcılığı: Karşılaştırmalı bir analiz. *Anatolia: Turizm Araştırmaları Dergisi*, *27*(1), 62–78.

Çıkmaz, E. (2024). Turizm sektöründe kadın girişimciliğin bibliyometrik analizi. *Gaziantep University Journal of Social Sciences*, *23*(3), 1214–1227.

Düzgün, S. S. (2021). Covid-19 salgını döneminde Türkiye'de kadın girişimcilik yazını. *Girişimcilik İnovasyon ve Pazarlama Araştırmaları Dergisi*, *5*(10), 148–165.

Filimonau, V., Matyakubov, U., Matniyozov, M., Shaken, A., & Mika, M. (2024). Women entrepreneurs in tourism in a time of a life event crisis. *Journal of Sustainable Tourism*, *32*(3), 457–479.

Gündüz, A. Y., & Karadeniz, B. (2022). Girişimcilik olgusunun tarihsel gelişimi ve kadın girişimciliği: Malatya ilinde yapılan çalışmanın incelenmesi. *Bingöl Üniversitesi Sosyal Bilimler Enstitüsü Dergisi*, *24*, 96–112. https://doi.org/10.29029/busbed.1119269

Işık, E. (2020). Covid-19 salgını ve kadın emeği: Türkiye'den kadın deneyimleri. *Türkiye'den kadın deneyimleri. Politik Ekonomik Kuram*, *4*(2), 219–241.

Kadının Güçlenmesi Strateji Belgesi ve Eylem Planı. (2018–2023). https://www.aile.gov.tr/ksgm/ulusal-eylem-planlari/kadinin-guclenmesi-strateji-belgesi-ve-eylem-plani-2018-2023/. Accessed on December 10, 2024.

Koh, K. Y., & Hatten, T. S. (2002). The tourism entrepreneur: The overlooked player in tourism development studies. *International Journal of Hospitality & Tourism Administration*, *3*(1), 21–48.

Kozak, N., Kozak, M. A., & Kozak, M. (2012). *Genel Turizm İlkeler ve Kavramlar*. Detay Yayıncılık.

Kumkale, İ (2015). *Kadın girişimciliğinin stratejik liderlik yetkinlikleri açısından incelenmesi ve bir araştırma*. Bursa.

Kutlu, D., Çimen, Z. A., & Güdekli, D. (2022). Küresel cinsiyet eşitsizliğinin istihdam, eğitim ve GSYH değişkenleri açısından değerlendirilmesi. *Yaşar Üniversitesi E-Dergisi*, *17*(68), 857–877.

Nxopo, Z., & Iwu, C. G. (2015). The unique obstacles of female entrepreneurship in the tourism industry in Western Cape, South Africa. *Commonwealth Youth and Development*, *13*(2), 55–71.

Özkaya, M. O. (2009). Kadın girişimcilere yönelik "strateji geliştirmede" yerel yönetimlerle işbirliği içinde olmak, mümkün mü? *Journal of Management and Economics Research*, *7*(11), 56–72.

Republic of Turkey Ministry of Development. (2020). *Tourism special commission report*. Ministry of Development.

Republic of Türkiye Ministry of Labour and Social Security, National Employment Strategy (NES). (2014–2023). https://www.csgb.gov.tr/Media/y1vlqieo/ulusal-istihdam-stratejisi-2025-2028-1.pdf. Accessed on December 11, 2024.

Seçkin Halaç, D., & Meşe, G. (2021). Toplumsal cinsiyet bakış açısından Türkiye'de kadın girişimciliğinin durumu. *Dumlupınar Üniversitesi Sosyal Bilimler Dergisi*, (68), 255–270. https://doi.org/10.51290/dpusbe.838567

Soysal, A. (2010). Türkiye'de kadın girişimciler: Engeller ve fırsatlar bağlamında bir değerlendirme. *Ankara Üniversitesi SBF Dergisi*, *65*(01), 83–114. https://doi.org/10.1501/SBFder_0000002153

Turkish Hoteliers Association (TUROB). (2021). *Report on tourism sector and female employment in Turkey*. TUROB.

Türkiye Cumhuriyeti Cumhurbaşkanlığı Stateji ve Bütçe Başkanlığı. Kalkınma Planları. Accessed on December 10, 2024. https://www.sbb.gov.tr/kalkinma-planlari/, https://www.sbb.gov.tr/wp-content/uploads/2022/07/Kalkinma_Plani_Birinci_Bes_Yillik_1963-1967.pdf, https://www.sbb.gov.tr/wp-content/uploads/2022/07/Ikinci_Bes_Kalkinma_Plani-1968-1972.pdf, https://www.sbb.gov.tr/wp-content/uploads/2022/08/Yeni-Strateji-ve-Kalkinma-Plani_Ucuncu-Bes-Yil_1973_1977.pdf, https://www.sbb.gov.tr/wp-content/uploads/2022/08/Dorduncu-Bes-Yillik-Kalkinma-Plani_1979_1983.pdf, https://www.sbb.gov.tr/wp-content/uploads/2022/08/Besinci-Bes-Yillik-Kalkinma-Plani-1985-1989.pdf, https://www.sbb.gov.tr/wp-content/uploads/2022/07/Altinci_Bes_Yillik_Kalkinma_Plani-1990-1994.pdf, https://www.sbb.gov.tr/wp-content/uploads/2022/07/Seventh_Five_Year_Development_Plan_1996-2000.pdf, https://www.sbb.gov.tr/wp-content/uploads/2022/07/Long-Term_Strategy_and_Eight_Five_Year_Development_Plan_2001-2005.pdf, https://www.sbb.gov.tr/wp-content/uploads/2018/11/Ninth_Development_Plan_2007-2013.pdf, https://www.sbb.gov.tr/wp-content/uploads/2022/07/The_Tenth_Development_Plan_2014-2018.pdf, https://www.sbb.gov.tr/wp-content/uploads/2022/07/Eleventh_Development_Plan_2019-2023.pdf, https://www.resmigazete.gov.tr/eskiler/2023/11/20231101M1-1.htm.

Tayhani, İ. (2009). Türkiye Cumhuriyeti'nin Temeli: Laiklik. *Ankara Üniversitesi Türk İnkılâp Tarihi Enstitüsü Atatürk Yolu Dergisi*, (43), 517–529.
Tekeli, N., & Yılmaz, G. (2021). Women's entrepreneurship and tourism under the scope of sustainability ın Turkey; Swot analysis of the current problems. *Journal of Social, Humanities and Administrative Sciences*, *7*(36), 120–134.
Turkish Statistical Institute (TURKSTAT). (2022a). *Household labour force survey*. TURKSTAT. https://webapps.ilo.org/surveyLib/index.php/catalog/8236
Turkish Statistical Institute (TURKSTAT). (2022b). *Women in statistics*. TURKSTAT. https://eca.unwomen.org/sites/default/files/2023-05/tuik_statistic_2022_en_0.pdf
Turkish Statistical Institute (TURKSTAT). (2023a). *Household labor force survey*. TURKSTAT. https://webapps.ilo.org/surveyLib/index.php/catalog/8237
Turkish Statistical Institute (TURKSTAT). (2023b). *Women in statistics*. TURKSTAT. https://data.tuik.gov.tr/Bulten/Index?dil=2&p=Women-in-Statistics-2023-53675
Turkish Statistical Institute (TURKSTAT), Türkiye İstatistik Kurumu (TÜİK). İşgücü İstatistikleri. https://data.tuik.gov.tr/Kategori/GetKategori?p=Istihdam,-Issizlik-ve-Ucret-108. Accessed on December 10, 2024.
Turkish Statistical Institute (TURKSTAT), Türkiye İstatistik Kurumu (TÜİK). İstatistiklerle Kadın. https://data.tuik.gov.tr/Bulten/Index?p=Istatistiklerle-Kadin-2022-49668. Accessed on December 10, 2024.
Turkish Statistical Institute (TURKSTAT), Türkiye İstatistik Kurumu (TÜİK). İstatistiklerle Kadın. https://data.tuik.gov.tr/Bulten/Index?p=Istatistiklerle-Kadin-2023-53675. Accessed on December 14, 2024.
Turkish Statistical Institute (TURKSTAT), Türkiye İstatistik Kurumu (TÜİK). Kazanç Yapısı. https://data.tuik.gov.tr/Bulten/Index?p=Kazanc-Ya(pisi-Istatistikleri-2022-49750. Accessed on December 10, 2024.
Ünsay, B. (2017). *Mucize Dirilişin Önderi Gazi Mustafa Kemal Atatürk*. Ceres Yayınları.
Ünüvar, O. (2020). *Turizm girişimcilik eğiliminin belirlenmesi ve coğrafi bilgi sistemi ile haritalandırılması* Ph.D. Thesis. Selçuk University.
World Economic Forum. (2023). *Global gender gap report 2023*. https://www3.weforum.org/docs/WEF_GGGR_2023.pdf. Accessed on December 20, 2024.
Xu, H., Wang, C., Wu, J., Liang, Y., Jiao, Y., & Nazneen, S. (2018). Human poverty alleviation through rural women's tourism entrepreneurship. *Journal of China Tourism Research*, *14*(4), 445–460.
Yadav, V., & Unni, J. (2016). Women entrepreneurship: Research review and future directions. *Journal of Global Entrepreneurship Research*, *6*(1), 12. https://doi.org/10.1186/s40497-016-0055-x
Yangil, F. M., & Başpınar, N. Ö. (2022). Mustafa Kemal Atatürk'ün Liderlik Tarzının Sürdürülebilir Liderlik Açısından Değerlendirilmesi. *Kırklareli Üniversitesi İktisadi ve İdari Bilimler Fakültesi Dergisi*, *11*(2), 323–350. https://doi.org/10.18092/ulikidince.1052731

Web Links

https://biruni.tuik.gov.tr/medas/?kn=72&locale=tr. Accessed on December 10, 2024.
https://data-explorer.oecd.org/?pg=0&bp=true&snb=247&tm=women. Accessed on December 12, 2024.

Section 3

Tourism and Economic Development

Chapter 10

Sports Tourism: Modern China's Economic Development Through the Little White Ball

Yu-Feng Lin Lee

New Mexico State University, USA

Abstract

Is golf a sport or an entertainment in China? Since its debut in the mid-1980s, the development of golf is newfangled but flourishing, although it is prohibitively expensive, exclusively restrictive, and authoritatively forbidden for Chinese politicians. Due to scant intellectual analysis, this paper unveils golf in modern China pertaining to (1) its perception in the eyes of Chinese, (2) its growth as an industry in sports tourism, (3) its political dilemma, (4) golf economics—demand and supply, and (5) the future of "Chinese golf." In conclusion, it offers the implication of golf growth in the course of forthcoming Chinese economic development.

Keywords: Golf; economic development; conspicuous consumption; sports tourism; Chinese economy

Introduction

The following press recording (National Public Radio, 2017) depicts the dialogues of Robert T. Jones Jr., world's top golf course designer and architect, and Deng, Xiao-Ping, national leader of People's Republic of China (PRC; as known as mainland China, or China), as Deng visited US President Jimmy Carter in the United States in 1979 for China's "Open Door Policy" to further US–China bilateral trade.

Economics and Tourism, 163–179

doi:10.1108/978-1-83662-916-020251011

Deng: "What is golf?"
Jones: "It's a small ball hit over a big field into a hole, and people gamble about it and they buy each other drinks."
Deng: "Oh perfect, the Chinese will love it!"

The introduction of golf was not until 1984, when the first golf course—Zhongshan Hot Spring Golf Club—was built in the coastal city of Zhongshan in Guangdong province, along the Pearl River Delta (PRD) region, thanks to the launch of the 1979 economic reformation and openness by Deng. Given China's outstanding and incessant economic growth since then, not only has the Chinese per capita income increased substantially, which advances the overall domestic consumption power, but it has also broadened and enhanced lifestyle of Chinese, in part from influences of the West, through various leisure activities, including foreign travel, fine arts and upscale dining, and luxury entertainment and recreation such as F1 car racing, horse riding and racing, and golfing.

Who plays golf in China? Since the 1980s, golf has almost always been equated with the class of the rich. Nevertheless, with the burgeoning Chinese middle class,[1] who resembles China's rapidly growing and powerful consumption troop, the increase in their daily income from $2 or less a day to now $10 (lower-middle class) to $50 (higher-middle class) a day[2] has prompted a propensity to consume sports and entertainment beyond their spending on essentials. The growth-induced urbanization[3] as another catalyst also enhances the growth of golf and leisure markets, which thenceforth supports Chinese's adaption to diverse urban lifestyle (China Power, 2017).

The debut of golf in Deng's "New China" has attested to mainland Chinese economic growth. From no or a niggling number of golf courses and players to now the aggressive building and training of national golf teams for international events, and from prohibitively expensive golfing costs and exclusively restrictive membership to now more middle-high and high-income earners who could afford to play, golf (industry) witnesses China's continuous economic development and endogenously supports the growing interests of those who pursue diverse living. In recent years, golf was even used to reflect the positive change of Chinese political culture—the anti-corruption initiative of the Chinese government commanded by its President Xi, who outlawed all golf-related activities connected between businesses and Chinese bureaucrats for the pledge of "clean" government.

[1]Chinese middle class shared 4% of its population in 2002 but rose to 31%, or over 420 million people in 2012, and it is forecasted to reach 550 million in 2022.
[2]According to Chinese governmental definition, middle-class annual income is ranged between $7,250 and $62,500.
[3]China's skyrocketed urban population from 19% in 1980 increases to 58% in 2017 and is projected to 75% in 2022.

Literature Review in Chinese Golf

Although relevant intellectual study is still scant, the rise of golf in China has followed leading factors of politics, economics, cultural, and globalization movements. Since Deng's "Open Door Policy," playing golf has fulfilled part of the political needs between Chinese officials and their foreign diplomats when China's first golf club of Guangdong was opened (Shao, 2013). It then rides with China's decades-long outperforming economy, during which foreign capital was injected into Chinese golf investment, matching many elite Chinese and the "new middle income" class, their mindset of golfing to express social prestige and rising financial ability (Shao, 2013; Wang, 2011; Zhang et al., 2009, 2016; Zhou, 2014). Though golf is culturally controversial among Chinese whose self-indulgence through golfing with ample time and money is de-emphasized in the culture of collectivism, as proposed by Zhou (2014), golf can be made "culturally correct" if promoted in an "accurate" way for self-discipline, self-cultivation, equity, and equality, fitting to Confucius' teaching favored by Chinese. Meanwhile, in modern business underpinning service and product value, Wu and Ai (2016) suggested developing Chinese golf culture on equitable tactics to promote experiential quality and satisfaction.

Theoretical Framework: Veblen's Golf Market Equilibria in China

Thorstein Veblen (1899)'s theory of conspicuous consumption, also known as the "Veblen Good," notably classifies consumption behavior of the wealthy as "a means of reputability to the gentleman of leisure." It illustrates the dual golf market equilibria in China where dichotomized consumers are the elite Chinese who display their ostentatious wealth and swagger social prestige by golfing more when facing higher prices, in contrast to their ordinary counterparts who consider golf a normal good following the law of demand. Of Fig. 10.1, the disjointed c-shaped golf demand would traverse the conventional golf supply in two points to infer the wealth gap between the rich and its opposite. As the "Veblen good" of higher golf price tends to enfold more golf consumption from rich Chinese, the "Normal good" of lower price would potentially appeal to more of the commons.

"Golf Is the Apple of the Rich's Eye."—The Perception of Golf in Modern China

Is golf a sport or an entertainment in China? In the 20th century, as some Western media noted, it was the "green opium" (Krich, 2003), golf was labeled the "sport for millionaires" by Mao Zedong (also known as Chairman Mao of China) after assuming his political hegemony in 1949. Ever since, like a daunting curse, ordinary Chinese have perceived golf as an immoral and luxurious pastime of the bourgeois. It is not recognized as a sport, but rather the elite's leisure due to its incredibly high costs summed from the gear price, the activity and field fee, and the club and membership dues. Under the practice of Chinese socialism, it is believed that resources should be reserved and utilized for the production of all

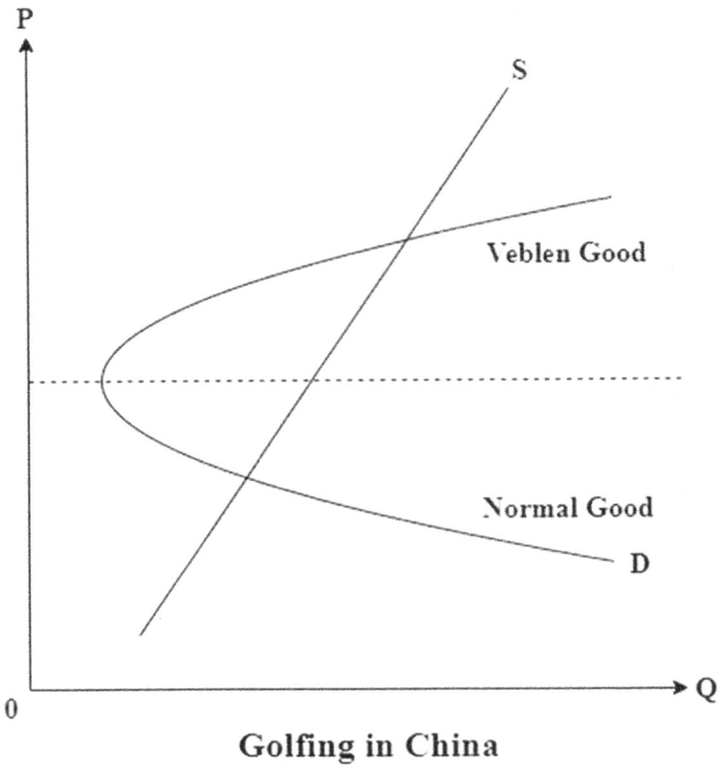

Fig. 10.1. Golf as the "Veblen Good" in China. *Source:* The diagram is drawn by the author.

and by the proletariat class, while golfing by capitalists is reckoned resource-wasteful and unproductive. The contentious image has made golf a bipolar status as the rich minority perceives it as socioeconomic preeminence, contradictory to the disdain of the less-wealthy majority seeing its fruitless societal contribution.

Based on the statistics generated by the *Forward Group—China Golf Industry Report* (2018; https://mp.weixin.qq.com/s/wTd9jr5uymtIi3jxg_165Q), 84% of modern Chinese golfers are young college-educated males with entrepreneurial or business executive ranks, aged between 21 and 25 years, and earn annual income between US$15,000 and US$45,000 (i.e., from RMB 100,000 to RMB 300,000, as compared with China's estimated per capita nominal GDP of around US$10,000 in 2019). Thanks to their relatively higher income, many have played golf for three or more years and participated in indoor, outdoor, and driving range activities, while spending nearly US$4,500 (or RMB 30,000) annually and at least 50% of their sports budgets on golfing all year round.

On the contrary, regarding the primary reasons for golf being an unpopular activity among Chinese surveyed in 2015 (by *Forward Group—China Golf Industry Report*) (2015; https://zhuanlan.zhihu.com/p/97302164, in Chinese language, under "Baidu" search engine), most Chinese consider golf undesirable owing to a lack of time (golf as a time-consuming activity) (32%); golf as an over-priced activity (26%); inadequate and inaccessible ways of golf participation (23%), and consequently, insufficient golf attraction (19%).

Golf Growth in Modern China

Golf has been booming in China. Even if, to the majority of Chinese, it is an inordinately expensive activity, the construction of new golf courses is in swiftness across China, with currently around 500 sites, especially clustered in the first-tier globalized metropolitans like Beijing, Shanghai, and Shenzhen (of Guangzhou), and spreads to resort provinces like Hainan facing the South China Sea, hosting its world-famous "Mission Hills – Haikou" game. Of recent statistics, golf courses are located all over China across all 33 divisions, including provinces, municipalities, autonomous regions, and Hong Kong and Macao, the Special Administrative Regions (SARs), while in 2017, the last region in Tibet was also covered with an international-standard golf course over 3,000 meters in elevation by Hilton Hotels and Resorts as a foreign direct investment in China (Dudley, 2017). By 2010, these courses attracted over 350,000 of both professional and amateur golfers, who were either top-ranked and highly paid business personnel, entrepreneurs, or government officials to play more than eight rounds a year. Almost a decade later, in 2018, the golf industry was worth US$1 billion, and collectively near 1.1 million Chinese golfers played around China (see Abkowitz, 2014; Forward Group – China Golf Industry Report, 2011; Marketing to China, 2018). After the reinstatement of golf at the 2016 Rio Summer Olympic Games (SOG) and its election as a feature for both men- and women's golf at the 2020 Tokyo SOG, the Chinese government has spent numerous resources to form and train its national teams in hopes of golf medaling. China's central authority carefully delineates its aim as it is for the national pride, but not for its promotion as a sport, especially among the governmental sectors.

Following the studies by *Forward Group—China Golf Industry Report* (2018; https://max.book118.com/html/2024/1226/5120120231012020.shtm, in Chinese language, under "Baidu" search engine; https://max.book118.com/html/2023/0826/7032154133005150.shtm, in Chinese language, under "Baidu" search engine), the rapid growth of golf facilities in China has started since 1980s, while it also revealed the decrease in golf course operation facing the Chinese government's authoritative shutdown in 2011. The increase in golf courses was exponential (from 22 to 538) in just over two decades (1994–2014) and was in sharp decline to around 380 courses in 2017, while golfers playing golf rounds show a steady growth from 2009 to 2013 (from 8,720,000 rounds of 2009 to 12,150,000 rounds of 2013), along with an uneven surge of average 18-hole rounds (from an average of 20,115 18-hole rounds between 2009 and 2012 to an average of 19,040 18-hole rounds between 2013 and 2015, followed by an increase of 21,300 18-hole rounds in 2017).

Concerning the rise of professional golf talents, the *PGA Tour* (at https://www.pgatour.com/stats/stat.186.2020.html) keeps its records publicly available for the international professional golfers' performance, which allows this study to assemble and disclose the chronicles of Chinese professional golfers made to the Top 100 All-Around (AA) and Official World Golf (OWG) rankings (see Table 10.1), accredited by major championships and professional golf tours associated with the International Federation of PGA Tours. Before the advent of the new millennium, the prematurity and unpopularity of golf in China had hardly earned its international presence and recognition. Nonetheless, the Chinese golf honor roll started to surface, although slowly, and at the turn of the last

Table 10.1. All-Around (AA) and Official World Golf (OWG) Ranking, Top 100, Selected Years.

Ranking Includes Chinese Golf Players and Their Profiles				
Year	**Player's Name**	**Ranking**	**Total Prize (US$)**	**Scoring Average (Par 72)**
2020	Xinjun Zhang	81 (AA)	$1,218,354	70.932
	Haotong Li	53 (OWG)	$1,209,934	71.436
	C.T. Pan[a]	54 (OWG)	$5,576,892	73.006
2019	Haotong Li	50 (OWG)	$1,209,934	N/A
	C.T. Pan[a]	51 (OWG)	$5,799,036	71.660
2018	Haotong Li	56 (OWG)	$1,209,934	N/A
	C.T. Pan[a]	51 (AA)	$5,799,036	71.660
	C.T. Pan[a]	100 (OWG)	$5,799,036	71.660
2017	Haotong Li	65 (OWG)	$1,209,934	N/A
2016	No Chinese golf players made to the Top-100			
2015	No Chinese golf players made to the Top-100			
2010	WC Liang	66 (OWG)	$445,366.00	70.479
2005	No Chinese golf players made to the Top-10			
2000	No Chinese golf players made to the Top-100			
1995	No Chinese golf players made to the Top-100			
1990	No Chinese golf players made to the Top-100			
1985	T.C. Chen[a]	57 (AA)	$616,303.00	71.084

Source: PGA Tour. https://www.pgatour.com/stats/stat.186.2020.html

[a]Players representing Chinese Taipei (TPE).

decade, more Chinese professional golfers were placed in the top world ranks than ever before.

The Golf Dilemma: Authoritative Golf Crackdown

While golf in the West may simply be an outdoor sport for all people, in China, it often resembles social prestige or is even linked to corruption.[4] In the Chinese public sector, playing golf is seen as taboo among government officials. Especially since the 2013 inauguration of the current President Xi, who has persisted in the declaration of his preceded Premier Wen, on suspending new golf course construction, which resulted in waste and misuse of public capital and illegal use and crowding out of agrarian lands, Xi impels the Chinese Communist Party (CCP) to ban all its members from joining golf clubs so as to support the incentive of China's anti-corruption. Of its new rules on golf, no CCP members are supposed to "obtain, hold or use membership cards for gyms, clubs, golf clubs, or various other types of consumer cards, or entering private clubs" (BBC News, 2015). Since 2011, the order of authoritative shutdown has rendered more than 110 golf courses inoperable (see France-Presse, 2017; Ross, 2017) whereas such a political pledge has reaffirmed the effort of the Chinese government for being "clean" and ethical as it tries to advance its political image in the global society, even if critics have referred such acts as short-lived and contrived.

Of the statistics of golf closure and authoritative shutdown reported by China Daily (2015; http://www.chinadaily.com.cn/sports/2015-03/31/content_19964426.htm),China's national English newspaper, between 2014 and 2015, 66 golf course closures, covering 23 provinces and municipalities, ordered by China's Ministry of Land and Resources (MLR) were to reflect the massive misuse of lands and water due to illegal golf course constructions and the pesticide and chemical pollution of water. Among them, golf course closure was topped in provinces or municipal districts of Shandong (8 closures), Guangdong (6 closures), Yunnan (6 closures), Liaoning (5 closures), Inner-Mongolia (4 closures), Hubei (4 closures), Jiangxi (4 closures), Hainan (3 closures), Guizhou (3 closures), Tianjin (3 closures), and Beijing (3 closures).

Golf Economics: Golf as a Luxury—How Pricy Is It?

High Price—The Golf Demand

Beyond the Chinese elites, playing golf can be pricy—as the "rich people's game." A typical round (or 18 holes) of golf can cost US$500 or more, as opposed to one-tenth in an American or European course, compared with the per-person monthly disposable income in Shanghai and Beijing[5] of approximately US$900 in 2019 (China Daily, 2019). Such a high price tempts the

---

[4]In China, golf may hint corruption since individuals such as businessmen or politicians sometimes gather to solicit or settle dubious business or political deals through playing golf.
[5]In 2019, Shanghai is the highest-income metropolitan in China, followed by Beijing.

Chinese government to levy a 24% tax on golf clubs, equally heavy as the toll on nightclubs (see Sirak, 2008), purposefully to fragment the golf market by discouraging common golf consumption. Two phases of golf course crackdown aiming to conserve water and land space were executed, with one in 2004 when less than 200 courses were built, and another of over 110 courses following the CCP's anti-corruption declaration since 2011. Though facing the imposed closure, golf demand remains strong in the nonpublic sector given China's continuous domestic growth and improving income. Since 2000, all of the new and old courses combined have nearly quadrupled (ESPN, 2017).

Playing golf among the affluent Chinese, in particular the businessmen and entrepreneurs, is deemed to satisfy both physical and spiritual demands. Physically, they play golf for their body build-up, while the prestigious image of golfing reflected in monetary aptitude fulfills their mental desire to be in the upper-class society. Paying a club or membership fee, as high as or more than US $100,000 annually, is often not a challenge to the affluent, whereas getting to the upper social preeminence through golf fellowship to fortify their status or reach more and bigger business deals is what matters to them.

According to the report of China Central Television (CCTV; China's official TV network) (2011), as a Chinese person's average annual income exceeds US $20,000, or above US$25,000 to be the "rich-beginner," they hypothetically would start to play or consider playing golf. Over 90% of golf activities in China are club-membership oriented, with the average club (initial membership) fee of US$53,000 (it can be paid as an individual or commonly paid as a corporate membership), four to five times higher than the charge in Europe. In many cases, golf courses are built around the deluxe resort housing or a wealthy neighborhood with elaborate amenities. Given such an upscale setting, as one purchases the housing unit, they could probably be granted the (free) golf club membership. In addition to the club fee, each member-golfer playing a round is subject to pay per-round (18 holes) activity fee (e.g., green fee) ranging from US$100 to $200 (higher weekend and holiday fees than those of weekdays). In short, playing golf is still perceived as "the rich's game," with its exceptionally high price as a sumptuous symbol, while condemned as a profligate pursuit by the commons.

High Cost—The Golf Supply

Despite the high levy on golfing and the recent authoritative shutdown, golf development in China is still at its peak, particularly from the business viewpoint. Golf scrambles are common public relations tools in business, emphasizing relaxation and fun while achieving business deals and networking among the players. Often seen across China, golf and golf courses are not only a standalone activity and facility, but they also are derived products in the business of real estate. Many estate developers add the golf courses to create value-added properties and cater to luxurious villa- and condo-living. Surrounding the golf facility, these luxury residence districts are embraced with high-end boutiques, club houses, spa and massage lounges, sports complexes, and other amenities at the price of half to a couple million dollars per housing unit to attract affluent Chinese buyers for their conspicuous consumption (see Abkowitz, 2014).

In a recent study by KPMG (2014), golf course building is often costly, from design to construction, ranging from an average of US$3 million to a high end of US$10 million. Though building golf courses is key to bringing in golf players, the large-scale golf events such as international tournaments with sizable prizes[6] are equally elemental to attract top-ranked golfers around the world to China. In 2006, when the world's largest golf course, Mission Hills—Haikou, claimed 1.5 times to the size of Manhattan (New York) was built, China's standing in golf became unneglectable since global players would seek to conquer the field for the proof of their skills. With other top golf facilities built elsewhere nationwide, where some make the "Top 100 Courses in the World" of *Golf Magazine* or *Golf Digest*, Chinese golf supply is globally competitive, offering world-class services to East and West players (see BBC Travel, 2017).

Following various publicly available news and statistics regarding golf competitions and top-ranked golf courses in China (see *Golf Digest* at https://www.golfdigest.com/story/china-best-golf-courses; *World Golf Championships* at https://www.hsbcgolf.com/; *GOLFLUX* at https://www.golflux.com/best-golf-courses-in-china/; *PGA Tour* at https://www.pgatour.com/stats/stat.186.2020.html; *Pantheon World* at https://pantheon.world/profile/occupation/golfer/country/china), Table 10.2 synopsizes China's golf supply, which entices event hosting by various multinational corporations such as HSBC, Volvo, BMW, and Buick, along with local Chinese conglomerates (e.g., Grand China Air, Midea). Many of these competitions were held in the municipal and resort cities such as Shanghai and Haikou with ample event prizes. In order to attract golf enthusiasts and amateurs, more golf courses are being built and advanced, while

Table 10.2. Top 10 Golf Competitions and Top 10 Golf Courses in China.

Top 10 Golf Competitions in China				**Top 10 Golf Courses in China**	
Tournament Name	**Est./Final Years**	**Prize: US$ Million (Prize Year)**	**Most Golf Course Held for Event**	**Ranks (2017–2018)**	**Golf Course/ Location**
HSBC Champions	2005 (ongoing)	$10.25 (2019)	Sheshan Golf Club/ Shanghai	1	Spring City Golf & Lake Resort/ Yunnan

(Continued)

[6]Various "Golf Open" games and champions are usually prized in millions of US$ per game.

Table 10.2. *(Continued)*

Top 10 Golf Competitions in China				**Top 10 Golf Courses in China**	
Tournament Name	**Est./Final Years**	**Prize: US$ Million (Prize Year)**	**Most Golf Course Held for Event**	**Ranks (2017–2018)**	**Golf Course/ Location**
Volvo China Open[a]	1995 (ongoing)	$2.81 (2019)	Shanghai Silport Golf Club/ Shanghai	2	Haikou Mission Hills Golf Resort-Blackstone/ Hainan
BMW Asian Open	2001/ 2008	$2.30 (2008)	Tomson Shanghai Pudong Golf Club/ Shanghai	3	The Dunes at Shenzhou Peninsula (East)/Hainan
Buick LPGA Shanghai	2008/NA	$2.10 (2009)	Qizhong Garden Golf Club/ Shanghai	4	Tiger Beach Golf Links/ Shandong
Grand China Air LPGA	2007/ 2008	$1.80 (2008)	Haikou West Golf Club/ Hainan	5	Sanya Blue Bay Golf Club/Hainan
Mission Hills Star Trophy	2010/ 2010	$1.20 (2010)	Mission Hills Haikou/ Hainan	6	Yulongwan Golf Club/ Yunnan
TCL Classic[b]	2002/ 2007	$1.10 (2007)	Yaolong Bay Golf Club/ Hainan	7	Kunming Sunshine Golf Club/Yunnan
Midea China Classic	2007/ 2010	$1.00 (2010)	Royal Orchid International Golf Club/ Guangdong	8	Enhance Anting Golf Club/ Shanghai
Luxehills Chengdu Open	2008/ 2010	$1.00 (2010)	Luxehills International Country Club/Sichuan	9	Tianjin—The 27 Golf Club/ Tianjin

Table 10.2. *(Continued)*

Top 10 Golf Competitions in China				Top 10 Golf Courses in China	
Tournament Name	**Est./Final Years**	**Prize: US$ Million (Prize Year)**	**Most Golf Course Held for Event**	**Ranks (2017–2018)**	**Golf Course/ Location**
Suzhou Taihu Ladies Open	2008/ 2013	$.39 (2013)	Suzhou Taihu International Golf Club/ Jiangsu	10	Shanqin Bay Golf Club/ Hainan

Source: Various news and statistics sources compiled by author; available upon request.

[a]Prize of Volvo China Open is recorded on the monthly average exchange rate of Chinese Yuan per US$ in September 2019: ¥7.1147 per US$; https://www.x-rates.com/average/?from=EUR&to=CNY&amount=1&year=2019.

[b]Prize of TCL Classic and Suzhou Taihu Ladies Open is recorded on the monthly average exchange rate of US$ per Euro in September 2019: US$1.1019 per Euro.

many meet or exceed the international standard, as ranked in the 2017–2018 Top-10 Golf Course list (also see Sina Magazine, 2018).

Golf Future in China: Golf Promotion and Development

Golf as an Affordable Sport

Unlike badminton and table tennis, commonly played by Chinese, golf is controversial, with somewhat fallacious impressions reliant on different social classes of people who see it. Due to its excessive cost and social exclusiveness, making golf ubiquitous among the general public in China may not be realistic, especially as it needs vast land space and natural resources to support the activity. The lands used for golf courses face large opportunity costs as the arable spaces are dwindling. Meanwhile, the amount of water typically consumed by one golf course can alternatively be used to support 600 rural villages, not to mention the possible pesticide pollution of groundwater from golf lawn maintenance (Kershaw, 2018). Given that growth of golf in China is anticipated, to feasibly make golf more affordable and environmentally approachable, a few proposals may be considered as follows:

- Golf Landscaping
  To make golf more affordable to the common Chinese, governmental planning and involvement may be inevitable. With properly reviewing and revising of

scales of land for uses of business and production, farming, dwelling, and leisure, the government should consider permitting golf facilities to be built and operated in the designated leisure sites. Golf course sizes in urban areas should be limited so as not to crowd out living and commercial spaces. Alternatively, city-operated golf courses can be extended to existing parks as part of the public property, whereas the sizable and world-class golf courses taking large lands and having higher facility standards could be directed to the less-populated rural or resort communities. Apposite golf landscaping between urban center and rural periphery could not only potentially support effective urban land use, but it also could enhance overall development in rural areas.

- Golf Pricing
  The pricing strategy of golfing across metropolitans should be economically oriented, as the city government could operate the golf courses as a publicly owned entity, like the facilities for tennis, table tennis, basketball, and badminton, funded and maintained through the finance of property taxes or other public outlays. Government may impose customary activity or facility fees on the users comparable to those charges on facilities of other sports to remunerate related spending and sustain budget balance. If golf privatization is of governmental goal to promote a fair market price, generating competitive golf pricing is vital while exercising an administrative "price ceiling" if market distortion occurs. Once an affordable golf price prevails, offering Chinese an alternate sport may increase the likelihood and willingness of participation.
- Golf-induced Rural Economic Development
  In the countryside, golf facilities that qualify for international standards may be made the hosts for large and global golf events. Being advantageous in the landscape, golf facilities could be extended with other amenities and operated as a resort destination. Local and state governments could work with the private sector to undertake public–private partnership (PPP) to invest, build, operate, and improve rural infrastructure such as road construction and refinement, transportation networks, lodging and food services, and other business logistics to attract visitors and golf players while advancing peripheral living. Aside from large and global-standard golf facilities, smaller-scale communal golf routes could also be added, as well as tennis courts and badminton and table tennis pavilions for common use. Improved rural living through golf may in turn encourage rural citizens' golf participation when employed in the golf-related workforce or playing golf as a pastime.

Golf as an Education

Thanks to thriving golf interest among the rising Chinese affluent class, professional golfers from organizations like the American Professional Golf Association (APGA) are recruited to give private or membership-based lessons to the wealthy learners. In recent years, schools for golf have been established independently or affiliated with academic institutions, including universities and colleges. In Beijing and Shanghai, golf class is increasingly added to the elementary school curriculum or extra-curriculum,[7] with some making it mandatory for the youth to learn and play, while others, such as colleges, develop golf (e.g., professional golf management) into a major study. Regardless of the institutional level, public or private, primary or advanced, the promotion of golfing is to connect the Chinese to the world, to introduce and train Chinese learners in international etiquette, and to build and improve them with character (see Connor, 2017; Horwitz, 2016).

- Golf Curriculum in the School System
  To increase golf popularity in China, golf education may become rudimentary, although, should it be "the rich's game," pairing with a high training price could be debatable. If Chinese governments, from central to local level, desire to make golf a common sport like badminton or table tennis, they may need to consider instituting a golf curriculum into the public-school system, and scheduling regular golf classes and practice time, to hire golf personnel and trainers, and supplying golf facilities. Practically, of the schools with limited land, regular golf lessons can be associated with indoor simulation or miniature golf, while outdoor golfing is given in the golf course encircled by the city parks (as proposed in Section "Golf as an Affordable Sport"). Of the rural area, school golfing is deemed less restrictive, facing land abundance as long as communal golf facilities are available and supported by the rural government.
- Golf Education Through Community Outreach
  Above and beyond school golfing, community golf events such as golf match can be appended to enhance golf fellowship, either supported by local government or by corporate public relation sponsorship. Consequently, through curricular planning and community engagement, the growth in golf education not only offers an optional recreation to common Chinese but also exhorts golf enthusiasts to promote wider golf participation.

Golf as Tourism

- Golf Tourism as a New Tourist Affection

From the business outlook, golf tourism is winning its stake in China. Increasingly, travel agencies joint-venture with the airlines, golf clubs, and resorts and villas to sell the luxurious golf tours and travel packages, thanks primarily to the real estate and upmarket recreational development (see Asian Golf Industry Federation, 2019). Since the last decade, the rise of golf tourism has promoted golf as a global sport, making "golfing in China" a new recreational getaway for many Westerners. It also injects tourist revenue in to the domestic Chinese economy, which was rather unforeseen before.

---

[7]As one of the first few institutions, The Experimental School of Foreign Languages affiliated to East China Normal University added golf curriculum in 2016.

Given the current lavish image of golf in China, golf tourism is packaged in such a way as to resemble the prestige and aptitude, especially the monetary power. It is aimed more at attracting foreign players and affluent Chinese than regular domestic tourists. Thanks to the Internet and social media, golf-tour companies either owned by Chinese in China or by foreign owners overseas are flourishing and competing to provide "golf holiday" sprees and "golf vacation" deals. Many believe that China's rapid growth in the golf industry could entice foreigners' "Chinese golf zest" while also appealing to the local wealthy class by making golf tours sumptuous.

As China's economy sustains its stable growth, golf tourism has the potential to soar. Economic growth empowers higher income, allowing more Chinese to allocate time between work and leisure. Along with the upscale market segment, if golf tourism could also be targeted for affordability, bolstering domestic plays would mean expanding revenue in the tourism industry. Likewise, the role of government in promoting affordable golf tourism is essential. Its support for developing free-market golf supply and demand could theoretically result in fair golf pricing, crucial to buttress market mechanisms and potentially to encourage golfing among Chinese.

Implication of China's Golf Growth

Since Deng's strategic "Open Door Policy" in the late 1970s, economic development in China has been described as "ten thousand arrows shot at once"—aiming at the growth of every and all industries simultaneously. The golf industry is no exception, even if it is relatively a "growth-latecomer." Generally speaking, public and private golf investments, along with other sectors, may become crucial, as such investments often increase domestic and foreign consumption tied to improving the Chinese standard of living. Under such a goal, China's golf growth implies (1) openness and connectivity of Chinese to the world, (2) growing longingness of Chinese for quality, diversity, and balance of life, and (3) sectoral growth (e.g., golf tourism) contributing to future economic advancement.

The growth of golf opens and connects the Chinese to the world. As a global sport, playing golf is no longer limited to Westerners' pursuit. The building and operation of golf courses invite non-Chinese businesses to establish foreign direct investment while enticing players to golf in China. Conversely, through domestic golf promotion, Chinese players may connect themselves to global professional and amateur golfers and increase their visibility in the golf arena.

The affluence of Western living is a goal for many Chinese in the emerging China, where playing golf may resemble one of the indicators of quality of life. In spite of golf being a sport or an entertainment, Chinese who yearn for a balanced life may partake in golfing, among other materials and means, to promote their contemporary living, show their financial ability, and endorse their social status.

The growth of golf tourism in China is believed to support its overall national growth. An increase in golf tourism revenue is not only likely to create golf- and tourist-related employment, but it also may generate growth by a multiplier effect in other sectors such as travel and transportation, hotel and lodging, restaurant and food services, and other business chains. Such cross-sectoral growth is deemed one of the key catalysts to further China's national development and its advanced economy.

Conclusion

Disparate from how Westerners see golf, its current view among most Chinese is associated with money and power as "the game of the wealthy." To make golf more "friendly" and affordable and accessible like badminton and table tennis in China, both public and private involvement in developing golf is essential and equally important. Promoting the golf industry as one of the growth engines while advancing and connecting Chinese living to the world, the following approaches are recommended as follows: (1) having pragmatic golf landscaping to create balanced urban and rural land and resource uses, (2) introducing market mechanisms to generate fair golf prices, (3) integrating golf curriculum in formal (e.g., school) and informal (e.g., community) physical education, and (4) promoting golf tourism to spur cross-sectoral growth. These golf-incorporating schemes are believed to result in a positive-sum welfare outcome in China's future economic development.

References

Abkowitz, A. (2014, May 15). China's golf boom. *The Wall Street Journal*. https://www.wsj.com/articles/the-golf-boom-in-china-1400193992

Asian Golf Industry Federation. (2019, May 18). Hainan alliance aims to promote inbound golf tourism to China's tropical island. https://www.agif.asia/2019/05/hainan-alliance-aims-to-promote-inbound-golf-tourism-to-chinas-tropical-island/

BBC News. (2015, October 22). *China golf: Communist party bans club membership*. https://www.bbc.com/news/world-asia-china-34600544

BBC Travel. (2017). *Golf in China has gone from outlawed to seemingly ubiquitous in just a few decades*. http://www.bbc.com/travel/bespoke/specials/sun-and-sanya/golf/china-vs-golf.html

China Central Television. (2011, August 13). Golf club fee is as high as US$53,000, multiple times higher than that of Europe. http://news.cntv.cn/special/uncommon/11/0813/index.shtml (in Chinese language)

China Daily. (2015, March 31). China's golf closure and authoritative shutdown. http://www.chinadaily.com.cn/sports/2015-03/31/content_19964426.htm (in Chinese language)

China Daily. (2019, May 03). Shanghai's Q1 per capita disposable income highest in China. http://www.chinadaily.com.cn/a/201905/03/WS5ccbfb95a3104842260b99bb.html

China Power. (2017, April 26). *How well-off is China's middle class?* Center for Strategic and International Studies. https://chinapower.csis.org/china-middle-class/

Connor, N. (2017, October 21). *The rise of "green opium: Golf made compulsory in Chinese schools to instill manners*. The Telegraph. https://www.telegraph.co.uk/news/2017/10/21/rise-green-opium-golf-made-compulsory-chinese-schools-instill/

Dudley, S. (2017, March 28). New Hilton resort includes Tibet's first golf course. *Golf Course Architecture*. https://www.golfcoursearchitecture.net/content/new-hilton-resort-includes-tibets-first-golf-course

ESPN. (2017, January 23). China swings back at golf, shutting down 111 courses. https://www.espn.com/golf/story/_/id/18536868/china-cracks-golf-closes-111-courses

Forward Group. (2011). *China golf industry report*. https://www.scmp.com/news/china/policies-politics/article/2064613/more-100-chinese-golf-courses-ordered-shut-graft

France-Presse, A. (2017, January 23). More than 100 Chinese golf courses ordered shut in graft. *South China Morning Post*. https://www.scmp.com/news/china/policies-politics/article/2064613/more-100-chinese-golf-courses-ordered-shut-graft

Horwitz, J. (2016, March 21). *Golf is now mandatory at a Chinese elementary school*. Quartz. https://qz.com/640572/for-one-public-school-in-shanghai-golf-is-a-mandatory-course/

Kershaw, T. (2018, October 27). In China, golf has come to encapsulate a country grappling with its own identity. *Independent*. https://www.independent.co.uk/sport/golf/wgc-hsbc-china-golf-courses-sheshan-pga-tour-country-clubs-a8604211.html

KPMG. (2014). *From North Cape to Cape Town: Golf course development cost survey 2014 in Europe, Middle East and Africa*. https://www.eigca.org/uploads/documents/originals/KPMG%20Cost%20Survey.pdf

Krich, J. (2003, November 08). Green opium addiction. *The Wall Street Journal*. https://www.wsj.com/articles/SB106996501362118300

Marketing to China. (2018, August 22). *The massive growth of golf industry in China*. https://www.marketingtochina.com/massive-growth-golf-industry-china/

National Public Radio (NPR). (2017, June 23). *China's government tightens its grip on golf, shuts down courses*. https://www.npr.org/sections/parallels/2017/06/23/534052842/chinas-government-tightens-its-grip-on-golf-shuts-down-courses

Ross, E. (2017, March 30). *Xi Jinping's 'war on golf' could leave Donald Trump with no sports buddy*. Newsweek. https://www.newsweek.com/xi-jinping-donald-trump-golf-meeting-mar-lago-china-576636

Shao, X. (2013). Reflection on development process of Chinese golf. In *Conference Paper, International Workshop on Computer Science in Sports (IWCSS)* (pp. 52–56).

Sina Magazine. (2018, October 25). *China's 2017~18 Top-10 golf course list*. (in Chinese language). http://sports.sina.com.cn/golf/industry/2018-10-25/doc-ifxeuwws7807742.shtml

Sirak, R. (2008, July 13). Ready to shine. *Golf Digest*. https://www.golfdigest.com/story/gw20080718sirak?currentPage=1

Veblen, T. (1899). *The theory of the leisure class*. Macmillan.

Wang, L. (2011). Research about golf in China's future development. In International Conference on Advances in Education and Management (ISAEBD) (ed.), *Advances in education and management* (pp. 564–569). Springer.

Wu, H., & Ai, C. (2016, December). Synthesizing the effects of experiential quality, excitement, equity, experiential satisfaction on experiential loyalty for the golf industry: The case of Hainan island. *Journal of Hospitality and Tourism Management*, *29*, 41–59.

Zhang, Y., Deng, J., Majumdar, S., & Zheng, B. (2009). Globalization of lifestyle: Golfing in China. In H. Lange & L. Meier (Eds.), *The new middle classes: Globalizing lifestyles, consumerism and environmental concern* (pp. 143–158). Springer.

Zhang, C., Omar, M., & Tiandra, N. (2016, March). An investigation of key market growth factors that influence the "luxurisation" of golf industry in China. *Journal of Business*, *1*(2), 20–28.

Zhou, X. (2014). Compatibility of golf culture with Chinese culture and suggesting ways to promote its development. *International Journal of Liberal Arts and Social Science*, *2*(4), 75–81.

Chapter 11

Challenges in Embracing Digital Payments: Insights From Street Vendors Across Different Tourists' Destinations of Odisha

Smruti Rekha Sahoo[a], *Sweta Leena Hota*[b] *and Alaka Panda*[c]

[a]Samanta Chandra Sekhar Autonomous College, India
[b]Kalinga Institute of Industrial Technology, India
[c]Biju Pattnaik Degree College of Science and Education, India

Abstract

With more and more people moving to the digital payment system, many populations are yet to adopt this system in both urban and rural areas and urban street vendors being one of them. Street vendors play a vital role in the economy, providing essential goods and services to urban populations. However, the penetration of digital payment systems within this segment remains uneven and presents barriers that hinder the widespread adoption. This research aims to identify and analyze the challenges faced by street vendors at different tourist locations of Odisha in integrating digital payment methods to its transactions. A structured questionnaire-based survey was conducted across key urban tourists' destinations like Bhubaneswar, Cuttack, and Puri in Odisha with a sample size of 220 street vendors. The study utilizes a combination of descriptive statistics and logistic regression to analyze the collected data, providing insights into the demographic characteristics of street vendors and the extent to which barriers impact their adoption of digital payment systems.

Keywords: Barriers; digital payment; transformation; tourists' destination; perception

Economics and Tourism, 181–191

doi:10.1108/978-1-83662-916-020251012

Introduction

India has been undergoing a significant transformation in its payment landscape with a rapid shift toward the digital payment system. The proliferation of smartphones has acted as catalysts for change. The sudden announcement of the withdrawal of high-denomination currency in 2016 led to the exploration of digital payment options. Further, the use of digital payment systems gained momentum during the spread of COVID-19, where contactless transactions were the need to curb the spread of the virus. During this period, people turned to online shopping, digital wallets, and Unified Payments Interface (UPI)-based transactions for their everyday needs, strengthening the foundation of India's digital payment ecosystem. Moreover, online shopping platforms often incentivize digital transactions and customers prefer the convenience of digital payment methods.

As per RBI data (PwC, 2023, p. 9), there has been an increase of more than 500% in the increase of digital payments by merchants from the period 2019–2021. The introduction of UPI has become a game changer in the Indian digital payment system, as it allows users to link multiple bank accounts to a single mobile application, facilitating seamless transfers and payments. Apps like Google Pay, PhonePe, Paytm, and others have gained widespread acceptance, as these platforms also allow users to store money digitally and make transactions at various outlets, online merchants, and even for utility bill payments. As per RBI records (PwC, 2023, p. 9), during the same period, that is, 2019–2021, the UPI payments increased by 1,200%. The Indian government has been actively promoting digital payments as a part of its push for a cashless economy by introducing schemes and incentives like cashback offers, discounts, and other promotions to encourage digital transactions. This has led to the adoption of digital payment systems by the informal sector as well. Adoption of the digital payment system by street vendors also contributes to financial inclusion. Moreover, it also reduces the risk of handling and storing physical cash. It is also very convenient, as it facilitates quick transactions.

It is important to note that the progress in digital payment adoption by street vendors varies across different regions and cities. Despite the evident benefits, many urban street vendors in India have not been able to adopt the digital payment system. The reasons behind nonadoption are many, starting from lack of awareness to reluctance to change, too much dependency on cash, etc. In the state of Odisha as well, the penetration of digital payment system has been rampant; however, a large number of street vendors, in spite of the benefits, have not been able to switch to the digital payment system. This study is an attempt to study the different barriers that obstruct the adoption of the digital payment system by urban street vendors across multiple leisure destinations in Odisha.

Review of Literature

Almousa (2013) studied the tangible barriers influencing consumers in adopting e-commerce in Saudi Arabia, where no after-sale support, followed by unavailability of international shipping, lack of previous experience, and website language were identified as major barriers, and advised that the government should take necessary measures for its redressal. The attitude of street shops toward digital payments and receipts was done post demonetization (Pal et al., 2018), and the results reveal that the choice of payment or receipt method was dependent on customer preference. Customers' unwillingness to adopt cashless payment methods impacted shopkeepers' technology adoption decisions. The studies also reveal that the digital payment method option increased significantly due to demonetization; however, it significantly went down after the introduction of new notes by RBI. A study on the possible reasons for the low level of digital payment adoption among merchants in Jaipur (Ligon et al., 2019) reveals that adoption is both feasible and inexpensive, and lower adoption results from the demand-side factors like customers unwilling to pay digitally and concerns related to tax liability or taxes from the customers side, which prevent the adoption of digital payment methods among merchants. In order to evaluate the factors influencing the adoption of digital payment applications by street vendors (Prasad et al., 2023), the PLS technique was used, and the results revealed digital literacy strongly influenced the behavioral intention among street vendors. Factors like privacy risk and security had little significance in influencing behavioral intention, as the street vendors are unaware of it and exposed them to fraud and data leaks.

Research Gap

The above literature reveals that there have been many studies on the barriers to the digital payment method system across the world, but very few studies have been made on the Indian context, therefore making it a relevant topic to study. Furthermore, studies that analyze the postdemonetization surge in digital transactions have not extensively examined the long-term sustainability of digital payment adoption among street vendors.

Objectives of the Study

The main objective behind this study is to identify the barriers that prevent the street vendors at travel destinations like Bhubaneswar, Cuttack, and Puri of Odisha from adopting the digital payment system. The research will delve into underlying factors contributing to these barriers.

Scope of the Study

The study will primarily focus on the selected points of interest within the state of Odisha. It shall target those street vendors who operate in urban areas, including markets, streets, and public spaces within the state. By doing so, the research aims to capture the experiences and perspectives of individuals directly involved in informal street vending activities.

Limitations of the Study

The sample taken in the study is 220, which may be considered relatively small. This could limit the generalizability of the findings to the broader population of street vendors. Moreover, the sampling process is only from specific geographic locations, which could skew the results and not capture the diversity of street vendors in Odisha. It is also possible that the respondents have provided socially desirable responses, especially when reporting their use of the digital payment system. The study may not have included all relevant variables that could influence the adoption of the digital payment system by street vendors. The measurement of trust and security is subjective in nature and could vary among respondents.

Hypothesis of the Study

H_0. Barriers have no significant impact in the adoption of the digital payment system by urban street vendors.

H_1. Barriers significantly impact the adoption of digital payment system by urban street vendors.

Research Methodology

This study is based on primary data where a structured questionnaire has been prepared and the responses have been collected from a total number of 220 respondents. The sample consisted of street vendors who sell convenience goods daily in urban areas of tourists' interest like Bhubaneswar (75), Cuttack (73), and Puri (72) of Odisha, out of which 123 are male respondents and 97 are females (Fig. 11.1). The sample was selected using a cluster sampling method to find suitable respondents at random. In order to know the basic characteristics of

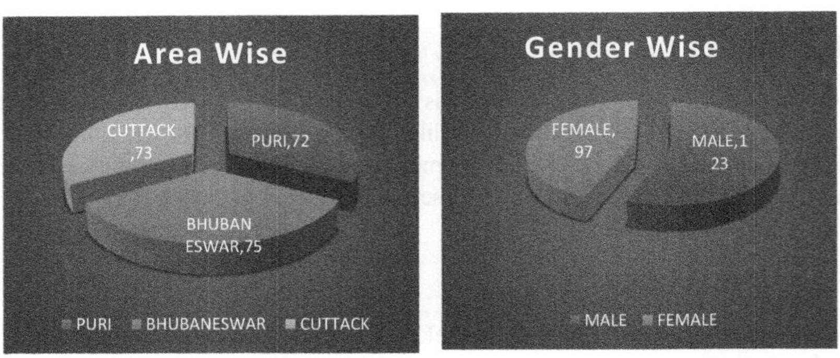

Fig. 11.1. Sample Size—Area Wise and Gender Wise. *Source:* Primary Data.

each predictor, descriptive statistics have been done. The barriers were identified from existing literature. Further, logistic regression has been used to predict the extent to which the barriers impact the adoption of the digital payment system. The data collected has been analyzed using JASP 0.18.0.0.

Analysis and Interpretation

To proceed with analysis, first, the reliability of the data was tested with Cronbach's alpha, and the value is 0.828. The general rule of thumb is that a Cronbach's alpha of 0.70 is good; thus, these data may be considered reliable for further analysis.

From the review of literature, it may be ascertained that variables like age, educational qualification, having a smartphone, necessary infrastructure (internet connectivity and affordability), ease of use, security, and trust have a role in the adoption of the digital payment system by street vendors of Odisha.

For a better understanding of different variables, descriptive statistics have been done, giving us more information on different measures of central tendency and skewness (Table 11.1). The maximum and minimum value ranges between 1 and 5, as the questionnaire contained close-ended questions to be answered in the Likert scale (Table 11.1). The skewness value is within the range of -1 and 1 whereas the kurtosis value ranges between -2 and $+2$ which may be considered a normal distribution (Hair et al., 2010).

In order to assess the extent of impact of independent variables like age, gender, education level, smartphone ownership, necessary infrastructure, ease of use, trust, and security on adoption of digital payment by street vendors, the logistic regression technique is used.

The model summary in logistic regression (Table 11.2) provides key information about the overall information and the fit of the regression model. In this case, the deviance value of alternate hypothesis (H_1) is 82.057, which is lower as compared to the null hypothesis (H_0) of 259.758, suggesting that the H_1 model provides a better fit to the data. The Akaike Information Criterion (AIC) is a measure of a model's goodness of fit, adjusted for the number of predictors, and, in this case, H_1 model is 98.057 lower than H_0 261.758, indicating a better fit model. Similarly, the Bayesian Information Criterion (BIC) value in H_1 (125.206) is lower than H_0 (265.152), indicating a better fit model. The chi square value 177.701 X^2) suggests that the predictors in the model are related to the adoption of the digital payment system. The p-value of 0.001 indicates that the model is statistically significant. McFadden R square, Nagelkerke R square, Tjur R square, and Cox and Snell R square are measures to explain the proportion of variance in the model. Thus, all values (0.684, 0.800, 0.745, and 0.554) indicate moderate to strong explanatory power.

In logistic regression, the coefficients represent the log-odds of the probability of the event occurring.

Table 11.1. Descriptive Statistics.

Statistics	Gender	Smart Phone Ownership	Age	Education	Infrastructure	Ease of Use	Trust & Security	Digital Adaptation
Valid	220	220	220	220	220	220	220	220
Missing	0	0	0	0	0	0	0	0
Mode	1	2	2.016	2	2.999	2.005	2	2
Median	1	2	3	3	3	3	3	2
Mean	1.455	1.545	2.368	2.836	2.841	2.814	2.758	1.723
Std. deviation	0.499	0.499	1.246	1.089	0.925	1.277	0.905	0.449
Skewness	0.184	−0.612	−0.67	0.113	0.089	0.089	0.516	−1.002
Std. error of skewness	0.164	0.164	0.164	0.164	0.164	0.164	0.164	0.164
Kurtosis	−1.984	−1.64	−0.751	−0.75	−1.123	−1.13	−0.825	1.002
Std. error of Kurtosis	0.327	0.327	0.327	0.327	0.327	0.327	0.327	0.327
Shapiro-Wilk	0.633	0.605	0.902	0.893	0.902	0.902	0.871	0.56
P value of Shapiro-Wilk	<0.001	0.009	<0.001	<0.001	<0.001	<0.001	<0.001	<0.001
Minimum	1	1	1	1	1	1	1	0
Maximum	2	2	5	5	5	5	5	1

Source: Primary Data.

Table 11.2. Model Summary and Coefficients of Logistic Regression.

Model	Deviance	AIC	BIC	df	X^2	p	McFadden R^2	Nagelkerke R^2	Tjur R^2	Cox and Snell R^2
H_0	259.758	261.758	265.152	219	—	—	—	—	—	—
H_1	82.057	98.057	125.206	212	177.701	<0.001	0.684	0.8	0.745	0.554

Coefficients for Logistic Regression

Predictor	Estimate	Standard Error	z	Wald Statistic	df	P
(Intercept)	−6.91	3.323	−2.079	4.324	1	0.038
Age	−0.494	0.512	−0.965	0.932	1	0.334
Gender (2)	0.652	0.674	0.967	0.934	1	0.334
Education	1.32	0.393	3.364	11.263	1	0.001
Smart phone ownership (2)	3.3	0.654	5.041	25.416	1	0.001
Infrastructure	0.246	0.519	0.479	0.229	1	0.632
Ease of use	1.536	0.455	3.375	10.723	1	0.001
Trust & security	0.45	0.607	0.742	0.551	1	0.458

Source: Primary Data.

The interpretation of the coefficients is as follows:

- Age (−6.910): The negative coefficient for age suggests that as the age of a street vendor increases, the odds of adopting digital payments decrease. However, the *p*-value of 0.038 indicates that this relationship is statistically significant, meaning that age has a significant impact on adoption.
- Gender (−0.494): The negative coefficient for gender implies that the female gender is less likely to adopt digital payments than the other. However, the *p*-value of 0.334 is above the typical threshold of 0.05, indicating that this effect is not statistically significant. Thus, gender does not have a significant impact on digital payment adoption in this model.
- Education (0.652): The positive coefficient for education suggests that street vendors with higher levels of education are more likely to adopt digital payments. However, with a *p*-value of 0.334, this result is not statistically significant. Therefore, education does not significantly affect adoption in this model.
- Smartphone Ownership (1.320): The positive coefficient for smartphone ownership suggests that vendors who own smartphones are more likely to adopt digital payments. The *p*-value of 0.001 indicates that this effect is statistically significant. Hence, smartphone ownership does significantly impact digital payment adoption.
- Infrastructure (3.300): The positive coefficient for infrastructure suggests that better infrastructure (possibly referring to internet access or payment system availability) increases the likelihood of adopting digital payments. With a *p*-value of 0.001, this is statistically significant, meaning infrastructure is a significant factor in the adoption of digital payments.
- Ease of Use (0.246): The positive coefficient indicates that vendors who find digital payments easier to use are more likely to adopt them. However, the *p*-value of 0.632 is high, indicating that this factor is not statistically significant in influencing adoption.
- Trust (1.536): The positive coefficient for trust suggests that higher trust in digital payment systems increases the likelihood of adoption. The *p*-value of 0.001 indicates that trust is statistically significant and has a strong impact on adoption.
- Security (0.450): The positive coefficient for security suggests that vendors who feel that digital payments are secure are more likely to adopt them. However, the *p*-value of 0.458 is high, indicating that security does not have a significant effect on adoption in this model.

Summary of Findings

- Significant factors: Age, smartphone ownership, infrastructure, and trust are significant predictors of digital payment adoption among street vendors, with *p*-values of 0.038, 0.001, 0.001, and 0.001, respectively.
- Nonsignificant factors: Gender, education, ease of use, and security have *p*-values greater than 0.05, meaning they do not significantly affect the adoption of digital payments in this model.

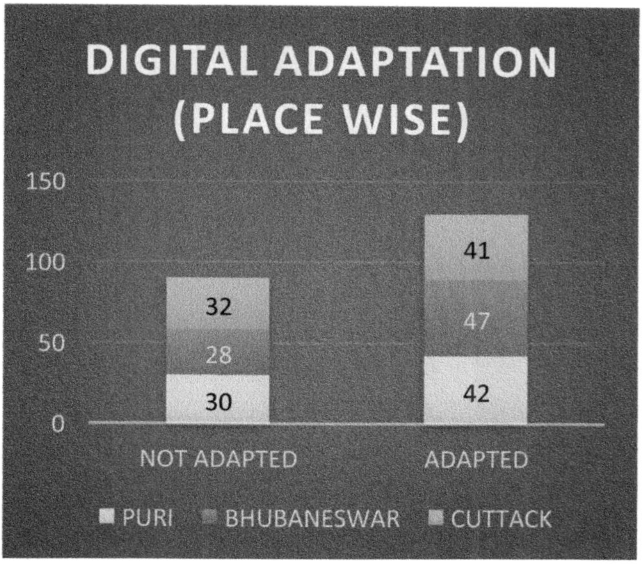

Fig. 11.2. Digital Adaption by Respondents—Place Wise. *Source:* Primary Data.

It may also be noted from the above (Fig. 11.2) that out of 75 street vendors surveyed in Bhubaneswar, 47 were found to have adopted the digital payment system, followed by 41 in Cuttack and 42 in Puri, respectively. In all three places, the male respondents were more digitally inclusive as compared to female counterparts (Fig. 11.3).

Conclusion

Overall, the logistic regression analysis provides insights into the factors influencing the adoption of digital payment systems by street vendors in Odisha. Based on the model, the significant barriers to adoption of digital payments among street vendors appear to be related to age, smartphone ownership, infrastructure availability, and trust. These factors should be prioritized in efforts to promote digital payment adoption in this context, while other factors like gender, education, ease of use, and security may not have a strong impact according to this analysis. The logistic regression analysis in this study aligns with the UTAUT framework, as variables like infrastructure and trust significantly impact digital payment adoption. Additionally, social influence plays a role, as indicated in past studies where customers' preference for cash transactions deterred vendors from adopting digital payments (Pal et al., 2018).

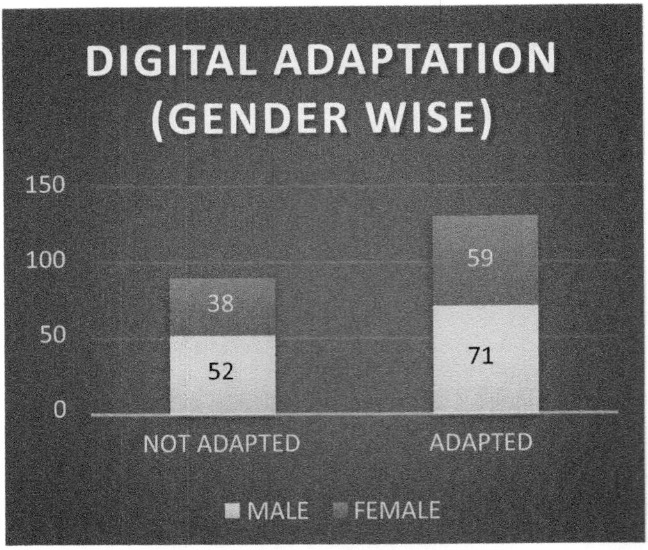

Fig. 11.3. Digital Adaptation by Respondents—Gender Wise.
Source: Primary Data.

The adoption of digital payments among street vendors across various tourist destinations in Odisha represents both opportunities and challenges. While digital transactions offer potential for greater financial inclusion, increased convenience, and enhanced customer satisfaction, many vendors face obstacles such as limited digital literacy, inadequate infrastructure, and concerns over transaction security. In order to make India digitally inclusive, it is important that digitalization penetrates to the grassroots level. It is essential to recognize the barriers that prevent the adoption of the digital payment system by street vendors across different parts of the country and overcome them through a collaborative effort involving government bodies, financial institutions, technology providers, and the street vendor community itself. Tailoring solutions to the specific needs and context of street vendors will enhance the effectiveness of these efforts. By addressing these challenges, the benefits of a cashless economy can be more widely realized, empowering street vendors to thrive in an increasingly digital marketplace.

Acknowledgment

This study is a part of Minor Research Project sponsored by OURIIP–2022, Odisha State Higher Education Council (OSHEC).

References

Almousa, M. (2013). Barriers to e-commerce adoption: Consumers' perspectives from a developing country. *iBusiness*, *05*(02), 65–71. https://doi.org/10.4236/ib.2013.52008

Ligon, E., Malick, B., Sheth, K., & Trachtman, C. (2019). What explains low adoption of digital payment technologies? Evidence from small-scale merchants in Jaipur, India. *PLoS One*, *14*(7), e0219450. https://doi.org/10.1371/journal.pone.0219450

Pal, J., Chandra, P., Kameswaran, V., Parameshwar, A., Joshi, S., & Johri, A. (2018). Digital payment and its discontents: Street shops and the Indian government's push for cashless transactions. In *Proceedings of the 2018 CHI conference on human factors in computing systems* (pp. 1–13). https://doi.org/10.1145/3173574.3173803

Prasad, S., Sharma, Y., & Suri, A. (2023). Dynamics of technology adoption during street vendors acceptance of digital payment apps: An extension of UTAUT2 using PLS-SEM. *Vision: The Journal of Business Perspective*. https://doi.org/10.1177/09722629231187260

PwC. (2023). The Indian payments handbook – 2022–2027. https://www.pwc.in/assets/pdfs/the-indian-payments-handbook-2022-2027.pdf

Chapter 12

The Impact of Tourism Revenues on Economic Growth in Türkiye

Sidar Atalay Şimşek

Batman University, Türkiye

Abstract

In this chapter, the relationship between economic growth and tourism revenues in Türkiye between 2004 and 2023 is investigated by econometric analysis. The Johansen cointegration test reveals the existence of a long-run cointegration relationship between the variables. The full modified ordinary least square (FMOLS) test reveals that the effect of tourism revenues on economic growth is statistically significant. A 1% increase in tourism revenues increases economic growth by approximately 0.75%. According to the dynamic ordinary least square (DOLS) result, the effect of tourism revenues on economic growth is statistically significant. A 1% increase in tourism revenue increases economic growth by approximately 0.89%. Finally, according to the canonical cointegrating regression (CCR) parameter estimation result, the effect of tourism revenues on economic growth is statistically significant. A 1% increase in tourism revenues increases economic growth by approximately 0.78%. It is possible to say that the results of the three parameter estimations are similar. According to the joint results of the FMOLS, DOLS, and CCR methods, tourism revenues increase economic growth in Türkiye.

Keywords: Economic growth; tourism; time series; Türkiye; cointegration test

Introduction

Economic growth is one of the most important indicators that increase the welfare level of a country. In this respect, there is an increasing number of studies

Economics and Tourism, 193–202

Published under exclusive licence by Emerald Publishing Limited
doi:10.1108/978-1-83662-916-020251013

investigating the contributions of different sectors to analyze the dynamics of economic growth. The tourism sector is one of the most strategically important sectors for many countries due to its potential for economic growth, both in terms of foreign exchange earnings and employment generation advantages. Türkiye's geopolitical position, having bays on the seashore, having clean beaches, and experiencing all four seasons, the tourism sector, which is called the "chimneyless industry," is very important for Türkiye. The number of international tourists visiting Türkiye between 2004 and 2023, and the tourism revenue ($1,000), and the average expenditure per visitor ($) are shown in Table 12.1. According to the table, except for the COVID-19 pandemic period that affected the whole world, it is observed that both the number of tourists arriving and tourism revenues have increased year by year.

Table 12.1. Number of Tourist Arrivals to Türkiye, Tourism Revenues, and Average Expenditure by Years (2004–2023).

	Total		
Years	**Number of Tourists**	**Tourism Revenue (1,000 $)**	**Average Expenditure ($)**
2004	20,753,734	17,076,607	843
2005	25,045,142	20,322,111	842
2006	23,924,023	18,593,951	803
2007	27,239,630	20,942,500	770
2008	31,137,774	25,415,067	820
2009	31,759,816	25,064,482	783
2010	32,997,308	24,930,997	755
2011	36,769,039	28,115,692	778
2012	37,715,225	35,717,337	980
2013	39,860,771	40,186,327	1,024
2014	41,627,246	41,316,834	998
2015	41,114,069	37,700,923	906
2016	30,906,680	26,539,007	846
2017	37,969,824	31,253,835	809
2018	46,112,592	35,920,910	787
2019	51,747,199	42,851,778	826
2020	15,971,201	15,169,371	958
2021	30,038,961	30,309,722	1,032
2022	51,387,513	49,857,030	971
2023	56,693,837	55,874,176	979

Source: Turkish Statistical Institute, Central Bank, Ministry of Culture and Tourism, 2024.

The tourism sector has both direct and indirect effects on the Turkish economy. This study investigates the nature of the relationship between tourism revenue and economic growth and the existence of a cointegration relationship between these two variables. The study aims to contribute to similar studies in the literature with the most recent data and to better understand the effects of Türkiye's tourism policies on economic growth. In this context, the findings of the study provide important implications for both policy-makers and sectoral actors.

Literature

According to Table 12.2, which summarizes the literature on the relationship between economic growth and tourism revenues in Türkiye, it can be stated that

Table 12.2. Literature Review.

Author(s)	Period	Variables	Method	Results
Kasman and Kasman (2004)	1963–2002	Tourism revenue, economic growth	Granger causality	Causality is found from tourism income to economic growth
Yıldırım and Öcal (2004)	1962–2002	Tourism revenue, economic growth	VAR analysis	Long-run causality is found from tourism income to economic growth
Bahar (2006)	1963–2004	Tourism, economic growth	VAR analysis	A positive long-run relationship was found between the variables
Yavuz (2006)	1992–2004	Tourism revenue, economic growth	Granger causality	No causality was found
Yalçınkaya and Karabulut (2017)	1965–2006	Tourism revenue, economic growth	Granger causality	No causality was found
Aslan (2008)	1992–2007	Tourism, economic growth	Johansen cointegration, Granger causality	A long-run causal relationship was found between the variables

(Continued)

Table 12.2. *(Continued)*

Author(s)	Period	Variables	Method	Results
Yıldırım et all. (2017)	2005–2015	Tourism, inflation	Johansen cointegration	There is no relationship between the variables in the short run, but there is a relationship in the long run
Dilber and Kılıç (2018)	1995–2016	Tourism revenue, economic growth	Granger causality, VAR analysis	A positive long-run relationship was found between the variables
Altıner (2019)	1969–2018	Tourism, economic growth	ARDL	A positive long-run relationship was found between the variables
Sarıdoğan (2020)	1987–2018	Tourism revenue, economic growth, labor, and capital	Zivot Andrews Testi, Gregory-Hansen cointegration	There is a statistically significant positive long-run relationship between the variables
Özkurt and Bilgir (2022)	1980–2020	Tourism revenue, economic growth	ARDL	A positive long-run relationship was found between the variables
Sari and Aydın (2022)	1998–2021	Economic growth, tourist arrivals and exchange rate	ARDL	A positive long-run relationship was found between the variables
Ülker (2023)	1995–2020	Tourism, economic growth, and trade openness	ARDL	In the long run, the effect of tourism and trade openness on economic growth is positive and significant

Source: Compiled by the author.

the studies differ from each other in terms of periods, variables, and econometric methods used.

Most of the studies in the literature summary concluded that there is a positive and statistically significant relationship between tourism revenues and economic growth. The results obtained from this study, which aims to determine the relationship between economic growth and tourism revenues for Türkiye between 2004 and 2023 are consistent with the results obtained from the studies in the literature. Both the results obtained from the studies in the literature and the results obtained from this study are consistent with the views on the relationship and impact between tourism and economic growth predicted by the theory.

Data Set and Model

In this chapter, which examines the impact of tourism revenues on economic growth in Türkiye between 2004 and 2023, economic growth is selected as the dependent variable, and tourism revenues are included in the model as the explanatory variable. Data on the variables are obtained from the World Bank database. The analysis was carried out by taking the natural logarithms of the variables used in the model. Table 12.3 shows the definitions of the variables included in the model.

The regression equation of the model is as follows:

$$GDP_t = \beta_0 + \beta_1 TOUR_t + u_t \tag{12.1}$$

According to the equation, GDP is the dependent variable of the model, TOUR is the independent variable of the model, and u_t is the error term of the model. Descriptive statistics of the variables used in the model are presented in Table 12.4.

Methods and Findings

In the analysis, the stationarity of the variables was tested first. Because non-stationarity of the series will prevent obtaining accurate results as it will cause the problem of spurious regression. Therefore, the unit root test of the variables was performed with the Phillips–Perron test, which is the most preferred test for testing the stationarity of time series. The results are shown in Table 12.5. According to the results of the unit root test, both GDP, which

Table 12.3. Definition of Variables Used in the Model.

Variable	Definition
GDP	Gross domestic product per capita ($ in 2015 constant prices)
TOUR	Tourism revenue ($)

Source: Created by the author.

Table 12.4. Descriptive Statistics for Variables.

	GDP	TOUR
Mean	8.11E+11	31,157,933
Median	7.96E+11	29,212,707
Maximum	1.26E+12	55,874,176
Minimum	4.82E+11	15,169,371
Std. Dev.	2.36E+11	11,102,490
Skewness	0.330078	0.533391
Kurtosis	1.919996	2.526799
Jarque-Bera	1.335179	1.134951
Prob.	0.512943	0.566955

Source: Created by the author.

Table 12.5. Phillips–Perron Unit Root Test.

PP	Constant Prob.	Constant and Trend Prob.
Level		
GDP	0.912	0.320
TOUR	0.287	0.190
First Difference		
lnGDP	0.007**	0.028**
lnTOUR	0.000***	0.000***

Source: Created by the author.

Note: ***, ** denotes significance at 1% and 5% levels, respectively.

represents the dependent variable, and TOUR, which represents tourism revenue, were found to be I(1), that is, stationary in difference.

For the GDP series, the null hypothesis "the series has a unit root" cannot be rejected for both the models with constant and the models with constant and trend. Therefore, the series is not stationary at the level. When the first difference of this series is taken, it is concluded that the series is stationary in both fixed and fixed and trended models, that is, it does not have a unit root. When the unit root result for the TOUR series is analyzed, it is concluded that the series has a unit root at the level, but after taking the first difference, the series becomes stationary in both the fixed and fixed and trended models, that is, it does not have a unit root.

Before performing cointegration analysis, the appropriate lag length should be determined. The appropriate lag length for Table 12.6 model is found to be 1.

Table 12.6. VAR Model Determination of Lag Length.

Lag	LogL	LR	FPE	AIC	SC	HQ
0	−2.336131	NA	0.005896	0.542016	0.638590	0.546962
1	28.09191	**49.44557***	**0.000219***	−2.761489	**−2.471768***	−2.746653
2	32.30672	5.795353	0.000220	−2.788339	−2.305471	−2.763613
3	36.56656	4.792324	0.000232	−2.820820*	−2.144805	−2.786202*
4	39.58506	2.641189	0.000310	−2.698133	−1.828970	−2.653624

Source: Created by the author.
Note: *denotes significance of LR, FPE, and SC.

After the unit root test, both variables were found to be stationary at the same degree, and the precondition for cointegration analysis was met. Before proceeding to the co-integration analysis, the appropriate lag length should be determined by constructing the VAR model.

According to Table 12.6, the model selection criteria (LR, FPE-Final Prediction Error, SC-Schwarz Information Criterion) indicate that the optimal lag number is "1." After determining the number of lags, the cointegration relationship was analyzed. The long-run relationship between the variables was investigated by Johansen and Juselius (1990) cointegration test. The results of the Johansen co-integration test are shown in Table 12.7.

According to the trace statistics, it is possible to say that there are at least two cointegrated vectors between economic growth and tourism revenues. Parameter estimation can be done after the cointegrated relationship between the variables. For this reason, the extent to which and in which direction the independent variable, tourism revenues, affects the dependent variable, GDP, will be determined with the help of FMOLS, DOLS, and CCR estimators.

According to the FMOLS result shown in Table 12.8, the effect of tourism revenues on economic growth is statistically significant. A 1% increase in tourism revenues increases economic growth by approximately 0.75%. According to the DOLS result, the effect of tourism revenues on economic growth is statistically significant. A 1% increase in tourism revenue increases economic growth by approximately 0.89%. Finally, according to the CCR parameter estimation result, the effect of tourism revenues on economic growth is statistically

Table 12.7. Johansen-Juselius Cointegration Test Result.

Ho	Eigenvalue	Trace Statistic	0.05 Critical Value	Prob.
$r = 0$	0.694005	31.55635	25.87211	0.008
$r \leq 1$	0.545285	12.60935	12.51798	0.048

Source: Created by the author.

Table 12.8. FMOLS, DOLS, and CCR Cointegration Parameter Estimation Results.

Variable	Coefficient	Std. Error	*t*-Statistic	Prob.
FMOLS				
LNTOUR	0.754177**	0.229853	3.281127	0.0044
C	14.42821	3.959350	3.644085	0.0020
DOLS				
LNTOUR	0.891747**	0.388230	2.296957	0.0404
C	12.07340	6.675198	1.808696	0.0956
CCR				
LNTOUR	0.785041**	0.241430	3.251630	0.0047
C	13.90684	4.148965	3.351882	0.0038

Source: Created by the author.

Note: ** denotes significance at 5% level, respectively.

significant. A 1% increase in tourism revenues increases economic growth by approximately 0.78%. It is possible to say that the results of the three parameter estimations are similar. According to the joint results of the FMOLS, DOLS, and CCR methods, tourism revenues increase economic growth in Türkiye.

Conclusion

Tourism is defined as a set of economic and social activities that enable people to travel from one place to another for different purposes. The tourism sector not only creates economic vitality in the places visited but also supports economic growth through both direct and indirect effects in many areas such as employment, income distribution, foreign exchange inflows, and infrastructure investments. In this respect, tourism stands out as an important growth engine in developing countries.

In this chapter, which examines the relationship between economic growth and tourism in Türkiye between 2004 and 2023, the effect of tourism revenues on economic growth is statistically significant according to the FMOLS results. A 1% increase in tourism revenues increases economic growth by approximately 0.75%. According to the DOLS result, the effect of tourism revenues on economic growth is statistically significant. A 1% increase in tourism revenue increases economic growth by approximately 0.89%. Finally, according to the CCR parameter estimation result, the effect of tourism revenues on economic growth is statistically significant. A 1% increase in tourism revenues increases economic growth by approximately 0.78%. It is possible to say that the results of the three parameter estimations are similar. According to the joint results of the

FMOLS, DOLS, and CCR methods, tourism revenues increase economic growth in Türkiye.

The statistically significant effect of tourism revenues on economic growth reveals that the tourism sector has a strategic importance for Türkiye. Therefore, tourism should be considered not only as a foreign exchange earner but also as a tool to support sustainable economic growth. Türkiye, with its natural beauties, historical and cultural heritage, and geographical advantages, has always needed comprehensive and multifaceted policy steps to achieve a more competitive position in the tourism sector on a global scale. Some policy recommendations can be listed as follows. First of all, it is critical to increase diversity in tourism and keep tourism alive throughout the year. Increasing Türkiye's investments in different types of tourism will free the sector from seasonal dependency. Moreover, it is possible to attract more tourists from new target markets through strategic steps such as strengthening international promotion campaigns and visa facilitation. In this process, infrastructure investments and improving the quality of tourism services are also essential for sustainable growth. In addition, adopting environmental and sustainable tourism policies will allow Türkiye to increase tourism revenues while preserving its natural and cultural heritage. Investments in the training of tourism workers and service quality will also contribute significantly to the sector in the long run. Thus, Türkiye will be able to further strengthen its contribution to economic growth by increasing both the number of tourists and per capita tourism income.

References

Altıner, A. (2019). Turizm Ve Ekonomik Büyüme İlişkisi: Türkiye Örneği (1969–2018). *Anadolu İktisat Ve İşletme Dergisi, Sayı, 3*(2), 114–133. https://Dergipark.Org.Tr/Tr/Download/Article File/219443. Erişim Tarihi May 22, 2022.

Aslan, A. (2008). *Türkiye'de Ekonomik Büyüme Ve Turizm İlişkisi Üzerine Ekonometrik Analiz.* https://dergipark.org.tr/tr/pub/erusosbilder/issue/23757/253190. Erişim Tarihi May 09, 2023.

Bahar, O. (2006). Turizm Sektörünün Türkiye'nin Ekonomik Büyümesi Üzerindeki Etkisi: VAR Analizi Yaklaşımı. *Yönetim Ve Ekonomi Dergisi, 13*(2), 137–150. https://web.archive.org/web/20171202064303id_/.http://www2.bayar.edu.tr/yonetimekonomi/dergi/pdf/C13S22006/OB.pdf. Erişim Tarihi March 06, 2023.

Dilber, İ., & Kılıç, J. (2018). Türkiye'de turizm gelirleri ile ekonomik büyüme ilişkisi: Engle Granger eşbütünleşme testi ve VAR model. *TESAM Akademi Dergisi, 5*(2), 95–118.

Johansen, S., & Juselius, K. (1990). Maximum likelihood estimation and ınference on cointegration with applications to the demand for money. *Oxford Bulletin of Economics and Statistics, 52*(2), 169–210.

Kasman, A., & Kasman, S. K. (2004). Turizm gelirleri ve ekonomik büyüme arasındaki eşbütünleşme ve nedensellik ilişkisi. *Iktisat Isletme ve Finans, 19*(220), 122–131.

Özkurt, İ. C. & Bilgir, B. (2022). Türkiye'de Turizm Gelirleri Ve Ekonomik Büyüme İlişkisi: Ardl Yaklaşımı . *Uluslararası Yönetim İktisat Ve İşletme Dergisi, 18*(1),

277–303. https://doi.org/10.17130/ijmeb.960782. https://dergipark.org.tr/tr/pub/ijmeb/issue/69067/960782. Erişim Tarihi December 20, 2023.

Sari, S., & Aydin, S. (2022). Turizm-Ekonomik Büyüme İlişkisi: Türkiye Ekonomisi Üzerine Bir Uygulama. *Çukurova 8th Nternatıonal Scıentıfıc Researches Conference, 15*(17), 320–337.

Sarıdoğan, H. Ö. (2020). Turizm gelirlerinin ekonomik büyümeye etkisi: Türkiye için yapısal kırılmalı birim kök ve eşbütünleşme analizi. *Eskişehir Osmangazi Üniversitesi İİBF Dergisi, 15*(3), 829–848.

Ülker, B. (2023). Ekonomik büyüme, turizm ve ticari açıklık ilişkisi: Türkiye örneği. *Kastamonu Üniversitesi İktisadi ve İdari Bilimler Fakültesi Dergisi, 25*(1), 254–270.

Yalçınkaya, Ö., & Karabulut, K. (2017). Turizm Gelirlerinin Ekonomik Büyüme Üzerinde Etkileri; Türkiye Üzerine Dönemsel Ve Yapısal Kırılmalı Bir Zaman Serisi Analizi (1965-2016). *Journal of International Social Research, 10*(52).

Yavuz, N. Ç (2006). Türkiye'de turizm gelirlerinin ekonomik büyümeye etkisinin testi: Yapisal kirilma ve nedensellik analizi. *Doğuş Üniversitesi Dergisi, 7*(2), 162–171.

Yıldırım, J., & Öcal, N. (2004). Tourism and economic growth in Türkiye. *Ekonomik Yaklaşım, 15*(52–53), 131–141.

Yıldırım, B. I., Yıldırım, F., & Gülmez, M. (2017). Türkiye'de Enflasyon Ve Turizm Gelirleri İlişkisi Üzerine Ekonometrik Bir Analiz. *Uluslararası İktisadi Ve İdari Bilimler Dergisi, 3*(1), 69–81. https://dergipark.org.tr/tr/pub/uiibd/issue/27470/268548. Erişim Tarihi May 15, 2023.

Chapter 13

Impact of Social Media on Tourism Demand

Sana Muhammad Tariq[a], *Yasir Rasool*[a], *Nohman Khan*[b] *and Gobinathan Manickam*[b]

[a]Asia Pacific University of Technology and Innovation (APU), Malaysia
[b]The Millennium Universal College, Faisalabad Campus, Pakistan

Abstract

Social media has transformed the tourism industry fundamentally by impacting traveler behavior, tourism demand, and destination marketing. Viral content that made destinations famous on platforms like TikTok and Instagram helped the growth of tourism. Travel trends are now shaped by user-generated content (UGC), influencer marketing, and data-driven strategies. Nevertheless, social media has certain drawbacks, like misinformation, overtourism, and privacy concerns. This chapter studies the transformative power of social media in the field of tourism with a perspective on both risks and opportunities and provides suggestions for sustainable strategies for the destination.

Keywords: Social media tourism; destination marketing; user-generated content; influencer marketing; overtourism; digital tourism trends

Introduction

Social media has completely altered the tourism and hospitality industry in the past decade. The strategies for marketing, promotion, and experiencing tourism destinations have changed due to the proliferation of digital platforms (Nusair et al., 2019). With social media, travelers can interact with destinations, feel their joy, and influence them through electronic word-of-mouth (eWOM) (Kanje et al., 2020). Traditional marketing methods only allow one-way communication,

Economics and Tourism, 203–218

doi:10.1108/978-1-83662-916-020251014

whereas platforms like Instagram and Facebook offer real-time interaction and content sharing. User-generated content (UGC) in the form of travel blogs, vlogs, or online reviews helps establish the consumer's perception of a destination (Tran & Rudolf, 2022). Additionally, eWOM is now more important for tourists who rely increasingly on other traveler's recommendations and reviews than official tourism promotion (Y.-F. Chen & Law, 2016).

In addition, the viral nature of social media also suggests that social media trends can reach viral levels, which birthed the concept of "viral tourism." Some destinations that were previously not much known suddenly become popular worldwide overnight just because of a post doing rounds on social media (Zhang & Huang, 2024). For instance, social media exposure has resulted in tourism booms for places such as Bali, Santorini, and Iceland, with many economic benefits. However, this sudden influx of tourists has challenges, such as overtourism, environmental degradation, and commercialization of local culture (Utama et al., 2024). Moreover, "Instagrammable" travel has caused overcrowding at some destinations, where tourists choose to take pictures instead of experiencing the culture itself (Karyatun et al., 2021).

Nevertheless, social media is a curated space, and its content raises authenticity and representation issues. Heavily edited images and influencer collaborations that increase a tourism business' digital presence can set unrealistic expectations among travelers (Jani et al., 2024). The phenomenon of "staged tourism" has developed, where destinations or attractions are deliberately created to appear visually appealing on social media at the cost of authenticity (cultural or historical) (Gardiner et al., 2022). In addition, the issue of privacy has grown as businesses become increasingly able to collect user data for personalized marketing campaigns (Yallop et al., 2021). Although it is something that tourists may unknowingly do to help the data collection practices, it brings up questions regarding digital security and consent in the tourism industry.

The adoption of social media by travelers poses challenges regarding their behaviors during travel experiences. Digital engagement in tourism creates stronger travel experiences, yet it produces two problems: "overtourism fatigue" and digital dependency. It is also believed that contemporary travelers dedicate more time to social media content creation than to a cultural exploration of their destinations (Munar & Jacobsen, 2014). Society criticizes this current trend because it reduces genuine travel experiences when people choose visual content instead of genuine social connections with local people. Travelers experience stress alongside unrealistic expectations due to pressure related to producing social media content (Pellegrino et al., 2022), which negatively impacts their satisfaction levels and complete travel experiences.

The power of social media as a marketing tool and branding instrument for tourism continues to grow despite its challenges. Destination marketing organizations (DMOs) and businesses that use social media successfully create high consumer engagement levels while building dedicated customer bases, enabling them to outperform their competitors globally (McKee et al., 2021). The tourism industry can extract maximum social media value through responsible, ethical marketing, adequate privacy protection, and responsible tourism promotion.

The following chapter will explore the complex relationship between social media and tourism, where social media impacts traveler behavior, driven marketing measures, and opportunities and challenges in the tourism environment.

The Evolution of Tourism Marketing in the Digital Era

In the past few decades, tourism marketing has been transformed from traditional to digital. Traditional tourism marketing was driven by print advertisements, television commercials, brochures, and word of mouth (Dolnicar & Ring, 2014). However, the reach of these channels was limited, the costs were high, and considerable time was spent on their distribution and the gathering and feedback of information. As a result, marketers often depended on travel agencies, billboards, and direct mail campaigns to attract tourists.

With digital technology being introduced, the tourism marketing landscape has completely changed. The Internet has facilitated rapid, cost-effective, and targeted marketing strategies, providing businesses with powerful tools to engage travelers. Unlike traditional marketing, digital platforms allow real-time interaction, personalized recommendations, and direct engagement with potential tourists (Buhalis & Sinarta, 2019). As a result, businesses can now track consumer behavior through website analytics, search engine trends, and social media engagement, optimizing their marketing strategies accordingly (Theodorakopoulos & Theodoropoulou, 2024).

Social media has revolutionized tourism marketing, enabling businesses to reach global audiences instantly. Platforms like Facebook, Instagram, YouTube, TikTok, and TripAdvisor have become essential tools for promoting destinations, accommodations, and travel experiences (Chourasia, 2024). On the other hand, digital marketing campaigns, which use social media platforms, can use targeted advertising where they can target a specific demographic depending on their interests, location, and online behavior. Travel bloggers and vloggers have also become a part of influencer marketing, which involves joining with the tourism brands to promote services and destinations (Irfan et al., 2022). Tourism businesses can leverage the authenticity of social media influencers to increase brand credibility and hence attract more travelers.

Major Platforms Influencing Tourism Demand

Instagram

Instagram has emerged as a dominant force in tourism marketing, with visually appealing content driving travel inspiration. The platform's emphasis on high-quality images, stories, and reels allows tourism businesses to showcase destinations in an immersive way. Hashtags, location tags, and partnerships with influencers further enhance visibility and engagement (Kilipiri et al., 2023). Additionally, Instagram's algorithm prioritizes content that receives high engagement, meaning popular travel posts have the potential to reach millions of users organically. The introduction of Instagram Shopping has also enabled tourism businesses to offer direct booking links, making it easier for users to convert interest into action.

Facebook

Facebook remains a key player in tourism marketing due to its extensive user base and diverse advertising options. Businesses use Facebook Pages, groups, and ads to share travel promotions, updates, and customer testimonials. Furthermore, Facebook Live and virtual tours are interactive features that offer users real-time travel insight and are valuable tools for destination marketing (Neuburger et al., 2018). Travel groups found on Facebook are incredibly powerful due to their communal nature, and many huddle together in groups to discuss travel, swap tips, and share recommendations and experiences.

TikTok

TikTok has quickly become a favored marketing tool for younger travelers. Travel experiences, challenges, and itineraries featured in short, engaging videos have been good in influencing travel decisions (Zhou et al., 2023). However, TikTok's algorithm is designed to promote content discovery, meaning that smaller businesses and less well-known locations can grow organically. #TravelTok has amassed billions of views, while #Wanderlust has created tons of views in its hashtags. Also, there are interactive challenges and trends in TikTok that encourage users to actively engage with destinations, and that can become viral tourism marketing opportunities.

YouTube

Being the second biggest search engine after Google, YouTube is a vital travel marketing platform. Long-form video content, including travel vlogs, destination reviews, and documentary-style explorations, provides tourists with in-depth insights into travel experiences (Wadhwa & Bansal, 2022). Tourism boards and businesses use YouTube to publish official promotional content and collaborate with travel influencers. The platform's ad capabilities, including skippable ads and sponsored content, allow businesses to target potential travelers effectively. Additionally, live streaming on YouTube has gained traction, allowing real-time engagement between travel brands and audiences.

TripAdvisor

TripAdvisor remains a trusted platform for user-generated travel reviews and recommendations. Tourists frequently rely on the platform to read hotel, restaurant, and attraction reviews before making travel decisions. Businesses use TripAdvisor to manage their online reputation, respond to customer feedback, and showcase their services through advertisements and promotional content.

Beyond reviews, TripAdvisor's forums and ranking system heavily influence tourism demand, as higher-rated destinations and accommodations receive increased bookings (Kladou & Mavragani, 2015). The platform also integrates direct booking options, providing an end-to-end travel planning solution.

Pinterest

Pinterest has emerged as a unique platform for travel inspiration, particularly among those who prefer visual trip planning. Users create "travel boards" where they save destination images, itineraries, and recommendations, making it a powerful tool for long-term engagement (McMullen, 2020). Unlike other platforms, Pinterest content has a longer lifespan, as pins remain searchable and relevant for extended periods. Many tourism brands use Pinterest to drive website traffic by linking pins to travel blogs, booking pages, and informational resources.

UGC and Tourism

UGC has revolutionized the tourism industry by enabling travelers to share their experiences and influence others' travel decisions through platforms such as TripAdvisor, Instagram, YouTube, and TikTok. Unlike traditional marketing, UGC provides authentic, firsthand perspectives that impact travelers' destination choices, accommodations, and activities (Dogan & Kaurav, 2022).

Online reviews, travel blogs, and vlogs are among the most influential forms of UGC. Reviews on TripAdvisor, Google Reviews, and Yelp significantly impact potential travelers' decisions. Research suggests that 81% of travelers consult online reviews before finalizing bookings (Roelen-Blasberg, 2025). Positive reviews help create the image of a destination, while negative reviews discourage visitors.

In travel blogs, in-depth narratives allow potential travel destinations to learn about cultural experiences, itineraries, and travel tips. Blogs are more relatable than other guidebooks because they are constantly updated and customized to the individual. Moreover, vlogging on YouTube and TikTok is also gaining popularity, and video storytelling makes the content more accessible and desirable (Hussain et al., 2024).

Impact of User Experiences on Destination Reputation

Tourist-generated content has a great impact on the reputation of a destination. Positive UGC increases trust and desirability, whereas negative experiences online may discourage visitors. The volume, tone, and credibility of UGC are what affect people's perception of a destination worldwide (Pantano & Pietro, 2013).

Proactive review engagement, feedback response, and UGC integration into marketing strategies have a positive impact on a brand's digital presence. Viral social media trends may help amplify destination popularity, as is the case of places that are suddenly popular due to viral posts (Fjelldal et al., 2022). On the contrary, negative UGC (for example, overcrowding or bad service) can damage the reputation and interest in tourism.

Case Studies of Viral Travel Destinations

Bali, Indonesia

The rise of tourism in Bali is attributed to the visual content that influencers and travelers share on Instagram and TikTok, which is engaging and visually captivating. Significant online engagement of the island's scenic landscapes, cultural experiences, and luxury resorts has been driven (Rahjasa et al., 2024). However, this popularity has also come with overtourism and consequent environmental concerns due to the rising number of visitors (The Conversation, 2024). The solution, as it has been, is for local authorities to implement sustainable tourism policies such as visitor caps at popular sites and conservation fees.

Santorini, Greece

Santorini is one of the most photographed destinations with its iconic whitewashed buildings and picturesque sunsets, and has been transformed into one of the most popular tourist destinations (Stavrianea & Kamenidou, 2021). This exposure has aided in improving the local economy; however, it has also brought overcrowding, a high cost of living for residents, and environmental stress. To regulate tourism, cruise passengers will be subject to visitor quotas to preserve the island's heritage and infrastructure (Chadha, 2024).

Machu Picchu, Peru

The amount of UGC of Machu Picchu, with its stunning landscapes and historical significance, has led to a massive increase in tourism to the site. It has become a must-see location thanks to the travel vlogs and blog posts that explain how to hike routes and where to find cultural heritage. Nevertheless, the number of visitors has stirred fears for the preservation of the site, which prompted restrictions on the number of daily visitors and obligatory guided tours to save the area from wear and tear (Lau, 2023).

Role of Social Media Influencers in Travel Decisions

Social media revolutionized the travel industry by establishing influencers as vital agents who control the preferences of tourists and affect destination image creation. Travel influencers now serve as essential promotion assets for tourism boards and businesses since they create content focused on destinations, accommodations, and experiences (Pop et al., 2022). Social influencers connect mainstream marketing approaches to individual endorsements by producing content that creates authentic yet persuasive material, leading people to book vacations.

Social media influencers play a crucial role in shaping travel trends and consumer preferences (W.-K. Chen et al., 2022). Their content, which often includes reviews, destination guides, and travel itineraries, influences the perception of places and services. Several key factors contribute to their impact on tourism marketing:

- *Increased Destination Visibility:* Influencers introduce lesser-known destinations to global audiences, driving interest and boosting tourism (Pettersen-Sobczyk, 2023). For instance, destinations such as Cappadocia, Turkey, and Bali, Indonesia, have experienced a surge in visitors due to widespread influencer promotion.
- *Authentic Engagement:* Unlike traditional advertisements, influencer content often appears more genuine and personal, making it more persuasive to potential travelers. Studies suggest that consumers trust influencer recommendations more than traditional brand marketing (Rachmad, 2024).
- *UGC as a Marketing Tool:* Many travelers document their experiences inspired by influencers, further amplifying the destination's appeal. This cycle of content creation generates organic reach and long-term engagement.
- *Shift in Travel Preferences:* Influencer marketing has shifted travel preferences toward experience-based and luxury tourism. Many travelers now seek unique, Instagram-worthy locations and immersive travel experiences, such as eco-tourism and adventure tourism, influenced by social media trends (Thirumaran et al., 2021).

Ethical Concerns and Authenticity Issues in Influencer Marketing

Despite its advantages, influencer marketing raises ethical concerns regarding transparency, authenticity, and consumer trust. Several key issues need to be addressed:

- *Sponsored Content and Disclosure Issues:* Many influencers receive payments, free stays, or incentives to promote destinations without clear disclosure, leading to concerns over biased reviews. Regulatory bodies, such as the Federal Trade Commission (FTC), require influencers to label sponsored posts, yet enforcement remains inconsistent (Musiyiwa & Jacobson, 2023).
- *Exaggerated and Unrealistic Representations:* Some influencers curate highly edited, unrealistic portrayals of destinations, setting false expectations for travelers. This often leads to dissatisfaction when real experiences do not match online content (Jani et al., 2024).
- *Overtourism and Environmental Impact:* The popularity of influencer-promoted locations has led to overtourism, environmental

degradation, and strain on local communities. Destinations like Santorini and Venice have struggled with overcrowding due to excessive influencer exposure.
- *Lack of Cultural Sensitivity:* Some influencers engage in culturally insensitive behavior, such as inappropriate attire or disregard for local customs, leading to backlash from communities and ethical concerns regarding responsible tourism.

Social media influencers have significantly reshaped travel decisions, destination branding, and consumer engagement in tourism. While their impact is largely positive in terms of increasing awareness and promoting travel, ethical concerns regarding authenticity, responsible marketing, and overtourism must be addressed. Since influencer marketing is still evolving, both influencers and tourism brands have to be more ethical to have a sustainable, authentic travel experience for the audience.

Social Media as a Tourism Demand Predictor

Tourism demand forecasting relies heavily on social media because digital platforms have become the primary sources that travelers use for sharing experiences while also obtaining recommendations and planning trips. UGC on Instagram, Facebook, TikTok, and Twitter produces massive amounts of content that functions as an immediate quality indicator for travel trends and customer emotions (Y. Li et al., 2022). Tourism stakeholders improve their marketing strategy forecasting through the analysis of these operational trends.

Over 24 hours, social media platforms generate a flow of travel-related data that can provide insights into consumer behavior and tourism trends. DMOs can monitor which of their destinations, attractions, or travel experiences are raking in followership (Roque & Raposo, 2014).

Along the same lines, viral travel challenges on TikTok or trending hashtags on Instagram (#TravelGoals, #Wanderlust) signify a rise in interest for certain places. Likewise, the timing of surges in tourism demand can also be predicted before these turn into actual bookings. It allows tourism boards to be prepared for visitor number fluctuations, allocate resources efficiently, and target promotional campaigns (Wu et al., 2025).

Use of Big Data and Artificial Intelligence (AI) in Tourism Analytics

The revolution that took place to forecast tourism demand is through big data and artificial intelligence. AI-powered tools process a large volume of social media data and predict social media data patterns as well as future tourism trends with high accuracy (Shah Alam et al., 2024). The machine learning algorithms and the ability to conduct sentiment and predictive analysis help businesses understand traveler preferences and change their marketing tactics.

For example, Google Trends can show businesses that the search volume for some travel destinations is spiking, predicting demand. Also, Expedia and

Airbnb use AI-powered recommendation engines that help in analyzing past travelers' behavior, offer personalized offers, and predict future bookings (Nugroho et al., 2024). AI-powered virtual assistants and chatbots enhance customer engagement by suggesting personalized travel routes based on real-time data (Babu Reddy et al., 2024).

Social media has emerged as a powerful predictor of tourism demand. Using big data and AI-driven analytics, tourism businesses and governments can use data to make informed decisions, improve destination management, and enhance visitor experience. The incidence of social media shaping tourism demand is set to grow even more as digital technology continues to evolve.

Challenges and Risks of Social Media in Tourism

Tourism has been influenced by social media to provide real-time information sharing, share destination marketing, and facilitate UGC. However, this also comes hand in hand with social media's challenges of spreading misinformation, overtourism, and privacy issues. Social media is an excellent tool when it comes to travel planning, and while social media adds value to travel planning, it is also important as a means of tourism sustainability, security, and authenticity.

Spread of Misinformation and Fake Reviews

Spreading misinformation and fake reviews are some of the risks found in social media in tourism. Given that many people rely on online reviews (TripAdvisor, Google Reviews, Yelp, among others) to help make travel decisions, research has found that a large proportion of these reviews are fraudulent or manipulated (Abdallah, 2021). Fake reviews can skew the impression of the quality of accommodations and attractions, resulting in visitor dissatisfaction and a decrease in trust in online travel platforms (Ismail et al., 2024).

Second, misleading promotional content and heavy editing of content lead to misinformation. Travel influencers and marketers then apply some false, unrealistic portrayals of some destinations and set false expectations for tourists (Shahidul Islam, 2025). The phenomenon of "Instagram vs. Reality" has caused growing ethical concerns about digital tourism marketing.

Over-Tourism and Environmental Impact

Viral travel trends triggered by social media are leading to significant issues related to tourism where excessive visitor numbers surpass the environmental and infrastructure capacity of a destination. For example, viral posts have caused spikes in tourist arrivals in places like Santorini, Bali, and Venice, which resulted in overcrowding, pollution, and disruption of local communities (Dodds & Butler, 2019).

Social media-driven tourism has environmental consequences such as increased carbon footprint, biodiversity loss, and destruction of fragile ecosystems. The studies indicate the correlation between the spikes in tourism and social media engagement, which often leads to pressure on local resources that need to be intervened by the authorities (Dhiraj & Kumar, 2021). However, in response, governments have imposed visitor caps, started eco-tourism initiatives, and imposed higher tourism taxes to counter the negative effects of mass tourism (Chadha, 2024; Lau, 2023).

Privacy and Security Concerns for Tourists

Sharing personal travel experiences on social media on a broad scale represents a serious privacy and security risk. As a result, many tourists unwittingly publish their location and personal data on the internet in real-time, thereby becoming susceptible to identity theft, cyberstalking, and physical threats (Ioannou et al., 2021). Criminals have utilized features of social media platforms that geotag to "target" unsuspecting travelers.

In addition, travel companies' AI-driven data collection creates further privacy risks. There are many tourism apps and online booking platforms that do not have transparent policies regarding data security and track user activity, which is a concern for users' personal information being misused. Travelers should limit their social media sharing, adjust privacy settings, and access travel-related services from secure networks.

Case Studies of Social Media Impact on Tourism

However, social media platforms have also played a key role in the transformation of tourism landscapes, spreading word of mouth about previously unknown locations, making them extremely popular tourist hotspots through viral content. This is particularly evident for this phenomenon in cases of platforms such as TikTok and Instagram that have had a great impact on travel behavior and destination popularity.

Example 1: How a Viral TikTok Video Boosted Tourism in a Specific Destination

TikTok's algorithm works uniquely and embraces highly engaging content quickly, thus making the featured locations spread rapidly. For instance, the influence of short food videos on the image of Chengdu's tourism is a pertinent example. According to research, Chengdu's cognitive, affective, and conative images as a travel destination have improved among potential tourists as a result of the TikTok videos on Chengdu fare (Y. Li et al., 2020)

The city of Harbin in China went through a similar transformation in its tourism scene on account of TikTok (CGTN, 2024). With Harbin becoming popular for its ice attractions, reopening the Ice and Snow World without visitor planning caused a crisis that caused the public to be "not happy." The government acted quickly and brilliantly capitalized with the help of TikTok's power to make good publicity programs that improved the city's image. As indicated in this example, social media platforms are used to help destinations handle crises and improve their tourism appeal.

Example 2: The Role of Instagram in Making a Hidden Gem a Tourist Hotspot

Instagram's visual-centric platform has become a powerful tool for destination marketing, where hidden gems are getting international recognition. The Algarve region in Southern Portugal is a case in point. DMO used Instagram to promote the Algarve's picturesque landscapes and cultural heritage. Through the creative production of content and interaction with the users, the online community was co-produced with the region's image to attract interest in the region and increase the number of tourists (Iglesias-Sánchez et al., 2020). In this case, Instagram proves itself to be a very successful model for creating an interactive and visually related narrative to turn destinations that have not been heard of before into tourist hotspots. These examples demonstrate how TikTok and Instagram function as social media platforms that support the significant development of the tourism sector. Destinations face unanticipated challenges when it comes to tourist number control together with quality visitor experience stewardship, while obtaining massive promotional potential. Social media influencer marketing opportunities will only benefit destinations that implement proper proactive strategies to manage crowds and environmental impacts.

Conclusion

The tourism industry faces an undeniable social media influence regarding its market promotion, while tourism consumers make choices that affect demand levels. Viral content from TikTok combined with Instagram successfully promotes new destinations that once received minimal interest to become highly sought-after travel destinations. Digital transformation provides numerous market opportunities alongside problems of misinformation, excessive tourist numbers, and privacy concerns.

Having analyzed the shift from traditional to digital tourism marketing strategies, we have witnessed the strength of UGC, influencer marketing, and even data-driven decisions. To demonstrate positive economic impacts and sustainability concerns associated with viral tourism trends, case studies of viral tourism trends are presented.

With that, destination management organizations, policymakers, and tourism businesses must find the balance between using social media's promotional power and responsible tourism. The healthy relationship between social media and tourism will need sustainable marketing strategies, ethical influencer collaborations, and better data security measures to keep the relationship alive.

However, social media is going to remain a key player in shaping of tourism's future. Stakeholders can use their power to develop positive travel experiences while mitigating their downsides through proactive and adaptive strategies. Innovation, regulation, and a desire for sustainability are the keys to this increasingly digital tourism landscape.

References

Abdallah, A. (2021). Fake news, false advertising, social media and the tourism industry. *International Journal of Development Research*, *11*(7), 48999–49003.

Babu Reddy, S., Kathpalia, R., Sil, R., & Nag, A. (2024). Tourism companion: Enhancing travel experiences with AI chatbot and soft computing. In C. K. K. Reddy, T. Sithole, M. Ouaissa, Ö. Özer, & M. M. Hanafiah (Eds.), *Soft computing in industry 5.0 for sustainability* (pp. 301–317). Springer Nature. https://doi.org/10.1007/978-3-031-69336-6_13

Buhalis, D., & Sinarta, Y. (2019). Real-time co-creation and nowness service: Lessons from tourism and hospitality. *Journal of Travel & Tourism Marketing*, *36*(5), 563–582. https://doi.org/10.1080/10548408.2019.1592059

CGTN. (2024). China's tourism boom after Harbin goes viral. *CGTN website*. https://radio.cgtn.com/news/recommend/Chinas-tourism-boom-after-Harbin-goes-viral/2427. Accessed on February 22, 2025.

Chadha, S. (2024). Your Greek holiday just got costlier, especially a trip to Santorini | Personal finance—Business standard. *Business Standard website*. https://www.business-standard.com/finance/personal-finance/your-greek-holiday-just-got-costlier-especially-a-trip-santorini-mykonos-124090900185_1.html. Accessed on February 22, 2025.

Chen, Y.-F., & Law, R. (2016). A review of research on electronic word-of-mouth in hospitality and tourism management. *International Journal of Hospitality & Tourism Administration*, *17*(4), 347–372. https://doi.org/10.1080/15256480.2016.1226150

Chen, W.-K., Silaban, P. H., Hutagalung, W. E., & Silalahi, A. D. K. (2022). How Instagram influencers contribute to consumer travel decision: Insights from SEM and fsQCA. *Emerging Science Journal*, *7*(1), 16–37. https://doi.org/10.28991/ESJ-2023-07-01-02

Chourasia, Dr B. (2024). The influence of emerging social media trends on the evolution of the travel and hospitality industry. *Educational Administration: Theory and Practice*, 1110–1116. https://doi.org/10.53555/kuey.v30i7.7069

Dhiraj, A., & Kumar, S. (2021). Overtourism: Causes, impacts and solution. In A. Sharma & A. Hassan (Eds.), *Overtourism as destination risk* (pp. 49–56). Emerald Publishing Limited. https://doi.org/10.1108/978-1-83909-706-520211004

Dodds, R., & Butler, R. (2019). The phenomena of overtourism: A review. *International Journal of Tourism Cities*, *5*(4), 519–528. https://doi.org/10.1108/IJTC-06-2019-0090

Dogan, G., & Kaurav, R. P. S. (2022). *Handbook on tourism and social media*. Edward Elgar Publishing.

Dolnicar, S., & Ring, A. (2014). Tourism marketing research: Past, present and future. *Annals of Tourism Research*, *47*, 31–47. https://doi.org/10.1016/j.annals.2014.03.008

Fjelldal, I. K., Kralj, A., & Moyle, B. (2022). Profanity in viral tourism marketing: A conceptual model of destination image reinforcement. *Journal of Vacation Marketing*, *28*(1), 52–63. https://doi.org/10.1177/13567667211020497

Gardiner, S., Vada, S., Yang, E. C. L., Khoo, C., & Le, T. H. (2022). Recreating history: The evolving negotiation of staged authenticity in tourism experiences. *Tourism Management*, *91*, 104515. https://doi.org/10.1016/j.tourman.2022.104515

Hussain, K., Didarul Alam, M. M., Malik, A., Tarhini, A., & Al Balushi, M. K. (2024). From likes to luggage: The role of social media content in attracting tourists. *Heliyon*, *10*(19), e38914. https://doi.org/10.1016/j.heliyon.2024.e38914

Iglesias-Sánchez, P. P., Correia, M. B., Jambrino-Maldonado, C., & de las Heras-Pedrosa, C. (2020). Instagram as a co-creation space for tourist destination image-building: Algarve and Costa del Sol case studies. *Sustainability*, *12*(7), 2793. https://doi.org/10.3390/su12072793

Ioannou, A., Tussyadiah, I., & Miller, G. (2021). That's private! Understanding travelers' privacy concerns and online data disclosure. *Journal of Travel Research*, *60*(7), 1510–1526. https://doi.org/10.1177/0047287520951642

Irfan, M., Malik, M. S., & Zubair, S. K. (2022). Impact of vlog marketing on consumer travel intent and consumer purchase intent with the moderating role of destination image and ease of travel. *Sage Open*, *12*(2). https://doi.org/10.1177/21582440221099522

Ismail, S., Hattingh, M., & Matthee, M. (2024). Understanding the challenges of fake news in the tourism and travel industry: A systematic literature review. In R. van de Wetering, R. Helms, B. Roelens, S. Bagheri, Y. K. Dwivedi, I. O. Pappas, & M. Mäntymäki (Eds.), *Disruptive innovation in a digitally connected healthy world* (pp. 371–382). Springer Nature. https://doi.org/10.1007/978-3-031-72234-9_31

Jani, D. A., Ratnoday, N. R., & Bajpai, S. (2024). Social media influence on travel choices. *International Research Journal of Humanities and Interdisciplinary Studies (IRJHIS)*, *5*(7), 1–14.

Kanje, P., Charles, G., Tumsifu, E., Mossberg, L., & Andersson, T. (2020). Customer engagement and eWOM in tourism. *Journal of Hospitality and Tourism Insights*, *3* (3), 273–289. (world). https://doi.org/10.1108/JHTI-04-2019-0074

Karyatun, S., Efendi, S., Demolingo, R. H., Wiweka, K., & Putri, A. P. (2021). Between instagrammable attraction and selfie tourist: Characteristic and behavior. *South Asian Journal of Social Studies and Economics*, *12*(4), 314–324. https://doi.org/10.9734/sajsse/2021/v12i430338

Kilipiri, E., Papaioannou, E., & Kotzaivazoglou, I. (2023). Social media and influencer marketing for promoting sustainable tourism destinations: The Instagram case. *Sustainability*, *15*(8), 6374. https://doi.org/10.3390/su15086374

Kladou, S., & Mavragani, E. (2015). Assessing destination image: An online marketing approach and the case of TripAdvisor. *Journal of Destination Marketing & Management*, *4*(3), 187–193. https://doi.org/10.1016/j.jdmm.2015.04.003

Lau, E. (2023). Peru shuts parts of Machu Picchu from tourists due to erosion. *The National website*. https://www.thenationalnews.com/travel/2023/09/29/peru-machu-picchu-overtourism/. Accessed on February 22, 2025.

Li, Y., Lin, Z., & Xiao, S. (2022). Using social media big data for tourist demand forecasting: A new machine learning analytical approach. *Journal of Digital Economy*, *1*(1), 32–43. https://doi.org/10.1016/j.jdec.2022.08.006

Li, Y, Xu, X., Song, B., & He, H. (2020). Impact of short food videos on the tourist destination image—Take Chengdu as an example. *Sustainability*, *12*(17), 6739. https://doi.org/10.3390/su12176739

McKee, J., Evans, D., & Bratton, S. (2021). *Social media marketing*. A G Printing & Publishing.

McMullen, M. (2020). 'Pinning' tourist photographs: Analyzing the photographs shared on Pinterest of heritage tourist destinations. *Current Issues in Tourism*, *23* (3), 376–387. https://doi.org/10.1080/13683500.2019.1568399

Munar, A. M., & Jacobsen, J. K. S. (2014). Motivations for sharing tourism experiences through social media. *Tourism Management*, *43*, 46–54. https://doi.org/10.1016/j.tourman.2014.01.012

Musiyiwa, R., & Jacobson, J. (2023). Sponsorship disclosure in social media influencer marketing: The algorithmic and non-algorithmic barriers. *Social Media + Society*, *9*(3). https://doi.org/10.1177/20563051231196870

Neuburger, L., Beck, J., & Egger, R. (2018). The 'phygital' tourist experience: The use of augmented and virtual reality in destination marketing. In M. A. Camilleri (Ed.), *Tourism planning and destination marketing* (pp. 183–202). Emerald Publishing Limited. https://doi.org/10.1108/978-1-78756-291-220181009

Nugroho, I. S., Priyanto, D., & Purnama, Y. (2024). Exploring the role of artificial intelligence (AI) in designing and optimizing personalization strategies to enhance customer experience in the tourism industry. *Technology and Society Perspectives (TACIT)*, *2*(3), 292–298. https://doi.org/10.61100/tacit.v2i3.247

Nusair, K., Butt, I., & Nikhashemi, S. R. (2019). A bibliometric analysis of social media in hospitality and tourism research. *International Journal of Contemporary Hospitality Management*, *31*(7), 2691–2719. https://doi.org/10.1108/IJCHM-06-2018-0489

Pantano, E., & Pietro, L. D. (2013). From e-tourism to f-tourism: Emerging issues from negative tourists' online reviews. *Journal of Hospitality and Tourism Technology*, *4*(3), 211–227. https://doi.org/10.1108/JHTT-02-2013-0005

Pellegrino, A., Abe, M., & Shannon, R. (2022). The dark side of social media: Content effects on the relationship between materialism and consumption behaviors. *Frontiers in Psychology*, *13*. https://doi.org/10.3389/fpsyg.2022.870614

Pettersen-Sobczyk, M. (2023). Influencer marketing in the promotion of cities and regions. *European Research Studies Journal*, *XXVI*(4), 35–43. https://doi.org/10.35808/ersj/3270

Pop, R.-A., Săplăcan, Z., Dabija, D.-C., & Alt, M.-A. (2022). The impact of social media influencers on travel decisions: The role of trust in consumer decision journey. *Current Issues in Tourism*, *25*(5), 823–843. https://doi.org/10.1080/13683500.2021.1895729

Rachmad, Y. E. (2024). *The future of influencer marketing: Evolution of consumer behavior in the digital World*. PT. Sonpedia Publishing.

Rahjasa, S. L., Prasasti, G., & Apriliani, K. M. (2024). How travel influencer and social media influence tourist travel decision to ubud. *TRJ Tourism Research Journal*, *8*(1), 127–141. https://doi.org/10.30647/trj.v8i1.243

Roelen-Blasberg, T. (2025). Online review statistics every hotel needs to know in 2025. *Mara-Solutions website*. https://www.mara-solutions.com/post/online-review-statistics-every-hotel-needs-to-know. Accessed on February 22, 2025.

Roque, V., & Raposo, R. (2014). Social media as a communication and marketing tool in tourism: An analysis of online activities from international key player DMO. *Anatolia: An International Journal of Tourism and Hospitality Research*, *27*(1), 58–70. https://www.tandfonline.com/doi/abs/10.1080/13032917.2015.1083209

Shah Alam, S., Ahsan, M. N., Masukujjaman, M., Kokash, H. A., & Ahmed, S. (2024). Adoption of big data analytics and artificial intelligence among hospitality and tourism companies: Perceive performance perspective. *Journal of Quality Assurance in Hospitality & Tourism*, 1–35. https://doi.org/10.1080/1528008X.2024.2442674

Shahidul Islam, M. (2025). Deconstructing deception: Exploring misleading practices in tourism marketing. *Journal of Travel Research*. https://doi.org/10.1177/00472875241312177

Stavrianea, A., & Kamenidou, I. (2021). Memorable tourism experiences, destination image, satisfaction, and loyalty: An empirical study of Santorini Island. *EuroMed Journal of Business*, *17*(1), 1–20. https://doi.org/10.1108/EMJB-10-2020-0106Eirini).

The Conversation. (2024). Bali gives a snapshot of what 'overtourism' looks like in the developing world. *The Conversation website*. https://theconversation.com/bali-gives-a-snapshot-of-what-overtourism-looks-like-in-the-developing-world-235550. Accessed on February 22, 2025.

Theodorakopoulos, L., & Theodoropoulou, A. (2024). Leveraging big data analytics for understanding consumer behavior in digital marketing: A systematic review. *Human Behavior and Emerging Technologies*, *2024*(1), 3641502. https://doi.org/10.1155/2024/3641502

Thirumaran, K., Jang, H., Pourabedin, Z., & Wood, J. (2021). The role of social media in the luxury tourism business: A research review and trajectory assessment. *Sustainability*, *13*(3), 1216. https://doi.org/10.3390/su13031216

Tran, N. L., & Rudolf, W. (2022). Social media and destination branding in tourism: A systematic review of the literature. *Sustainability*, *14*(20), 13528. https://doi.org/10.3390/su142013528

Utama, I. G. B. R., Suardhana, I. N., Sutarya, I. G., & Krismawintari, N. P. D. (2024). Assessing the impacts of overtourism in Bali: Environmental, socio-cultural, and economic perspectives on sustainable tourism. *TourismSpectrum: Diversity & Dynamics*, *1*(2), 81–92. https://doi.org/10.56578/tsdd010202

Wadhwa, R., & Bansal, R. (2022). Exploring the role of YouTube as a tourism marketing tool. In *New learning technologies of leadership & role of media management*.

Wu, D. C., Zhong, S., Wu, J., & Song, H. (2025). Tourism and hospitality forecasting with big data: A systematic review of the literature. *Journal of Hospitality & Tourism Research*, *49*(3), 615–634. https://doi.org/10.1177/10963480231223151

Yallop, A. C., Gică, O. A., Moisescu, O. I., Coroş, M. M., & Séraphin, H. (2021). The digital traveller: Implications for data ethics and data governance in tourism and hospitality. *Journal of Consumer Marketing*, *40*(2), 155–170. (world). https://doi.org/10.1108/JCM-12-2020-4278

Zhang, T., & Huang, X. (2024). Viral marketing: Influencer marketing pivots in tourism—A case study of meme influencer instigated travel interest surge. *Current Issues in Tourism*, *25*(4), 508–515. https://www.tandfonline.com/doi/abs/10.1080/13683500.2021.1910214

Zhou, Q., Sotiriadis, M., & Shen, S. (2023). Using TikTok in tourism destination choice: A young Chinese tourists' perspective. *Tourism Management Perspectives*, *46*, 101101. https://doi.org/10.1016/j.tmp.2023.101101

Section 4

Cultural, Social, and Global Dimensions of Tourism

Chapter 14

Challenges and Solutions for Sustainable Tourism Development: Identifying Gaps in Narrative Crafting Beyond the Tourist Gaze

Keith Kay Hin Tan and Sze-ee Lee

Taylor's University, Malaysia

Abstract

This qualitative study examines challenges to sustainable tourism development at a marginal tourist site. It highlights how content creation in a poorly documented location can create isolated silos of information, which, rather than providing rich layers of interest, instead produces disconnected narratives. By reviewing print, audio, and online media, the research explains how gaps in narrative-crafting are significant stumbling blocks to the growth of a tourism-based economy. The findings address the gap between resident self-identity and visitor expectations that, if unresolved, can damage a location's social and cultural sustainability. The findings propose localized, narrative-based solutions for sustainable tourism development.

Keywords: Sustainable tourism; narrative crafting; tourist gaze; gatekeepers; identity

Introduction

Storytelling plays an important role in human consciousness and peoples' ability to accept and appreciate information. This is particularly important for destinations on the fringe of what Urry (1990) famously described as the "Tourist Gaze." These places often lack strong tourist "attractors" (Mattsson et al., 2005) capable of drawing visitors across long distances regardless of expense. These

Economics and Tourism, 221–236

doi:10.1108/978-1-83662-916-020251015

often overlooked places therefore mostly rely on a series of secondary attractions which require skilled marketing to compete for tourism visibility in an industry already crowded with multiple products catering for every imaginable visitor type across the world.

Where cultural tourism is concerned, the packaging of history as either a collection of facts, a celebration of local or national achievement, or simply a collection of interesting stories is an area of study that has grown in recent years (Harrison, 2013; de la Torre, 2002). When the packaging of history is linked to tangible objects, the need to curate a suitable narrative surrounding these objects becomes important, as shown in recent discussions regarding the return of historical artifacts from former colonial centers to their former colonies. Even the most famous objects, like the Parthenon/Elgin marbles in the British Museum, have been subject to much debate about the rights or wrongs of keeping them in a "safe" museum away from their place of authentic origin (King, 2006).

This paper documents how tangible items preserved by a newly constructed gallery were grouped into five categories, which were then curated as an audio-guide linked to a mini museum to encourage sustainable tourism in a small, historic former mining town in Malaysia. The research then explores the multiple sources of data that can contribute to good storytelling for tourism. The findings highlight the importance of recording and transmitting the collective memories of older generations to younger people in a way that is not just accessible but also socially and technologically relevant to young, 21st century lifestyles.

The findings will identify the gaps in narrative crafting that exist in a location just beyond the mainstream tourist gaze, as well as their causes. In particular, they will address the gap between local self-identity and visitor expectations that, if left unresolved, can shift the role of tourist gatekeepers away from residents to outsiders, which carries the risk of profound long-term damage to a small-scale location's social and cultural sustainability. It will finally propose strategies emphasizing localized, narrative-based approaches that respect unique and sensitive local contexts as a suitable solution for sustainable tourism development in a secondary tourist site.

Problem Statement

A loss of identity often sets in when the authentic roots of a place have disappeared due to changing commercial, social or demographic reasons (Li & Chan, 2018). This is the case in many settlements around the world that derived their origins from extractive industries and finite commodities. Once these are exhausted, the settlement's original "reason for being" disappears, in some cases taking the settlement with it. In other cases, such as San Francisco (gold mining), Newcastle (coal mining), or Ipoh (tin mining), re-orientations toward other industries have successfully maintained or enlarged the settlement's economic viability, leaving behind their original roots as merely important footnotes of history.

Although many large cities tracing their distant history to extractive industries are now involved in multiple other commercial activities, small towns with a more recent experience of mining in particular sometimes struggle with directional or even existential problems once mining ceases to be a viable proposition. In Malaysia, once the world's largest producer of tin, small towns like Papan and Sungai Lembing have become semi ghost-towns since the collapse of tin mining in the 1980s, and towns like Batu Arang (literally "coal") have similarly struggled since the end of coal mining (Ramele Ramli et al., 2022).

Faced with the threat of decline, some small towns in Malaysia have turned to tourism as a way to sustain their fortunes in a postcommodities economy. When tangible objects are available to explain the town's historical origins to a new generation of visitors, curation of those objects then becomes necessary to communicate history in a way that is relevant across different generations with different experiences and expectations about authenticity. In Malaysia, due to the multi-ethnic makeup of the country's population, and the historical ties of the different communities to particular industries, questions of authenticity are even more complicated due to debates about memory, heritage, and what is emphasized, suppressed, or reshaped by different communities and the government (Blackburn & Hack, 2012).

Methodology

This qualitative study examines the challenges to sustainable tourism development faced by the secondary tourist site of Serendah in Malaysia's central Selangor state. Despite being the custodian to a rich historical legacy linked to the country's past as the world's largest producer of tin, the district of Serendah is today located just beyond the mainstream tourist gaze. This research will examine three sources of narratives describing the cultural, natural, and historical significance of the site, as it seeks to diversify its economy away from extractive industries toward tourism:

(1) audio media (a resident-sponsored audio-guide developed to welcome visitors to the town);
(2) printed media (the only extant resident-created guidebook written about Serendah);
(3) online media (online visitor reviews for "*Sekeping Serendah*")—the best-known eco-friendly accommodation available in the district.

The data collection began with a descriptive study of historical items that had been donated to the *Hock Leng Keng* temple gallery in Serendah from 2016 to 2022, which had then been arranged to support a narrative story regarding the town in 2023. Based on various visits conducted in 2022 and 2023, the researchers arranged the items on display into five broad categories (shown later in Table 14.1). In turn, these five categories were curated into narrative

Table 14.1. Categorization of Items on Display at the Serendah Temple Gallery via the Audio-Guides.

Category	Related Gallery Items	Importance to Serendah
1. Tin mining	Scale models of mining structures	The town was founded in the 1890s by immigrant tin miners from Southern China
2. Rubber tapping	Sections of rubber trees, forestry, and tapping equipment	The invention of the automobile increased the demand for natural rubber, which became an important industry in Serendah, especially between 1900 and 1920.
3. Public health and commerce between the wars	Traditional medicine cabinet; trade items, water dispensaries, gas lamps	The prevalence of opium use among early immigrants, together with a dependence on traditional remedies, made public health an important early issue for the town
4. Daily life in the mid-20th century	Time-capsule items creating a mock-up of 1960s life	The years surrounding Malayan independence in 1957 and the formation of Malaysia in 1963 are memorialized via the display of household items once used in the town
5. Hock Leng Keng temple—linking the past to the future	Sedan chairs for deities, decorative panels, ceramics, statuettes	The second-oldest temple in Serendah is an important archival center for the town's Chinese community in particular.

audio-guides in three languages—Mandarin, English, and Malay (with the Mandarin version taking precedence).

By reviewing the above audio, print, and online media, the research will explain how gaps in narrative-crafting are significant stumbling blocks to the growth of a tourism-based local economy. It highlights how content creation in a poorly documented site can create silos of information with little or no overlap between them, which, rather than creating rich layers of interest, instead produces disconnected narratives, with each catering to different types of visitors. It explains the challenges associated with delivering an intergenerational transfer of ideas in the face of this lack of cohesive narrative, particularly in a location affected by rural–urban migration, socioeconomic change, and language shift, a phenomenon occurring throughout Malaysia's ethnic Chinese population (Ong & Troyer, 2022; Wang, 2009).

Background

Although the rural district of Serendah has been inhabited by an indigenous, forest-dwelling tribe known as the *Temuan* for many centuries, the small town of Serendah at its center traces its origins to tin mining (Ee, 2020). Indeed, the discovery of rich and easily recoverable tin deposits and prospecting for the metal in the late 19th century led to the gradual expansion of British colonial control over Malaya in general and its tin-producing lands in particular. This culminated in the signing of the Anglo-Malay "Pangkor Treaty" in 1874, which established de facto British control over approximately half the Malay peninsula via a political entity known as the Federated Malay States, or FMS (Moore, 2004). Commodities were vital to the country's economy from then until long after the country's independence.

Malaysia indeed remained the world's leading producer of tin and natural rubber until the 1980s, with both forming the backbone of its economy. A subsequent collapse in the price of both commodities caused the country to initially enter a deep recession, before it transitioned to become the world's leading producer of palm oil. A rapid industrialization of the economy then followed in the 1990s, permanently altering Malaysia's socioeconomic direction (Leete, 2007).

The historic legacy of being a formerly commodity-dependent economy, however, had a lasting effect on the country's demography via the use of immigrant labor, because sociopolitical factors combined to link particular industries to particular immigrant groups. Tin mining became associated with immigrants from China, rubber tapping with immigrants from India, and palm-oil production with immigrants from Indonesia. Of these three primary industries, the oldest, but also now the most extinct, is tin mining. Whereas tin accounted for nearly 20% of the value of Malaysia's exports in 1970, by 2005 that value had fallen to a mere 0.2% (Leete, 2007) with a similar fall in employment numbers.

Although some Malaysian mining settlements achieved their peak population around the time when the mines were most active before going into gentle decline (Khor et al., 2017), others, such as Kampung Pulai in Kelantan as well as Serendah, have managed to maintain a more or less stable population despite the transition from one dominant enterprise to another (Carstens, 1980; Tan et al., 2020). In the case of Serendah, its mining heyday occurred during the first three decades of the 20th century. This was especially following the completion of a tarred "high street" in the 1890s, which supported the construction of the first brick shophouses. The settlement was then shaped by a mostly ethnic Chinese population of working men who were migrants from Southern China (Ee, 2020).

The entry of Chinese immigrants created an urbanized core in a previously rural district. These immigrants were Cantonese speakers who embarked from the then Portuguese colony of Macau, as well as Hokkien speakers from Amoy (modern day Xiamen) (Ee, 2020). Although Malaysia's Cantonese and Hokkien speakers had historically engaged in violent competition with each other prior to the signing of the Pangkor treaty, their subsequent peaceful coexistence in Serendah allowed for their clan temples to be built side by side just off the center of the old town.

Clan Temples

Serendah is home to two Chinese clan temples, which can trace their history to the 1890s. These are the *Sin Sze Si Yah* temple, founded by Cantonese-speaking migrants, and the *Hock Leng Keng* temple, started by Hokkien-speaking migrants. Unlike many of the newer Chinese temples in Malaysia, which are mainly Taoist and/or Buddhist, these temples, like most of the earliest immigrant temples, cater to a form of ancestor worship focusing on deities. The *Hock Leng Keng* temple houses a trinity of these—which link the Hokkien community in China to the medieval legend of the "Three kingdoms" as well as the Goddess of Mercy, *Kwan Yin*. Of the three deities, *Kwan Yin* is perhaps the most well-known in Southeast Asia. Oral sources among some Taoists, in fact relate to her akin to how the Virgin Mary is venerated by Roman Catholics.

The Cantonese temple, on the other hand, venerates local deities, who lived in colonial Malaya at the end of the 19th century. According to a plaque in front of the similarly-aged *Sin Sze Si Ya* temple in Kuala Lumpur, the deities were said to have guided one of the founding fathers of Kuala Lumpur, Yap Ah Loy. According to local oral history, legends surrounding their deaths included stories of white blood, which led Yap Ah Loy to offer prayers toward them, and the setting up of three *Sin Sze Si Yah* temples in places where he had business or clan interests. This included Kuala Lumpur, Semenyih, and Serendah.

Economic and Social Transition

The mining boom, although responsible for much of the colonial-era architecture of Serendah, was relatively short-lived. It created a town that was male-dominated, with an unsustainable socioeconomic pattern also containing elements of gambling, prostitution, and opium that marked many of the early immigrant communities in British Malaya (Rimmer & Allen, 1990). The town's population peaked after the First World War, after female immigration from China became more widespread, but then stagnated in the 1920s due to the general collapse in tin prices after the World War and exhaustion of easily obtainable surface deposits of the metal. This period also saw new restrictions being imposed on the entry of male immigrants from China and the voluntary repatriation of thousands of able-bodied men and their saved monies back to the mainland, even as the influx of Chinese women continued. As a result, the over 5:1 ratio of males to females in Malaya's Chinese population at the beginning of the 20th century became less than 2:1 by the 1930s (Loh, 1975).

This gradual "normalization" of the gender balance across British Malaya eventually led to a significant drop in demand for prostitution in most Chinese-majority settlements, including Serendah. The 1920s also saw the first of several changes in the town's economic focus, away from mining toward rubber tapping, which also encouraged a growth in the Indian population, not only in the town but also in British Malaya as a whole, in the years preceding the Second World War (Moore, 2004).

Unlike tin mining, rubber tapping produced fewer tangible structures of note in Serendah town, as the focus of the activity, as well as Indian settlement, was in the nearby "Serendah Estate," mostly owned by colonial interests via the "New Serendah Rubber company Ltd" (Ee, 2020). The eventual decline of that industry as well by the 1980s left Serendah with no obvious source of employment to retain its working-age population. It thus transitioned to become a dormitory settlement for the larger nearby town of Kuala Kubu Bharu as well as the Malaysian capital of Kuala Lumpur, located approximately 40 kilometers away by increasingly well-appointed roads.

Recent Developments

Improvements in domestic road connectivity coupled with increasing demand for leisure travel by Malaysia's urban population have, however, resulted in many of the country's small towns seeing a renaissance in visitor and tourist interest in recent decades (Tan et al., 2022). Apart from the unexpected downturn caused by the COVID-19 pandemic between 2020 and 2021, that trend has continued apace, aided in no small part by social media networks and the Internet, to bring many places previously considered off-the-map into the outer edges of the "tourist gaze" (Urry, 1990).

Cultural tourism focusing on Malaysia's urbanized Chinese community has indeed grown in recent years (Phua & Tan, 2022). This is in part because of the community's own efforts to promote an understanding of and appreciation for their contribution toward nation-building in the late 19th and early 20th centuries through industrial development in general and tin mining in particular.

At the same time, the history and culture of Malaysia as presented in the country's public museums has been criticized for downplaying the contribution of non-Muslim communities (Abu Talib, 2015; Teo, 2010). This has acted as a catalyst for the formation of several private museums of different sizes around the country that focus on the contribution of the Chinese community in particular. This is often via the adaptive re-use of old buildings, such as the *Baba-Nyonya Heritage Museum* in Penang, or via the construction of dedicated community museums, such as at the former gold-mining town of Pulai village in Kelantan (Tan et al., 2020).

The deep historical links between Malaysia's ethnic Chinese population and tin mining, although now a thing of the past, are indeed a point of pride for the community. This was especially the case for the committee members of the *Hock Leng Keng* temple in Serendah, who commissioned an extension to their 19th century temple as a cultural annex and gallery in 2022. This gallery houses items of historical importance not just to the temple but also to the broader community in general and Serendah in particular.

The local temple committee chairperson explained that

> Since around fifteen years ago, the Malaysian Chinese community has generally become more interested in curating its history… as proof that the Chinese community played a very important role in the development of the country. We are doing the same thing in Serendah, because we have many historical artefacts to share with the public.

Recording oral and family history to trace the origins of tangible items was indeed one of the goals of the temple committee when it commissioned the creation of associated audio-guides in 2023.

Data Collection, Comparison, and Analysis

Audio Media

Although each audio narrative was dedicated to its highlighted topic, it was designed to support an overall storyline, which in turn was designed to bring visitors on a journey from the origins of the town to its present state. As such, the narrative was curated according to a numbered sequence that highlighted its five sections (Table 14.1).

Although the audio-guides were recorded in three languages (Mandarin, English, and Malay), the Mandarin recording was the "control version" which most closely matched the items on display, where written descriptions were also primarily captioned in Mandarin, with partial English translations.

Printed Media

By contrast, the only extant resident-created guidebook written about Serendah (Ee, 2020) is available only in English. It was written in a data-driven format without chapters. Its highlights are described in Table 14.2.

Online Media

Whereas Serendah town is located on the fringes of the tourist gaze, the nearby eco-resort of "*Sekeping Serendah*" (literally, "*A slice of Serendah*") is, by comparison, a well-known tourist attraction catering to middle-class visitors from nearby Kuala Lumpur and its surrounding suburbs. Located very near the town,

Table 14.2. Highlights From Printed Serendah Guidebook.

Category	Description	Importance
Historical context	Tribal people, colonialism	Intangible heritage
Major buildings	Colonial and cultural buildings	Tangible heritage
Infrastructure	Colonial transport and engineering works	Access and liveability
Contemporary context	Contemporary road and rail links, Contemporary agriculture Contemporary tourism projects	Access and liveabiliy

online visitor reviews for "*Sekeping Serendah*"—mostly written in English—show a further disconnect between the audio and printed media with respect to branding the Serendah district for tourism. Based on the search phrase "*Sekeping Serendah Retreats*" there were 499 Google reviews written until November 2024, of which over 90% were written in English.

Of the top 10 keywords mentioned by these reviews (*see* Table 14.3), only 1 (atmosphere) can be linked to the sections identified as important by the Serendah Gallery described in Table 14.1, as the descriptions of "location" tended to focus on access and convenience, whereas "atmosphere" also dealt with the unique atmosphere of the Serendah district and what it offers to visitors—although for visitors to *Sekeping Serendah*, the surrounding forest was a far greater draw than history.

Table 14.3. Top 10 Keywords Mentioned by Google Reviews.

	Category	Number of Reviews	Unfavorable	Positive	Difference
1	Property	99	18%	14%	4
2	Services	70	37%	54%	17
3	Nature	66	6%	86%	80
4	Cleanliness	60	37%	55%	18
5	Sleep	53	55%	26%	29
6	Room	51	43%	39%	4
7	Fitness	48	10%	73%	63
8	Location	46	11%	59%	48
9	Bathroom	44	43%	34%	9
10	Atmosphere	40	3%	93%	90

Analysis

As the different industries that contributed to the development of the town had ceased operations by the turn of the 21st century, a simple thematic grouping of the five areas under the audio-guides revealed just two broad themes covering history and culture. Conversely, the top 10 narrow categories discussed in the online reviews can be grouped into 2 different broad themes covering guest comfort and experience. The guidebook, in turn, had sections covering the colonial and postcolonial narrative of the town as well as recent developments, which could be loosely linked to the themes of History and Experience presented in the audio-guides and online reviews, as shown in Fig. 14.1.

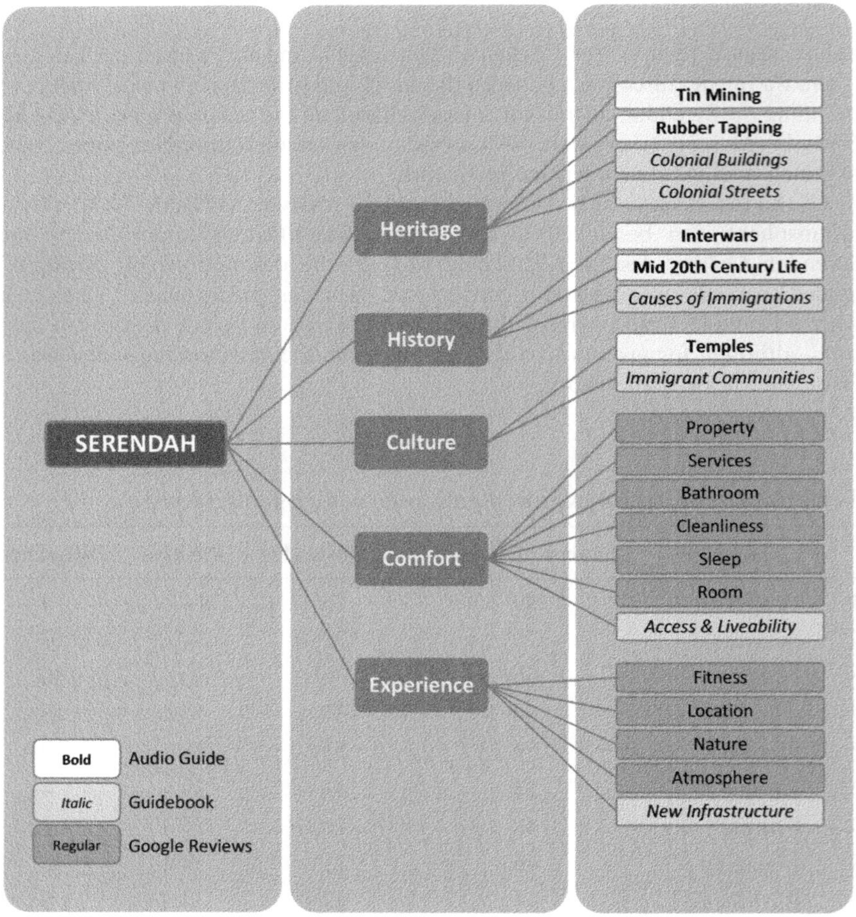

Fig. 14.1. Thematic Grouping of Keywords Highlighted in the Audio-Guides, Printed Guidebook, and Google Reviews.

Identified Themes

Heritage

The audio-guide celebrated the early contribution of tin mining and rubber tapping to Serendah as an important part of the town's intangible heritage. The guidebook did likewise but expanded the discussion of heritage to include the tangible heritage of the town's streets and old buildings. By contrast, heritage was not mentioned by any of the online reviewers. Instead, visitors to *Sekeping Serendah* were attracted by the branding of the resort as a forest retreat and its convenient location, accessible by road in an hour from the center of Kuala Lumpur. This was encouraged by the resort's website, https://www.sekeping.com/serendah/home which described Serendah as a "sleepy one street town," and which did not provide any services to visit the town or the surrounding *Temuan* villages.

History

Whereas the main focus of the audio-guides and guidebook was either heritage or history, there were noticeable differences in approaches between the two. The audio-guide utilized a story telling technique, whereas the guidebook was more data-driven, focusing on the causes and statistics of immigration into Serendah. Both were challenged by the fact that the history of Serendah is missing the major tangible monuments or the exciting/dark intangible history of dramatic events, which often attract tourists (Leiper, 1990). Indeed, the town's history is similar to many other tin mining towns or Chinese New Villages in Malaysia, where the tangible remains of old shop-houses are relatively common. Indeed, the only unique tangible monument to exist in the district is the "Seven Wells of Serendah" a still functioning sluice dam with seven spillways and sinkholes dating from colonial times. This is accessible via privately guided walking tours but is not actively promoted.

Culture

Although the guidebook briefly explained the cultural background of Serendah, it did so mostly from a historical perspective by explaining the growth of immigrant communities in the town prior to the First World War and how these communities were responsible for building their temples and laying out the town's streets in collaboration with colonial authorities. By contrast, the audio-guide walked visitors through the temple rituals and explained the importance of its enshrined deities for visitors who would otherwise be ignorant of their importance. The goal was to highlight culture as being important to the present and not merely a marker of the past.

Comfort

Neither the audio-guide nor the guidebook mentioned visitor comfort, although it is of paramount concern in online reviews of *Sekeping Serendah*. This is linked to high expectations of customer experience due to the relatively high cost of staying at the resort. Indeed, visitors were more satisfied with the pristine nature surrounding the resort than with its buildings or "created" experiences. This would imply that a better review rating could in fact be achieved via the provision of more experiences connected to the resort's surroundings, for example, visits to the old town, *Temuan* villages, or the Seven Wells.

Experience

The guidebook describes recent infrastructure developments linking Serendah to greater Kuala Lumpur by new highway and railway routes and suggests that it has a bright future as a worthy destination for urban visitors seeking history, interesting cuisine, and nature. *Sekeping Serendah* reviews, however, mostly focus on the experience of "glamping" in the jungle, overlooking any mention of Serendah town completely. By contrast, the audio-guide's focus on heritage and history essentially ignores the *contemporary* experience of visiting the town, apart from a few references to friendly locals and food toward its conclusion. This contradicts the fact that travel experience is ideally a complete package, beginning from departure and ending with the visitors' return home. To be comprehensive, a destination should therefore include not just accommodation and food, but also internal transport from one attraction to another and related activities. Only via *unique experiences* unavailable elsewhere will visitors then report satisfaction and encourage others to follow in their footsteps.

Findings

Although the research identified the five themes of *heritage, history, culture, comfort,* and *experience* as the current representation of Serendah from three different sources of visitor-friendly narratives, it also shows that none of the three different sources currently represents Serendah across all five themes by itself. For example, although both the audio-guides and the written guidebook focus on history, the deeper Chinese cultural aspects of the former are mostly missing from the latter. In turn, the guidebook's background about the *Temuan* tribes inhabiting the nearby forest as well as its statistically rich colonial history of the town are only mentioned briefly by the audio-guides. Conversely, while the guidebook describes the nature of the site in passing, natural attractions are in turn missing from the audio-guides. By contrast, visitor reviews of *Sekeping Serendah* ignore history almost completely, preferring instead to focus on the district's importance as an eco-friendly, nature-based attraction.

As a result of this "silo-based" approach to describing and experiencing Serendah for visitors, there has been a noticeable challenge toward establishing an "inter-generational transfer of ideas" from old to young in the town, where tourism is concerned. This can be attributed to several interconnected factors highlighted in this chapter:

(1) *Language shift.* Among the Chinese community in Malaysia generally, and in Serendah in particular, there has been a noticeable language shift away from regional dialects toward standardized Mandarin. This is especially true of the "millennial generation" under the age of 30. As a result, although Serendah was originally a town where different dialect groups had their own temples and where these different ancestries are still celebrated, the slow demise of traditional dialects has been accompanied by a gradual loss of each community's distinct cultural identity. This is also evidenced by the fact that Mandarin was the primary language used in the audio-guides, while the guidebook and online reviews were in English, thereby marginalizing some of the town's older residents who are fluent in neither language.

(2) *Shifting occupations.* Whereas the temple gallery and audio-guides celebrate the historical connection of the town to tin mining and rubber tapping, the disappearance of meaningful jobs in both industries means that any meaningful explanation of Serendah's industrial past is increasingly dependent on the oral histories of a shrinking pool of elderly residents. Indeed, the desire to meaningfully document these from primary sources was one of the main motivations for creating the audio-guides, which adopted a narrative approach to create stories for the millennial generation in their preferred languages.

(3) *Social separation.* Due to the rapid changes to Malaysia's economy from the 1980s to the present day, there now exists a relatively sizable and prosperous urban population centered around greater Kuala Lumpur (referred to by the government as the "T20" group, or the top 20% of households when measured by annual income). This group, which comprises many English-speaking families engaged in "white collar" and professional occupations, in turn dominates the demand for high-end domestic travel and leisure within the country, and certainly to exclusive, bespoke locations like *Sekeping Serendah.* As a result, there is now a separation between the *Temuan* tribes who traditionally lived in and cared for the forest around Serendah and the weekend "urban eco-warriors' who have become concerned about the district's flora and fauna for somewhat different, leisure-based reasons.

These three factors have shifted the role of potential tourist gatekeepers away from the traditional, dialect-speaking cultural custodians of the Chinese community, the forest-dwelling *Temuan* people of the district, and the townspeople themselves toward English-speaking urbanites whose interests are far removed from the traditional livelihoods of Serendah. Even where localized attempts have been made to control the narrative (via the audio-guides or the written guidebook), the languages used have further reinforced the pattern of language shift that has been gathering pace since the turn of the 21st century.

This chapter has shown, however, that although local people have a strong interest in sharing their *heritage, history,* and *culture* with visitors, this interest is primarily being led by older residents keen on celebrating historical achievements, which are increasingly being forgotten by younger generations. By contrast, visitors themselves are mainly concerned about their *comfort* and *experience.* The data, however, implies that visitors' lofty demands are fueled by the high price of accommodation at *Sekeping Serendah,* leading to a desire among visitors for high levels of comfort and service to justify their expenditure.

This suggests that the gap between the culturally based local desires and lofty visitor expectations can be bridged by stronger engagement between the local community (especially those from the younger generation who are currently mostly working outside Serendah in greater Kuala Lumpur), visitors, and the *Temuan* people. A sensible goal would be to produce more competitively priced eco-experiences using locally sourced labor and raw materials, which emphasize the unique culture and historical traditions of settlement in the area, while not ignoring the younger generation's desire for interesting experiences not only tied to history or culture.

If successful, this would encourage longer-term visitor stays both in the forest surrounding Serendah and in the town itself. This in turn could encourage day trips from forest lodges to the town and vice versa, as well as broaden the district's appeal toward other less wealthy visitor groups. This would allow the town to express its heritage, history, and culture to visitors who currently bypass it, while also offering a different, more accessible version of comfort and experience to a wider group of travelers who are not currently enthralled by Serendah. This will go some way toward breaking down the barriers between the different stakeholders currently populating the different silos identified in this chapter.

Conclusion

The chapter highlighted challenges associated with delivering an intergenerational transfer of ideas for tourism without the presence of a cohesive narrative, particularly in a location affected by rural–urban migration, socioeconomic change, and language shift. The findings identify the gaps in narrative crafting that exist in a location just beyond the mainstream tourist gaze, as well as their causes. In particular, the findings address the gap between local self-identity and visitor expectations that, if left unresolved, can shift the role of tourist gatekeepers away from residents to outsiders, which carries the risk of profound long-term damage to a small-scale location's social and cultural sustainability.

By suggesting the creation of new, forest-based accommodation by a younger generation of locals, albeit with an appreciation for the town's history, the findings point to ecotourism with urban links as a solution that combines the historical knowledge of older residents of Serendah with the social and professional networks of their descendants, who are now mostly working in Kuala Lumpur. It also celebrates the traditional knowledge of the forest-dwelling

Temuan people with local service providers keen on sharing their town's stories to visitors. Successfully combining these different skillsets will build bridges between the existing silos that, if left isolated, will prove unsustainable for the future of the district and its community.

Acknowledgments

The authors would like to thank the *Persatuan Hokkien Hoay Kuan Serendah, Selangor,* for sponsoring this research in collaboration with Taylor's University, Malaysia.

References

Abu Talib, A. (2015). *Museums, history and culture in Malaysia*. NUS Press.

Blackburn, K., & Hack, K. (2012). *War, memory and the making of modern Malaysia and Singapore*. NUS Press.

Carstens, S. (1980). Pulai: Memories of a gold mining settlement in Ulu Kelantan. *Journal of the Malayan Branch of the Royal Asiatic Society*, *53*, 50–67.

Ee, Y. C. (2020). *Serendah, Then and Now*. Ee Yoke Chan.

Harrison, R. (2013). *Heritage: Critical approaches*. Routledge.

Khor, N., Isa, M., & Kaur, M. (2017). *The towns of Malaya*. Editions Didier Millet.

King, D. (2006). *The Elgin marbles*. Hutchinson.

Leete, R. (2007). *Malaysia: From Kampung to twin towers: 50 years of economic and social development*. Oxford Fajar.

Leiper, N. (1990). Tourist attraction systems. *Annals of Tourism Research*, *17*(3), 367–384.

Li, T. E., & Chan, E. T. H. (2018). Connotations of ancestral home: An exploration of place attachment by multiple generations of Chinese diaspora. *Population, Space and Place*, *24*(8), e2147.

Loh, P. F. S. (1975). *Seeds of separatism: Educational policy in Malaya 1874–1940*. Oxford University Press.

Mattsson, J., Sundbo, J., & Fussing-Jensen, C. (2005). Innovation systems in tourism: The roles of attractors and scene-takers. *Industry and Innovation*, *12*(3), 357–381. https://doi.org/10.1080/13662710500195967

Moore, W. K. (2004). *Malaysia, a pictoral history*. Editions Didier Millet.

Ong, T. W. S., & Troyer, R. A. (2022). The double-edged sword of Mandarin: Language shift and cultural maintenance among middle-aged Chinese-Malaysians. *Manusya: Journal of Humanities*, *25*(1), 1–20.

Phua, J. S., & Tan, K. K. H. (2022). Local perspectives on the cultural significance of rejuvenated heritage shophouses in George Town, Penang. *Archnet-IJAR*. *17*(1), 43–69. https://doi.org/10.1108/ARCH-01-2022-0003

Ramele Ramli, R., Ali, M. H., Anas Abu Bakar, A., & Widyawati Madzhi, N. (2022). Designation of Batu Arang, Selangor as the coal mining and geological heritage site: Issues and challenges. *Journal of Cultural Heritage Management and Sustainable Development*, *15*(3), 441–461.

Rimmer, P. J., & Allen, L. M. (1990). *The underside of Malaysian history: Pullers, prostitutes, plantation workers*. NUS Press.

Tan, K. K. H., Lee, S. E., & Choy, C. W. (2020). 'Academic tourism' and art: Student submissions as a means of capturing meaning at Pulai Village, Kelantan. In P. Mura, K. K. H. Tan, & C. W. Choy (Eds.), *Contemporary Asian artistic expressions and tourism* (pp. 39–57). Springer Nature.

Tan, K. K. H., Lee, S. E., & Fu, Y. H. (2022). The role of academic field-trip organizers as gatekeepers for emerging heritage sites in Malaysia. *Journal of Tourism and Cultural Change*, *20*(3), 436–456.

Teo, E. (2010). The proclamation of independence memorial in Melaka: History, memory and silences. In B. Lockhart & T. S. Lim (Eds.), *Studies in Malaysian and Singaporean history*. MBRAS.

de la Torre, M. (2002). *Accessing the values of cultural heritage*. The Getty Conservation Institute. https://doi.org/10.2979/aft.2003.50.2.66

Urry, J. (1990). *The tourist gaze: Leisure and travel in contemporary societies*. SAGE.

Wang, X. (2009). The spread of Mandarin in Malaysia: Evidence in language choices in public settings. *Journal of Modern Languages*, *19*(1), 207–224.

Chapter 15

Tourism and Climate Change: Adoption Strategies

Ihtisham Ullah[a], *Muhammad Farooq Akhtar*[b], *Wondemsew Mesafint Kebadie*[c] *and Ravindra Kumar Perumal*[a]

[a]Asia Pacific University of Technology and Innovation (APU), Malaysia
[b]The University of Faisalabad, Pakistan
[c]Samara University, Ethiopia

Abstract

The role of tourism is established in the economic development of the country. Along with the positive impacts of tourism on the economy, this industry creates dangerous impacts on the climate of the world. This chapter highlights the negative impacts of tourism on climate and provides different strategies in the form of eco-friendly transport, waste management, and residential services to overcome and reduce the negative influence of tourism on climate and to gain sustained benefits from the gifts of nature. The last portion of this chapter highlighted the political and behavioral hurdles in the way of adopting eco-friendly strategies.

Keywords: Tourism; climate change; adoption strategies; transportation; waste management; residential management

Introduction

In recent years, the tourism industry has gained substantial popularity worldwide (Socratous et al., 2025). Tourists gain different kinds of benefits from this industry in the form of education (Meng et al., 2024), medical (Wong et al., 2024), spiritual (Ohlan & Ohlan, 2024), adventurous (Rojas et al., 2025), business (Liu et al., 2024), and leisure (Akhtar et al., 2021; Awan et al., 2025). These tourism activities contribute significantly to the economy of the country

Economics and Tourism, 237–249

Published under exclusive licence by Emerald Publishing Limited
doi:10.1108/978-1-83662-916-020251016

and the local community. The local community earns money in exchange for products and services. In addition, tourism is a great source of cultural and educational exchange activities (Pedersen & Stanoeva, 2024, pp. 1–17).

The delegates from different countries visit other places to discuss educational ideas and participate in indigenous cultural activities. On the other side, the literature dealing with sustainable consumption and production shows the negative impacts of tourism on the environment (Postma & Schmuecker, 2017). The world has faced severe environmental problems in the form of air, water, waste, and noise pollution (Akhtar & Suki, 2022, pp. 863–871). This pollution caused many dangerous diseases in humans, such as respiratory (Bălă et al., 2021), stomach (Mohammadnezhad et al., 2023), hearing loss (Tsai et al., 2021), and cancers (W. Li & Wang, 2024). The government has to spend a huge amount of budget to cure people's diseases by way of medicines, doctors' fees, equipment, surgical treatments, buildings, and other operational expenses (Garg et al., 2024; Kousar et al., 2023).

Besides the importance of tourism, the interdisciplinary literature on tourism and climate change shows that excessive tourism creates multiple environmental concerns for the people living in destination places and on the way to tourist spots. The study of Esteban-Cantillo et al. (2024) shows that building materials create environmental problems in the local communities. Further, tourists travel from distant places toward these places in specific seasons, which causes residential issues. To avoid these issues, the local community creates big hotels and restaurants that are used for a short period of time for accommodations and remain vacant for the remaining time. Tjilen et al. (2022) discussed that local residents destroy trees and plants for the creation of buildings for tourists. This activity damages the natural beauty of the town, where buildings replace the trees and plants, which reduces the sources of oxygen for humans.

Additionally, Xu et al. (2021) conducted a study on the negative impacts of tourism, showing that tourists throw waste on beautiful places. This waste creates stinky smells and destroys the natural beauty of these places. In addition to residential and waste management problems, the literature highlighted that excessive travel toward these destinations creates pollution. Based on the importance of the tourism sector and the environmental problems caused by this sector, the authors of this chapter talk about the importance of tourism, the climatic impacts of tourism, and measures to reduce the environmental impacts of tourism (residential planning, waste management, and eco-friendly transportation). Further, the authors discuss the challenges in the adoption of climate management efforts.

This study provides theoretical grounds for academics and researchers in a way to give a clear picture of the relationship between tourism and climate change. In addition to theoretical support for academicians, this chapter guides policymakers, tour planners, and governmental organizations dealing with tourism-related matters.

Current Trends of Tourism and Climate Change

Tourism

Tourism is one of the fastest-growing sectors in the world, and it has lots of different parts that come together to create the overall experience. Because it is so closely linked to the environment and climate, this industry is particularly sensitive to the impacts of climate change (Qiu et al., 2023). Take climate, for example. It really affects the resources that are available for tourism and how people experience it, such as their feelings about the weather, comfort levels with temperature, and safety concerns (Fang et al., 2018). Njoroge (2015) has identified that climate is a major factor that influences tourism in many ways, both directly and indirectly. Climate change affects our daily weather, the patterns of the seasons, how weather varies from year to year, and even how often extreme weather events happen. All these elements play a role in shaping the preferences of tourists and the decisions made by tourism operators and the demand at various destinations (Matthews et al., 2021; Noome, 2020). The World Travel and Tourism Council reported that the COVID-19 pandemic knocked the travel industry down by nearly $4.5 trillion in 2020 (Lee & Chen, 2022; Škare et al., 2021). Its contribution to global GDP dropped from 10.4% in 2019 to 5.5% in 2020 due to restrictions on mobility (Leal Filho, 2022). However, keep in mind that the tourism industry has faced some major challenges beyond just the pandemic. Climate change, for example, brings rising temperatures, shifting humidity, increased flooding, droughts, and weather that can be pretty unpredictable (Atasoy & Atasoy, 2020).

Recent studies reveal that the tourism industry contributes about 8% of global greenhouse gas emissions, which is a pretty important impact (Lenzen et al., 2018; Russo et al., 2020). The main factors contributing to this notable impact are accommodations, transport, and various tourism activities (Khatib, 2023). Projections suggest that without intervention, tourism-related emissions could rise markedly in the coming decades (Banerjee et al., 2025). The link between climate change and tourism is complex (Knowles & Scott, 2021). The tourism industry's planning, operations, and investment are already being impacted by climate change (Ma & Kirilenko, 2020). These trends emphasize the energetic relationship between tourism and climate change, simplifying the challenges faced by the industry and the innovative solutions being developed for a more sustainable future (Serio et al., 2024).

Climate Change

These days, climate change is a pressing issue that greatly affects our community's ecosystem and poses challenges to the sustainability of the tourism industry (Mohd Shariff, 2022). This topic often sparks debate in the tourism industry. People believe it could change the way things work, touching everything from infrastructure and hospitality to land, culture, and the economy (Hall et al., 2015). A major concern for the tourism industry when it comes to climate change is moving toward a low-carbon economy (H. Li et al., 2017). This entails imagining what tourism could look like in the global economy by the middle of this century. We will be aiming for net-zero emissions, and we will need to go through a big process to decarbonize the industry to hit those emission reduction goals (P. Peeters et al., 2024).

Climate change is having a growing impact on how tourists make their choices and behave (Lin & Wang, 2023). It affects where people decide to travel, what attractions and activities are available, the timing of tourist seasons, and overall enjoyment during trips (Font & Hindley, 2017). Climate change can impact the sustainability and long-term health of global tourism (Lam-González et al., 2020). Studies have shown that different climate factors, like temperature and humidity, greatly influence how much people want to travel. On the flip side, when the weather turns bad with rain or storms, it can put a damper on travel plans (Zhang & Kulendran, 2017). A recent meta-analysis showed that places affected by climate change might see shifts in tourist numbers. Bad weather can make certain spots a lot less attractive (Zhou et al., 2024). There is still insufficient study about how climate change might impact the growth of the tourism industry and its ability to advance the Sustainable Development Goals, particularly (Becken, 2019).

The Relationship Between Tourism and Climate Change

Tourism is one of those industries that feels the effects of climate change. At the same time, it's also contributing to the problem (Michailidou et al., 2016). While the environment plays a big role in tourism, research on this topic has only started to grow over the past few decades (Hoogendoorn, 2014). A plethora of recent research has been looking into the connection between tourism and climate change. It is emphasizing how much the tourism industry contributes to worldwide emissions and how vulnerable it is to the impacts of climate change (Amelung & Nicholls, 2014; Rosselló-Nadal, 2014).

Lately, there's been a growing conversation around how tourism impacts climate change, especially within the world of sustainable tourism (Fang et al., 2018; P. Peeters et al., 2024), because tourism accounts for about 8% of the world's greenhouse gas emissions, and most of this comes from traveling, staying in hotels, and other activities that tourists engage in (Scott, 2021). This large carbon footprint worsens climate change, creating real challenges for the tourism industry (Lenzen et al., 2018). As international travel demand grows, tourism-related emissions are projected to increase by 25% between 2016 and 2030 (Becken & Scott, 2024). Studies on the impacts of climate change have highlighted several implications for tourism, for instance, shifts in tourist flow, shifts in destination choice of tourists and discomfort in transportation (Ngxongo, 2021). Weather and climate are important determinants of the success of tourism in a given location and arguably, the predominant factor controlling tourist flows on a global scale (Fitchett & Hoogendoorn, 2018).

Thus, it is clear that tourists, industry players, and governments need to band together and tackle the ever-changing relationship between tourism and climate change (Luthe & Wyss, 2016). The tourism industry can make a positive impact on the environment while still offering visitors fun and enjoyable experiences (Scott & Gössling, 2022). By welcoming sustainable practices, using technology wisely, and adapting to new environmental challenges, we can create a win-win situation for everyone involved (Qiu et al., 2023).

Adoption Strategies

The tourism industry is stepping up to play its part in helping the environment (Becken et al., 2020; Sinclair-Maragh, 2016, pp. 7–24). The Glasgow Declaration on Climate Action in Tourism is all about bringing people together to reach net-zero emissions by 2050 (Higham & Miller, 2018; Scott & Gössling, 2021). Over the past two decades, there has been a growing trend in research exploring how tourism relates to climate change, especially when it comes to the global challenge of adapting to and lessening these effects (Hoogendoorn & Fitchett, 2018). This includes cutting down on carbon emissions, encouraging sustainable practices, and lending a hand to local communities (Hall, 2021, pp. 18–34).

It is important to adopt well-rounded solutions to make sure the tourism industry can thrive and withstand challenges, especially given the tricky relationship between tourism and climate change (Moyle et al., 2018). As climate change gets worse, we are starting to see its impact on tourism. Because of this, the stakeholders involved in the industry are stepping up and looking for ways to adapt that address both environmental and social issues (Papageorgiou, 2025). It is interesting to note that when it comes to climate change adaptation, the tourism industry hasn't received as much attention as other economic sectors. There is a surprising gap in research here that deserves more focus (Scott & Becken, 2010), even though research on climate change mitigation in the tourism sector has been conducted since the mid-1980s, with substantial growth in the last 15 years (Scott et al., 2019).

The existing researchers highlighted and encouraged the upcoming researchers to work on the low-carbon transition in every aspect of the tourism system, including international travel, destination management, and traveler behavior (Gössling & Higham, 2021; Scott & Gössling, 2018).

Transportation

Research on how tourism might help alleviate climate change lacks a number of essential tools, such as commonly used vocabulary, well-defined system boundaries, and appropriate data collection about modes of transportation and tourism transportation (P. Peeters et al., 2024; Scott et al., 2012). Only with this data can comprehensive inventories of CO_2 emissions be created (P. Peeters et al., 2024). Tourism-related transportation, especially air travel, is the source of the majority of emissions (Gunter & Wöber, 2021). The distance traveled between home and destinations is the primary factor influencing emissions (P. M. Peeters, 2017). Significantly reducing greenhouse gas emissions linked to tourism can be achieved by promoting the use of electric cars, trains, and other low-carbon means of transportation (Leal Filho et al., 2023). The carbon footprint of tourism can be lowered by putting demand management policies into place and enacting regulations like frequent flyer charges or aviation taxes to help reduce excessive travel demand (Rocchi et al., 2024). Developing sustainable tourism practices, such as Investing in ecotourism and nature-based travel, supports conservation efforts and promotes environmental awareness among tourists (Agyeman, 2019).

Waste Management

Increased garbage creation from tourism frequently presents problems for waste management systems (Obersteiner et al., 2021; Prabhakaran et al., 2016). Incorporating cutting-edge technologies is essential to updating waste management in the travel and tourism industry. (Rahman et al., 2024). Data analytics, Geographic Information Systems (GIS), and remote sensing are examples of innovations that improve environmental change monitoring and management (Fatorić & Seekamp, 2017). These tools facilitate real-time tracking of waste generation and disposal patterns, enabling more responsive and efficient waste management strategies (Perkumienė et al., 2023). Adaptive strategies in waste management are integral to aligning tourism practices with climate change mitigation and adaptation goals (Mdoda et al., 2024). The tourism sector may greatly lessen its environmental effect and increase resistance to climate change by adopting sustainable practices, technological advancements, strategic planning, and cooperative initiatives (Banerjee et al., 2025; Papageorgiou, 2025; Rahman et al., 2024; Tehseen et al., 2024, pp. 69–94).

Residential Services

Reducing the carbon footprint of lodging facilities for tourists requires the implementation of energy-efficient technologies and the integration of renewable energy sources (Rahman et al., 2024). Water scarcity, exacerbated by climate change, poses significant challenges. Accommodations are adopting water-saving technologies and practices to address this issue (Brandão et al., 2018). In order to overcome the issues posed by climate change, the tourism industry must implement adaptive solutions for residential services (Michailidou et al., 2016). Hotels may improve their resilience and support the growth of sustainable tourism by emphasizing energy efficiency, climate-responsive designs, water conservation, and stakeholder collaboration (Hoogendoorn & Fitchett, 2018; Jain, 2025, pp. 271–288).

Challenges in the Adoption of Sustainable Initiatives

The chapter previously discussed tourism, the influence of tourism on climate, and measures to reduce the effects of tourism on environmental degradation. This section of the chapter deals with the issues that hinder the progress on these burning issues. The vision and direction of the governmental agencies about tourism and climate change are crucial for the successful management of this whole process of tourism and environmental management (Lu et al., 2024; Yüksel et al., 2012). The literature dealing with tourism and politics discusses that low-income countries have many other problems in the form of corruption, favoritism, education, and political instability (Şanlı et al., 2024).

All these basic-level concerns hide the holistic concerns related to tourism and climate change. These countries have fewer laws to protect the environment, which more specifically deal with residence, transport quality, and waste management (Atta et al., 2024). On the other side, law enforcement agencies failed to strictly implement environmental laws in true letter and spirit (Salamba, 2024). Moreover, the behavioral literature highlighted that people in third-world countries are illiterate, which creates ignorance among the people about environmental issues (Ismail, 2024; Mahasan & Akhtar, 2024).

Conclusion

As we draw this discussion to a close, tourism plays a significant role in the growth of the country and the world. Moreover, the extensive traveling of tourists from one place to another creates environmental problems in the form of air, water, and noise pollution. This chapter suggested different adoption strategies in the form of transportation, residence, and waste management to overcome these pressing issues. These adoption strategies are helpful to improve the weather conditions and provide a clean environment (pollution-free) to the tourists and the local community. Besides the importance of these strategies, the literature shows the reluctance in the adoption of sustainable options by the local community and the government. Consequently, the success of tourism and sustainable practices is possible with the collaboration of local communities and the government. The successful adoption of sustainable strategies is helpful for the local community in the form of local business development (food, transport, residence, and tour guides). In addition to the local community, the government may get benefits from these initiatives in the form of tax collection, royalties, and the projection of indigenous tourism in international media and the world.

References

Agyeman, Y. B. (2019). Ecotourism as an adaptation strategy for mitigating climate change impacts on local communities around protected areas in Ghana. In *Handbook of climate change resilience* (pp. 151–159). Springer.

Akhtar, M. F., Saeed, S., & Waheed, M. (2021). Smart tourism: An alternative approach to clench overtourism. *Overtourism, technology solutions and decimated destinations* (pp. 217–225). Springer Nature Singapore.

Akhtar, M. F., & Suki, N. M. (2022). *Green consumer behaviour: Integration of theory of planned behaviour and technology acceptance model Research Anthology on measuring and achieving sustainable development goals.* IGI Global Scientific Publishing.

Amelung, B., & Nicholls, S. (2014). Implications of climate change for tourism in Australia. *Tourism Management*, *41*, 228–244.

Atasoy, M., & Atasoy, F. G. (2020). The impact of climate change on tourism: A causality analysis. *Turkish Journal of Agriculture-Food Science and Technology*, *8*(2), 515–519.

Atta, N., Sharifi, A., & Ying Lee, C. (2024). The relationship between the rule of law and environmental sustainability: Empirical evidence from the analysis of global indices. *The International Journal of Sustainable Development and World Ecology*, *31*(8), 1023–1039.

Awan, A., Hussain, K., Zafar, M., & Bajwa, S. U. (2025). Is tourism conducive to green growth? An investigation of the role of tourism-based economic expansion in the nexus of leisure tourism and business tourism. *Journal of Hospitality and Tourism Insights*, *8*(1), 120–137.

Bălă, G.-P., Râjnoveanu, R.-M., Tudorache, E., Motişan, R., & Oancea, C. (2021). Air pollution exposure—The (in) visible risk factor for respiratory diseases. *Environmental Science and Pollution Research*, *28*(16), 19615–19628.

Banerjee, A., Mahmudov, T., Adler, E., Aisyah, F. N., & Wörndl, W. (2025). Modeling sustainable city trips: Integrating CO2e emissions, popularity, and seasonality into tourism recommender systems. *Information Technology & Tourism*, 1–38.

Becken, S. (2019). Decarbonising tourism: Mission impossible? *Tourism Recreation Research*, *44*(4), 419–433.

Becken, S., & Scott, D. (2024). Tourism and climate change stocktake: A call to action. *Journal of Sustainable Tourism*, *32*(9), 2018–2038.

Becken, S., Whittlesea, E., Loehr, J., & Scott, D. (2020). Tourism and climate change: Evaluating the extent of policy integration. *Journal of Sustainable Tourism*, *28*(10), 1603–1624.

Brandão, C. N., Barbieri, J. C., & Araújo, M. F. (2018). Tourism and climate: A substantive theory on adaptation strategies in the accommodation sector in "Águas Paulista" circuit, São Paulo, Brazil. *WIT Transactions on Ecology and the Environment*, *227*, 163–174.

Esteban-Cantillo, O. J., Menendez, B., & Quesada, B. (2024). Climate change and air pollution impacts on cultural heritage building materials in Europe and Mexico. *Science of the Total Environment*, *921*, 170945.

Fang, Y., Yin, J., & Wu, B. (2018). Climate change and tourism: A scientometric analysis using CiteSpace. *Journal of Sustainable Tourism*, *26*(1), 108–126.

Fatorić, S., & Seekamp, E. (2017). Are cultural heritage and resources threatened by climate change? A systematic literature review. *Climatic Change*, *142*(1), 227–254.

Fitchett, J., & Hoogendoorn, G. (2018). An analysis of factors affecting tourists' accounts of weather in South Africa. *International Journal of Biometeorology*, *62*, 2161–2172.

Font, X., & Hindley, A. (2017). Understanding tourists' reactance to the threat of a loss of freedom to travel due to climate change: A new alternative approach to encouraging nuanced behavioural change. *Journal of Sustainable Tourism*, *25*(1), 26–42.

Garg, S., Tripathi, N., & Bebarta, K. K. (2024). Cost of care for non-communicable diseases: Which types of healthcare providers are the most economical in India's Chhattisgarh state? *PharmacoEconomics-Open*, 1–11.

Gössling, S., & Higham, J. (2021). The low-carbon imperative: Destination management under urgent climate change. *Journal of Travel Research*, *60*(6), 1167–1179.

Gunter, U., & Wöber, K. (2021). Estimating transportation-related CO2 emissions of European city tourism. *Journal of Sustainable Tourism*, *30*(1), 145–168.

Hall, C. M. (2021). *Climate change and tourism: Emerging transformations emerging transformations in tourism and hospitality*. Routledge.

Hall, C. M., Amelung, B., Cohen, S., Eijgelaar, E., Gössling, S., Higham, J., & Scott, D. (2015). Denying bogus skepticism in climate change and tourism research. *Tourism Management*, *47*, 352–356.

Higham, J., & Miller, G. (2018). *Transforming societies and transforming tourism: Sustainable tourism in times of change* (Vol. 26, pp. 1–8). Taylor & Francis.

Hoogendoorn, G. (2014). Mapping fly-fishing tourism in Southern Africa. *African Journal of Hospitality, Tourism and Leisure*, *3*.

Hoogendoorn, G., & Fitchett, J. M. (2018). Tourism and climate change: A review of threats and adaptation strategies for Africa. *Current Issues in Tourism*, *21*(7), 742–759.

Ismail, W. N. A. T. (2024). Challenges and opportunities for implementing innovative green tourism practices: Evidence from Indonesia. *Planning Malaysia*, *22*.

Jain, R. (2025). Building climate resilience adaptation strategies for sustainable development in the UAE. In *Exploring pillars of sustainability for modern age improvements*. IGI Global.

Khatib, A. N. (2023). Climate change and travel: Harmonizing to abate impact. *Current Infectious Disease Reports*, *25*(4), 77–85.

Knowles, N. L., & Scott, D. (2021). Media representations of climate change risk to ski tourism: A barrier to climate action? *Current Issues in Tourism*, *24*(2), 149–156.

Kousar, S., Ahmed, F., Afzal, M., & Segovia, J. E. (2023). Is government spending in the education and health sector necessary for human capital development? *Humanities and Social Sciences Communications*, *10*(1), 1–11.

Lam-González, Y. E., Galindo, C. G., Hernández, M. M. G., & León, C. J. (2020). Understanding the heterogeneity of tourists' choices under climate change risks: A segmentation analysis. *Atmosphere*, *12*(1), 22.

Leal Filho, W. (2022). Will climate change disrupt the tourism sector? *International Journal of Climate Change Strategies and Management*, *14*(2), 212–217.

Leal Filho, W., Ng, A. W., Sharifi, A., Janová, J., Özuyar, P. G., Hemani, C., & Rampasso, I. (2023). Global tourism, climate change and energy sustainability: Assessing carbon reduction mitigating measures from the aviation industry. *Sustainability Science*, *18*(2), 983–996.

Lee, C.-C., & Chen, M.-P. (2022). The impact of COVID-19 on the travel and leisure industry returns: Some international evidence. *Tourism Economics*, *28*(2), 451–472.

Lenzen, M., Sun, Y.-Y., Faturay, F., Ting, Y.-P., Geschke, A., & Malik, A. (2018). The carbon footprint of global tourism. *Nature Climate Change*, *8*(6), 522–528.

Li, H., Song, H., & Li, L. (2017). A dynamic panel data analysis of climate and tourism demand: Additional evidence. *Journal of Travel Research*, *56*(2), 158–171.

Li, W., & Wang, W. (2024). Causal effects of exposure to ambient air pollution on cancer risk: Insights from genetic evidence. *Science of the Total Environment*, *912*, 168843.

Lin, C.-H., & Wang, W.-C. (2023). Impacts of climate change knowledge on coastal tourists' destination decision-making and revisit intentions. *Journal of Hospitality and Tourism Management*, *56*, 322–335.

Liu, J., Mai, H., Zhao, X., & Zhou, Z. (2024). Business tourism: A bibliometric visualization review (1994–2023). *Tourism Review*, *80*(9). https://doi.org/10.1108/TR-11-2023-0813

Lu, Y., Bashir, H., Ayub, A., Hasnain, A., & Akhtar, M. F. (2024). Green knowledge sharing and green innovative behavior: The roles of transformational leadership and green shared vision. *Journal of the Knowledge Economy*, 1–25.

Luthe, T., & Wyss, R. (2016). Resilience to climate change in a cross-scale tourism governance context: A combined quantitative-qualitative network analysis. *Ecology and Society*, *21*(1).

Ma, S., & Kirilenko, A. P. (2020). Climate change and tourism in English-language newspaper publications. *Journal of Travel Research*, *59*(2), 352–366.

Mahasan, S. S., & Akhtar, M. F. (2024). The effect of CSR on organizational performance: Mediating role of corporate image and moderating role of corporate activism. *International Journal of Contemporary Issues in Social Science*, *3*(2), 182–192.

Matthews, L., Scott, D., Andrey, J., Mahon, R., Trotman, A., Burrowes, R., & Charles, A. (2021). Developing climate services for Caribbean tourism: A comparative analysis of climate push and pull influences using climate indices. *Current Issues in Tourism*, *24*(11), 1576–1594.

Mdoda, S. S., Dube, K., & Montsiemang, T. (2024). Tackling water and waste management challenges within the tourism and hospitality industry: A sustainable development goals perspective. *Water*, *16*(24), 3545.

Meng, L., Yan, F., Fang, Q., & Si, W. (2024). Research on the educational tourism development of intangible cultural heritage: Suitability, spatial pattern, and obstacle factor. *Sustainability*, *16*(11), 4647.

Michailidou, A. V., Vlachokostas, C., & Moussiopoulos, N. (2016). Interactions between climate change and the tourism sector: Multiple-criteria decision analysis to assess mitigation and adaptation options in tourism areas. *Tourism Management*, *55*, 1–12.

Mohammadnezhad, K., Sahebi, M. R., Alatab, S., & Sajadi, A. (2023). Investigating heavy-metal soil contamination state on the rate of stomach cancer using remote sensing spectral features. *Environmental Monitoring and Assessment*, *195*(5), 583.

Mohd Shariff, N. (2022). Adaptation strategies for impacts of climate change on sustainable tourism in Malaysia. *GeoJournal of Tourism & Geosites*, *45*.

Moyle, C.-l. J., Moyle, B. D., Chai, A., Hales, R., Banhalmi-Zakar, Z., & Bec, A. (2018). Have Australia's tourism strategies incorporated climate change? *Journal of Sustainable Tourism*, *26*(5), 703–721.

Ngxongo, N. A. (2021). The impact of climate change on visitor destination selection: A case study of the central Drakensberg region in KwaZulu-Natal. *Jàmbá: Journal of Disaster Risk Studies*, *13*(1), 1161.

Njoroge, J. M. (2015). Climate change and tourism adaptation: Literature review. *Tourism and Hospitality Management*, *21*(1), 95–108.

Noome, K. (2020). *An assessment of the climatic suitability of Namibia for tourism using the Tourism Climate Index (TCI)*. University of the Witwatersrand.

Obersteiner, G., Gollnow, S., & Eriksson, M. (2021). Carbon footprint reduction potential of waste management strategies in tourism. *Environmental Development*, *39*, 100617.

Ohlan, R., & Ohlan, A. (2024). Religious tourism scholarship: Current state and future research directions. *Journal of Islamic Marketing*, *15*(3), 800–818.

Papageorgiou, M. (2025). Spatial planning for tourism destinations resilient to climate change. *Tourism and Hospitality*, *6*(1), 8.

Pedersen, S. B., & Stanoeva, E. (2024). *Tourism diplomacy in cold war Europe: Symbolic gestures, cultural exchange and human rights*. Contemporary European History.

Peeters, P. M. (2017). *Tourism's impact on climate change and its mitigation challenges: How can tourism become 'climatically sustainable'*.

Peeters, P., Çakmak, E., & Guiver, J. (2024). Current issues in tourism: Mitigating climate change in sustainable tourism research. *Tourism Management*, *100*, 104820.

Perkumienė, D., Atalay, A., Safaa, L., & Grigienė, J. (2023). Sustainable waste management for clean and safe environments in the recreation and tourism sector: A case study of Lithuania, Turkey and Morocco. *Recycling*, *8*(4), 56.

Postma, A., & Schmuecker, D. (2017). Understanding and overcoming negative impacts of tourism in city destinations: Conceptual model and strategic framework. *Journal of Tourism Futures*, *3*(2), 144–156.

Prabhakaran, S., Nair, V., & Ramachandran, S. (2016). Community participation in mitigating marine waste to reduce climatic change in tourism destinations. *Worldwide Hospitality and Tourism Themes*, *8*(5), 569–577.

Qiu, X., Kong, H., Wang, K., Zhang, N., Park, S., & Bu, N. (2023). Past, present, and future of tourism and climate change research: Bibliometric analysis based on VOSviewer and SciMAT. *Asia Pacific Journal of Tourism Research*, *28*(1), 36–55.

Rahman, T. U., Saud, D., & Nawaz, T. (2024). Sustainable tourism in a changing climate: Strategies for management, adaptation, and resilience. *Penrose: International Journal of Interdisciplinary Studies*, *1*(2), e24001.

Rocchi, L., Rizzo, A. G., Paolotti, L., Boggia, A., & Attard, M. (2024). Assessing climate change vulnerability of coastal roads. *Mitigation and Adaptation Strategies for Global Change*, *29*(5), 43.

Rojas, N. S., Sand, M. S., & Gross, S. (2025). Regenerative adventure tourism: Going beyond sustainability–a Horizon 2050 paper. *Tourism Review*, *80*(1), 270–285. https://doi.org/10.1108/TR-12-2023-0874

Rosselló-Nadal, J. (2014). How to evaluate the effects of climate change on tourism. *Tourism Management*, *42*, 334–340.

Russo, M., Relvas, H., Gama, C., Lopes, M., Borrego, C., Rodrigues, V. & Eusébio, C. (2020). Estimating emissions from tourism activities. *Atmospheric Environment*, *220*, 117048.

Salamba, Y. P. (2024). The effectiveness of law enforcement against the perpetrators of tourism object vandalism. In *North Toraja* (pp. 48–62). Journal of Court and Justice.

Şanlı, D., Gülbay Yiğiteli, N., & Ergün Tatar, H. (2024). Do economic complexity drivers differ by income level? Insights from a global perspective. *Sage Open*, *14* (2). https://doi.org/10.1177/21582440241239412

Scott, D. (2021). Sustainable tourism and the grand challenge of climate change. *Sustainability*, *13*(4), 1966.

Scott, D., & Becken, S. (2010). Adapting to climate change and climate policy: Progress, problems and potentials. *Journal of Sustainable Tourism*, *18*(3), 283–295.

Scott, D., & Gössling, S. (2018). *Tourism and climage change mitigation: Embracing the Paris agreement: Pathways to decarbonisation: European travel commission*.

Scott, D., & Gössling, S. (2021). From Djerba to Glasgow: Have declarations on tourism and climate change brought us any closer to meaningful climate action? *Journal of Sustainable Tourism*, *30*(1), 199–222.

Scott, D., & Gössling, S. (2022). A review of research into tourism and climate change-Launching the annals of tourism research curated collection on tourism and climate change. *Annals of Tourism Research*, *95*, 103409.

Scott, D., Hall, C. M., & Gössling, S. (2019). Global tourism vulnerability to climate change. *Annals of Tourism Research*, *77*, 49–61.

Scott, D., Hall, C. M., & Stefan, G. (2012). *Tourism and climate change: Impacts, adaptation and mitigation*. Routledge.

Serio, R. G., Dickson, M. M., de Graaff, T., & Pels, E. H. (2024). *Environmental policies as a pull factor for tourists? Insights from Italy* [Preprint]. arXiv. https://doi.org/https://doi.org/https://doi.org/https://doi.org/https://doi.org/https://doi.org/https://arxiv.org/abs/2404.08696

Sinclair-Maragh, G. (2016). *Climate change and the hospitality and tourism industry in developing countries climate change and the 2030 corporate agenda for sustainable development*. Emerald Publishing Limited.

Škare, M., Soriano, D. R., & Porada-Rochoń, M. (2021). Impact of COVID-19 on the travel and tourism industry. *Technological Forecasting and Social Change*, *163*, 120469.

Socratous, M., Thrasyvoulou, G., & Stylianou, C. (2025). Technology-driven sustainable tourism destinations: Perspectives from key policymakers. *Worldwide Hospitality and Tourism Themes*, *17*(1), 77–90. https://doi.org/10.1108/WHATT-12-2024-0298

Tehseen, S., Hossain, S. M., Ong, K. Y., & Andrews, E. (2024). *Sustainable tourism in a changing climate: Balancing growth and environmental responsibility the need for sustainable tourism in an era of global climate change: Pathway to a greener future*. Emerald Publishing Limited.

Tjilen, A. P., Sahetapy, W., Tambaip, B., & Betaubun, M. (2022). Ecotourism development policy, supporting capacity and development of sustainable tourism facilities and infrastructure in Raja Ampat Regency, West Papua Province. *The International Journal of Science in Society*, *4*(03).

Tsai, S. C.-S., Hsu, Y.-C., Lai, J.-N., Chou, R.-H., Fan, H.-C., Lin, F. C.-F., & Chang, K.-H. (2021). Long-term exposure to air pollution and the risk of developing sudden sensorineural hearing loss. *Journal of Translational Medicine*, *19*, 1–7.

Wong, A. K. F., Vongvisitsin, T. B., Li, P., Pan, Y., & Ryan, C. (2024). Revisiting medical tourism research: Critical reviews and implications for destination management and marketing. *Journal of Destination Marketing & Management*, *33*, 100924.

Xu, X., Feng, C., Zhen, D., Tan, Y., & Lai, Q. (2021). Evaluation of the environmental costs of tourism based on an emergy analysis of tourism waste disposal: A case study of Yarlung Zangbo grand Canyon National Park in Motuo county, Tibet. *Environmental Science and Pollution Research*, *28*, 32708–32720.

Yüksel, A., Yüksel, F., & Culha, O. (2012). Ministers' statements: A policy implementation instrument for sustainable tourism? *Journal of Sustainable Tourism*, *20*(4), 513–532.

Zhang, H. Q., & Kulendran, N. (2017). The impact of climate variables on seasonal variation in Hong Kong inbound tourism demand. *Journal of Travel Research*, *56*(1), 94–107.

Zhou, W., Faturay, F., Driml, S., & Sun, Y.-Y. (2024). Meta-analysis of the climate change-tourism demand relationship. *Journal of Sustainable Tourism*, *32*(9), 1762–1783.

Chapter 16

Trends in the Development of Tourism Associated With Indigenous Culture

Nguyen Thi Minh Tien[a] *and Nguyen Thi Thanh Thuy*[b]

[a]Hanoi University, Vietnam
[b]Vietnam Women's Academy, Vietnam

Abstract

This chapter delves into the intricate interplay between indigenous cultures and tourism, emphasizing the evolving trends that shape their relationship. As globalization accelerates, indigenous communities find themselves at a crossroads where the preservation of cultural heritage is increasingly intertwined with the tourism sector. The chapter highlights the rise of cultural and eco-tourism, where travelers seek authentic experiences that connect them to the indigenous lifestyle. The current status of cultural tourism in the world and Vietnam is also analyzed, providing a panoramic view of its current and future development trends. The chapter also discusses critical challenges faced by indigenous communities as well as suggested solutions for the development of tourism associated with indigenous culture.

Keywords: Indigenous culture; sustainable tourism; Vietnamese indigenous tourism; eco-tourism; culture preservation

Introduction

In recent years, tourism associated with indigenous cultures has evolved from a niche interest to a dynamic and rapidly growing sector within the global travel industry. According to the World Travel & Tourism Council (WTTC), the indigenous tourism market is projected to reach $67 billion by 2034, growing at a compound annual growth rate (CAGR) of 4.1%. This surge is driven by travelers' increasing desire for authentic, immersive experiences that connect them

Economics and Tourism, 251–265

doi:10.1108/978-1-83662-916-020251017

with the rich cultural heritage of indigenous communities.[1] Indigenous tourism represents a unique intersection of economic opportunity and cultural preservation. In Canada, the indigenous tourism sector supports nearly 2,000 businesses and over 39,000 jobs, contributing CA$1.7 billion to the economy as of 2017. Similarly, in Western Australia, the indigenous tourism sector added AU $63.8 million to the Gross State Product in 2021–2022.[2] This growth reflects successful governance models that prioritize community participation and equitable benefit distribution. According to Smith (2009), these initiatives frequently integrate cultural tourism with other sectors, including ecotourism, culinary experiences, and environmental conservation. This chapter explores the significances and benefits of tourism development associated with indigenous culture through multiple case study analysis, examining how indigenous communities navigate tourism development while protecting cultural identity and advancing community well-being.

The Significance of Indigenous Culture in Tourism Development

Concepts of Indigenous Culture

Culture is a broad concept that is interpreted differently and relates to all aspects of human life. According to James et al. (2015), components of culture include knowledge, faith, art, morals, law, practices, and any customs or practices that a person acquires as a member of society. The perspectives on these constitutive aspects are also affirmed by UNESCO in the Universal Declaration on Cultural Diversity (2001), as "a set of distinctive spiritual, material, intellectual and emotional features of society or a social group, and that it encompasses, in addition to art and literature, lifestyles, ways of living together, value systems, traditions and beliefs."

Indigenous peoples[3] are special populations, which can be called by many different names, such as first peoples, aboriginal tribes, and autochthonous/native peoples. It is the group of people originating from and identified as the original inhabitants who lived and settled for a long time in a certain area, distinguished from other groups that have settled or occupied the region in recent times (Sanders, 1999). This group is often described as indigenous when they maintain customs or other components of an early culture tied to a given area. They have a set of rights based on their cultural and historical identity and territory, which is protected by international or national law from other population groups (Coates, 2004).

Indigenous culture is the cultural identity of indigenous people formed during their community development process. Cultural identity is the vibrant sum of

---

[1]https://wttc.org/news/indigenous-tourism-to-inject-67bbn-usd-into-global-economy-says-wttc-report?

[2]https://hotelbizlink.com/indigenous-tourism-a-67-billion-opportunity-for-global-economic-growth/

[3]Sanders, D. E. (1999, January). Indigenous peoples: Issues of definition. *International Journal of Cultural Property*, *8*(1), 4–13.

creative activities that constitute the value system, traditions, tastes, aesthetics, and lifestyle of people that have taken place in the past as well as are taking place at present through which people assert their own identities. Indigenous culture refers to the unique, traditional, historical practices, beliefs, languages, and customs of indigenous peoples, which are often characterized by a deep connection to the land, community-based ways of living, oral traditions, and spiritual beliefs that have been passed down through generations. It holds invaluable knowledge systems that have evolved over time, offering insights into sustainable living and community resilience.

The Roles of Indigenous Culture in Tourism Development

Indigenous cultures play a significant and multifaceted role in tourism development. As unique expressions of cultural heritage, traditions, and lifestyles, indigenous cultures attract tourists seeking authentic experiences and insights into different ways of life.

Indigenous cultures offer rich historical narratives, traditional knowledge, art forms, and rituals that can enhance the authenticity of tourism experiences, and cultural tourism uses these cultural resources as a foundation to build its products. Tourists often seek special, novel experiences in places with cultural differences and genuine interactions with local communities, or join in various activities associated with the livelihoods and daily customs of the indigenous people at the destination, which makes cultural heritage a key attraction. Indigenous culture combined with tourism will promote the comparative advantage of a locality, and many places consider cultural heritages as special assets to improve their competitiveness in tourism development.

Indigenous peoples are considered the ones who were originally born, coexist with the natural environment over time, and often possess unique cultural practices, languages, art, and traditions that can enhance the authenticity of tourism experiences, drawing visitors interested in learning about and engaging with local customs. Meanwhile, cultural features encourage tourists to join in cultural events, festivals, ceremonies, and traditional crafts. Cultural tourists often have a deep understanding of local ecosystems and sustainable practices, which can improve ecotourism initiatives, leading to sustainable tourism development that respects the environment and local customs.

Benefits of Tourism Development Associated With Indigenous Culture

Tourism, with its continued growth and diversification encompassing an increasing number of new destinations, has become a key driver for socio-economic development (Kajzar, 2013). Tourism development associated with indigenous culture can yield significant benefits, promoting economic growth, cultural preservation, and social well-being, while also encouraging sustainable practices and greater autonomy for indigenous communities. Developing tourism associated with indigenous culture not only brings great economic and social benefits but is also an effective way to preserve cultural heritage values that are increasingly being lost or destroyed by time or by the neglect of indigenous communities.

One of the core elements to develop products of cultural tourism is the cultural heritage resources (Boniface, 2003), which include the richness, diversity, and uniqueness of cultural elements crystallized in the development process of each nation and locality, passed down from generation to generation (Boniface, 2003; McKercher & Du Cros, 2002), and become the main driving force of cultural tourism development (Boniface, 2003).

One significant advantage of tourism associated with indigenous culture is its potential to boost local economies. Visitors' spending for local services such as accommodation, food, entrance tickets, transportation and souvenirs can make a great contribution to the growth and development of the locality. A part from that, cultural tourism can also create job opportunities for local people working in relevant services including guides, performers, artisans, etc..., who bring authentic cultural experiences to tourists.

Economic Benefits

Revenue Generation

Visitors engaged in cultural tourism contribute significantly to the local economy through spending on accommodations, food, souvenirs, and entrance fees to cultural sites, which stimulates production and develops infrastructure systems and technical materials to serve tourism development associated with indigenous culture. The influx of tourist dollars can boost economic growth in the region and make a contribution to the international payment balance of a country. In addition, *by participating in community-based tourism, local people can* generate their income through entrance fees, cultural performances, selling local handicrafts, or *working for different tourism providers.* Tourism associated with indigenous culture can also provide income during peak seasons (of festivals, for instance) and contribute to a more stable economic base for communities by encouraging year-round visitation, particularly if cultural offerings are diversified.

Job Creation and Local Budget Increase

Tourism associated with indigenous culture promotes employment opportunities in different sectors such as hospitality, arts and crafts, travel services, guiding, and cultural performances. New jobs can emerge in restaurants, hotels, museums, tour companies, and local residences, as those who serve tourists will be trained in relevant skills and subsequently enhance their employability. In another way, indigenous people can start their own business by leveraging local cultural assets like craft shops or guided tours, and souvenir shops. In villages with traditional craft, local people can not only introduce and sell handicraft products to tourists but also potentially export. This contributes to "on-the-spot export" of industrial commodities, consumption goods, handicrafts, agricultural, and forestry products... with higher retail prices while sellers do not have to pay for shipping, insurance, or export—imported taxes. Tourism associated with indigenous culture, on the other hand, generates revenue for local governments through sales taxes, lodging taxes, and other fees. This revenue can be reinvested in community services, infrastructure, and cultural preservation efforts.

Local Business Support

Tourism associated with indigenous culture encourages the growth of local businesses such as artisan shops, restaurants, and tour operators. It creates a market for locally made products, allowing communities to control their economic destiny and benefit from their cultural resources. It also promotes other economic sectors because tourism needs interdisciplinary support like manufacturing, accommodation, insurance, construction, transportation, and retail and financial services. By developing tourism associated with indigenous culture, respective localities can diversify their economies, reducing reliance on traditional industries like agriculture or manufacturing. This diversification helps to buffer against economic downturns.

Investment in Infrastructure

The development of tourism associated with indigenous culture often leads to investments in infrastructure, including roads, public transportation, utilities, and community facilities, which can improve the local residents' life quality as well as enhance tourist experiences. Tourism associated with indigenous culture brings high profit margins with low-risk investment, uncomplicated techniques, and fast capital return. This makes it easy to attract capital from domestic and foreign investors. Successful models of indigenous cultural tourism development can raise regional and national profiles, which, in return, attract investment and showcase cultural heritage to a wider audience, leading to an ongoing influx of tourists and related economic benefits.

International Economic Relations Promotion

Tourism associated with indigenous culture encourages intercultural dialogue and experiences, leading to a better understanding of different cultures that can foster goodwill and create opportunities for international partnerships and collaborations. Cultural heritage on a country's territory is a big card to attract foreign tourists, which generates other trade relationships accordingly. Expanding relationships helps local tourism service suppliers learn and exchange experiences to create rich, diverse, and distinctive products, while indigenous people can learn about different cultural values from visitors.

In addition, tourism associated with indigenous culture makes a contribution to increasing labor productivity. It improves indigenous people's knowledge, enables them to learn new techniques, and strengthens their health and spirit, which, as a result, brings higher efficiency and creativity in work.

Social Benefits

Besides economic benefits, tourism associated with indigenous culture also brings local communities social and environmental benefits (Aref et al., 2010). Through tourism, international visitors have better insights into the cultural heritages and values of a country, which can awaken the hidden cultural values of and bring benefits to the country and indigenous people.

Tourism associated with indigenous culture creates a unique opportunity for visitors to submerge themselves in a region's history and traditions. Through experiencing the local customs, they can gain an authentic understanding of indigenous cultures that enables them to enjoy the cultural diversity and uniqueness of the world. Cultural heritage preservation and revitalization are also other benefits of tourism associated with indigenous culture. Local people are encouraged to protect and maintain their cultural assets to attract more visitors who are seeking authentic experiences of different traditions and history. This, in combination with the promotion of diversified cultures, creates a sense of ownership, pride, and belonging for indigenous people, and it subsequently strengthens cultural exchange, enabling them to learn about other cultures while acknowledging their values and beliefs. Many countries around the world have retrieved and enhanced historical and material cultural relics as well as other spiritual values, which have been neglected or immersed in other national events. This helps maintain a sense of identity that allows future generations to benefit from those valuable resources.

Through tourism, people can immerse themselves in diverse cultures and become more appreciative of other cultures, which helps them build broader mindsets and respect for cultural differences. This will increase tolerance among different groups of people and societies. The trips associated with the indigenous culture of tourists are usually more memorable than conventional holidays, as they enable them to learn something new through their visits to various tangible cultural attractions such as national parks, art galleries, archeological sites, historical buildings, and museums, or their real experiences and participation in local craft making, dances, or traditional events. By interacting with local artists and performers, cultural tourists can establish an appreciation for numerous artistic expressions, which contributes to the general vitality of the art world and supports the preservation and maintenance of performing arts and other creative activities. The increase in recognition of indigenous cultures through tourism can lead to better representation in policy-making processes, allowing indigenous voices to be heard on issues affecting their communities. This would make better changes for local people, visitors, and tourism destinations as well as for the whole country.

Environmental Benefits

Tourism associated with indigenous culture has the potential to bring significant environmental benefits when approached with sustainability and community involvement in mind. By emphasizing the connection between culture, heritage, and the environment, it can foster a better acknowledgment of both and stimulate responsible behaviors among tourists and host groups. This connection makes a great contribution to preserving both cultural and natural heritages for future generations. In many cases, natural landscapes and biodiversity are encouraged to be preserved by local people and governments to attract visitors. These, in return, generate new income to support conservation initiatives, protect habitats, and foster responsible land management practices, which will contribute to improving biodiversity and enhancing the resilience of local ecosystems. By integrating these practices into tourism, visitors can learn about sustainable agriculture, fishing, and land use, fostering an appreciation for environmentally friendly methods and instilling a sense of responsibility toward conserving natural resources. In many regions, various educational tours that highlight traditional ecological knowledge are offered, which can promote understanding of sustainable practices and environmental ethics. Increased awareness will lead to more environmentally conscious behaviors among tourists, both during their travels and upon returning home.

In addition, tourism associated with indigenous culture usually encourages local communities to take ownership of their environmental and cultural resources. This empowerment often leads to community-led conservation initiatives, where locals develop strategies to protect their natural and cultural heritage. Involvement in tourism associated with culture creates economic incentives for communities to engage in sustainable land-use practices that benefit both the environment and their livelihoods. Apart from that, indigenous cultural tourism can help with dispersing visitors away from heavily urbanized areas and concentrating them in rural regions or cultural sites. Encouraging travel to less populated areas, it will alleviate the pressures of urbanization on local environments and ecosystems, reducing pollution, overpopulation, and habitat destruction typically associated with urban development. The growth of indigenous cultural tourism can drive investment in green infrastructure that benefits both the community and the environment. This includes initiatives such as eco-lodges, the use of sustainable materials for construction, renewable energy sources, and waste management systems that minimize environmental impact. Such infrastructure not only supports sustainable tourism but also enhances the overall ecological health of the area.

Trends in the Development of Tourism Associated With Indigenous Culture and Typical Models in the World

Within the global travel market, tourism associated with indigenous culture is expanding quickly, appealing to tourists who want to fully experience the rituals, traditions, and lifestyles of the local populace. It blends leisure activities with a genuine exploration of the distinctive historical, architectural, cultural, and gastronomic features of a place. Demand for indigenous tourism has increased recently due to a growing awareness of the importance of celebrating and conserving varied cultures as well as increased curiosity in foreign customs and cultural experiences outside of the usual tourist destinations. Studies have shown that demand for cultural tourism has grown into various segments (McKercher & Du Cros, 2002), that people are increasingly looking for cultural "experiences"

(Prentice, 2001), and that cultural tourism is increasingly being integrated with other tourism industries, including religious, culinary, and literary tourism (Smith, 2009). According to a 2014 OECD assessment, this transition is causing a significant realignment of the relationship between the creative industries and tourism as well as significant changes in how "sustainable cultural tourism" is created for and enjoyed by travelers.

The intersection of indigenous culture and tourism has evolved significantly over recent years, driven by a growing recognition of the value of cultural diversity and the rights of indigenous people. This trend has manifested in various ways across the globe, leading to both opportunities and challenges for indigenous communities. International pronouncements like the United Nations Declaration on the Rights of Indigenous Peoples (UNDRIP) have contributed to a greater understanding of indigenous peoples' rights. Numerous indigenous tribes now have the authority to claim their land and cultural rights thanks to this acknowledgment, which has an impact on the travel and tourism industry. Many indigenous groups are now increasingly prominent in the tourism industry, exhibiting their own cultures, traditions, and legacy as interest in cultural preservation develops globally. Eco-tourism and community-based tourism, which prioritize sustainability and moral behavior, are growing in popularity, while initiatives conducted by indigenous peoples frequently prioritize protecting the environment, maintaining cultural traditions, and making sure that financial gains benefit the community directly.

The rise of digital platforms has enabled indigenous communities to promote their cultural experiences more broadly. Social media and travel websites allow for storytelling and sharing of cultural practices that attract tourists. Some indigenous communities are providing virtual tours, workshops, and cultural events as a result of the efforts to respond to the COVID-19 epidemic, which has accelerated the adoption of online experiences and increased interest in indigenous traditions. In order to support sustainable tourism practices, fight for their rights, and obtain funds for cultural preservation initiatives, numerous indigenous groups are partnering with governmental and non-governmental organizations (NGOs). More frameworks that acknowledge the role of indigenous people in the development and governance of tourism are the result of increased lobbying for indigenous rights in tourism regulations.

Tourism Associated With Indigenous Cultures in the World

In Asia

Tourism associated with indigenous culture in Asia demonstrates the exceptional diversity and richness of the world's largest geographical region. In Southeast Asia, tourists have a unique opportunity to experience the life of the Hmong people in Sa Pa (Vietnam) with traditional linen weaving and unique Hindu culture in Bali (Indonesia) through spiritual rituals and the traditional Kecak dance, as well as learn about the weaving profession of the Karen people in Thailand. Central Asia and Mongolia are famous for their nomadic culture, where visitors can sleep in yurts, enjoy fermented horse milk, and participate in traditional horseback riding activities. In South Asia, Nepal and Bhutan attract visitors with their unique Buddhist culture, while East Asia offers the opportunity to explore Tibetan Buddhism in China and Ainu culture in Hokkaido, Japan. Notably, many countries are developing sustainable community tourism models, which not only help preserve traditional culture but also create livelihoods for local people and organize traditional craft workshops such as weaving, pottery, and cooking, which helps visitors gain a deeper understanding of the intangible cultural values of Asia's indigenous communities.

In Europe

Tourism associated with indigenous culture in Europe has unique characteristics, reflecting the long history and cultural diversity of Europe's indigenous peoples. The highlight is the combination of traditional preservation and modern development, creating unique travel experiences. In Scandinavia, visitors can experience the culture of the Sami people—indigenous people living in Norway, Sweden, and Finland. They can participate in reindeer herding activities, sleep in traditional Lavvu tents, enjoy Sami cuisine such as reindeer meat and smoked salmon, learn about traditional arts and crafts and listen to Joik—the traditional song of the Sami people. In Scotland, the Hebrides islands are the places where visitors can discover Gaelic culture, where the Gaelic language is still spoken every day. Visitors can attend Ceilidhs—gatherings with traditional music and dance, learn about Harris tweed weaving, and explore the history of Scottish clans. In Maramureş, visitors can admire ancient wooden churches, visit traditional villages with unique architecture, and participate in folk festivals. In Ireland, in the Gaeltacht region—where Irish is still the main language—visitors can take language courses, enjoy traditional music in pubs, and learn about ancient Celtic culture through heritage sites and relics like Ogham-engraved stone. The Baltic regions, Estonia, Latvia, and Lithuania, also have communities that maintain strong traditional cultures. Visitors can participate in folk festivals, learn about traditional crafts such as wool weaving, and participate in ancient spiritual rituals.

Many regions in Europe are developing sustainable tourism projects to preserve local culture. These projects often combine homestay accommodation, learning about traditional crafts, and participating in the daily life of the community. This not only brings a unique experience to visitors but also contributes to maintaining and developing traditional European cultural values.

In Africa

Tourism associated with indigenous culture in Africa reflects the diversity of more than 3,000 ethnic groups on this continent. Coming to Tanzania, visitors can live with the Maasai people in traditional villages and learn about how they raise livestock and perform typical high-jumping dances (Adumu) in bright red Shuka costumes. Meanwhile, Ethiopia is the land of ancient stone churches in Lalibela, where visitors can participate in unique Orthodox Christian ceremonies and enjoy traditional, hour-long coffee ceremonies. In Senegal, Gorée Island is not only a historical relic of the slave trade period but also a place where visitors can learn about contemporary Senegalese art and enjoy vibrant mbalax music. In Ghana, visitors are immersed in the atmosphere of the Ashanti Adae festivals at the Kumasi palace, where chiefs in bright kente costumes demonstrate the solemnity of ancient royal culture. In Namibia, visitors can learn about the way of life of the Himba people in the Kalahari Desert, learn about their survival knowledge, and the art of ochre red clay makeup. Morocco in northern Africa offers a taste of Berber culture in the Sahara Desert, where visitors can spend the night in traditional tents, enjoy Gnawa music, and learn how to cook tagine.

Many African countries are currently also developing community-based tourism models, where local people directly manage and benefit from tourism activities, ensuring sustainable development and preserving traditional culture.

In the Americas

The journey of discovering tourism associated with indigenous culture in the Americas stretches from North to South America, with unique experiences about the lifestyle, beliefs, and traditions of communities and ethnic groups. Coming to North America, visitors can explore Native American culture through preserved areas such as the Navajo Nation in Arizona, where they can learn about the traditional art of carpet weaving and admire impressive architectural works such as cliff dwellings at Canyon de Chelly and enjoy local cuisine like fry bread. The Pacific Northwest is famous for its First Nation villages, where visitors can admire iconic totem poles and join in traditional potlatch festivals. Mexico offers a rich experience of Mayan and Aztec culture. In the Yucatan Peninsula, visitors can not only visit monuments like Chichen Itza but also participate in purification rituals in cenotes—sacred wells of the Maya or experience traditional healing rituals.. In Oaxaca, Zapotec culture is still alive and well preserved through weaving, pottery, and festivals such as Día de los Muertos. In the Amazon region, indigenous communities such as the Shipibo-Conibo people in Peru or the Kichwa people in Ecuador are developing community ecotourism, allowing visitors to learn about indigenous knowledge of herbal medicine and rainforest ecology. In Bolivia, the La Paz witch market is where visitors can learn about traditional Aymara medicine, while the Altiplano highlands offer the chance to experience the lives of llama and alpaca herders. Guatemala is famous for its modern Maya communities in the Lake Atitlán region, where visitors can learn traditional chocolate making and participate in shamanic ceremonies.

A notable point is that many indigenous communities in the Americas are developing sustainable tourism models, both preserving traditional culture and creating a source of income for the community. These projects often combine the sharing of traditional culture with environmental conservation, creating meaningful and responsible travel experiences.

In Australia

Tourism associated with indigenous culture in Australia explores the Aboriginal and Torres Strait Islander culture—one of the oldest cultures in the world. Here, visitors learn about the special relationship between people and the earth in Australian Aboriginal culture.

In the Northern Territory, Kakadu National Park is a prominent destination where visitors can admire ancient cave paintings, learn about the Dreamtime—a creative period in Aboriginal religion—and participate in Aboriginal-led tours to learn about the use of traditional medicinal plants and survival skills in the wild. In Queensland, the Great Barrier Reef Island is not only famous for its coral reefs but is also a place where visitors can experience Torres Strait Islander culture through traditional dance performances, learn how to fish in traditional ways, and hear stories about the sea passed down from generation to generation. In Western Australia, the Kimberley region offers a unique opportunity to explore ancient cave art, especially the mysterious Gwion Gwion paintings dating back tens of thousands of years. Visitors can join Aboriginal-led tours to learn about the meaning of these works of art and their connection to contemporary culture.

Major cities such as Sydney, Melbourne, and Brisbane also have Aboriginal cultural centers, where visitors can participate in dot painting workshops, learn how to play the didgeridoo—a traditional musical instrument—and enjoy prizes. Indigenous cuisine with unique ingredients such as kangaroo, emu, and bush tucker. In particular, many Aboriginal communities are developing sustainable tourism projects, allowing tourists to stay at camps in their traditional lands and participate in cultural activities such as hunting, harvesting, and listening to stories around the campfire. These experiences not only bring income to the community but also contribute to preserving and promoting traditional cultural values.

Typical Models of Tourism Associated With Indigenous Culture in the World

Whakarewarewa Maori Cultural Village (New Zealand)

Located in the city of Rotorua, Whakarewarewa Maori Cultural Village (Te Whakarewarewa) is one of New Zealand's most unique destinations, where visitors can fully experience the culture of the Maori people—the indigenous inhabitants of the Kiwi region. This is not simply a tourist destination but a real inhabited village, where visitors have the opportunity to enjoy Hangi cuisine cooked in geothermal pits, watch traditional haka dancing and enjoy Waiata music, visit a wood carving workshop, and learn flax weaving and the art of Moko tattooing. In particular, visitors can also witness how Maori people take advantage of natural hot water and steam sources in daily activities. Traditional ceremonies such as powhiri (touching noses) and retold ancient stories help visitors gain a deeper understanding of the spiritual culture of the Maori people. Tourism development has had a positive impact on the Maori community, as shown by the number of Maori tourism staff increasing by 25% in 2023, reaching 3,450 people. In particular, the arts and entertainment industry increased by 46% to 1,050 people, and the accommodation and food services industry increased by 19% to 1,850 people. There are currently 537 Maori tourism businesses across the country, and in Gisborne, almost 85% of staff in Maori-owned tourism businesses are Maori people.[4] This model not only creates jobs and income for local people but also makes an important contribution to preserving and promoting traditional cultural values while helping the young Maori generation to be educated about their communities' cultural heritages.

Yucatan Peninsula, Mexico—Unique Cultural Tourism Model of the Mayan People

Mexico focuses tourism development on combining cultural and natural heritage, in which cultural tourism is the key product. In 2023, this country welcomed about 40 million international visitors. In the Yucatan Peninsula, since 2018, YTO (Yucatan Tourism Observatory) has been established as a support network for the Ministry of Tourism Development of the Government of the State of Yucatan (SEFOTUR), with the task of monitoring and managing sustainable tourism. According to the YTO report, in 2023 (2023), Yucatan welcomed 2.4 million visitors, an increase of 14.2%, and generated revenue of 715 million dollars, an increase of 34.9% compared to the previous year.

Tourism based on Mayan cultural heritage plays an important role in local economic development. The Mexican government has launched the "Pueblos Mágicos" (Magical Villages) program to develop sustainable cultural tourism. Mayan archaeological sites such as Chichen Itza attract a large number of tourists, with 1.76 million visitors as of July 2023.[5] This site, along with Tulum and Uxmal, forms the famous Maya heritage triangle.

In particular, the tourism model in Yucatan harmoniously combines ancient heritage and contemporary Mayan culture. Visitors can experience life in traditional Maya villages through homestays in "palapas" houses, participating in activities such as making tortillas, tending medicinal gardens, and weaving. Maya cuisine with signature dishes such as cochinita pibil and tamales, along with spiritual rituals such as temazcal and traditional rain ceremonies, are kept alive. Ecotourism combined with culture is also developed through tours to explore rainforests and cenotes—sacred underground lakes. Income from tourism is distributed equitably within the community and invested in cultural preservation, helping to maintain languages and traditional crafts for younger generations.

---

[4]https://camperchamp.com.au/statistics/newzealand/#:~:text=In%202019%2C%20over%203.89%20million,below%20the%202019%20peak%20figures

[5]https://mexiconewsdaily.com/travel/mexico-expects-to-receive-up-to-40-million-tourists-in-2023/

Ancient Capital Kyoto, Japan—A Balance Between Tourism Development and Traditional Culture Preservation

Kyoto, the ancient capital of Japan, is an excellent example of preserving and developing traditional cultural tourism. According to JNTO Japan Tourism Statistics (2024), in 2023, Japan welcomed 26.8 million international tourists, of which 29.8% came to Kyoto, making this city the fourth tourist destination of the country.[6]

Kyoto's success is based on the close cooperation between the government and enterprises. The government creates a solid legal framework to preserve cultural heritage, financially support the restoration of temples and pagodas, and maintain traditional craft villages. Meanwhile, local enterprises develop unique tourism products that combine tradition and modernity, such as cultural experience tours, craft workshops, and ryokan accommodation services.

The highlight of Kyoto's cultural tourism model is its system of more than 1,600 Buddhist temples and Shinto shrines, where visitors can experience meditation and participate in traditional rituals. Geisha culture in the Gion neighborhood, the art of tea ceremony (Sadō), and traditional craft villages such as kimono weaving in Nishijin and pottery making in Kiyomizu are still preserved intact. Kyoto cuisine (Kyō-ryōri) with kaiseki restaurants and the Nishiki traditional market also creates unique cultural experiences for visitors.

Bali Island, Indonesia: Tourism Development Through Cultural and Religious Activities

According to Statistics of the Central Statistical Office of Bali Statistics Center (2024) (Badan pusat statistick provinsi Bali), Bali tourism welcomed more than 15.4 million international and domestic tourists in 2023, including 5.27 million international tourists (accounting for 65% of total international tourists visiting Indonesia).[7]

The core factor of this success lies in the fact that the Balinese people always appreciate their traditional culture. Local people still maintain a rich cultural life through festivals, Hindu religious rituals, and traditional dances such as Kecak, Legong, and gamelan performances. They skillfully integrate cultural elements into tourism services, from designing resorts and hotels with traditional architecture to serving authentic local cuisine and applying traditional spa methods. Noteworthy is the development of craft villages into tourist destinations such as Ubud with wood carving and painting, Celuk with silver craft, and Mas with stone chiseling. In addition, the island government also has appropriate policies to protect indigenous culture, such as regulations on building height not being higher than coconut trees and strict protection of temples and sacred sites. This model not only brings economic benefits to people through cultural activities,

---

[6]https://statistics.jnto.go.jp/en/graph/#graph–inbound–travelers–transition

[7]https://bali.bps.go.id/id/statistics-table?subject=519#subjekViewTab3.html

crafts, and local experiences, but also contributes to preserving and promoting cultural identity.

Sa Pa, Vietnam—A Combination of Tourism Development and Indigenous Culture Preservation

Sa Pa, a famous tourist destination in Northwest Vietnam, has succeeded in combining tourism development with preserving the indigenous culture of the H'Mong, Dao, Tay, and Giay ethnic groups. According to statistics from the Department of Tourism of Lao Cai province, in the first 11 months of 2023, Lao Cai welcomed 6.9 million visitors, including nearly 471,000 international visitors and over 6.4 million domestic tourists, bringing impressive revenue of VND 21,146 billion.

The highlight of Sa Pa tourism is the homestay system in traditional villages, where visitors can experience the daily life of ethnic minorities from cooking to farming. Visitors can enjoy typical dishes such as Thắng Cố and grilled stream fish and participate in the process of preparing traditional dishes. Traditional crafts, especially weaving and embroidery of the H'Mong and Red Dao people, are preserved and developed through tourism. Traditional festivals and trekking tours through villages not only bring experiences of natural landscapes but also help visitors deeply understand local culture. Local authorities have implemented many solutions, such as planning for sustainable tourism development, training tourism human resources for local people, and supporting community tourism projects, to create a balance between tourism development and indigenous cultural preservation.

Conclusion

Tourism development associated with indigenous culture represents a dynamic intersection of economic opportunity, cultural preservation, and environmental stewardship. As demonstrated by successful models worldwide—from New Zealand's Maori villages to Vietnam's Sa Pa region—this form of tourism can generate substantial economic benefits while empowering indigenous communities to maintain their cultural identity. The key to sustainable indigenous tourism lies in balancing commercial viability with authentic cultural representation. Communities that maintain control over their tourism initiatives consistently report higher satisfaction and better preservation outcomes. Moving forward, the sector must address challenges including cultural commodification, equitable benefit distribution, and environmental impacts. Development frameworks that prioritize indigenous decision-making authority, community participation, and intergenerational knowledge transfer offer the most promising path forward. By implementing these principles, indigenous tourism can fulfill its potential as both an economic driver and a powerful mechanism for preserving the world's diverse cultural heritage, creating experiences that enrich visitors while strengthening the communities at destinations.

References

Aref, F., Gill, S. S., & Aref, F. (2010). Tourism development in local communities: As a community development approach. *Journal of American Science*, *6*(2), 155–161.

Bali Statistics Center. (2024). *Tourism statistics*. https://bali.bps.go.id/id/statistics-table?subject=519#subjekViewTab3.html

Boniface. (2003). *Managing quality cultural tourism*. Routledge.

Coates, K. S. (2004). *A global history of indigenous peoples: Struggle and survival*. Palgrave MacMillan.

James, P., Magee, L., Scerri, A., & Steger, Manfred, B. (2015). *Urban sustainability in theory and practice: Circles of sustainability (p. 53)*. Routledge.

Japan National Tourism Organization. (2024). *Japan tourism statistics*. https://statistics.jnto.go.jp/en/graph/#graph–inbound–travelers–transition

Kajzar, P. (2013). Greece as cultural destination. In *16 international Colloquium on regional science*. Masarykova Univerzita.

McKercher, B., & Du Cros, H. (2002). *Cultural tourism: The partnership between tourism and cultural heritage management*. Haworth Press.

Prentice, R. (2001). Experiential cultural tourism: Museums & the marketing of the new romanticism of evoked authenticity. *Museum Management and Curatorship*, *19*, 5–26.

Sanders, D. E. (1999). Indigenous peoples: Issues of definition. *International Journal of Cultural Property*, *8*(1), 4–13.

Smith, M. (2009). *Issues in cultural tourism studies*. Routledge.

UNESCO. (2001). *UNESCO Universal Declaration on Cultural Diversity (p. 2–3)*. https://unesdoc.unesco.org/ark:/48223/pf0000127162

Yucatan Tourism Observatory. (2023). *Annual report 2023*. https://www.observaturyucatan.org.mx/public/publicaciones/2024/Annual%20Report.pdf

Chapter 17

Bridging Borders: The Intersection of Forced Displacement, Economic Integration, and Tourism

Farhang Morady

University of Westminster, UK

Abstract

This chapter examines the causes and intersection of forced displacement, economic integration, tourism, and hospitality, contributing to the migration-sustainable development debate in the European framework. Exploring the travel and hospitality sectors offers a way of understanding the possibilities for refugees to integrate into society and contribute to the economic and cultural legacy. Drawing on examples from various European countries, with special attention to Greece, the chapter emphasizes the importance of education, training, and economic and political strategies to highlight the necessity for policies that effectively address the potential opportunities and the inherent challenges.

Keywords: Forced displacement; refugees; economic integration; sustainable development; tourism; social capital theory; human capital theory; eco-tourism

Introduction

Forced migration has become a crucial issue for media and politicians in the 21st century. A 2025 UNHCR report indicates that more than 120 million people have been displaced due to political conflicts, civil wars, economic instability, and climate change. However, one-third of the world's refugees have been hosted by countries like Turkey, Uganda, and Pakistan, while wealthier nations have

Economics and Tourism, 267–277

Published under exclusive licence by Emerald Publishing Limited
doi:10.1108/978-1-83662-916-020251018

admitted far fewer. By the end of 2022, European countries admitted 12.4 million refugees, 50.8% of whom were Ukrainian. In comparison, only 25,400 refugees came to the United States that same year (UNHCR, 2023).

Forced migration differs from voluntary migration because it is caused by war, persecution, natural disasters, or poverty and implies prolonged displacement and resultant humanitarian crises (Betts, 2013). Some scholars have identified capitalist development, neoliberal policies, and geopolitical conflicts contributing to displacement since the 1990s (Achcar, 2013; Chomsky, 2016). Others have pointed to environmental destruction, which makes climate refugees a product of ecological disasters, deforestation, and the exploitation of natural resources (Malm, 2020). Nevertheless, since conventional discourse treats forced migration as a humanitarian problem, the primary focus is on providing aid instead of tackling the key economic and political causes.

Contrary to common misconceptions, refugees can contribute positively to host economies, especially in rapidly aging European countries—the population aged 65+ has increased from 16.2% to 21.3% between 2003 and 2023, according to Eurostat (2025)—and need refugees to boost their labor markets. Bauder and Jayaraman (2020) and the OECD (2018) agree on their economic advantages, as does Becker (1964) in Human Capital Theory, which holds that appropriately prepared and socially assimilated immigrants add value to economic development. Portes and Zhou's (1993) Social Capital Theory also builds on the notion that strong networks are a key driver of refugee economic impacts.

Empirical evidence from Greece suggests that refugee-led social businesses, especially in tourism, are creating a basis for the economy and, at the same time, helping to maintain the culture of refugees.

This article critiques the prevailing perspective that perceives refugees as a burden to economic growth. It argues that, contrary to this belief, refugees possess the potential to contribute to sustainable economic integration and development, thus enhancing overall economic productivity and innovation within host communities. This paper consists of four sections: In the first, the trends in forced migration are reviewed; in the second, the economic integration literature is reviewed; in the third, the theory regarding refugees' participation in tourism is discussed; and, in the fourth, the present paper offers a case study of Greece as a model of inclusion of refugees in the industry. It is therefore argued that with the proper legal and social support, refugees can take their skills and networks and help grow the economies of host countries.

The Drivers of Forced Migration: Global Trends and Impacts

During the 1980s, a new development model emerged that relied heavily on neoliberal free market principles, deregulation, privatization, and reducing government intervention (Harvey, 2005; Saad-Filho & Johnston, 2005). This shift had particularly impacted countries in the Global South. Rapid industrialization in emerging countries led to enormous debt for nations like Mexico, Brazil, and Turkey, which found themselves in a cycle of borrowing. This, in turn, led them to seek help from organizations such as the World Bank (WB) and the International Monetary Fund (IMF), which required them to implement structural adjustment programs (SAPs).

These SAPs meant that the IMF requested debtor countries to implement policies that typically privatize public services (like transportation, healthcare, and education) and remove subsidies from essential goods such as bread, oil, and meat. This reduced social funding and subsidies within debtor countries exacerbated problems, leading to the closure of some industries with consequent rising unemployment and greater food insecurity. As a result of these economic changes, social and political disruptions occurred in countries across Latin America, Africa, and Asia. Hence, some people, desperate for a better livelihood, were forced to migrate due to the weakened local economies (Klein, 2007; Peck, 2010; Sassen, 2014; Smith, 1996).

The change in geopolitical situation became more complicated with the involvement of the great powers, spearheaded by the United States, which intervened to promote democracy and oust dictators from power. Two significant occurrences during this period include the Western intervention in Afghanistan in 2001 and the removal of Saddam Hussein in Iraq in 2003. Additionally, the Arab Spring that began in 2011 sparked movements advocating for reforms across the Middle East, ultimately leading to the civil war in Syria and Libya. Millions have had to leave their homes due to these conflicts, which have resulted in skilled young individuals seeking safety in countries like Turkey, Pakistan, and across Europe. The UNHCR estimates that between 2001 and 2021, over 27 million Afghans, 4 million Iraqis, and 6.6 million Syrians became displaced in neighboring countries and Europe (UNHCR, 2025).

From a theoretical perspective, Lee (1966) applies the Push-Pull Theory to analyze forced migration by listing the factors that make people *leave* their home countries (for example, war, poor economy) and the factors that attract people *to* other countries (for example, job opportunities, political stability). These forces seem ingrained in the modern global economy, so displacement remains persistent.

In response to the large influx of forcibly displaced people, governments and national and international organizations have had to respond. Inter-country agreements, such as the EU/Turkey deal, revealed how political and financial motives frequently influence the delegation of refugee responsibilities to parties. This deal was signed in 2016 as part of Europe's response to the refugee crisis. Under the terms of this agreement, Turkey agreed to host refugees and stop irregular migration to Europe. In return, the EU promised financial aid (6 billion euros), visa liberalization for Turkish citizens, and progress in Turkey's EU accession negotiations. The deal effectively shifted the responsibility for managing asylum seekers from the EU countries onto Turkey (Ovacik et al., 2024).

Yet, studies show the positive benefits of these influxes of immigrants – numerous immigrants actively participate in the economy by venturing into entrepreneurship activities despite sometimes facing stringent immigration regulations. Their economic contributions bring skills and traditions to the community, benefiting businesses and increasing employment opportunities.

Alongside this are cultural benefits, as diverse customs, foods, and cultural practices can enhance international communication and collaboration, leading to greater inclusivity (UNWTO, 2021).

A significant proportion of incoming European refugees fall into the 18–35 age group. Many young adults in their 20s and 30s become assets, especially those with labor skills (World Migration Report, 2024). According to a report by The Organization for Economic Co-operation and Development (OECD), in 2018, some became engaged in opening small businesses such as shops and working in hotels and catering industries (OECD, 2018). Several studies have highlighted the role played by refugees in rejuvenating struggling areas, leading to their redevelopment and the growth of local economies. For example, evidence from Poland indicated that Ukrainian refugees had contributed between 0.7% and 1.1% to Poland's GDP in 2023 (Dombrovskis et al., 2024). According to an article in *The Guardian*, immigration policies have helped Spain's GDP rise by 3.2% in 2024 (Kassam, 2025).

This trend is also evident in the United States, where, from 2005 to 2019 in the United States, a study by the Department of Health and Human Services revealed that refugees and asylees contributed $123.8 billion more in revenue than they received in expenditures (Ghertner et al., 2024). Refugees in the United States earned $93.6 billion in family income in 2019. They also paid a combined total of $25 billion in taxes, which includes $16.2 billion in federal taxes and $8.7 billion in state and local taxes (American Immigration Council, 2023).

However, refugees often face a struggle to be able to legally access the job market, vocational training, and education. If such legislation is implemented, it can have a positive economic effect and speed up economic integration. Sweden and the Netherlands are two countries that can be seen to have put in place the right inclusive economic policies: their strategic investments in refugee integration have resulted in better employment rates and higher tax collections (Fasani et al., 2021).

Refugees' Social Connections and Tourism Industry

The conceptual frameworks of Human Capital Theory and Social Capital Theory offer essential insights into how displaced populations move from being economically passive subjects, dependent on external assistance, to active participants in their host societies' economic lives. Human Capital Theory stresses the importance of education, skills, and training in increasing economic productivity. In the case of refugee integration, this theory favors policies that improve refugees' professional aptitudes to limit their reliance on social assistance. The "3+2 Rule" of Germany,[1] the Fast Track Program of Sweden, and

[1]The 3+2 Rule is commonly associated with Germany's asylum and immigration policies. It allows asylum seekers to complete vocational training (typically 3 years) and then stay for an additional 2 years for employment. This rule provides a pathway for integration into the labour market, particularly for those whose asylum applications might otherwise be rejected. See, INF Migrants.

the Refugee Hospitality Skills Program of Greece are successful investments in refugee skill development. These initiatives help refugees engage in key industries, especially tourism, hospitality, and construction, where labor shortages exist. A similar finding was made by Dustmann et al. (2017), who established that when refugees are given vocational training and a chance to learn, they can add value to national economies by filling labor gaps, increasing productivity, and easing the burden on public welfare expenses.

As Portes and Zhou (1993) have argued, Social Capital Theory focuses on the role of networks, trust, and community ties in economic integration. Employment, business partnerships, and cultural interchange are usually obtained through social networks, which help newcomers adapt to their new economic environments. *Refugee Walks* in Athens and *Refugee Voices Tours* in Berlin are businesses that create economic opportunities and promote cultural exchange between the displaced and local populations. The *Italy Migrants Food Lab Initiative* and the eco-tourism projects in Lesvos and Crete also show how social capital allows refugees to earn a livelihood while contributing to the economic recovery of tourism-dependent regions.

Thus, the combination of Human Capital Theory and Social Capital Theory can provide policy measures that promote the economic independence of refugees. In addition, it effectively taps into their value as agents of growth for nations and communities. Training programs, legal work permits, and strategic education investments encourage economic self-sufficiency while promoting social ties and accelerating community integration and long-term stability. Thus, it is possible to contemplate refugee-driven economic activity, in terms of workforce participation or entrepreneurship, as shifting the perception of forced displacement from a calamity to an opportunity. In the end, recognizing the economic subjectivity of the displaced populations in terms of human and social capital is a way of building sustainable integration in a challenge to the negative migration narratives and a reaffirmation of the positive economic role that refugees play across the world.

Education remains integral to fostering refugee participation in tourism and hospitality. Initiatives like Germany's DAAD[2] scholarships provide financial support, mentorship, and language instruction to equip refugees with critical customer service, culinary, and operational skills (DAAD, 2016). Similarly, vocational training programs in France and Italy incorporate sustainability-oriented modules, enabling refugees to adopt eco-friendly

[2]Since 2016, the German Academic Exchange Service (DAAD) provide financial support through programs like "Integra," DAAD has supported over 40,000 refugees in preparing for university studies in Germany. Most of these participants are from Syria, accounting for approximately 75% of the cohort, followed by individuals from Afghanistan and Iran (each constituting 6%), and Iraq (3%) (*DAAD*).

practices that advance the European Union's green tourism agenda[3] (OECD, 2018; UNWTO, 2021).

Eco-tourism has enabled initiatives headed by refugees to rejuvenate neglected rural areas. Projects in Spain, Greece, and Italy have transformed idle land into dynamic locations featuring renewable energy sources, permaculture, and organic farming. Such initiatives diversify rural companies, draw eco-aware tourists, and provide jobs for residents and refugees (OECD, 2018). Many refugee-led enterprises focus on conserving cultural traditions and implementing environmentally responsible methods, mirroring the global pivot toward responsible tourism. Examples include eco-lodges in rural Italy and Greece designed to reduce energy consumption and waste and urban culinary ventures that enrich Europe's gastronomic landscape (Betts et al., 2017; Williams & Hall, 2002). These projects help surrounding businesses attract tourists looking for distinctive and meaningful experiences: by combining cultural legacy with environmental sustainability, broader objectives of fair economic growth can be achieved.

In Spain, several projects have been created to employ refugees in rural areas to solve two problems: depopulation and economic decline. The Murcia region has a unique approach to this integration and a specific focus on helping refugees to gain employment. This provided refugees with the security and income they needed and attracted over 781,654 visitors. This has also contributed over €230 million to the economy and created 4,249 jobs in those rural regions. The data also shows how vital the ecotourism industry can be in restoring declining regions based on the sustainable growth of the economy. Therefore, Spain has developed a strong and diverse rural community for all citizens by integrating refugees and ecotourism (Soyecotourista, 2025).

Scheherazade, in Austria, is another example of an organization incorporating refugees into eco-hospitality projects and cultural tourism ventures that support the European Union's goals (Betts et al., 2019; Williams & Hall, 2002). This is a pioneering social enterprise: Magdas Hotel is located in the heart of Vienna and has the unique mission of integrating refugees into the workforce while being an environmentally friendly hotel. The hotel was established by Caritas, a prominent Catholic relief organization and is proof of a socially responsible and environmentally friendly approach. In addition, the hotel has a multicultural staff of immigrants, former refugees, and highly skilled professionals from 14 nationalities. Magdas Hotel not only provides job opportunities for those who have faced significant challenges in their lives, but it also enhances the guest experience, as they can engage

[3]The European Union's green tourism agenda focuses on sustainability through initiatives like the European Tourism Agenda 2030 and the Transition Pathway for Tourism, which promote eco-friendly practices, circular economy principles, and renewable energy use in the sector. Programs like European Destinations of Excellence (EDEN) highlight sustainable travel destinations, while policies encourage energy-efficient accommodations and smart mobility. These efforts aim to balance economic growth with environmental preservation, making tourism in Europe more resilient and sustainable, see European Commission (2020).

with people from different cultures. The hotel is set in a beautifully restored building that focuses on sustainability. It has been built with its environmental impact in mind, from energy conservation systems to environmentally friendly features. In this manner, Magdas Hotel is a perfect example of how sustainability and the integration of refugees can be combined in the hospitality industry (SPRING, 2022; BWM Designers & Architects, 2025).

The integration of refugees into host economies can be effectively understood through human capital theory, which emphasizes skill development and workforce participation, and social capital theory, which highlights the importance of networks and community support. Refugee-led initiatives in tourism and eco-hospitality, including vocational training programs and social enterprises, are advantageous for economic growth, cultural exchange, and sustainability.

Greece Refugee-Driven Social and Economic Enterprises: A Model for Integration

Due to the country's strategic location at the junction of Europe, Asia, and Africa, the flow of culture and trade has been evident in Greece for centuries. However, in recent years, with the ongoing political, economic, and environmental crises in the Middle East, North Africa, and the eastern part of Europe, it has also become the primary entry point for refugees fleeing conflict and hardship. Although the country has its share of economic problems, Greece, with a population of 11 million, has accepted more than 200,000 asylum seekers from Afghanistan, Syria, Iraq, Palestine, and Iran (International Rescue Committee, 2024). Greece has had to come up with new and creative social enterprises to enhance the integration of such migrants. The central idea of this approach is to leverage the travel industry to create employment for displaced persons. Most of the projects are based on cultural and culinary experiences; therefore, refugee-led businesses share stories of displacement and strength, offering refugees a chance to earn a living and be part of fostering global tolerance.

These initiatives, which are based on the Human Capital Theory and the Social Capital Theory, focus on the economic role of refugees and, at the same time, contribute to the promotion of understanding and acceptance of difference. The Greek approach is based on the idea that travel and cultural industries can create jobs for refugees and thus empower them economically. Most refugee-owned businesses are in the culinary sector and offer tourists a taste of the country's rich tradition of accepting and integrating immigrants through the emphasis on developing networks and trust while also building up the professional abilities and employability of the refugees.

One well-respected project, *Refugee Walks*, provides migrants with employment as tour guides to help people learn more about the history of Greece, migration, and contemporary refugee situations. The tours also pass through areas with a rich migration history, such as Victoria Square and Exarchia in Athens, where refugees and locals have been neighbors for many years. Through personal stories and historical information, the tours offer a practical approach to cultural interchange and improve the public's perception of refugees. *Refugee Walks* have positive economic effects for the refugee guides who gain employment and learn how to speak publicly and communicate with people from different cultures. Research shows that more than 90% of the participants on these tours have a better perception of refugees and have gained a better understanding of the migration issues (Planet Wonk, 2025). The program also helps the guides by providing language training in Greek and English and linking with cultural institutions to increase their visibility and participation.

Another successful project, *Taste of Home*, uses food as a tool to empower refugees and, at the same time, promote cultural interchange. This program enables displaced people to present their culture through food, organizing pop-up dining events, and partnering with local restaurants. Refugees are given the chance to relate their stories, prepare the food, and share it with other refugees and with local people. Cooking events and food festivals provide income for the refugee chefs and contribute to the relationship between the refugees and local people. Research from pilot projects in Greece shows that such programs can help refugees learn certain skills, such as menu planning, kitchen management, and entrepreneurship. Moreover, the Hellenic Refugee Integration Council found that 78% of the Greek participants in refugee-led culinary events had a better perception of the displaced population, according to the study conducted in 2022 (Infomigrants, 2023).

To increase the availability of *Taste of Home*, it could be beneficial to form partnerships with cultural institutions, museums, and educational institutions. For instance, schools and universities could include refugee-led cooking workshops in their studies, from the gastronomy and migration perspectives, to increase general cultural awareness. Also, working with tourism companies and hospitality associations could assist refugee chefs in getting jobs in the sector or even starting their own food-based businesses. Although these initiatives show refugee-owned businesses' vocational and social advantages, several challenges must be met to ensure sustainability. Legal and bureaucratic challenges, which include the availability of work permits and the complexity of obtaining business licenses, hamper refugees' chances of engaging legally in the labor market. Furthermore, there are constant funding problems, since many of these programs are wholly dependent on donations. Social reintegration measures are sometimes difficult to implement due to the existing xenophobic attitudes that need to be tackled through public enlightenment programs. To build up the scalability and sustainability of refugee-driven social businesses, Greece and other host countries should establish policies that permit work permits, offer financial benefits to firms for hiring refugees, and combine vocational training with business creation. Greece's experience identifies tourism and hospitality as sectors that can guarantee economic inclusion and cultural exchange. Thus, these initiatives change the perception of refugees from being passive subjects of assistance to active participants in programs that present displacement as a chance to enrich societies.

Conclusion

Over the past three decades, forced migration has risen sharply, changing the global discourse on displacement, economic integration, and sustainable development. This paper highlights the structural causes of refugee movements, such as geopolitical conflicts, capitalist economic policies, and environmental crises. It shows that forced migration is a humanitarian problem and an economic and social advantage. Nevertheless, the existing narratives are pejorative; that of refugees as a burden is one of them; however, the proof indicates that when provided with the proper support, they are an added advantage to the host economies, especially in the tourism and hospitality industry.

Applying human and social capital theories, this article demonstrated that refugees have the potential to be productive assets for economic growth and development. Successful refugee-led businesses in the tourism sector in Greece, Spain, and Sweden have been noted, creating employment and contributing to cultural enrichment and integration. Refugee Walks Athens, Taste of Home culinary activities, and eco-tourism activities in rural Europe are examples of how displaced populations can create value while maintaining cultural identity and supporting environmental stewardship.

Nevertheless, there are still existing challenges, including legal obstacles, the unavailability of the labor market, and prejudice. These challenges can only be met by concerted efforts by governments, businesses, and NGOs to enforce inclusive labor policies, vocational training, and financial incentives for refugee employment. International solidarity and the proper distribution of the burden between countries are also essential to ensure that host countries get the necessary support.

Ultimately, shifting the discourse from one that sees refugees as a humanitarian burden to one that highlights the economic and social development of the refugee issue will be necessary to change the perception of forced migration. The involvement of refugees in tourism and other sectors of the economy improves the quality of life and raises the prospects for inclusive and sustainable growth. Thus, using tourism as a two-way development process, communities affected by displacement can rebuild themselves as strong cultural and economic entities. The travel and hospitality industries provide a unique venue to reduce cultural barriers, promote financial stability, and increase social cohesiveness. Recognizing and supporting refugee contributions would enable societies to transform the global refugee crisis into an opportunity for mutual understanding and shared growth. Together, governments, businesses, and NGOs can help fully exploit this potential and build strong, varied, inclusive communities.

References

Achcar, G. (2013). *The people want: A radical exploration of the Arab uprising*. University of California Press.

American Immigration Council. (2023). *Starting Anew: The Economic Impact of Refugees in America*. American Immigration Council. https://www.americanimmigrationcouncil.org/sites/default/files/research/05.23_refugee_report_v3_0.pdf. Accessed January 16, 2025.

Bauder, H., & Jayaraman, S. (2020). Refugee integration and employment pathways in hospitality industries. *International Journal of Migration Studies, 42*(5), 523–545.

Becker, G. S. (1964). *Human capital: A theoretical and empirical analysis, with special reference to education.* University of Chicago Press.

Betts, A. (2013). *Survival migration: Failed governance and the crisis of displacement.* Cornell University Press.

Betts, A., Bloom, L., Kaplan, J., & Omata, N. (2017). *Refugee economies: Forced displacement and development.* Oxford University Press.

Betts, A., Bloom, L., & Weaver, N. (2019). Refugee economies and sustainable tourism: A case study of Uganda. *Refugee Studies Quarterly, 38*(1), 77–94.

BWM Designers & Architects. (2025). *Magdas HOTEL (project page).* https://integrationpractices.eu/data/practice/magdas-hotel/?utm_source=chatgpt.com. Accessed on October 1, 2025.

Chomsky, N. (2016). *Who rules the world?* Metropolitan Books.

DAAD. (2016). *Higher education programme for refugees extended.* Press release, Bonn/Berlin. 11 October. https://www2.daad.de/presse/pressemitteilungen/2016/en/49167-higher-education-programme-for-refugees-extended/

Dombrovskis, V., Obstfeld, M., Sologoub, I., Gorodnichenko, Y., Becker, T., Fedyk, A., Gérard, R., & Mauro, W. (2024). Stimulating growth in Ukraine and policies for migrants' return. *VoxEU.* https://cepr.org/voxeu/columns/stimulating-growth-ukraine-and-policies-migrants-return. Accessed on January 25, 2025.

Dustmann, C., Fasani, F., & Speciale, B. (2017). Illegal migration and consumption behavior. *Oxford Economic Papers, 69*(2), 235–257.

European Commission. (2020). Refugees and labour market integration in the European Union. *EU Policy Review, 12*(4), 56–72.

Eurostat. (2025). *Refugee statistics.* https://ec.europa.eu/eurostat. Accessed on January 20, 2025.

Fasani, F., Frattini, T., & Minale, L. (2021). Lift the ban? Initial employment restrictions and refugee labour market outcomes. *Journal of Economic Geography, 21*(3), 381–417.

Ghertner, R., Macartney, S., & Dost, M. (2024). *The fiscal impact of refugees and asylees at the federal, state, and local levels from 2005-2019.* ASPE Report. https://aspe.hhs.gov/reports/fiscal-impact-refugees-asylees. Accessed on February 18, 2025.

Harvey, D. (2005). *A brief history of neoliberalism.* Oxford University Press.

Infomigrants. (2023). https://www.infomigrants.net/fr/post/49651/greek-and-refugee-chefs-unite-for-world-refugee-day

International Rescue Committee. (2024). *Who we are.* https://www.rescue.org/who-we-are. Accessed on January 23, 2025.

Kassam, A. (2025). How Spain's radically different approach to migration helped its economy soar. *The Guardian.* https://www.theguardian.com/world/2025/feb/18/how-spains-radically-different-approach-to-migration-helped-its-economy-soar. Accessed on January 21, 2025.

Klein, N. (2007). *The shock doctrine: The rise of disaster capitalism.* Metropolitan Books.

Lee, E. S. (1966). A theory of migration. *Demography, 3*(1), 47–57.

Malm, A. (2020). *Corona, climate, chronic emergency: War communism in the twenty-first century*. Verso Books.
OECD. (2018). *Working together for local integration of migrants and refugees*. OECD Publishing. https://www.oecd.org/content/dam/oecd/en/publications/reports/2018/04/working-together-for-local-integration-of-migrants-and-refugees_g1g8b73d/9789264085350-en.pdf. Accessed on January 2, 2025.
Ovacik, G., Ineli-Ciger, M., & Ulusoy, O. (2024). Taking stock of the EU-Turkey statement in 2024. In *European journal of migration and law*. Brill. https://brill.com/view/journals/emil/emil-overview.xml
Peck, J. (2010). *Constructions of neoliberal reason*. Oxford University Press.
Planet Wonk. (2025). https://theplanetwonk.com/
Portes, A., & Zhou, M. (1993). The new second generation: Segmented assimilation and its variants among post-1965 immigrant youth. *The Annals of the American Academy of Political and Social Science*, *530*(1), 74–96. Accessed on January 18, 2025.
Saad-Filho, A., & Johnston, D. (2005). *Neoliberalism: A critical reader*. Pluto Press.
Sassen, S. (2014). *Expulsions: Brutality and complexity in the global economy*. Harvard University Press.
Smith, N. (1996). *The new urban frontier: Gentrification and the revanchist city*. Routledge.
Soyecoturista. (2025). https://soyecoturista.com/en
SPRING. (2022). *Magdas Hotel – Sustainable practices of integration*. Integration Practices database. https://integrationpractices.eu/data/practice/magdas-hotel/?utm_source=chatgpt.com. Accessed on October 1, 2025.
UNHCR. (2023). *Global trends: Forced displacement in 2023*. https://www.unhcr.org/us/global-trends-report-2023. Accessed on January 16, 2025.
UNHCR. (2025). *Refugee statistics: The latest trends and data*. United Nations High Commissioner for Refugees. https://www.unhcr.org/refugee-statistics. Accessed on January 23, 2025.
UNWTO. (2021). *Refugees and tourism: Creating pathways for economic inclusion*. World Tourism Organization. https://www.unwto.org/tourism-in-2030-agenda. Accessed on January 19, 2025.
Williams, A. M., & Hall, C. M. (2002). *Tourism, migration, circulation, and mobility: The contingencies of time and place*. Springer.
World Migration Report. (2024). *Chapter 2: Refugees and asylum seekers*. https://worldmigrationreport.iom.int/what-we-do/world-migration-report-2024-chapter-2/refugees-and-asylum-seekers. Accessed on January 20, 2025

Printed and bound by CPI Group (UK) Ltd, Croydon, CR0 4YY

15/09/2026

14962486-0003